RENEWALS 458-4574
DATE DUE

On the Nature of Cities

Toward Enduring and Creative Human Environments

Jossey-Bass Publishers
San Francisco • Washington • London • 1979

ON THE NATURE OF CITIES
Toward Enduring and Creative Human Environments
by Kenneth R. Schneider

Copyright © 1979 by: Jossey-Bass, Inc., Publishers
433 California Street
San Francisco, California 94104
&
Jossey-Bass Limited
28 Banner Street
London EC1Y 8QE

Copyright under International, Pan American, and Universal Copyright Conventions. All rights reserved. No part of this book may be reproduced in any form—except for brief quotation (not to exceed 1,000 words) in a review or professional work—without permission in writing from the publishers.

Library of Congress Catalogue Card Number LC 78-62556

International Standard Book Number ISBN 0-87589-391-0

Manufactured in the United States of America

JACKET DESIGN BY WILLI BAUM

FIRST EDITION

Code 7833

Kenneth R. Schneider

Preface

    This book challenges the way modern America builds its cities. Although urban environments represent society's most fundamental means of altering nature and organizing social life, we seem to think more fundamentally about the character of the Grand Canyon than about the form of our neighborhoods.
    I say this despite the recent flood of books about cities and the equally large literature on the natural environment. Indeed, the gulf between these two areas of modern concern helps explain why neither body of thought gets to the essence of human environments: urban space and its logistics, human community and cosmopolitan life, the many profound possibilities of human association, and—so critical today—a true basis for a sustainable human ecology. Both bodies of literature, I contend, miss the vastness of the problems and possibilities of human habitation on earth.
    Today we continually hear of the emergence of a profoundly

different paradigm of life in society. New images of great promise now appear regularly. To them, my question is: How can any vision of life be valid without reference to the physical and institutional forms of cities that not only organize behavior but also imprint themselves onto our patterns of thought and filter into the deepest sources of human aspiration and the modern ethos?

My aim in this book is to show how technological and corporate change in society is occurring chiefly in and through the forms and functions of cities. Although the urban result is revolutionary to the core, this transformation is yet hardly examined, appreciated, or argued. Our society has a sophisticated awareness of the special effects of machine technology and functional bureaucracy, but it lacks basic perception of the larger combined results, in particular the environments of cities.

The aim of *On the Nature of Cities* is to elevate questions of human habitation and urban organization to a higher and more central position in the human dialogue. However, this volume is but a first step, and I plan a second book exploring the wide promise of urban form. While the present volume describes the growing failure of cities to serve human ends, the projected work will emphasize the many creative possibilities of urban form. Society now shuns—and often reacts against—any urban inventiveness that is not a direct result of scientific technology or enterprise organization, the two spheres of innovation that we endow with full social legitimacy. Some books, to be sure, are beginning to appear that do emphasize creative urban form, and ultimately the more creative literature is necessary to found a higher dialogue of cities and more positive urban traditions. Nevertheless, because society now organizes change according to pragmatic evaluation on the one side and technical and enterprise inventiveness on the other side, a book striving to alert society to what has become a destructive urban dynamism is, in my estimation, a necessary prerequisite.

If readers are to understand or appreciate the book's message, they must free themselves, at least for a time, from many commonly accepted perceptions of the city. My own perspective, I must stress, evolved over a full quarter century, and I deeply appreciate the problems of communicating the compressed results of that evolution into a single volume. The image we Americans bring

*The Jossey-Bass Social and
Behavioral Science Series*

Contents

	Preface	vii
	The Author	xiii
	Introduction	1
1.	Getting on Top of the Revolution	7
2.	Urban Destruction by Development	21
3.	The American Way of Citymaking	45
4.	The Strategy of Urban Defeat	72
5.	The Environmental Toll	130

6.	The Economic Toll	154
7.	The Human Toll	184
8.	Unkind Traditions	220
9.	The Urban Implosion of the Population Bomb	261
10.	Can We Build Good Cities?	287
11.	The Urban Future	320
	References	334
	Index	341

Preface

to cities is at once conservatively rural and radically industrial—that is, sentimental in thought and revolutionary in practice.

Despite my criticism of *present manifestations* of social values, my approach is founded solidly upon established American values and, broadly speaking, empirical science. For example, I assume such values as spaciousness and privacy, and I use a simple geometry to examine the urban forms in which they are expressed. However, I do raise questions of opposable or corresponding values, such as spatial compactness and public participation. These are counterparts of a larger social freedom, and include such elements as opportunity *and* security, community *and* cosmopolitan life; but today they have suffered badly in the one-sided struggle for individual wealth and power. Implicit here is the idea that studies of social affairs should relate value and method. Social values are always present, and to simply set them aside or systematically exclude them is to discredit them. I think it is useful, perhaps vital, to openly link social value and social method.

Each chapter develops a separate perspective of cities. The first two overview and highlight the self-destructive paradox of cities. Chapter Three sketches the historic development of today's American cities. Chapter Four examines many specific elements of self-defeating urban form. Chapters Five, Six, and Seven summarize how today's cities damage the environment, economic system, and, most importantly, human value. Chapter Eight explores *why* we have been so destructive in citymaking in the past hundred years. Chapter Nine looks at some basic lessons of urban development in the Third World and points to their instructive worth to industrially advanced countries. Chapter Ten examines some central issues of urban societies: urban freedom, the organic imperative of cities, and cities as master mechanisms of society—why they are a very fundamental kind of social constitution. The final chapter looks to the future and hints at some of the exciting prospects of the human habitat that did not exist before this century.

I have written this book for a wide range of people. Academic, professional and research persons in the social and ecological sciences, design, education, health, business, and government should find it relevant to the extent they are concerned with the content, problems, and outlook of cities. And, in reflection of the vitality and variety of life encompassed and infused by cities, I also reach out to those persons who, whatever their station in life, may be provoked and dedicated to innovatively pursue a broader vision and ideal of cities.

Flagstaff, Arizona Kenneth R. Schneider
December 1978

On the Nature of Cities

Toward Enduring and Creative Human Environments

The Author

KENNETH R. SCHNEIDER, who earned a bachelor's degree in sociology and has done graduate work in sociology and city planning at the University of California, Berkeley, is currently devoting his time to writing and research in city planning.

Schneider's diverse career in city planning and international development began with teaching on the Hopi Indian Reservation, followed by four years of city and transportation planning in California's San Joaquin Valley. After an association with architect and planner Albert Mayer in New York, Schneider joined the Cooperative for American Relief Everywhere (CARE), where he studied CARE's community development work in the Philippines and was Chief of Mission in Sierra Leone and Jordan. In the late 1960s he took a number of consulting assignments with the United Nations in New York, including the writing and editing of reports submitted to the Committee on Housing, Building, and Planning, the Economic and Social Council, and the General Assembly. Schneider returned to California in 1971 to lecture, write, and consult on key issues of urban development.

The editor of *The Planning of Metropolitan Areas and New Towns* (for the United Nations, 1967), Schneider is also the author of *Destiny of Change* (1968) and *Autokind Vs. Mankind* (1971). His many articles on urban life have been published in such journals as *Architectural Forum, Traffic Quarterly, International Development Review, Journal of the American Institute of Planners,* and *Ekistics.*

To my five children:
Leslie Alynn, Lowell Alexis,
Mari Alane, Loren Paul, and
Matthew Arron—and to their generation

Introduction 3

chaos after the fall of the Roman Empire, people contracted with lords for protection. In time, they became bonded serfs in exchange for the security they so desperately wanted.

In our case, we have created an environmental situation in cities in which a constantly growing wealth is necessary to maintain an always precarious personal security. I do not refer to inflation (although that is relevant, according to both Toynbee and Schumacher) but rather to the rising physical imperatives of gross consumption. Where once, for example, we could conveniently walk or ride a public conveyance in almost any city, a family must now typically own two vehicles to maintain a reasonable membership in society. Although we are motivated by the Protestant ethic to work and accumulate wealth, we do not understand how it has compelled us to build urban environments so as to make cars mandatory.

Impelled to consume by our current ideology and then compelled to consume by the structure of urban environments, a continuous growth of input-output is guaranteed while we remain largely ignorant of the consequences. Nor do we do much to find out. The dynamic bureaucracy of corporations, which is bound by profits to promote an escalating input-output, also assures a kind of public orderliness needed for economic growth. But the order is bureaucratic only, not social or individual. The massive functionalism actually denies the more fundamental human orderliness required for personal security and growth.

Individuals, perhaps like those in the chaos after the fall of Rome, contract with an authority for a security responding to the chief domestic fears and dislocations of our time: financial security. Employment and the immense role played by work careers signify our bondage, for which we, too, pay a steep price. If our condition is a magnificently indulgent serfdom, it is a serfdom nevertheless. With it, environmental order is sacrificed. Deeper but less demanding human motives are buried or subtly pulverized under the economic mandate so peculiarly central to our time.

I have the feeling that it is the environmental disorder and the buried human needs—both created by the fragmented physical and social form of the modern city—that underwrite today's public psychosis. If so, there is good reason to believe that an ecological humanism of cities may well be the foundation for a renaissance of our time.

The psychosis, only decades old in its more obvious manifestations, may be the first sign of a momentous watershed. Our era is a product of over four hundred years of accelerating technical development. Now, quite suddenly in the closing decades of this century, our historic material deprivations are turning into a surfeit (even, ironically, as many material needs remain unmet). Now nature, which was once awesome and seemingly limitless, has abruptly become small and in danger of turning into a dustbowl. And gradually we are coming to realize that the old era cannot continue in its mindless accelerations.

At the same time, society is slowly becoming conscious that cities are in serious trouble. If the problems are truly basic to the way we make cities, we can suspect that they derive from the urban paradoxes suggested above. My observations lead me to believe that the paradoxes arise in an unusually wide schism between our *expressed urban values* (such as the popularity of the one-family house on a large suburban lot) and the *actual urban benefits* derived from the kinds of urban environments we build. And despite our wide range of sophistication in the sciences and professions, the gulf apparently still widens. Thus, strangely, it seems to me, our most progressive tools of society do not prepare us to understand the city.

In recognizing the many agonizing urban crises, we carry out special studies of particular problems and set special agencies into action. But when we look at only crime or traffic or schools, we do not look at the whole city. We seem to be oblivious to the interactive wholeness of urban life. I believe it is in the perception of urban wholeness that our mighty investigative and conceptual traditions fail us most in facing up to the treacherously dynamic nature of contemporary urban environments.

We are learning in other areas, such as natural ecology, health, and even education, that understanding anything less than a whole habitat, a whole being, or a whole system is likely to be ineffective and sometimes harmful, especially over the long term. What whole in society, we must ask, deserves understanding as an organic unity more than the city?

Introduction

Having had considerable experience with New York's subways, I am sympathetic to the observation that they represent the worst of man's built environments. One day, shortly after abandoning that underground passage, which daily intimidates both body and sensibility, I found myself sitting and watching people in San Francisco's Ghirardelli Square. While I was relaxing in the brisk yet sunny air so uniquely common to the Bay Area, and undoubtedly influenced by the bronze mermaids in the spouting waters of the lily pond, a profoundly biased observation struck me: *People are beautiful in beautiful environments, ugly in ugly environments.*

The power of my feelings that day in San Francisco later reminded me of an equally striking observation that had occurred years earlier, precisely while waiting for a train in New York's subways: *No other area in American cities has as much potential for dynamic development as Manhattan.* That is, I began to see that the closer things come together in the city the greater is the potential for people to build and share environments that are both beautiful and efficient. And subways are a part of that potential.

The two observations are not as radically opposed as one might first assume. Ghirardelli Square is quite efficient in itself, as well as an exciting place to be, and there is no outstanding reason why underground environments cannot be beautiful as well as useful. Some foreign subways, for example, display art, like some art galleries, using little or no natural light. So the bleak and threatening nature of the underground stations merely expresses our confined thinking about cities.

But more telling illustrations of our limited views of built environments exist. The American driving a superb Monte Carlo on a $10-million-per-mile freeway may consider outrageous the thought that he or she is making charges against nature that cannot be sustained long into the next century or that cannot be extended to the whole world's population for more than a decade or two. Equally outrageous to Americans is the thought that their immaculate suburban split-level homes are incompatible with a workable urban system. Nevertheless, bit by bit, these all-but-heretical propositions are being substantiated. There is increasing evidence suggesting that our urban living and travel arrangements are *intended* to be inefficient and monumentally consumptive. Even traffic accidents are tallied into the GNP.

Nor is simple waste the end of it. The American family, two sole adults raising two isolated children, may be spending much of its new-found wealth to assure its fundamental self-deprivation. Could it be that, through our inherited faith in endless frontiers, we are acting out a giant Promethean fallacy, becoming harried, bondaged, and estranged by gross consumptions and accumulations? This idea is being increasingly supported by hard evidence.

It would appear that a virtual psychosis is being formally introduced into one of the world's most rational and productive societies. Appearing normal, right, and even necessary for material abundance, the public psychosis seems to arise from pervasive insecurities, which are naggingly similar to those that underwrote the appearance of feudalism during the early Middle Ages. In the

1

Getting on Top of the Revolution

Although America has become a nation of cities, we did not really want it that way. Like Jefferson, we never quite trusted city life. But we did want industry, which we seemed to trust. The cities themselves were required to bring together the wealth, labor, materials, and consumers. So Carnegie built Pittsburgh, and Ford built Detroit, even though he detested the "unnaturalness" of city life.

Among many things, we did not learn that the city needs to be not only an efficient producer but an efficient consumer as well. Through the urban pattern that we established, we encouraged urban consumptiveness of land, materials, and energy. We did not know how the city could generate so much waste and chaos.

More importantly, we did not realize that encouraging urban consumption could destroy the very foundations of urban health. We forgot a cardinal rule of nature: Every species has its own best size and most efficient form, to which all organs are adjusted. We built on the notion that a city could grow to any population and expand to any area or could scatter indiscriminately without any form at all.

Then we decided that the city needed better transportation to overcome her vast formlessness. Our solution was automobiles, each requiring as much moving space as a phalanx on foot. Automobiles as a primary form of transportation raised to new heights the requirements to consume land and to waste already critical resources. With the extreme distances to be covered by automobiles came tortuous, bulging traffic.

In the end, the immense acreages in roadways, parking lots, and driveways became twenty to forty times greater than the land reserved for parks and usable open spaces. Creating breathing spaces or urban lungs was evidently considered to be far less vital than overcoming vacuous urban distances.

All along, we gave too much attention to innovations of producing and selling, which at first promoted the goods we really needed but then promoted more and more pointless consumption, more frenzied movement. We never really built neighborhoods with integrity. Each detached house, in time, became a command post for a family bus company.

Still, America does not yet fully accept urban life. We ignore the magnificent urban potential. Only the urban crises challenge us, and even here we tend to treat symptoms, which merely create higher levels of consumptiveness. One day we may realize, as did the ancient Athenians, that the good life means the good city. And when we understand that the city must also be human in scale and socially relevant, perhaps we then will make the city itself an ideal of society.

Ritual Sacrifice

In America our national exuberance and optimism have sharply faded. We look at the past and find that it worked; we look

Introduction

But what is the wholeness of the city? Unlike the human body, where wholeness has been defined by natural evolution and our task of learning is mainly to respect that wholeness, the city is completely created by human beings. If we are to have good cities, as whole and organic as our bodies, is it not necessary for us to somehow devise a kind of shorthand for the millions of years of evolution?

That shorthand is theory. Theory goes to the roots of form and function, means and ends, cause and effect, value and action. Theory, including design and experimentation, is society's substitution for millennia of accidental mutations. I doubt that we can devise an organic urban system, or any system at all, without first creating sound and penetrating urban theory. Of course, both theory and practice are tightly interwoven, especially in cities capable of intimately serving human ends. If good practice depends on good theory in any complex system, bad practice demands a search for sound theory.

As it stands, however, our minds, our organizations, and our made environments continue on their course of escalating rude materialism. This escalation seems to be our operating "theory" in building cities. How soon will we recognize that our concern for pollution or energy, for example, is tragically confined when our entire way of life is now structured—quite unnecessarily—so as to promote pollution and wasteful uses of energy? We do not seem to have learned that the power to do environmental and social damage increases exponentially with the growth of technological power.

The message of this book is that society continues to build exponential jeopardy into the cities, the basic form shaping human life and the core of our modernism. More than anything else, cities are the crucial structure of our physical, economic, and social being. And, I believe, an awakening to the nature of cities will lead better than anything else not only to an understanding of our jeopardy but also to the exciting potential of society made possible by the technological system.

I think we must now abandon our titanic approach to technology. That idea made sense only in the industrial start-up period. The beneficial role of technology in the future depends primarily on technology becoming an integrated and harmonious part of more efficient cities. Technology operating independently of a higher urban integration is the major impediment to what we now call *appropriate technology*. Being appropriate means restraint, balance, and synthesis—qualities achievable only with efficient cities.

Technology can become an articulate bridge between nature and society by using more leverage and less brute force. That possibility resides mainly in the unique organizing qualities of the city. A good city orchestrates all things that work well together, technology most of all. But, as we see in these pages, technology has come into conflict with the city and has largely supplanted its synthesizing qualities by destroying the contiguities and ligaments always associated with cities in the past. Then, when the city becomes consumptive and wasteful, technology rapidly accelerates its exploitation of both nature and society to overcome the inefficiencies.

What we speak of here, then, is nothing less than the direction of civilization. Normally we only talk about the particular things of civilization (such as its art, its medicine, or its engineering), not of its wholeness. On reflection, we know that the nature of cities largely defines the nature of civilization. Here, too, we only talk about the particular things of the city and fail to deal with its wholeness, its effect on the whole personality, or its effect on the course of society.

Despite our particularizations, the city does affect the wholeness of social life, far more than government, economics, or technology, especially in people's everyday life. The city represents the specific local form of society, that is, the organic or vital quality of environments, institutions, and behavioral patterns created by and for people themselves. When we can view the city as the setting in which self-determining personality can emerge, then I believe we will see its most creative potential.

I hope, therefore, that this volume will forcefully underscore how the city is among the highest creative works of society and how it is the formative setting for nearly all other creative human works.

of science and bureaucratic organization will resolve them. Yet the debilitations grow, are interwoven into the warp and woof of society, and really become a part of "progress" itself. Their penetrating destructiveness is camouflaged by the brilliant floral wreath of affluence. For many decades, the inner social decay has been the theme of philosophers, novelists, poets, and playwrights, as well as the subject of social scientists and the platform of reformists. The same conditions have also prompted the conservative mind to fall back on the fundamentalist, preindustrial faith in simple individualism and pure capitalism. The manifestations of social decay continue to be underestimated, seen either as eddies, when in fact they constitute the flooding mainstream, or as special solutions, when in fact they are a fundamental part of the general problem.

Consider the breadth and penetration of this historic predicament:

- Pervasive deterioration of human environments, physically, functionally, socially, and esthetically.
- A goods intoxication and a forced consumption, based on a social and environmental structure that demands purchases.
- A gross misapplication of technology, involving energy, consumer products, housing, construction, transportation, and food preparation.
- Exponential depletion of nonrenewable resources, especially energy and metals.
- Civic bankruptcy of democratic local government in metropolitan areas, including the nature of participation, control, and services.
- Rising health hazards and diseases—ranging from traffic accidents to nervous disorders, heart diseases, and cancer—combined with a malfunctioning system of health services.
- Misdirected education that emphasizes specialized productive-consumptive citizenship while excluding broader humanistic purposes.
- A spread of defensive privacy and an inability to establish creative intimacy, resulting in a self-deprivation of association, experience, and growth.
- A depreciation of the roles, values, and overall validity of family life.

- A decline in the importance and meaning of the *places* of work, play, and social interaction, the *social continuity and content* of events surrounding the individual, and the *psychosocial integrity* of the individual.
- Deepening social alienation, which calcifies human behavior, promoted by the fractured nature of urban life.
- Growth of crime—ironically paralleling the growth of affluence.
- Surges of drug abuse, alcoholism, mental illness, and suicide.

Taken together, these conditions highlight a massive inner human defeat that is overtaking the dramatic external successes of productive technology. No single cause can explain this counter-progress or its fundamental threat to life. But a common locus of causes is found in the forms and functions of the city. The disruptive conditions are physically contained there, had their genesis there, and have their greatest human impact there. Increasingly powerful evidence points to myriad conflicts, wastes, and debilitations imbedded in the very anatomy of the cities we make, their layout, their transportation network, and their pattern of commerce and industry. These conflicts penetrate a large part of our urban life, although they are disguised by high output and high income, that is, by wasteful production and consumption.

Ironies abound. Thousands of scientists, technicians, therapists, and police are employed, but fail to check the urban problems; budgets of health and welfare agencies grow out of control, but fail to ameliorate personal desperation. Meanwhile, wrecking yards, dumps, pollution, ugliness, and urban decay grow faster than ever. Finally, due to bad public accounting, the degenerative processes of the ill-formed cities are reported as increased product and service, material progress, economic growth, and a higher standard of living.

Making Revolution

Armies of observers have described our times as revolutionary. Since World War II, we have witnessed the atomic age, the computer age, the space age, and the bioengineering age. These have been suggested by some persons as being as epochal as the Iron and Bronze ages or the Renaissance and Industrial Revolution.

Getting on Top of the Revolution

to the future and find that it will not work, even while many old indexes of progress continue upward. We are dismayed that our struggle to tame nature is becoming a gigantic overkill. And we are shocked to discover that our so recently built cities and metropolitan areas have become technological rats' nests. Perhaps our shock and dismay are the metamorphoses of a new belief, a new faith, a new foundation of action. But right now our disenchantment runs deep.

Times are both good and bad, yet they have never been more promising. Buried in these words are the paradoxes that make old virtues into hard-core vices and old phobias into vast possibilities. We have to recognize, for example, that most of our modern problems arise not because we have failed, but rather because we have succeeded. Our success is affluence. The game we play is prosperity. Yet the game forces us to higher and higher levels of raw consumption, which ultimately mean waste and degeneration, the negation of a true human plenitude.

To obtain prosperity, we developed technology, bureaucracy, and economics to magnificence. To be sure that nothing stood in the way, we neutralized religion, stripped the family to its nuclear core, and killed community. We did, of course, create an exciting new cosmopolitan world in the early twentieth century, right in the cities we built so backhandedly. But the environmental and human trade-offs were enormous. As Robert Brady (1961, p. 3), late economics professor at Berkeley, once said, "we are prepared to sacrifice whatever stands in the way" of the technological process. The results that confine human behavior, however, are "extraordinary . . . as little understood in theory as they are revolutionary in practice."

When we consider human sensibilities, the cities we build have become socially bestial because the onward, upward, and endless standard of living does not recognize human consequences. Little wonder, then, that increasing numbers of people drop out of society or add to the hard statistics of social disorder.

With a mythical tenacity, we cling to rural self-reliance as our model of society in an age when corporate, interdependent production and consumption press themselves on us in mass metropolitan areas and chase each other in a spiral of pollution and waste. We have just not thought out the relationships between mass urbanism, high technology, growth economics, and what nature has left in her storehouse. Consequently, we are building environments of dangerous contradictions by continuing to consume at a rapid rate and by ignoring the fact that our environment is not a disposable commodity.

The environment that counts most for modern man is the city. And it is in the city that the American people continue to commit the highest rate of crimes and misdemeanors. And the environment of our cities appears to be getting worse. Consider some of the most common evidence:

- What mother is not now an enslaved chauffeur for her children and does not deprive them of some advantages because the trips are too many, the distances too long?
- What family outside New York or perhaps San Francisco is not forcibly bound to two, three, or four cars if it is to have full access to the privileges of contemporary life?
- What city is not ripped apart, decayed at the center, sprawled and environmentally destructive in the suburbs, or entwined with its neighboring cities?

We can be sure that the environmental struggle is only beginning. The environmental frontier is no longer air or water, or even land or transportation. It is, foremost, the city—the human environment that organizes behavior and virtually designs the circuitry of our mind, as well as determining our uses of nature. The biting issue today is the city, for it is the badly organized city that fouls the air and water, wastes land, enforces unwanted mobility and goods, and prompts escape to the mountains, lakes, rivers, and coasts. It is the environment of the city that we must confront.

Impasse of Progress

A stark and possibly tragic truth is bearing down on the Western countries, particularly America. Since about 1900, a lethal pall has gradually been cast over the highest achievements of science, technology, and human organization. The resulting debilitations are largely ignored on the tenuous faith that the momentum processes require unusual clarity and credibility? A giant awakening may be expected, for example, when the American people discover that their cherished values of privacy, private initiative, individual freedom, and individuality are denied by many of the very actions by which they are pursued, most particularly in the way they build cities.

Despite our disjointedness, inversions, and basic confusions, one consideration overrides and penetrates all others: Man has transformed himself into a man-God in a literal fulfillment of the Christian doctrine to subdue the earth and all of its creatures. Since World War II, human power to destroy nature has approached the absolute. The potential for indirect and unintended effects has exploded, ranging from unnecessary resource depletion and pollution to social disorder and nuclear blackmail.

With incredible new power, man's ego rules supreme when he can take control of 250 horsepower and maneuver it through the urban maze, jet across the continent for a two-hour meeting, or send a rocket to the moon. But miscalculations also rule with the ego. Note the blithe comment from a 1907 *Harper's Weekly:* "the automobile means that man has finally segregated a little bit of the giant forces of nature and hitched it to his individual chariot." Note also the innocence in a 1911 *Country Life:* The automobile "has brought green fields and pure air seemingly near our lives of industry."

How much control do we have over the powerful tools we create? Crude paleolithic weapons and fire, as well as the neolithic containers, shelters, and wheels, were the antecedents of the modern car, jet, and rocket. All were mind-directed changes, the first halting elements of a new super-evolution of a technical culture that takes complete leave of its biological chain of mutations and natural selections. In super-evolution, man is simultaneously the mutant force (experimenter) and object of evolution. In the period before 1945 and especially before 1800, the pace and impact of radical technical mutants was slow enough to permit reasonable integration into society, almost on the basis of one cause and one effect at a time.

But the pace of radical mutations quickened, spread to more fields, affected increasingly larger populations, created a more rapid impact (note the explosion of television in but one decade, the 1950s), had more complex effects, and sometimes had a calamitous effect on earlier evolutions (for example, the motor vehicle's impact on railroads, transit, and the hearts of our cities). As society became more complex and interdependent, the new mutations—such as atomic energy—became radically more sophisticated and created more basic social risks.

The acceleration of technical mutations inevitably produces greater instability. The danger of pollution, depletion of resources, and social breakdown arise more suddenly or accumulate more uncontrollably. But today, after the long evolution and sudden acceleration of technical power, our vital question is no longer the creation of new powers. The city, although it might have been a vital tool of selection and integration, has been instead the unrecognized receptacle of powerful mutations too easily adopted and too rapidly accumulated. The result is a dangerous and dehumanized condition in the radically new metropolitan and urban setting of life. Today's hard questions focus on intelligent selectivity and careful integration of all technical and social development. This is the revolution we await, and in it the city has a preeminent role to play.

Making Good Revolution

We are the creators of indescribable power; power capable both of magnificence and of treachery. Yet the power we create remains grossly uncontained, virtually assuring that it will be profligately consumed, environmentally degrading, and socially disruptive. The very fact that society wields such ominous power makes the creative abandon with which that power has been created dangerously obsolete. Future benefit, let alone survival, requires a renunciation of the linear, monolithic, and unstable revolution that put this power into human hands. Two other revolutions—equally profound and inherently stabilizing—are needed to absorb it. The first is human ecology within nature. The second is humanism within created environments and institutions.

The first revolution is inevitable because nature always charges society for its extravagances and indiscretions, although

Of course, it is the compaction of the new ages within half a life span that assures us that our time is indeed revolutionary.

The nature of the real revolution we make still escapes us, although it radically alters the basic terms of human life. Society's exotic new capacities with atoms, rockets, electrons, and genes are more dramatic than the deeper human transformations they help to detonate. But it is the human transformations, ranging from changes in the nature of work and marriage to new beliefs and higher expectations, that are fundamental. New technical and organizational capacities do not guarantee positive human results. Unfortunately, the brilliance of technical discovery is not matched by a brilliance of social uses. Alas, it seems that human direction of momentous human creativity has gone awry.

If the technical and organizational revolution we are making is to be sorted out and channeled to truly benefit humanity, to broaden and deepen every person's engagement in life, only the widest perception of the *human* potential offers us a reasonable basis from which to draw our course into the future. Old methods of organization and action, especially the bureaucratic method, and old criteria of measuring benefit, reliability, and compatibility, primarily the economic criterion, do evidently require fundamental reconsideration. In a rapidly changing human setting, old and seemingly faithful tools and methods, no less than new tools and methods, too often become erratic and easily reverse their expected benefits. This problem of sorting out our revolution, of channeling complex causes and effects, of converting as it were technical power into social grace, must, I think, be addressed in the form of the cities we make.

"No," said Norbert Wiener, in a provocative little book, *God and Golem, Inc.* (1964), "the future offers very little hope for those who expect that our new mechanical slaves will offer us a world in which we may rest from thinking . . . The world of the future will be an ever more demanding struggle against the limitations of our intelligence" (p. 60). To Socrates the unexamined life was not worth living. Today, must we not ask whether the unexamined life is simply dangerous?

The "good" revolution will occur only if humanizing thought is as daring as that found in the seismic movements of the technological revolution. Harnessing radical change for human benefit requires radical thought—thought that measures up to the power, complexity, speed, and utter novelty of our circumstances.

As our analysis of the city unfolds, we will show how old refuges, old symbols of human value, and old opportunities too often become dangerously exposed, inverted, and restrictive. Whether or not we make our revolution or merely happen to live in one, our profit, indeed our survival, necessarily rests on a self-conscious shaping of human behavior, human organizations, and human habitations within the limits of nature. No longer can we permit hand-me-down, preliterate, preindustrial, and preurban responses in a society that is already dangerously unified yet seriously underorganized, overpowered and future-shocked. In these times, the best we can expect is painful new adjustments.

It is indeed ironic that the technological and organizational forces that radicalize our lives are the same that wear the mask and carry the banner of "conservative" in economics and politics. These industrial and commercial forces of radical social transformation are corporate and centralized, and they quite thoroughly subscribe to what we may call the technoeconomic determinism of society. They are the most centralizing forces in history, and they may also be the most deterministic. Yet they are able to effectively cloak themselves in the preindustrial, preurban—and unquestionably worthy—social values of yeoman enterprise, social and physical mobility, and individuality. New and unprecedented wealth, with immense mechanical gadgetry, gives the ideology a compelling but largely false sense of fulfilled destiny.

Many confusions arise from this great ideological inversion. For example, we view the city as a mere collectivity, a vast open arena for the operation of these socially divisive forces, not as an organic whole deserving the same high integrity we plan for every industrial plant and underwrite in public laws, policies, and budgets. Put most simply, the individual has become lost in service to enterprise, and the misformed city is a primary manifestation of the confusion.

Mistaken language leads to a confusion of values and then to mistaken actions. How long can we tolerate such fundamental confusions when the terms describing critical social conditions and sometimes slowly and often indirectly, as with environmental devastation. If we do not undertake what might be called a "counter revolution," nature itself certainly will. The many warnings by an increasing number of authorities in a growing number of fields tell us very simply that time is fast running out.

The second revolution is necessary if society is to reasonably benefit from technological change. The kind of progress we have witnessed and the kind of problems we face preponderantly have a technical source. While siren songs attract us to the fantastic power of mechanical slaves, novel human experiences, or life-saving health services, that same power burns out many traditional social nutrients that have sustained what is most human about us and brought us to aspire with and for our fellow creatures.

A strong case can be made that both revolutions are really one. Whereas past efforts of ecology and of humanism have taken different paths, one responding to the devastated environment and the other to the devastated human being, we might now strive for their unification. A united philosophy of ecological humanism could recharge the essential ethical underpinnings of society.

A united philosophy having a common ethic does not preclude making a valid distinction between ecology and humanism, however. One stresses conservation and regeneration of the human habitat, the other full development of the human potential within that habitat. We dare not lose one by a miscalculated emphasis on the other. Both demand clearer social purposes than those formed in our rush to industrialization. Nor can we permit either to develop as blindly as urbanization did under the impact of industrialization, for our cities today are a rude throwback to such evolutionary dead-ends as the Mesozoic reptiles.

Both ecology and humanism have become potent social forces since 1965. The concept of ecology is rapidly influencing thought in public affairs, even entering into economics and engineering as crises constantly reappear in these fields. Strains between pollution and energy policies are appearing, but most of these will vanish with a larger perspective, for basic ecological validity of one is ultimately that of the other. And a new humanism is bursting out in dozens of unanticipated ways—although not always positively or creatively—despite the continuing power of raw economic growth.

A mere enumeration of liberation and humanistic movements—from the movements of women and minorities to the sexual revolution to the new interest in communes, sensitivity groups, and Eastern religions—reveals how human expectations are growing in areas unrelated to economic gain, not so long ago our nearly universal medium for human aspiration. Perhaps the freedom from economic determinism is the most significant liberation.

Just as clear, however, is the virtual absence of a fundamental philosophic direction for both ecology and humanism. Many Paul Reveres call for mobilization, but few are the trenchant John Lockes who build valid constitutional foundations for either ecology or humanism within industrial and bureaucratic society. Both movements remain gross movements, merely new levels of naive consciousness, and flounder against the self-aggrandizing methodologies of management and the powerful "worldly" philosophies of Adam Smith, David Ricardo, Karl Marx, and John Maynard Keynes.

The persistent unanswered question, the silent intruder in all of these matters—both oppressive and liberating—is the city, its environments, and its institutions. Virtually everything we say in the twentieth century speaks to or through the city. Yet we hardly recognize the city as the medium encompassing nearly all that is modern. We do not listen to it and do not understand its language.

As modernists, we are only beginning to understand the language of nature. Cities, like nature, speak to us in kind and constitute a new "natural" medium of life for most people in advanced countries. Cities today are composed of very exacting instruments but are formed without harmony or orchestration. As such, they reveal a primitive level of human order, comparable perhaps to the first crude cultivation of food grains or domestication of animals that foretold a long succession of immense possibilities.

Alas, since the city today remains a product of the marketplace—that is, created from random and generally isolated decisions without a form giving genetic development of the whole (despite all the motions of planning)—a basic theory of urban development speaking directly to human freedom and growth has failed to appear. Cities have been treated as a number of unrelated sectors subordinate to economics and industry. Cities then respond too easily to the power brokers who manipulate expertly and profitably within the disorder in dealing with land, public improvements, and trade. The city, although the dominant fact of civilization and the central organizer of both our most mundane behavior and our highest aspirations, thus remains a churning maelstrom of forces that serve the power brokers.

If we look on ecology and humanism as one, it is in the city that we must search for their most critical integration. In the city the natural environment and the made environment have their most creative and positive interplay. Humanism of cities, however, will rise no higher than the level set by urban form and organization. All the imagination that we can muster will be required to create the future city, for it constitutes the only possible foundation for what could become the first completely humane civilization.

Since our cities in the recent past were designed quite singularly—to the extent that they were consciously designed at all—to obtain a more productive society, they now speak to us beautifully only in the arts of industrial output. We can expect them to serve us beautifully in whatever way we build them with inspiration. Mostly, they have not been inspired, and they fail us dismally. We suffer while struggling to hoard the productive gold we so desperately mined in our earth and in ourselves.

Cities have done little for us because we have asked little of them. Now we must ask more of them if we are to save nature, our sanity, and even the productive power of the cities themselves. Getting more from the city will require learning its language or, better still, creating a valid ecological and humanistic language to build good cities.

Our minds are largely closed to the city. Our unwillingness to view it idealistically and objectively is one of the mysteries of this aspiring, investigative, scientific, and managerial age. The urban debasement seems to have resulted from what we may one day see as the typhoon of technology. The modern faith rests with what we are beginning to see as a narrow ideology of technology, management, and economics. This ideology provides in one alluring package the complete philosophy, goals, methods, and organization for man to become both Prometheus and Midas—that is, to ignore natural limits.

We are beginning to see the fall of this dangerous myth.

Such power, especially resting in science and carrying a sense of completeness, rightness, and goodness, grew slowly from Galileo's time to a swaggering authority bordering on religious infallibility. But the belief that science has, for example, *the* corner on truth, *the* inside track on reality, and *the* critical answers for the conduct of life is now fading. We are also seeing an end to the dangerous dogma that scientific truth should be pursued for its own sake, when inevitably it is pursued using vital social resources, for very human motives, and with very human consequences.

Knowledge itself has now been classified as a ranking human problem, being an integral part of the population explosion, energy depletion, environmental degradation, and atomic annihilation. Knowledge is legitimate and fundamental, of course. Its balanced acquisition is essential for stable human growth. But in the past we have sought knowledge for exploitive power and have equated exploitive power with development. And that power has now accumulated into a dangerous, chaotic mass and threatens the base of civilization. The challenge today is the creation of integrative knowledge, a larger wisdom that digests raw human power for fullest human benefit.

Ecology is inherently a sphere of integrative knowledge. So is humanism. Both represent revolutions in thought precisely because they demand a new perception of knowledge itself. And it is the city, more than any other environment, institution, philosophy, or methodology, that can unite the ecological and humanistic foundations of civilization.

Within the city resides the greatest concentration of *human* energy and aspiration. Up to now, the city has attracted broad imagination or inspiration only in its fragments, not in its wholeness. The whole city deserves attention as one of the most liberating integrators of human wisdom, sensibility and, inevitably, power.

The creation of the city is possibly the most revolutionary of all human revolutions. Conceivably it could be the best. For the most part, however, the deeper *urban* revolution has yet to begin.

2

Urban Destruction by Development

Cities have always been the heart of civilization. But now, for the first time in human history, cities are also becoming the universal medium of people's lives on earth. Only a century ago, the overwhelming setting of human life was the community village, which fit symbiotically with nature and shaped customary society. Now, with an almost frightening historic suddenness, urban life dominates most people. And our new cities have ushered in a radical transformation in which a mechanized, synthetic environment largely replaces nature and in which a bureaucratic, centralized social organization largely replaces folk processes. In an America dominated by cities, the fact of the city is resoundingly present, even to people on a New Jersey farm, a ranch in Montana, or in Yosemite Valley.

Yet, ironically, as much as cities represent the successful modernization of the American society, they are formed in chaos and defeat many of the real benefits of modernization. The old inner cities of Boston, Saint Louis, and Detroit are allowed to deteriorate in a spiteful contempt of the awesome wealth they helped to create. While sterile suburbs are wastefully strewn across the countryside, the hearts of our cities have become sharply less urban, less efficient, and less viable than a half-century ago.

Although cities grew with industry, industrialization seems to have severely limited our vision of urban development. The appearance of productive technology has seriously diverted our attention from environments and sustenance—or the total settings and processes of life—to products and consumption. The consequences are profound, and they are imbedded in every fibre of the city. Herein lies a great paradox of the industrial—or what more properly might be called the urban—age.

Urban Destruction and Creation

Aristotle once said that "People move to the city to live. They stay to live the good life." Modern urban development evidently remains at the earlier stage, still overwhelmed by the industrial foundations we have devised to live in cities, especially with such affluence. This characterization is especially true of development in the United States, where it has been observed that there was never an urban chapter in the American Dream. Indeed, we do not find an authentic urban philosophy underwriting Western development.

Few people understand how deeply destructive our urban environments are, especially the way they deny values we prize most. Since World War II we have suffered severe air pollution, traffic congestion, and intolerable levels of accidents. We face crises of transportation, schools, and sewer facilities. Taxes, municipal boundaries, and public services operate in a chaotic pattern and in contradiction to each other. We live with massive slums, watch our neighborhoods decline, and are dismayed at the cost and ineffective-

Urban Destruction by Development

ness of redevelopment. Housing remains basically inadequate for at least a quarter of the American population. Crime, alcoholism, and drugs threaten our children, our parents, and ourselves. Protests, riots, and bombings reveal a deep frustration with contemporary life. Most of us feel a profound personal isolation and helplessness. And now we are challenged with the probability of a permanent shortage of energy for our homes and cars.

Projecting these trends into the future, we may expect a dismal and constrictive life in forty or sixty years—precisely the sort of life we believed we were permanently leaving behind with the rising standard of living. Yet we do not recognize the central and dominating burden of modernity: the inarticulate power, massiveness, complexity, and interdependence of the urban environments we have constructed.

The lack of recognition extends even more pointedly to the positive *human* potential of cities. We know something of the flourishing humanity of cities by reflecting on the exuberance and élan of the ancient Greeks. They, more than anyone, defined the incisive, spirited thought and diverse excellence on which modern progress rests. Yet they were also townspeople who gloried in endless, highly charged *association,* from personal involvement in athletics and theater to the rich informalities of the *agora*. Their humanity appeared without great historic precedent and without technological foundations.

How great might our humanism become, we might ask, with today's assets? Is not the promise of urban humanism at least as great as the progress we have achieved in science and technology? Should we not be determined that it is broadly and profoundly attained? Once recognized and set into motion, this vision may also be easier to achieve. If what the psychologists tell us is true, the creation of urban humanism may be far more natural to our being and may flow more directly from our spirit of growth than did scientific progress and technological development in the past. Then, too, we may find that an urban renaissance will be necessary before we can fully benefit from our scientific advances.

We can identify four major ways in which new forms of urban humanism might arise:

First, we can imagine urban environments as having the

combined qualities of a resort hotel, a fair, a university campus, and a small town, all within the framework of metropolitan diversity. Analysis suggests that 90 percent or more of the urban land area can be preserved for varied natural settings and activity areas. Yet all common services, activities, and interests, including a job, a concert, or golf, could be within a few minutes of one's door. These services and activities would not require massive transportation, although mobility would be easier. The result could be a major expansion of environmental freedom: immediate access to nature, infinite personal opportunities, and varied association.

Second, a restructured physical environment such as that suggested above could complement a variety of new or renewed institutions, bringing them closer to the individual and thereby making them more responsive to personal growth and more democratic at the grass roots. In such an environment, individuals would be freer to initiate and to cooperate on a wider range of behaviors and endeavors. Festivities and traditions could develop a new richness, variety, and depth of human meaning. Local self-determination could become as real and as vital in the life of every individual as it was in the town-hall tradition.

Third, given a restructuring of both urban environments and institutions, we can imagine a broader and deeper base of cultural development and a dramatic increase of popular involvement. When encouraged and assisted in an appropriate setting, people love to sing, perform, play, dance, demonstrate, parade, draw, paint, design, form, build, fashion, read, study, theorize, write, search, compose, experiment, teach, recreate. They perform these activities best when individuals and groups can associate, interact, cooperate, and compete freely and creatively. Athens, Florence, Elizabethan England, and, more recently, Vienna provided such an environment at those momentous times when certain conditions of the urban habitat—which society could learn—came together in a fortunate way.

Fourth, we must realize that all urban potential rests on the potential of the individual person. Lewis Mumford has observed how we have transferred the responsibility for the liberal development of the person from the city as a whole to formal education. With Mumford, many consider this transference unfortunate because the inevitable formality, isolation, and lifeless sterility of the classroom imposes itself indelibly on the person. It is within the nexus of free interpersonal behavior—every day, all day, and throughout life—that the good city can help people to build relationships that are rewarding, stimulating, comforting, trusting, and truly liberating. The structure of a city determines why and how people come together. Whether or not the result is positive depends on conditions that are as discernable as those determining the utility of a machine, the effectiveness of a productive enterprise, the competitiveness of a basketball team, or the safety of a car or highway. Similarly, the good city can minimize the need for people to "use" each other for external or "selfish" ambitions and interests while supporting human association for its inherent human qualities.

Because the whole city has not been understood, particularly in terms of its potential, we think of cities largely in negative and fractured terms. Not only does this negativity prevent us from perceiving all of the city's impact on the growth of the individual but it also assures that we will be dominated by the debilitating problems and crises arising from such shortsightedness.

The city has become secondary to the special interests and benefits of each industry, business, or agency and to specific quantitative criteria, such as the number of housing units constructed or total capital invested. But these special interests and criteria do not make life in cities complete, meaningful, and exciting. Moreover, the statistics of isolated and measurable conditions (for example, income, housing, traffic) tend to become the only valid criteria of urban worth. Alas, we then emphasize statistics either of negative "goals" (such as reducing school *dropouts* or housing *deficiencies*) or of social disorganization (crime, drugs, alcohol).

Consequently, we become boxed in and respond only to the problems of city life, rarely to its potential. We Americans have prided ourselves on progressiveness and creativeness. In reality, the inherited patterns of our creative thinking—focused almost wholly on technical and enterprise development—exclude a broader creativity concerning our urban environments and institutions. Except when we borrow from our dominant and progressive technical and bureaucratic sectors of society, we have a powerful, almost automatic resistance to innovation in most areas of public life in cities.

Here, then, is the general setting for asking the underlying questions that beset cities or deflect their potential. Readers may judge my pessimism to be unbalanced, my optimism unrealistic. This view is fair, but one that I hope will be moderated by viewing the book as a whole, no less than viewing the city as a whole. My pessimism and optimism merge and should be so perceived. They give rise to a challenge to capture the fullest human opportunities of our time through the environmental and institutional determinants to be found in urban form.

David and Goliath

If a dominant fact of modern life is the pervasiveness of the city, that fact is recent in history. The newness of cities as we know them means that people bring values, beliefs, and traditions to them that remain almost entirely rural. These customary orientations to land, space, building, mobility, nature, and resources often clash violently when applied to the intense forms and functions that are necessary to a good urban environment. Unfortunately, it is precisely when the powerful energies of modern technology are combined with the rural inheritance of urban design that the most contradictory urban developments occur. These anomalies involve almost every element of our urban behavior: dwellings, automobiles, streets and blocks, industrial and commercial development, airports and railroads. When looking at the modern metropolis, therefore, we must recognize how severely limited our experience is in shaping and developing it to serve bewilderingly varied human purposes.

Although we may acknowledge its lineage, the twentieth-century metropolis is a new and unique artifact of human history. The general scale of urban population is ten times larger than it was in 1850. Urban land area has expanded more rapidly. A radically new urban anatomy is dominated by transportation, industry, and commerce—an enormous functionalism that could not have been conceived in 1800. At the foundation of the new metropolitan scale and form are two innovations whose effects are all-pervasive and deterministic: technology, with its physical imperatives, and systematic bureaucracy, with its sophisticated grasp of

Urban Destruction by Development

society. The new metropolis is unique, however, mainly because these radical transformations have redefined the entire existence of the individual.

For a demonstration we might imagine Horace Greeley reappearing among us, going West himself on a journalistic assignment to see what the young men he had advised to go West had actually accomplished in a little more than a century. Of course, he would take a jet and then a helicopter into Los Angeles. There he could examine the new, slick, unadorned buildings and observe the rule of the automobile in the downtown area. From the garage under Pershing Square he could then be driven on a tour over the country's most elaborate web of freeways, stopping at a shopping center, college campus, aerospace plant, drag race, television studio, and a scientific laboratory. The brief tour would end with a visit to Disneyland for a compressed summation of the striking contrasts he had seen.

Greeley would learn from his hosts that there are five million motor vehicles in the area and that a high proportion are used for commuting trips of up to thirty and forty miles. He would be told of the number of accidents and would have seen the congestion and smog himself.

Greeley's queries would reveal that the massive scale of development he had seen was hardly thirty years old and that few of their antecedents were beyond the memory of the oldest residents. Yet he would also see that such innovations plainly characterize the life of the people, if not dominate it.

After his tour Greeley would prepare his dispatch about twentieth-century Los Angeles; he might conclude it as follows:

> Such a reconstellation of urban life is quite a feat for any civilization. Of course Los Angeles didn't do it alone. This city of much land and much speed but little time or space and hardly an ounce of relaxed humanity is merely a decade or so ahead in the economically impelling momentum of monopolizing the environment by faster machines and stronger organizations.
>
> All that I have seen points to an astonishingly precise control over particular human and mechanical action. But, as much as I look, I do not find this matched

by a similarly precise control over the general results of action. Consequently, Los Angeles has had to extend the meaning of the handicapped to include all people who cannot afford a machine or who cannot manage the thing on a ten-lane rushway in high-speed congestion. As a consequence, the city has also had to extend the concept of welfare to include all forms of public transportation, which is not very popular.

The people of Los Angeles are thus struggling to create a freedom of the road for powerful machines and a freedom of action for powerful organizations. But in doing so they are horse-trading away their very liberty to shape a comfortable environment for themselves, to organize their own behavior, and to form their own associations. They utilize immense acreages of land but it is not theirs to use freely. They are fantastic travelers but don't seem to have much enjoyment in the going. And ironically they're doing it in the name of necessity.

All this the new society hardly cares to understand, though it is in a real predicament, and is quite happy to believe that the vast changes are the gift of affluence and that science will correct things in time. Yet, a bit nervously, they are beginning to realize that the new metropolis may also be a fearsome Goliath, which they call the urban crisis.

Goliath's threat is plainly becoming a struggle of metropolitan life or death. Part of the threat is that auto movement can never be satisfied. Part of it is that the fluid used to propel automobiles does not grow like hay. The earth's supply of petroleum is already showing signs of petering out, just at the time when Los Angeles finished its first network of freeways. These freeways assure that automobiles will be the only reasonable means of getting about. The dilemma was harshly presented one day during the fuel shortage when I saw six or eight cars waiting in line at a station for scarce gas and in the same view I could see an overhead freeway on which all movement was stopped because the huge roadway had an inadequate capacity.

The question I keep asking these moderns is "How can you ever win with so many people using so many machines which burn limited and irreplaceable fuels to travel such distances?"

The Goliath of the modern metropolis, Greeley might tell us, arises from its own gargantuan shapelessness. When is David—the people—to assert the valid social sovereignty? Is it not now time to reassess the first century of modern metropolitanism, to do so with new eyes and new tools, to strategically assemble the critical experience, and then to make the city an uncompromisingly good place to stay in and enjoy?

Paradox of Environmental Power

What is the nature of our urban disaster? The answer is very simple and yet very complex. Many parts of the problem are well known. But the core is clouded, confused, and misunderstood—expressed in simplicities that recognize neither the paradoxes of past failures nor the possibilities of the urban future. Otherwise our environmental behavior would inevitably change.

In "The Campus and the City," a report of the Carnegie Commission on Higher Education, Donald Canty (1972, p. 11) was quoted as portraying the American city as (1) profligate, (2) malfunctioning, (3) divided, and (4) unjust. One finds, says Canty, a "near anarchy of the metropolitan pattern." But the anarchy is also observed in other, equally disturbing ways. We may add that (5) the metropolis is antidemocratic: observe the acute political apathy in municipal affairs, counterposed against a virtual denial of any real, local self-determination of any practical use to the individual. Further, (6) the metropolis is inhuman in the scale and form of social interaction. Finally, (7) the metropolis is unsafe, both technically (such as in auto traffic) and socially (such as in aggravated crime).

The optimism occurring in the 1950s and early 1960s with the rapidly rising standard of living can now be seen as virtually a hollow illusion, a massive climax to a four-century drive for industrial development. Many profound contradictions were set in motion long ago but did not reach a critical mass until recently. To the wealthy, the problems arising with earlier stages of industrialization could simply be bought off: more cars, more homes, new neighborhoods, more servants, guards, and winter vacations in Florida. Now the whole society is being massively affected by issues, such as pollution and energy, from which escape is more difficult. Other complex issues, such as human alienation, resources, and natural ecology, also show signs of bursting out of the small, pained circles of humanists and conservationists.

Stewart Udall's now-famous lines graphically illustrate the commonly observable contradictions found in society: "This nation leads the world in wealth and power, but also leads in the degradation of the human habitat. We have the most automobiles and the worst junkyards. We are the most mobile people on earth and we endure the worst congestion. We produce the most energy and have the foulest air. Our factories pour out more products and our rivers carry the heaviest loads of pollution. We have the most goods to sell and the most unsightly signs to advertise their worth" (in Dubos, 1968, p. 192).

In urban America the paradoxes associated with the massive climax of raw industrial and economic growth are revealed in many easily observable, interlocking debilitations. A few:

- Why do American cities, the most spaciously endowed on earth, so strangle in congestion and lack openness?
- Why does auto transportation, the most elaborate and costly on earth, so nearly defeat itself?
- Why are commercial services situated at concentrations of traffic rather than at concentrations of people?
- Why do suburbs remain so sterile while city centers lose their cosmopolitan diversity and their ability to integrate the basic functions of the metropolis?
- Why do we give such high priority to movement (for example, freeways) and so little to neighborhoods (cut by freeways)?
- Why does urban deterioration spread so virulently in what was, until recently, the world's wealthiest country?
- Why have cities lost efficiency while industrial productivity has multiplied?

The irony cannot escape us that the great American wealth and technology are somehow used to defeat a quality of life in cities,

Urban Destruction by Development

destroy nature, and exhaust the elements. We do not trust cities, and we do not make a full commitment to them. But we do invite massive numbers of machines to despoil what urbanity there is, then use those same machines to escape to the outer suburbs, despoiling the countryside as well.

Technology's seemingly endless requirements, which force us to enlarge the city's area and to grasp for millions of private minispaces, further expand land consumption. The endless scattering then presents us with an unprecedented transport hurdle. Together, the undifferentiated population masses, the insubordinate technologies, and the infinite scale of the metropolis put an impossible burden on rationalizing the urban form. The planless chain of causes and effects is, nevertheless, formalized in plans and zoning statutes. Because zoning, the primary foundation of orderliness, segregates rather than integrates development, it creates massive long-distance movement. The resulting mass movement becomes more despoiling than the conflicting land uses ostensibly prevented by zoning: the dangers, noises, disruptions, ugliness, and fumes assure degeneration of huge sections of the metropolis. The commercial strips are tortuous examples of conflicting land use that zoning could not stop. Parking wastelands add their toll. It seems that conspiracy could not have worked better.

Something even closer to conspiracy is found in the automobile's defeat of public transit. With mountainous subsidies, the auto claims up to two thirds of the most important parts of cities. Unlike transit, which focuses movement on strong urban centers, the automobile bleeds urban centers outward along strip commercial boulevards, dispersing development radially and then circumferentially. The boulevards become clogged with commerce, useless for movement, and are replaced with freeways. As a result, the Beltway around Washington, D.C., and Route 128 around Boston make those cities into gigantic interchanges, more important for what goes on around them than within them.

A reckoning must come, of course. If the seventy million people who are expected to inhabit the Eastern megalopolis in the year 2020 should consume land at present rates of urban development (at twenty-five hundred persons per square mile or less), they will occupy a solid block of land four hundred miles long and seventy miles wide between Boston and Washington. And if present random patterns of development prevail, those twenty-eight thousand square miles—equal to nine hundred Manhattans—will become an unimaginable quagmire of human chaos.

Such a future is frightening to contemplate. The lack of sufficient concentrations in strong urban centers will produce wild patterns of movement in all directions and congest even twelve lane turnpikes. Unclear municipal boundaries and irrational growth (especially with stringent zoning) will make a nightmare of civic management. Small- and medium-sized urban parks will be precious. Regional-scale open spaces will be extremely rare.

The simplistic answer is that there are too many people for too little land. But this answer is one of the most dangerous myths of modernism, for there is a fatal self-fulfilling truth to it.

The environmentalists have yet to discover that the vital question is neither population nor land, and probably not even human selfishness, but rather the structured relationships between land and people. It is the habit of Americans to divide the natural landscape into mutually exclusive private domains and then to use exclusive transport vehicles. Exclusiveness of land and transportation mushrooms the need for both while denying environmental efficiency and common amenity, as well as casual interpersonal association. With present technologies, fifty million people can be far more environmentally destructive than an enlightened population of five hundred million. Canada, with one tenth of the U. S. population, has nearly identical kinds of environmental problems.

The grim challenge to our current model of civilization is clear. Life itself may be threatened. Human freedom is certainly at stake. The passing of each year without new and positive responses increases the possibility of deeper cleavages between the classes and segments of society that must fight over the decreasing islands of social privilege. Social stability is threatened as the options for constructive development diminish.

Irony of Modernity

Why have we, in this century, built ecological and humanistic destructiveness on an increasing scale into the deepest foundations of our cities, the most intimate and powerful human environments?

This question, to which we will allude frequently, presents an enigma in a society that is devoted to pragmatism and is served by a coterie of advanced professionals renowned for their abilities to objectively analyze, plan, and manage the affairs of society. To understand the cultural lapse we need to search in the recesses of our understanding and action.

One limitation is created simply by the enormity of our success in devising millions of particular technical "improvements" in the way we do specific things. Industrial progress is unique in history. The headiness of a society cresting on a mountainous wave of human productivity is not easy to put into balanced historic perspective. Why should we not believe that the spirit of empirical inquiry can override the challenges now facing us? Our chief hurdle was obtaining the tools of measurable, testable, and applicable scientific knowledge. Our technical sophistication and unprecedented wealth encourage us to buy off our problems, escape them, or resolve them only through the process of producing goods—that is, to ignore all limits of nature that do not immediately imperil us.

Another limitation leading to destructiveness is our specialized or divided way of doing and perceiving things. Of course, our concentrated attention to particular matters lies at the heart of our success. Yet, regardless of how constructive and efficient each industry or particular development appears independently, the broader framework is marked by incredible conflict, inefficiency, overhead, and effluence. Effective evaluation stops at the level of the individual enterprise, agency, or operating system. Above that—at the scale of cities and regions—a peculiar reversal takes place, and the promotion of consumption, inefficiency, and waste becomes the unstated purpose and order of things.

The limitations hiding behind success and specialized interest would be visible were it not for another, deeper limitation that will concern us frequently: Consumptive, wasteful cities are necessary to sustain economic growth. This equation has been true ever since the productive system became physically capable of more than meeting the immediate consumer needs of the population—gradually, between about 1900 and 1950—and increasingly depends on special stimulants to raise the demand for production, construction, and transportation. Even urban deterioration contributes to economic growth because it encourages abandonment, escape, and development at new, higher scales of consumption of land and machines. The city itself has become essentially a throw-away product in a system that knows only acceleration as its means of creating economic growth and relieving urban distress.

Probably our most fundamental lesson, then, is to realize that we do not yet have a grasp of the real issues that shape our destiny.

Despite the statements of many urbanists and environmentalists to the contrary, the central issues are not clean air and water, endangered species or environments, more money for housing and urban renewal, or even energy, certainly not in their separate capacities. These issues are relevant, perhaps necessary, but not basic. What is basic is the structure of the human environment, the city. Building a good city—a framework for all separate things to work harmoniously—is essential in order to alleviate each of the separate issues of development. Separate concerns considered separately merely trap us into building an even larger environmental destructiveness.

The second lesson is that our society simply does not know how to shape a congenial urban setting for human beings.

New York daily reminds us that we do not know how to functionally organize the metropolitan masses into a workable whole. Los Angeles amply demonstrates that we have not learned to apply technology, especially transportation, to improve rather than to reduce overall urban efficiency. Neither New York nor Miami nor Phoenix demonstrates that we know how to achieve the best of both the natural and the made environments. Whether in Watts, Bedford Stuyvesant, or the Portlands and Springfields, we all feel deeply, even if unconsciously, that cities have failed to create a socially valid environment for urban humanity. The crazy quilt of local governments and special districts in northeast New Jersey and the San Francisco Bay Area, as well as the bleak no-name vastness of Chicago's living areas, dramatizes our failure to come to terms with local democracy both physically and institutionally.

Urban Destruction by Development

We need not tour the Newarks of America to see the tragedies we build. Any city will do. The arduous journey to work is an outrage, whether on tense, bleak freeways, through blatant gasoline alleys, or along depressing industrial and railroad environments, because it numbs the commuters to ugliness and to the waste of their own most valuable resource: time. Shopping is not any better. With shops dispersed to all points of the compass or along miles of garish commercial roadway, the journey becomes the housewife's chief burden.

Some of the most tragic waste, barrenness, and deprivation of cities occurs in the wealthiest districts possessing the best possible quality of development. In these districts, the ideals of ostentatious consumption demonstrate an isolation and sterility that is completely contrary to what a city is or must be: a functionally efficient basis for production and exchange, a setting for stable human ecology, and a hospitable framework for human association and growth. The wealthy suburbs deny each. They espouse consumption in spirit and demand it in form while insulating themselves rigorously from the freely enriching millieu of true urbanity.

Cities are a multicause, multieffect failure of our society: the failure of science and technology, economics and bureaucracy, politics and democracy, tradition and philosophy. Although each of these spheres of endeavor has achieved success separately—spectacularly in some cases—together they have failed to create an efficient, congenial, and sociable environment for people in cities. If the environment we build will not threaten human survival within the span of a lifetime, it already questions many merits of survival.

The paradox of cities thus presents us with a tragic irony. Cities are necessary for the creation of wealth, leisure, and life-saving science. They have grown immensely in the process of industrialization and have expanded the possibilities of the good life into an entirely new realm. But these same cities have in the course of their development acquired the form and function of chaos. The chaos of the city denies true affluence; moreover, the misformed environments and institutions of the city undermine the deepest foundations of healthy human intimacy and trust.

Three broad, interwoven levels of urban conflict are evident. The underlying conflict involves misuse of land and space; construction of endlessly disconnected buildings that house miscellaneous activities; promotion of massive, diffuse transportation into a necessity; and a pervasive and oppressive divisiveness of roadways and vehicles serving individual transportation. The manifestations are general urban disorder and reduced urban performance in every district and sector (which people erroneously perceive as normal and unchangeable). The direct results are more trips and greater distances, traffic congestion and danger, air and noise pollution, and a disastrous quality of the human environment. Work, services, and social activities become less accessible, while transportation itself becomes a larger part of the work, services, and costs of urban life.

The second level of conflict is a reaction to, and a compounding of, the first. People revolt against bad environments whenever they can. They escape to the newer suburbs and abandon most older parts of the city, leaving these sections to massive deterioration. Partly consequence and partly cause, the reaction accelerates a game of the urban environment that has no end and cannot be won. Ultimately this game means a "Los Angelization" of the earth, turning it into a mass habitat of defensive privacy, incessant movement, environmental degradation, and resource depletion.

The third level of conflict exists within people themselves and represents an internalization of external disorganization. "Chaos in human relationships," writes Rene Dubos, "has the same origin as chaos in the relationships between man and his environment" (1968, p. 16). A large segment of modern writing reveals the deeply alienating influences of city life. Never before has the feeling of personal helplessness and emotional isolation so deeply pervaded the American people. The results are varied, and social problems are always difficult to relate to specific causes. But it is not difficult to perceive that aggressive responses of individuals to high levels of personal frustration are the foundation for rising levels of crime and for the sudden bursts of protest, rioting, and bombing that attained a legitimacy after 1965.

All of these conflicts reside in the form of the city. The whole city—its pattern, its function, its output, its immensity—has been built as an arena of chaotic conflict. The modern city exists as a tumultuous, churning eddy in the stream of Western progress.

Urban Destruction by Development

We cannot escape the awesome importance of the city, certainly not its recently inherited internal contradictions. Cities determine very largely what we consume and how we conserve or waste. They therefore determine the fundamental ecology of our lives. The influence of cities is pervasive in commerce, the arts, religion, and individual opportunity. Freedom today, I suspect, bends more crucially to the form of the cities than to constitutional interpretation or judicial precedent.

Unfortunately, the powerful urban regressions undermine many cherished elements of the American Dream: privacy, ownership, mobility, initiative, enterprise, inventiveness, and individual integrity. But it is precisely the American Dream, silent on cities, that has left us insensitive to the delicate physical and social environments of the cities that could sustain vitality in those values. We are left unequal to the problems of such environments, virtually oblivious to their vast potential, and unable to realize major elements of the Dream.

Today we have built an economy of goods—more precisely, an economy of accelerating output—rather than an economy of well being. We have sought industrial and economic order. But industrial order has been achieved through a dangerous disorder in the city. Now another kind of disorder is beginning to rise against the economic system itself, involving the instability inherent in any continuous acceleration. And neither resources, environment, nor human beings can stand endless acceleration.

The terms of acceleration—promotion of consumption, advanced resources exploitation, environmental degradation, and social disarray—are, increasingly, identical to the conditions of urban disorder. Cities were built first to promote gross production, but now they promote raw consumption. Climactic economic acceleration and rising urban turbulence form a fatal symbiosis, which, if we do not intervene, signals an inevitable human defeat on all levels: physical and functional, environmental, economic, and social.

As he so often does, Lewis Mumford brings us acute insight: "There is something self-defeating about our technological dynamism: it is unstable almost by definition, because those who further it believe in instability, and do not realize that without continuity nothing that can be called progress is possible. In economic terms, our dominant system calls for constant turnover and constant expansion, whereas organic changes are changes that tend to promote equilibrium and regulate orderly growth. Those who are now making critical decisions for us . . . make the mistake of equating power with life" (in Darling and Milton, 1966, p. 726).

Cities: The New Wilderness

Modern man is a peculiar animal. Uniquely purposive, he strives diligently to improve his conditions of life. He has been enormously successful in special ventures. Yet, as specific successes multiply and spread to larger populations, and as each country's population becomes more urban, purposive behavior has become confused and contradictions appear that undermine the human potential. Imbedded in the city are many of society's most notorious contradictions. Just as depression is built into the economic system, a subversive set of relationships are built into the city. This subversion is penetrating, regular, and potentially predictable. At this time in history, the contradictions are "natural" to the form of the city.

We do, of course, recognize problems of pollution, congestion, energy, transportation, open space, slums and neighborhood deterioration, and social deprivation. But by the tradition of thought that created our industrial and urban system, we consider each problem only unto itself, even as we speak of interdependence. Consequently, we think of solutions to urban problems as smog control devices, smaller cars, more freeways, hot meals for the elderly, or family crises intervention centers.

Cities, despite the struggle of planners, epitomize the traditional forces of chaotic particularization: a fragmentation maintained in the name of freedom, a material waste propelled for economic growth, and a defensive privacy supporting the myth surrounding individuality. It does not matter greatly that each fallacy may be associated with a valid social purpose or individual value. What is critical to understand is that the illusion of freedom or material growth or individuality becomes insidiously associated with deep social chaos in the forms and functions of the city.

Thus, for example, although cities are fundamental in

Urban Destruction by Development

organizing industry, transport, social behavior, and the content of culture, their own inherent, more human integration has largely disappeared. Greater urban unity was once demanded by the limited means available, as society could not afford the luxury of urban inefficiencies. But today, given gross productive wealth and the eyes of the specialist, we are unable to perceive the essence of urban integration. The expert's analysis of urban real estate, the planner's studies of land use, and the complex evaluations of transportation do little more than chart the ebb and flow of chaos. Their analyses nevertheless legitimize the observed phenomena of urban disintegration, some say, as "the price of progress." Hence, we seem to find explosive human creativity matched by an inexplicable blindness.

Cities are not yet, despite all the motions, the object of serious public policy. And, despite the facades of planning, we have not yet rid ourselves of the belief that cities are to be shaped by the random forces of their history, that is, by the unevaluated consequences of innumerable independent decisions. We understand cities as if they were a primeval wilderness, not a higher "natural" setting for man, quite contrary to the precise control we exercise in technology and management. We do not hesitate to study and modify nature itself, of course. But we do not control the broader ranges of the urban environment for which we are completely responsible. One must assume, therefore, that there is a deep reluctance to exercise adequate control for fear that it might disturb the specialized spheres where our past successes occurred.

Design for Freedom

Western man learned long ago that old answers to radically changing conditions place an individual, organization, or whole society in jeopardy. Sooner or later, a nation that long stands pat on its defenses, alliances, and even its economic and educational foundations will find itself in serious trouble.

Sometimes handy formulas suggest what questions must be asked and what new answers might provide the necessary effectiveness. But at times the formulas themselves turn out to be myths, and "Maginot Lines" are constructed that are irrelevant to the more basic changes occurring in society.

In recent history the frequency of such irrelevancies has increased and their impact has deepened. Whole industries have become superfluous, such as whaling and carriage making. Sometimes whole sectors of the economy are transformed so radically that most of its participants become superfluous. Agriculture, not long ago both the occupation and the way of life for most people, is now in a latter phase of such a revolutionary transformation. Sometimes radically new phenomena appear that deeply affect the whole of civilization. A society may not be ready to take it on or to control its new condition, let alone to make the most human use of it. Today, both advanced and traditional societies appear to be in such straits.

If we can say that the *initiation* of modern economic development in less-developed societies is an event of cataclysmic social transformation, we might also say that the *culmination* of gross economic development as we have known it is no less cataclysmic in advanced societies. The industrialized and urbanized social order does not seem to be any better prepared to reorder itself to take full human advantage of a steady-state economy than the nomads of the Middle East, the Hindus, or the tribes of middle Africa are culturally prepared to industrialize.

Failure of less-developed societies to establish and to maintain economic growth under present conditions will mean deprivation, starvation, and death, primarily because many critical conditions of modern development—especially population growth and urbanization—have overstepped industrialization and the output of food. Failure of the developed societies to reorganize and to terminate the growth of the crude input-output economy will mean that the earth's industrial carrying capacity soon will be exhausted. Disruption, war, profound deprivation, and death are then also to be expected.

Society is beginning to recognize the necessity of a stable world population, although achievement within a few short decades remains in question. Population growth soars as soon as the first ameliorative conditions accompanying development effectively reduce childhood death rates and extend the average age. This growth normally temporizes after a few generations. However, society now generally accepts the imperative that a stable population must be achieved at an early date, before the earth's carrying capacities are overstepped.

Exactly the same reasoning applies even more powerfully to industry. J. S. Mill understood this process a century ago, although his brief discussion of the matter did not have a fraction of the impact that Malthus had on population. Just as continued population growth threatens industrial growth in the less-developed nations, unabated economic growth equally threatens the Western nations and Japan. A general failure in either arena will certainly rock world stability.

The West was fortunate in being culturally prepared to undertake industrialization and had ample time to pioneer. But it is now quite unprepared to bring industrialization to a reasonable organic stability. Current efforts to translate the gross industrial and technical capacities into higher human benefits are exceedingly primitive and groping. Time is short.

In any case, radically new conditions and increasingly powerful forces of instability immediately confront Western society. Every oil worker knows that the oil he pumps cannot be replaced. Scientists know that tradeoffs and overhead become more difficult as inexpensive fossil fuels approach exhaustion.

For anything so complex, many fundamental issues are relevant. In this analysis we identify two.

First, we cannot avoid terminating material-based growth. That will occur sooner or later anyway. The question is whether human benefit or tragedy will accompany it. The new direction of technology implied will emphasize qualitative rather than the traditional quantitative industries and products.

Second and more difficult, we must learn to think positively and creatively in areas in which we have been simply exploitative and negative in the past. Only very recently have we been forced to recognize how rudely disruptive we have been with nature and how doggedly uncreative we have been in constructing human settlements.

This second imperative is not a new Walden etiquette, a modern monumentalism, or a recession to Roman technology. It is nothing less than a complete integration of the various elements of the human habitat. The term *integration* is meant profoundly:

(1) to unite technology with nature, so that natural limits are always respected; (2) to unite environments, facilities, and goods so that decreasing inputs can provide increasing benefit; and (3) to design all human artifacts, from whole cities to heart pacers, so as to enlarge human freedom rather than to create the appearance of choice in a setting of chaos.

All three aspects of integration demand the same thing: design. But the design we need is complex, multitiered, and multiphased, as smoothly performing as an aircraft becoming whole on the production line. Such design also demands new theory, as coherent and involved as our knowledge of evolution from the fields of genetics, archaeology, and ecology.

Design to integrate the human estate means the positive working of the paradox that has functioned so destructively in cities during the last sixty to eighty years. Creative unions of values normally considered to be mutually exclusive—for example, secure privacy and full public participation, natural and man-made environments, or vigorous community and cosmopolitan diversity—may become the future source for enormous human creativity and progress. Thus, design may be our only reliable means to consciously preserve and expand human diversity.

Conscious design has been recognized as vital in cities for roughly the same sixty to eighty years. Why, then, have the planners not accomplished more? Most urban plans are little used or are used only when they support the special interests. But, more important, the planners' concepts of design and integration hardly affect the exploitative and consumptive approaches to urban development. The same fundamental contradictions, with few exceptions, appear in the plans as occur without them.

To be reasonably thorough and effective in responding to the radical conditions of our time, the role of government unavoidably will be reevaluated, especially as it affects the individual at home base. Land tenure will necessarily change at important points. Corporate enterprise will take a new role and a new character.

Yet our challenge is perhaps even more radical: to balance achievements and to make certain that results are beneficial to the individual. For decades we have heard about the necessity to create an efficient, organic, international system of money, trade, manufacture, and resources. The need for such a macro system is no doubt urgent, but we cannot build a valid world structural anatomy without also concerning ourselves with the healthy micro development of the cells and tissue of world society. The point is not marginal. A macro order of concern will necessarily focus mainly on resource development and exchange, not on conservation. Conservation stems mainly from the efficiency of local consumption and production—the complete ecological efficiency of a city or a region. Given the dramatic rise of productive efficiency in this century, the urgent, frontier questions now facing advanced and even developing countries center primarily on issues of consumption rather than on production or development of resources.

This challenge focuses on how society functions at the micro social scale of the individual: his dwelling, movement, amenities, work. Critically needed is a science and a system moderating gross consumption (while raising the quality and freedom of life), and this effort cannot avoid the pattern and functioning of human environments. Moderating consumption is the natural and necessary counterpart of production and exchange in an efficient social system. An organic ecology for world society begins and ends at home, at the micro scale.

Of course, macro and micro organic developments are complementary and equally necessary. There is a serious risk, however, that attention to the global anatomy and the gross output of the world will monopolize concern and reduce attention to the cells and physiology. And the first issue to move onto center stage tends to set the limits of discourse and crowd out other questions and issues.

It is the unrecognized issues that we must fear. Without a balanced view that fully considers the local as well as the global dimensions of human concern, disturbed cells can become a cancer that even the healthiest world system cannot manage. In these days, when uncontrollable factors too easily shoot through society, the broadest perspective on our condition cannot be lost. The issue we must now face most squarely is the human habitat in which the course of human life is most completely and decisively determined.

When we look at the city, we find a tragic vacuum of purpose. There is no generally accepted basis on which to preserve an urban natural setting; our parks, for example, are really little more than environmental crumbs. There are no definitive ideals of urban form, scale, character, or function to integrate or give pointedness to environmental design. Even independent developments, such as university campuses, have become shapeless multitudes of separated structures and spaces. Extremely scarce are the genuinely superior achievements, such as Rockefeller Center or the new town of Reston. Nor are there deeply etched objectives of social or environmental opportunity and freedom; the only operative ideals are, again, technical and economic. Finally, we have no active objective of safeguarding or improving overall urban efficiency; rising productivity of industry is largely lost in the larger disintegrative urban framework.

Plainly, bluntly, the outcome of the human revolution on earth is undecided. The human successes are too often illusory, false, or accumulatively destructive, whatever particular benefits they may confer to particular people at particular times. The beauty of internal combustion is lost in injuries, death, congestion, pollution, energy waste, and a generally degraded environment. The promise of nuclear energy pales beside the threat of atomic accident or holocaust. Even abundant, safe, and cheap atomic electricity does not itself promise a better world. Taken together, the onrush of change is underselected, underdesigned, and underresponsive to human values and the imperatives of our earthly ecology. That is, we do not seek change within an orderly framework, especially within the city and its processes of integration and stabilization.

3
The American Way of Citymaking

Development of the modern American city is a historic drama as stirring as colonization and national development, independence and westward movement, or scientific and technological development. Starting as villages in the first days of continental settlement, cities have been essential to such developments. However, until recently, historians rarely treated cities as more than a corollary of the central themes of classical history.

The lack of historic focus on the American city as a unified and organic whole was prophetic of the ultimate defeat of the city as a workable instrument of a progressive society. The historic nonconcern paralleled the broadly accepted view that the city was mainly a public arena for expression of private values and private power. The nonconcern also indicated the serious lack of ideals of civic form and public excellence, the barely visible efforts to understand and energize the dynamics of urban life, the rarity of teaching of urban subjects, and the necessity of corruption before urban reform could be undertaken. There is perhaps good reason, therefore, to say that the city historically has been a nonentity, almost a nonfact, merely a collective manifestation of the "real" facts of social history.

Also prophetic perhaps was the likelihood that the first English word to be Americanized was *lots,* which were drawn on the Mayflower to determine ownership of land parcels in the new town of Plymouth. In any case, American city-making from its beginning always emphasized physical division and separation over unity and integration. Of course, these distinctions were of little consequence in the earliest days when towns were small and constructed mainly of burnable wood. The spatial form of towns was largely determined by the extremely limited capacities of transportation and industry.

Medium for Endless Expansion

New lands forced settlers to make conscious decisions about forming their new towns, a matter that rarely occurred in the very slow accretions of urban growth in England and Europe. However, the settlers had removed themselves psychologically as well as physically from old environments. On new soil with a new social climate, many traditional restraints disappeared. In European towns with slow growth, a tree or a protruding building would normally result in a slight modification of the urban form. But in a new land with thousands of settlements to be built, a sweepingly simple and uniform arrangement was needed.

That simple scheme was the gridiron plan. No other arrangement could have been more rational: It was universally applicable and endlessly expandable, accommodated virtually any activity admissible to the city, was easily laid out, enabled parcels to be marketed by mail, and was manageable without much management at all. The gridiron assured easy access to every property and set forth the image of democratic equality. No plan could have met the unknown requirements of industrialization and rapid urbanization as flexibly. The straight streets forming square or rectangular blocks could be set out and surveyed without agonizing decisions. As a starting point, the gridiron could be an intersection of two roads in the wilderness. Or it could be superimposed on an existing layout of irregular streets, such as New York's gridiron plan of 1811, which systematized the city's northward expansion.

The orthogonal layout was first generally used by the rational Greeks, although they always modified it to accommodate the proper public functions of their acropolis and agora or to build walls. The use of the grid system is attributed to Hyppodamos, who planned Peiraeus and other towns, after which the method became widely used.

The uniform right angles increasingly prevailed in American city-making. They were prominently applied by William Penn in founding Philadelphia in 1682, used in town schemes approved by Thomas Jefferson, and completely dominated American urban growth during the crucial years of the nineteenth century. The outward reach of streets embodied growth and progress in urban geography. It did not matter whether the application was to large blocks or wide streets in the flat Salt Lake valley of Utah or to a smaller pattern on the steep inclines of San Francisco—there was an unquestioned faith in the gridiron. In 1797 an English traveler, Francis Baily (Reps, 1965, p. 294) was critical of our straight urban lines as a "sacrifice of beauty to prejudice, particularly when . . . streets cross each other at right angles, *without any regard to the situation on the ground.*" Today, the urban historian John Reps (1965, p. 314) views the three centuries of straightness and squareness with equal disdain: "The gridiron plan stamped an identical brand of uniformity and mediocrity on American cities from coast to coast. . . . Their lack of beauty, their functional shortcomings, their overwhelming dullness and monotony, cause us to despair."

But the pressure was on—U.S. Census figures for American cities of 2500 people or more show that the urban population literally exploded, growing no less than 450 times between 1800 and 1970 (see Table 1).

The common conception of streets and blocks, the subdivision of salable lots, offered another frontier for exploitive growth,

Table 1. Urban Growth in the United States

Year	Urban Population	Percent of Total Population
1800	322,000	6
1860	6,217,000	20
1920	54,158,000	51
1970	149,325,000	73

along with good agricultural lands, rich ores, and strategic ports and railheads. With gold and industry, real estate promotion and city-building gave great opportunities to ambitious men.

After the Civil War and until the grip of the automobile on American cities became evident between 1910 and 1920, the promoters of lots and the promoters of horsecars were often the same people. Each activity depended on the other and both were profitable. This coordination between land development and transportation would later break down with the domination of the auto.

City-making was specifically an economic activity offering huge profits to those who could best maneuver in strategic acreages, lot promotion, and speculative building. Yet the urban free market seemed to be a fulfillment of democracy and a system of self-improvement for the masses. Apparently, it did not matter that land values always pressed against the worker's ability to pay, that tenements built after 1835 often covered 90 percent of each parcel and contained many rooms without ventilation or sunlight, or that health conditions constantly threatened epidemics. Economics ruled our social concern, and the economics of crowding were very profitable. Such profits were firmly within the American system of city-making. Social Darwinism justified an urban survival of the fittest in the name of social progress.

In 1906 Max Weber visited America and stopped in Chicago, then a metropolis of over one million inhabitants and yet hardly more than fifty years removed from village status. He observed that "the whole city, more extensive than London, is like a man whose skin has been peeled off and whose entrails one sees at work" (1958, p. 15). This perception of Chicago, later memorialized by Carl Sandburg's poetry, conveys the vital forces of

American urbanization at work and, seemingly, its reason for existence, because Americans built cities to produce more consumable goods, not to build a better environment.

Gathering Urban Mass

The fifty years following the Civil War may well be the most dramatic and pivotal in American urban history. Sheer urban population growth was nearly eightfold. True metropolitanism appeared, not only in one or two centers but in more than a dozen. Nearly a majority of Americans were living in urban areas by 1915.

In 1865 most immigrants came from northern Europe and settled on farms, but by 1915 most of them came from southern Europe and settled directly in the cities. Railroads completed a national network and established unified national markets in this period. Simultaneously, major urban centers effectively acquired regional domination in the national exchange system. As regional production became more specialized, New England farms declined in favor of the more productive lands of the Midwest. Cities were the midwives of the broad social transformation of the nineteenth century, no less than the railroads and industry. The multiplying industrial output demanded a concentration of population as much as it relied on the interweaving of the Bessemer steel-making process, the railroads' demand for rails and rolling stock, the increasing use of more varied farm machinery, and a growing demand for factory-made consumer products by an expanding population.

Whether in the area of transportation, national markets, or industrialization, the only medium capable of accommodating and organizing that change was the ever growing city.

The industrial city of America that emerged around the turn of the century was like no other in history. Urban populations had grown to a new order of magnitude, and not in just a few places, as in earlier civilizations, but in many metropolitan centers, each with its hinterland of smaller cities and towns. Industrial and financial tycoons replaced the landed aristocracy; factories replaced the home artisans. Markets, no longer characterized by teaming plazas of traders and buyers, took on the diverse forms of grain or stock exchanges, department stores, corporate offices, and huge stockyards. Large parts of the city no longer housed people, but were devoted exclusively to factories, stores, offices, and railroad yards. The city of 1915 also brought to the country the first modest demonstrations of mass consumerism, including perhaps the most portentous consumable of the twentieth century: the automobile.

The historic uniqueness of the new cities and metropolitan areas extended far beyond their new industrial roles. Many new facilities and improvements were created in these years that made the growing cities minimally safe, more functional, and—for many—more tolerable. Of foremost importance were measures to assure the survival of the growing concentrations of people, many of whom were crowded into dismal apartment boxes that threatened health and spurred crime. Sanitation and housing improvements were, some authorities claim, just one step ahead of epidemic or disaster.

Only ten cities had sewer systems at the time of the Civil War. By 1875 the number increased to one hundred. The first sewage treatment began in the 1880s. Water was first filtered in the 1870s and chlorinated a decade later. New York, with the most dismal tenements, instituted important building-code improvements in 1867, 1887, and 1901. Bathrooms began to be standard components in new homes during the 1880s and 1890s. Regular uniformed police, adopted in eight cities by 1865, were common soon thereafter.

With a new scale of population, new distances of urban travel, and larger, more concentrated work centers, formal urban communications became a major area of innovation. New York claimed four elevated railroad lines in the 1870s, reflecting its larger population and higher densities, which these lines helped to promote. Horsecar lines claimed over 4000 miles by 1890. Electric trolleys were first installed in 1887. By 1900 they included 15,000 miles of tracks and 48,000 cars, demonstrating the speed and dynamics of change in the period. Costly subways, introduced in Boston in 1897, grew only to a few hundred miles by the 1920s when extension and improvement came to a virtual halt.

Improved surface transportation complemented new building technologies, which together made more compact and efficient urban patterns possible in some locations and caused crowding in

The American Way of Citymaking

others. Steel-framed structures were first erected in the 1850s, and these made possible safe high-rise buildings. High-rise buildings also required elevators, which were not long in coming. Hydraulic elevators were first imported from England in 1866; two decades later, electric elevators were available.

Powerful changes in urban life also appeared with electricity and telephone service. New York recorded the first steam electricity in 1882; this electric plant, built by Thomas Edison, primarily lit his newly invented incandescent lights. Telephone lines were first strung in the late 1870s. The 48,000 telephones in 1880 increased dramatically to 250,000 in 1890 and 2,000,000 in 1900.

Possibly the sense of progress and the emerging uniqueness of this first stage of modern urban life are revealed as much in recreation and entertainment as in the new anatomy and physiology demanded by the city's growing scale and complexity. For it was in the post-Civil War period that today's prevalent pattern of sports, leisure, and cultural behavior appeared.

Of the major American competitive sports, only baseball, derived from cricket, developed its present form in an earlier period (between 1839 and 1845). The first professional baseball team was organized in 1869 at Cincinnati. Football evolved from soccer in the 1860s and 1870s. Basketball was invented in Springfield, Massachusetts in 1891 specifically as a winter indoor sport, and complemented the increasing number of gymnasiums since the 1880s. Tennis was introduced from England in the 1870s, and golf came from Scotland in 1888. Croquet, roller skating, and cycling all appeared soon after the Civil War and were subject to fads and decline by turns throughout the period. Boxing was very popular.

Playgrounds developed slowly after the mid 1880s. City parks had a slower development, spurred by the prestige and status of Central Park in New York, which was planned in 1858. Two other developments—amusement centers and resort hotels—reflected the specific nature of cities. The amusement centers simply extended technological possibilities and commercialization from work to play. Resort hotels, sometimes in groups that formed urban centers, such as Atlantic City, afforded the urban well-to-do with a means of "getting away from it all."

Although development of sports and outdoor recreation by no means depended on the cities and was in some cases pursued more actively in the smaller towns where playing arrangements were often easier to make, most sports we play today developed and grew during America's most important period of industrialization and urbanization.

The changes wrought with new urbanism extended to education. Industry required increasing skill and better education and ultimately a great variety and depth of professional training. Urban schools led the way, inventing the night school. American higher education came into its own, especially in the last two decades of the nineteenth century, partially due to the creation of major private universities—such as Cornell, Johns Hopkins, Stanford, Northwestern, Chicago, Boston, Vanderbilt—and partially due to the steady ground swell of state universities. But it was the appearance of graduate schools in this period that advanced American education most. The first Ph.D. degrees were awarded soon after the Civil War. It was in those postwar decades that the diverse foundations of higher education began to be integrated, a process that slowly imprinted the model of the university on the institutes of technology, the land-grant colleges, and, later, the normal schools. Although some of the important universities were rural, such as Cornell at Ithaca or the University of Illinois at Urbana-Champaign, most of the more vigorous universities—as well as the primary university momentum, resources, needs, and outlook—were solidly urban.

Public libraries and museums were even more closely tied to the size and wealth of the cities. In 1870 only seven libraries out of 161 had over 50,000 books. Just 30 years later, 144 libraries had over 50,000 volumes and 54 boasted more than 300,000, while 1729 others claimed more than 5000 books. After 1907, Andrew Carnegie, whose life was devoted to building industry and cities through steel-making, helped finance over 1000 library buildings throughout the country. Similarly, from negligible development before 1865, museums made their first major stride toward today's level of accomplishment. The American Museum of Natural History, founded in 1869 in New York, and the Field Museum of Natural History, established at Chicago in 1893, were two of the

The American Way of Citymaking

most important. The Smithsonian Institution, although founded in 1846, did not reach importance as a museum for over a half century.

The aspirations, optimism, and sense of progress during this remarkable period seemed to many people to be synthesized in Chicago's Columbian Exposition of 1893. The common plan of this "White City" inspired civic improvement for over twenty years. Novelty, if not inspiration, was found in constructing many buildings articulated in form and function while retaining individual design. The exposition gave the observer a unique appreciation of a unified urban environment. "Chicago was the first expression of American thought as a unity," concluded Henry Adams.

Optimism between the Civil War and World War I was boundless. The many achievements were indeed fundamental and gave our urban life much of the prevailing industrial, commercial, and proprietary character we know today. Both the optimism and the achievements were intimately interwoven with the urban explosion. The American city of 1890 or 1910 almost seemed to invent "success." Henry Ford could never have built his cars without the vast resources of Detroit and other cities, despite his hatred of city life. Cattle barons depended no less on Kansas City or Chicago than wheat farmers relied on Minneapolis. Silver was discovered on the barren slopes of Virginia City, Nevada, but its developers resided in and brought the wealth back to San Francisco, two hundred miles away.

Any problem seemed resolvable with unending growth. Success and growth were one. Problems could be handled along the way with more knowledge or postponed until the next round of growth. The American Dream emphasized the onward and upward. Although cities were not a part of the Dream, they were instrumental in its fulfillment.

Sub-Urbanizing City Life

If after 1920 American cities began to show the first signs of a lower level of urbanity—along with a lower urban efficiency—it was undoubtedly because of another unprecedented development of American life: the sub-urbanization of the metropolis.

The earliest official use of the word *suburb* is associated with the census of 1880, and it occurred with one of the earliest official uses of the word *metropolitan* by the Bureau of the Census. Both words applied at that time only to New York City. The suburbs of the late nineteenth century usually consisted of row houses or tightly spaced detached dwellings served by trolleys and local stores. Most were also still within walking distance of the urban center or a major subcenter. And most were within urban corporate limits. The limited scattering that occurred usually appeared near the trolley lines, which were often extended into open country to attract land sales. For these reasons, the early suburbs are a genre apart from the suburbia we know today.

The term *sub-urb* is a very accurate description of the chief phenomenon characterizing recent metropolitan transformation. Sub-urb, or something less than completely urban, is the only valid description one can give to a process that first produces low-density, single-use decentralization or sprawl, then achieves the same low level of urban amenities with the high-density apartment boom, and finally reduces the ability of the urban center to perform its integrative functions and to provide a cosmopolitan setting for the excitements of urban living. Hence, the term has begun to imply the whole of the metropolis, both its core and the entire inner city, as well as the newer low-density growth on the urban periphery.

Although urban statistics are exceptionally arbitrary in giving a satisfactory picture of modern suburbia, being tied to municipal jurisdictions rather than the kind or location of development, post–World War II census figures do reveal some of the dynamics of growth outside central cities (Table 2).

Table 2. U.S. Metropolitan Population

	1950	*1960*	*1970*
Central Cities	48,377,000	59,975,000	63,921,000
Urban Fringes	20,871,000	37,873,000	54,524,000

The already large urban fringes of 1950 grew 161 percent in twenty years. Since many large suburban areas are a part of central cities through extensive annexations, such as in Los Angeles,

The American Way of Citymaking

Phoenix, Oklahoma City, and Jacksonville, the actual scale of suburbia now likely exceeds the population of the older, still relatively compact, and diversely developed central areas of the metropolis.

It is difficult to precisely define the term *suburbia*. Here it refers simply to post-1920 growth on the open urban fringes. Four factors generally account for suburbia as we now know it. First, there was rapid and massive urban growth. The possible forms of external growth were many, but the system of land tenure and the nature of private development demanded random, market-oriented, hop-and-skip growth on any available land. This pattern of growth was influenced, of course, by climate and topography, industrial location, transportation, and status.

Second, the rural image of life that Americans have carried into the making of cities has always been basic to urban development. It was, after all, one of the country's most renowned architects, Frank Lloyd Wright, who wrote and propagandized the *Broadacre City* in 1933. Some writers have suggested that the struggle to achieve this ideal resulted in the tract house of the 1950s.

Third, the low densities, whether in lots of six thousand square feet, a quarter acre, or the prestigious acre itself, were impossible to achieve on a metropolitan scale without the motorcar. And it is the car, operating with the one-family dwelling, that now forms the micro structure of the metropolis today.

Fourth, escape from the old inner city is perhaps the most illusive factor to understand and yet it is one of the most obvious forces of sub-urbanization. Most old housing became obsolescent by the rising standards of interior space, heating, lighting, bathrooms, kitchens, and appliances. Remodeling and rebuilding were discouraged by the low resale values, especially when set against the many governmental, banking, social, and ethnic biases favoring single-family suburban housing. The suburban escape also promoted ghetto formation until the minorities acquired a degree of affluence and broke the force of segregation in the 1960s. The spread of ghettos added an unfortunate climate of fear to the escape.

At first the escape seemed to be largely from the unpleasant remains of the nineteenth-century city. But after 1945 the higher levels of affluence combined with the ethic of consumption and planned obsolescence to drive people away from the growing debilitations of the twentieth-century metropolis itself. Thus, when the middle class moved to suburbia, "one could escape the urban condition—crime, grime, congestion, poverty, high taxes and bad services, inadequate schools, pollution, deterioration," writes the student of suburbia, Louis Masotti (in Masotti and Hadden, 1973, p. 20).

The great postwar flight could not have taken place without seemingly unlimited land, energy, time, mobility, and productivity. Only now are we beginning to understand how the consumptive applications of wealth and technical power, which are built into the city, are on a collision course with the deeper realities of urban life and the limits of nature.

Suburbia greatly modified the classic American grid pattern. The new profession of traffic engineering was established to improve what became the more important part of the gridiron scheme: the streets, not the blocks. Whereas the nineteenth-century grid provided a free and democratic equality to both the uses of land and the needs for movement, as well as a ready exchange between the uses of land and transport, the ascendance of mobility meant that traffic on streets would prevail in public policy over the uses of land on each block. Land development as such received little public innovation, skill, or assistance. Subsidies to movement seemed to characterize the limits of public interest; all else was a corporate or private matter.

Then, responding to the increasing scale of urban functionalism, an entirely new level of gridiron appeared. Major boulevards were developed from the 1920s on, usually on section and midsection lines, that formed huge blocks of 160 acres superimposed over the older blocks of three to five acres. Then, as the freeways began working their way through the metropolis in the 1950s, a third and larger grid was formed, especially in Los Angeles, where huge blocks five miles square have been evolving.

The three levels of roadway virtually reduced walking to a physical absurdity, involving puzzling and uninviting patterns of interior streets, noisy and dangerous boulevard crossings, blocked passage across freeways, and exploded distances. Shopping errands could no longer accompany a pleasant recreational walk or be its excuse. Seeing other pedestrians, a cherished but unrecognized joy of most walks, all but disappeared. The three traffic patterns dominated the urban plan and forced nearly all movement onto motorized, high-capacity, high-speed, long-distance routes.

The specialization and new scale of roadways arose simultaneously with the major functional separations and new scale of urban districts guaranteed by zoning. Shopping centers sometimes reached eighty or one hundred acres; industrial districts ranged beyond five hundred acres; new residential areas with only minimal services normally reached more than a thousand acres. Every major zoned district, in order to be connected to the others, required its freeway, its boulevard connections, and its interior street pattern. Journeys accordingly required an escalation up through the local street and boulevard systems to the freeway network, followed by a deescalation down through the boulevards and streets to an off-street parking stall. Urban exchange increasingly conformed to this mountainous overburden of access.

The new scales of land and distances, which followed the automobile's hold on city-making after 1920, formed a symbiotic relationship in the early stages of urban development. Although land development and roadway development were separated, one private and promotional and the other public and responsive, the two acted almost as a perfect team to create a kind of sprawl that would be inconceivable if either party were independently liable for the exorbitant costs, the excruciating traffic, and the self-confining living conditions appearing in the end product.

Wherever the developer could obtain an acreage or a whole section of land for development within commuting distance, often miles beyond existing development, it became the public responsibility to widen the rural highways into urban boulevards and eventually to build the freeways that such great urban distances and massive volumes of traffic demanded. The private initiative and public reaction were instruments of perpetual urban inflation, a physical mushrooming of the conditions of life that siphoned away much of the growing productive wealth. And it was practically impossible to correct.

Urban development became a huge game among the land developers and planners to see which land would be zoned for the more lucrative urban activities. Initiative and power resided primarily with the developers. And to an important degree, every distant development signaled an escape from the old inner city. And every development had to be followed by public subsidies, not only for roadways but also for sewers, schools, and protective services.

The financial stakes also rose with the new scale of urbanism. The single resident, the shopkeeper, and the small industrialist were each swept into much larger social forces channeled by and for the dominant industrial, commercial, and development enterprises. Many shopkeepers simply succumbed to the chain store in the harsh transformations that multiplied spaces and distances and created the new giant access imperatives.

Parallel events occurred in other areas of urban life. For their part, municipalities succeeded in annexing most new growth until about 1900. But big bureaucracies and big political machines prompted a negative reaction from the voters: They began to veto the annexations. The residents that vetoed themselves out of the big city said in effect that democracy in the vast metropolitan expanses was not working right. Subsequently, many suburban areas incorporated separately, often mainly in defiance of absorption by the central city. Many of the new cities became too large themselves to achieve a human scale or relevance in the manner of their administration. Democratic grass roots simply withered in both the central city and its suburban offspring. A physical distance of ten or even two miles to city hall is light years away from effective involvement for most people. How can a resident out in the San Fernando Valley expect reasonable attention to local needs by the Los Angeles City Council, regardless of how conscientious that council may be?

The suburbanized metropolis suffers a more basic incoherence. If, as some planners say, problems and possibilities define their own community of interest, the crazy quilt of municipal jurisdictions assures that that purposeful community cannot be created, that very little community interest will be perceived, and that even less will be acted on—primarily the issues of desperation. Public interests suffer. Since talented leaders will not tolerate the failure to get at the real public issues, those that would truly enhance urban living, they abdicate to less vigorous persons and those with special interests.

Another contradictory phenomenon has begun to occur.

The American Way of Citymaking

Until 1960, only a small percentage of new dwellings were multi-family units. In the late 1970s, however, even as Americans continue to assert their preference for one-family living, an increasing number of families are moving into apartments. Most apartments are being constructed on the distant periphery of the metropolis, near the beltways and radial freeways. Whereas high-density living heretofore was always close to the urban center and its great range of offerings, we now find that apartment blocks are being built on raw suburban land, far from almost every useful urban activity and dependent on the space-consuming and energy-consuming automobile.

Urban development has thus come full circle. We are building on the periphery the high density we thought we were escaping from near the center of the city. We are doing so with the same distances from work and services and the same social isolation and sterility as that characterized by the suburban one-family house. The high density that should afford the benefits of urbanity is reduced to the same antiurban characteristics created by the detached house, a direct transplant from the farm.

The full circle affects the older urban districts no less profoundly. There population declines, commerce evacuation, and rapid decay are the chief conditions of changes. Note the population decline in three central cities presented in Table 3.

Table 3. Recent Population Decline in Central Cities

	1950–1960	1960–1970
Detroit	− 9.7%	− 9.5%
St. Louis	−12.5%	−17.0%
Boston	−13.0%	− 8.1%

An assistant secretary of the Department of Housing and Urban Development has predicted that by 1980 we will actually have lower densities in our central cities than in large areas of suburbia. And while the large, highly specialized zones, the large-scale functionalism, and the jurisdictional fragmentation have prevented a genuine urbanity from arising in suburbia, suburbia has also been robbing the old city of whatever urban charm it had. We can hardly question, then, Louis Masotti's statement that the metropolis has been "suburbanized on such a scale and in such a way as to threaten the viability of the historic city" (in Masotti and Hadden, 1973, p. 16).

Moreover, individual suburbs do not develop a full range of services or employment nor are they integrated for convenience or efficiency. One must go from suburb to suburb, commercial strip to shopping center, or back into the central city for one's needs. The individual is forced into a diffuse, wearisome engagement with the whole metropolis to maintain a minimal personal viability. One's lifestyle is seriously reduced to a function of money, markets, and status. People are open to transport, commercial, and civic exploitations, and even become addicted to them. Personal social life is dependent on appointments and formal arrangements, either to entertain or be entertained. Casual social interaction—that is, association without the burdens of being a host or the tensions of both host and guest—is greatly diminished.

The suburb has thus overturned the metropolis, denying to itself and its inner city the expansive qualities of urbanity. This is today's meaning of sub-urb.

Functionalism on a Massive Scale

The seemingly irrepressible optimism and momentum of the period from 1865 to 1915 carried powerfully into the interwar years. Slowly, however, aspirations and events began to have entirely new results and new meanings.

The American city grew rapidly with few constraints of history or tradition, and its nature closely reflected the growing forces of industry and commerce, the new traditions that shaped the new ethos and carried the initiative. Industry and commerce controlled the content and direction of technology. Their power was reflected in the early railroads that cut right through town and into the smoke-belching steel mills. Yet until after World War I their effect on basic urban form was relatively mild, despite the smoke, filth, and grisly living conditions that had activated the first generation of urban reformers. In its primitive way, the gridiron layout functioned reasonably well.

But very basic changes were well under way. As people left the farms, they became less self-sufficient in food, clothing, and

The American Way of Citymaking

housing while becoming more dependent on jobs and wages. Work shifted away from the house and family. As kitchens acquired more labor-saving appliances, store bread, produce in tin cans, and other prepared foods became common purchases. As stoves were converted from wood and coal to electricity or gas, as furnaces and bathrooms were installed, and as refrigerators and other appliances appeared, the money economy became more powerful. Building a house became more dependent on occupational skills and contract construction. To obtain the new industrial conveniences, wives went to work full time in stores, offices, and assembly plants or seasonally in canneries and packing houses. Economics became more deterministic, that is, closer to the motivations of people and the ends of society.

The phenomenal industrialization and commercialization of city life soon ushered in the world's first mass consumer society, partly between 1900 and 1930, then more forcefully after 1945. A fundamental economic change began to occur as a growing number of people reached this first consumer plateau—almost a satiation—of goods. From the 1920s on, the *promotion* of consumption began its ascendance to a position in economic growth almost as important as that of production itself, and it would become increasingly essential to that growth.

In urban terms, mass consumerism had two principal effects. The first was simply the increase in personal goods, both traditional and newly invented. Since a considerable amount of new wealth went into new plumbing, electricity, heating, and appliances, housing obsolescence accelerated. Old structures do not easily accommodate household mechanization, and this fact propelled residential mobility.

The second effect was in transportation and appeared mainly in one product: the automobile. No other product except the dwelling ever influenced the city's form, function, and meaning more; and none in so short a time. Nor did any other product so powerfully propel popular consumption. The automobile not only injected another product into the city, it restructured the whole city to make the city a built-in escalator of consumption.

The automobile industry, barely in existence in 1900, grew with incredible speed. For example, until 1917, annual production each year averaged more than one-third of that year's entire registration. Note the exponential growth of the first twenty-five years given in Table 4.

Table 4. U.S. Automobile Production and Registration

Year	Production	Registration
1900	4,192	8,000
1905	24,250	78,800
1910	181,000	468,500
1915	895,930	2,490,932
1920	1,905,560	9,239,161
1925	3,735,171	19,940,000

Both automakers and motorists bitterly complained about the city's inability to accommodate traffic and parking needs. What they were asking and what they eventually achieved was nothing less than a complete remaking of every city to accommodate a gigantic new scale of motorization through the largest construction enterprise in history.

The watershed for the American automobile occurred between 1920 and 1930. In those years the industry reached the general order of production it would maintain for over a half century. This order of production was accompanied by developments that still characterize the industry: a regular system of auto loans, an organized used-car market, general production of closed bodies, and a shift from engineering alone to styling (and from "a mass market to a mass-class market," as Alfred Sloan phrased it).

More fundamental to the city were the changes creating an environment completely suited to the automobile. Based on the Federal Road Act of 1916, unprecedented amounts of money were budgeted for state highways after 1921, enough to build a complete national network of paved highways before 1940. In the city the same years saw the first development of "auto suburbs"—large tracts of detached houses with integral garage and driveway—reversing the trend toward row houses and multistory apartments. The first "superhighways" in or near cities were built late in the 1920s, helping to encourage the first urban sprawl. That decade also saw the first general development of off-street parking and the introduction of parking garages. (Parking meters were slower, first appearing in 1934). The service station, repair garage, automobile dealers, and wrecking yards also became universal in those years.

These revolutionary changes in the urban anatomy were mere steps to many other, more inventive means to bring the motor car into every cell of the city. It is hardly surprising that every major urban innovation appearing between the two world wars served or responded to the automobile in some basic way: the road house or tavern, which set off a long list of drive-ins, including theaters, banks, and in a few cases, churches; the supermarket and its more recent counterpart, the discount department store; the shopping center; the industrial district; and the most inventive form of urban blight, the strip commercial boulevard.

But the most rigorous, costly, and revolutionary invention was the freeway, a motorway design attempting to give perfect integrity to the line of vehicular movement. A freeway exists when a roadway has (1) at least two lanes in each direction separated by median dividers, (2) limited or controlled access, and (3) grade separations with interchanges. These features are intended to avoid conflicting patterns of movement and to maintain capacities and speeds at their theoretic limits, which the older superhighways could not do as they became commercial strips. Freeways have been billed as the only highway equal to the performance of the motor vehicle itself. Norman Bel Geddes, who designed General Motors' Futurama exhibit at New York's World's Fair in 1939, envisioned and effectively propagandized the city as completely transformed for motorization via principles of the freeway (see Bel Geddes, 1940). It was a fantasy, but it was largely realized in thirty years.

Since 1939 over four thousand miles of freeways have been built through American cities at five to fifty million dollars per mile. These costs are important not merely because they outscale nearly every other kind of urban investment but because they basically promote "automobility," the most costly and cumbersome form of movement in the urban environment. The tragedy of what we see every day but hardly perceive or understand is that the automobile disintegrates urban environments and that the disintegration then demands greater mobility: more feeder boulevards, more parking, more people escaping from auto-impacted parts of the city to more distant suburbs, more second and third family cars, longer utility lines, more school buses, and, in the end, more freeways. Freeways supremely magnify urban consumption, always pressing on our ability to pay, undermining the environment, and exhausting energy.

Freeways are revolutionary in another basic way. New York's Robert Moses, speaking in 1964, aptly stated the point: "When you operate in an overbuilt metropolis you have to hack your way with a meat ax." How could one be more explicit? To achieve an integrity of automobile movement one must destroy living environments.

The debasement of the city is not caused only by the motor car, of course. The car's incessant movement and vast speedways are but a part of the massive scale of functionalism that began with the railroads and industries of the nineteenth century, a pervasive and exorbitant mechanistic order that now threatens to overwhelm us.

Not all sources of this massive level of functionalism were strictly industrial. Some were founded in the changing conception of the city. Between 1915 and 1930, for instance, a profound shift occurred from the ideals of the "city beautiful" movement to land-use zoning. Most planners view the change as broadening the urban development approach and suggest that the ideals of urban aesthetics were never really lost. These attitudes are now difficult to sustain.

Two major facts about zoning are paramount. First, although zoning is now central in planning practice, it is based entirely on a *negative vision* of the city: to segregate and protect the bewildering variety of conflicting functions created by industrialization. Mixed or incompatible land uses, such as foundaries, machine shops, auto dealers and parts warehouses interspersed with shops and residences, destroy healthy neighborhoods, pleasant shopping, and, not least, property values. Avoiding such conflicts is the mission of zoning. The fear of industrial blight was great and produced a deep "separation reaction" that still permeates urban thinking. That fear was powerful enough to become the principal methodology of "comprehensive" planning after 1920.

Second, the separations demanded by zoning were nearly as

instrumental as roadways and automobiles in creating the inordinate distances underlying the functionalism of cities. As noted earlier, by forcing the separation of urban activities and requiring larger land parcels for each of them, zoning helped propel movement to a scale that demanded the wider boulevards, elaborate freeways and massive parking spaces. When zoning required lower densities to avoid the abuses of overcrowding (through the underorganization of the city) it also assured that transit on tracks would become impossible. The only response to the dispersed activities, low densities, and vehicular congestion accompanying zoning was more urban highways, expanded parking, and a vast back-up establishment of manufacture, repair, and service.

The significance of zoning is that the separations and high-space consumption central to it mean dispersion, distance, and travel. These have become the simple facts of urban disintegration.

When zoning is set alongside the distance-spanning and space-consuming automobile and its roadways, we put together the critical components of the oversized functionalism at the root of urban disintegration. Although huge urban populations, which occupy great spaces and travel great distances, help to underwrite the wonders of high production, they have the opposite effect on the organic quality of cities.

Society has struggled for many generations to boost industrial output. It is therefore extremely difficult for us to understand the self-defeating conflicts of excessive output and their detrimental effect on the city. This difficulty is to be expected, especially when we have built without an urban ideal that could give us intense feelings about what our cities *should be* for us, as well as how they produce for us.

The contradictions apparent in cities and industries—always appearing as "material rewards"—only become serious in large masses. We observe how wonderful the automobile is when we are on a lonely—and relaxing—road. But put even two cars together and there can be a collision; put ten together and there can be congestion. Build signals and lane divisions, boulevards and parking, then freeways and drive-ins, and traffic seems to grow by being served so well. So do the higher costs, accidents, incessant congestion, and energy shortages and pollution that inevitably follow.

Given our tradition of the boundless frontier and our faith in individual action, each problem is faced singly and pragmatically. Thus we build exhaust control devices and struggle to raise gas mileage by forty percent. But still the problem grows. Saving forty percent does not matter if we must drive more cars longer distances more frequently. We still run out of fuel. Cities are still disunited. A "tragedy of the common" still occurs, implicit in the immediate, pragmatic, specialized, and fragmented responses we make.

If we project the gridiron plan, our inheritance from a simple and forgiving urban past, into our less forgiving urban present, we can perceive that the mass and complexity suggest a live but vegetating urban body supported by machines that do little more than maintain pulse and vital functions. Ironically, it was industrialization that undermined the urban vitality, and now we must depend on industry to sustain the urban burdens. It helps us hardly at all to realize that we are materially "better off" when so much of that materialism overburdens our lives.

And it is here that we see most clearly the deep conflict between our rural heritage and our mushrooming technological capacities. It was precisely when the car came into general use in the 1920s that the American people reversed the trend to build cities compactly (even if they had been doing it badly). Reasserting their rural values when the automobile appeared, Americans chose to return to the detached one-family house on the largest lot they could afford and as far away from the city as they could manage.

Rather than turning our inventiveness to improving the range of possibilities of multiple dwellings, preserving more nature within the city, exploring the varied securities and opportunities of community, and developing cosmopolitan diversity, we quite literally turned our backs on the city and built isolation abodes in the sterile tracts of suburbia. Most people thought they were achieving the best of both town and country. In reality they diminished or destroyed both—along with the rural ideals of independence, choice, and privacy.

It is astounding that Americans favor exactly the same kind of dwelling in the city that they built on the farm. No less astounding is the fact that they prefer the same kind of transportation in urban and rural environments. As yet, neither the energy and environment crises nor the many urban crises have taught Americans that there are massive and fundamental contradictions among their pastoral values, their strident technologies, and the way they are structuring their cities.

A city is by necessity a quantity, quality, variety, and intensity of services, activities, and interests readily available to all. Any action that diminishes these conditions also diminishes the viability and benefits of the city itself. This, I contend, is the great central problem of American city development today.

Civic Depression

The American city, which has taken a progressively greater hold on American life, especially since 1865, might be characterized in two very different ways. The first description highlights the city's population growth, productivity, technological improvement, affluence, and surges of self-respect (such as the city-beautiful movement), and the city's remaking of itself for industry, air travel, and especially the automobile. Such changes reveal an unprecedented dynamism. Since 1865 each twenty-year period has produced major improvements in income, housing, health, and education. These improvements remain today as the most visible manifestations of change.

The second description highlights an equally broad failure and is almost an underground scenario. Very slowly but undeniably a creeping sense of inner defeat has grown from the same soil as success. A great public concern now centers on pollution and energy. Yet many know, or feel, that the critical questions and the accompanying malaise are far wider and deeper than these and other specific issues. Deeper questions are needed to get to the roots of all that we have done and all that we have learned in the first hundred years of modern metropolitanism, which encompasses and organizes the lives of most of us.

I am not blind to the glaring faults of the American urban environment of 1900 when I suggest that it was vigorous and progressive, at least impulsively, in the way private interests and aspirations found public expression. The so-called city-beautiful movement spurred into being a number of important civic achievements, from San Francisco's Civic Center to Philadelphia's Ben Franklin Parkway, and showed promise of a broader flowering of the city.

Many arenas revealed a great promise at that time. Public transportation, especially the elevated railways and subways, were expanding rapidly and appeared to be capable of giving spine and clear form to metropolitan growth. Although reformers were concerned about the filth, ugliness, and unrelieved squalor, industrial parks and garden cities with uncontaminated residential areas then seemed to be a realistic prospect. Even the automobile, then making its first appearance, seemed to hold great urban promise. No one yet needed to worry about the strength and viability of the urban centers. Civic reformers believed they could beat corruption and lead municipal government to higher goals. New housing laws had been enacted, and further improvements were in sight. Many were optimistic that slums and blight could be eliminated by concerted action, supported by the growing base of wealth. And in the newly established settlement houses and YMCAs one could find hope for a socially congenial way of life for the urban masses as well as for the cultured and wealthy.

Utopian movements were not in style in 1900 to be sure. Ebenezer Howard's Garden City movement was overseas and its American devotees were few in number. Yet the growing urban environments and new urban experiences were being explored alike by the university graduate from the small town, the farm youth, and the foreign immigrant, each in a practical workaday search for the diverse utopias the cities seemed to be developing, at least in material output.

But even as wealth was increased, back-breaking drudgery was reduced, and living conditions were slowly ameliorated for large numbers of people, most of the high prospects of the city of 1900 became hollow or quietly slipped away in the massive complexities arising during the ensuing seventy-five years. Instead of the city-beautiful movement diversifying into new visions and coalescing with other strands of urban improvement, goals seemed to narrow down to quantitative measures of material enlargement, as in zoning and housing. Quite ignored were the qualities of public environments, the needs for social integrity, and the necessity to promote

The American Way of Citymaking

urban efficiency. Urban filth and squalor declined with rising productivity and improved wages, but a large part of the higher income was lost in forced expenditures (such as commuting or yard equipment) or marred by air pollution, noise, and general decline of reasonably sound neighborhoods.

Blake McKelvey has noted the growing disparity between private economic growth and the lagging civic development in the 1920s, stressing how urban "problems were becoming more insistent and more complex" (1968, p. 108). But the old emphasis on private wealth continued, although today we commonly speak of private wealth and public poverty, as John Kenneth Galbraith phrased it. The issue remains a social enigma.

Both the Depression and World War II necessarily focused attention on the problems of production. The sheer scale of productivity occurring after 1945 became truly awesome in a world struggling for economic revival or industrial takeoff. The massive output and the resulting power it gave America between 1945 and 1965 was a national triumph, proving to most citizens the superiority of the American system and its vaunted know-how. Although the attitude that America had found the formula for a brighter world remained untainted, economists pointed to the serious gaps in private wealth that the productive system had not filled. These gaps, it was assumed, would be taken care of in time. And so the unstated answer to Galbraith's argument for a balance between public and private goods was that the growing private abundance would reduce—rather than increase—the need for public amenities and services.

The answer meant, for example, that a vigorous private housing industry was "preferable" to housing programs, necessarily public in origin and organization, that could renew cities and structure their form to create optimum and stable human environments. A large private boat that had to be towed fifty or a hundred miles by car to a lake was "preferable" to having a great urban park for local boating. The possibility of having good boating *and* good parks close by at a much smaller overall cost is difficult to understand when public dialogues are framed to exclude urban or public ideals. In any case, the events and circumstances by which

America came to its affluence seemed to cloud or directly avoid the best *uses* of the whole society's wealth.

Wilfred Owen commented in a news interview that "the American city lacks everything from which no profit is possible." The problem is more profound than what is missing, argues Owen. "Instead of seeing land as a public trust, we believe everyone has the constitutional right to exploit it. When anyone demands public controls on the pursuit of the dollar, we cry that our freedom is in danger. But we use the freedom only to despoil and destroy."

Moreover, the renewed emphasis on the large family between 1945 and 1965, together with its ideal of intense activities with boats, skis, and two cars, was founded solidly on the image of a suburban split-level domain—all the family's own. Automatic washers, television, and high-fidelity relieved the burdens and injected new interest into the single-family isolation cells of city life, but they also made it much easier to ignore and to suppress true urbanity. More ominous, the pleasant scene of a clean, white, wood-frame house with two cars in the driveway could not directly reflect the affluent-escape psychology of the urban middle class it represents nor the ultimate antithesis it establishes: the built-in deterioration of the whole metropolis, the life-threatening pollutions, and the precipitously declining energy resources.

Nevertheless, by the late 1960s the American infatuation with growth and high personal consumption began to disintegrate. Freeway revolts became common and shifted from fights over location to resounding rejections of the freeways themselves. Liberation movements flowered, although reform remained stunted. And, despite all the movements and the many shrill cries of crises, we still failed to recognize the fundamental urban condition. At best the movements brought forth traditional pragmatic solutions—specialized actions that often responded to special interests. These solutions did not answer the deeper meanings of the urban riots and bombings or the hippy's taking leave of virtually the whole cultural heritage.

Despite obvious awakenings, therefore, there remains an inability to recognize the urban roots of what may be modern man's first great debacle outside war. Today there are grave signs of society's first major confrontation with nature and symptoms pointing to what many believe may result in a complete breakdown of the urban and industrial order. The heart of many major issues—such as the structure and function of the metropolis—remains plain to see in the front and back yards of every city. Yet we use old and distorted telescopes and continue to look beyond our setting of life to the scientific heavens for answers promised by the old theology of progress.

4

The Strategy of Urban Defeat

Two structural elements dominate the form of the American city: the single-family house on an exclusive parcel and the single-family automobile on exclusive roadways. All other elements either reflect or respond to these overwhelming facts of American urban development.

The characteristics normally associated with this pattern of urban development are:

- Private decision-making for the uses of land and the design of buildings.
- Segregation of major urban activities.
- Two-dimensional organization of activities.
- Nonclustering of buildings (separated by lots and blocks).

The Strategy of Urban Defeat

- Nonintensive use of land.
- Long-distance travel for employment, services, and personal interests.
- High frequency of motorized trips.
- Elaborate access arrangements between places (from parking through collector streets and boulevards to freeways).
- Allocation of major quantities of urban land to transportation.

The sum of these characteristics is a granular city organized for easy exchange of property and endless expansion on the open market of land, buildings, and equipment. Schools, roads, sewers, and other public improvements are also built singly in response to the private "market directives" of urban development. By blindly following such directives, they too deny the vision of a general inner coherency of environments, of citywide economics, of communities, and possibly of a cultural identity.

The city is mainly the result of buyer, seller, and commodity operating independently. Although cities are very special human creations, the cities we create today arise almost solely in response to amorphous economic forces. The more granular or nonorganic the city becomes, the more it increases the scope and scale of the "urban" real estate market and consequently of durable and consumer goods as well. And the larger and "freer" the urban market becomes, the more that price fluctuation, speculation, and real estate opportunities are promoted.

Market values thus supersede all other urban values and become their common denominator. Market values verge on becoming the sole measure of opportunity and freedom. Zoning and planning laws, rather than directing urban development, act instead like a securities and exchange commission to prevent obvious market abuses and direct public debilitations, such as health and fire hazards. Otherwise such laws have little effect.

The power of the market also forces families to become small corporate conglomerates that must operate complex independent housing and transportation systems. Homes are purchased with a sharp eye on investment and resale. Neighborliness or social values are almost ignored, especially since most neighborhoods are largely inhabited with similarly estranged families.

Here, then, is another profile of urban disintegration, a condition resulting from massive populations and complex and powerful technologies. Let us examine the elements more closely.

House and Lot

We have noted the anomaly of building a structure in the city exactly as if it commanded a farm or ranch: a structure housing one family, free standing, made of wood or brick, and with a manicured front yard facing a roadway and a backyard with utility functions. Symbolically, the urban lot is a compressed farm based on an ideal of openness, privacy, and independent self-help (sometimes including the construction of the dwelling itself). Each family is organized to be a little Swiss Family Robinson.

Recall that the American custom of living directly on the farmstead is relatively unique. In most European countries, by contrast, farmers normally live in small compact villages, inhabiting attached or closely set dwellings. Where farmers do live on the farm itself, the dwelling is very often one part of the farm building complex: where the dwelling begins and the barn ends is not always easy to determine from the outside. Hence, the European rural tradition is psychologically urban and our urban tradition is psychologically rural.

The one-family house is an artifact of the rural past, a technical and functional anachronism in the industrial and urban present. Despite the range of sophisticated devices installed within it, the house itself remains simply a stick-built box designed for shelter and constructed by hand. Construction, man's oldest technology, has been labeled the most backward by the United Nations. And no form of building requires more archaic construction than the one-family house. Although some assembly-line techniques have been applied to tract housing, the one-family dwelling remains fundamentally ill adapted to industrialized construction. There are many particular reasons, but all reasons generally derive from the fact that small separate structures demand a fragmented and inefficient urban form.

The American house is a model of separateness and fragmentation in a society that has learned that these are conditions of inefficiency and waste. Its foundation, walls, and roof are individ-

The Strategy of Urban Defeat

ually exposed to the elements, resulting in a gigantic loss of materials and heat. Its utilities and appliances must comprise a complete system—undersized, overbuilt, and inefficient. Each element requires separate manufacture, installation, service, repair, and demolition. The general effect is a miniature industrial system built for consumption.

The economies found in sales volumes are lost in the mass duplications of equipment, low levels of usage (for example, washing machines), small and inefficient size of operations (heating, cooling), special facilities resulting from the larger inefficiencies (two-car garages and utility rooms), and machines that tend excessive urban spaces (mowers, rototillers).

The commanding fact of the one-family dwelling, however, is not just that it is separated, but that it is simultaneously connected. In the end, the connections to the city may be more burdensome and costly than the appliances that permit the separation. Each separated house must be joined with water, sewer, gas, electric, and telephone lines, as well as with sidewalks, wide streets, and storm drains made necessary by the impervious roofs and pavements. The 260,000 residents served by the city of Fresno, California, for example, have invested in more than 5600 miles of costly, energy-demanding linkages for sewer and other utility and transportation lines on *public* rights of way or easements.

The space utilization of the typical family parcel illustrates the waste and the isolation of the one-family dwelling. If we consider an average lot of eight thousand square feet (six thousand square feet is normally minimum), its use is likely to be divided as shown in Table 5.

Table 5. Typical Urban Lot

Use	*Square Feet*
Dwelling/Porch/Veranda	2000
Patio (outdoor living room)	800
Garage (two-car)	400
Driveway	600
Front yard	2000
Side yards	800
Backyard	1400
Total	8000

Excluding the space allocated to the garage and driveway, the typical family rarely makes effective use of more than about twenty-eight hundred square feet (the dwelling and patio), hardly more than one third of the land. The rest is an unwelcome burden to most people most of the time, maintained largely for status or social pressure; consequently, between one half and two thirds of every parcel is essentially wasted. As a result, the city's residential area is at least twice as large as it should be; services are twice as far removed as they should be; and children have only half as many playmates within walking distance. The waste evident in the typical urban lot thus sets in motion a greater waste beyond its boundaries. I do not suggest that merely cutting the size of the lots is the answer, or even appropriate. As we will see, far more dynamic solutions to urban space are possible.

Many lots are much larger than eight thousand square feet, of course, and require larger subsidies for longer urban connections, more machinery, paid gardeners, school busing, vehicular mail delivery, and the like. Yet when the lots expand up to fivefold, to an acre or more, they still do not provide sufficient space for all family recreation or allow a complete natural setting. A tennis court requires about six thousand square feet, for example, and therefore becomes reasonably feasible only on lots with thirty thousand square feet or more. But other running sports, walking, and horse riding require many acres in a pleasant setting. Only a wooded acre can provide a secluded or natural setting; in the desert, a house on each twenty acres completely disrupts the open vistas.

Thus, although even small parcels waste immense quantities of urban space, larger lots are cramped for most open-space purposes. The result is a monotony of minispaces. A larger openness, an urban pastoral quality, and a wide variety of park and recreation spaces are either absent or only distantly available.

People cling to the one-family house as their grip on privacy. Yet windows look on each other or are visible from the street. Walls are but a thin shield for family squabbles. Loud garden parties command neighborhood attention. To strengthen the flimsy privacy, fortifications are constructed with fences and high vegetation. Yet real privacy inevitably remains marginal.

The American house, although organized to be a separate

The Strategy of Urban Defeat

unit of ecology, nevertheless portrays little of the organic qualities of a valid ecological system. It does not produce. It is not an efficient consumer. It does not stand up to the environmental and social qualities attributed to it. It is built for independence, but it lacks the completeness and self-sufficiency on which independence rests. The forty- to eighty-year degeneration cycle of residential areas attests to a crippling impermanence of the city. All facets of the single-family home suggest that it plays a negative role in the creation of truly beneficial urban environments.

Car and Road

The one-family automobile and the one-family house are necessary counterparts to each other in the suburbanized metropolis. Without the car, the urban geometry of large houses on large lots in large cities is impossible. And it was the automobile, ultimately an equal consumer of space in the metropolis, that regenerated the one-family house. The car's mobility made it an unprecedented agent of city sprawl as long as wider and costlier thoroughfares were built. Many American cities of 1890 or 1910 were growing too large to make the separate house practical. Then autos appeared in strength in the 1920s to force-feed a half century of dispersed urbanism—although not without a wide variety of subsidies and supports.

The land and material extravagance of the automobile underwrote an almost unbelievable array of excesses in the city and influenced every facet of urban life. A thorough review of the auto's transformation of the city is given in an earlier book of mine, *Autokind vs. Mankind* (1971); here is a brief overview.

The extravagance stems from the automobile's mammoth dimensions forced onto urban environments that otherwise were developed on a reasonable human scale. Compare, for example, the space demands of the car to those of a person. A person requires a minimal standing space of 2 square feet (in a tight elevator) to 6 square feet (conversation space), whereas a car requires a minimal standing space of 250 square feet (if parked by an attendant) to 400 square feet (if parked by owner). Similarly, a person requires a minimum of 10 square feet for walking at an impeded pace and

25 square feet for walking at a normal pace, but a car requires at least 1000 square feet for stop-and-go movement and at least 3000 square feet for movement on an open freeway. Put simply, a car requires approximately the same area as a hundred persons in comparable situations.

Beyond these basic space requirements, the car's demand is always above that of the pedestrian, because walking is always required in addition to driving. When such figures are incorporated into the realities of the contemporary American city, the consequences are startling. Examine, for example, the percentage of space normally given to the auto in various sections of the city. (Table 6).

Table 6. Estimated Spaces Devoted to Automobiles

City section[a]	Percent
One-family lot	8–15
Apartment complex	15–25
Shopping center	60–80
Office complex	40–80
Downtown core[b]	45–60
Industrial district	10–50
Stadium/sports arena	70–90
Drive-ins	60–90

[a]Constructed since World War II or not served by a rapid transit station.
[b]Includes adjacent dedicated streets.

The figures in Table 6 strikingly illustrate the penetration and domination of the automobile on "nontransport" land. Moreover, the more valuable the land and the more intensively it is normally developed, such as in the downtown area or in shopping centers, the greater is the domination by four-wheeled mobility. And these figures only begin to tally the automobile's subjugation of the American city. Residential streets generally occupy between 20 and 25 percent, or more than 120 acres per square mile, of new subdivisions. Boulevards in newer urban districts, typically 80 to 120 feet wide at half-mile intervals, occupy about 40 acres per square mile. In a city of one million persons, therefore, approximately 50,000 acres are covered by paved residential streets, excluding alleys. When freeways are added, spaced about five miles apart, another 3500 acres are consumed.

The Strategy of Urban Defeat 79

Automotive services—new- and used-car dealers, repair shops, parts and accessory stores, service stations, wrecking yards, and the many parallel facilities for the trucking industry—occupy a large part of the activities along many commercial strips. These garish streets assure a gruesome travel experience, since they are pockmarked with signs and billboards, streaked with white lines and flashing signals, strained with bumper-to-bumper movement, and burdened with endless parking lots.

Such evidence of the motor vehicle's total impact on the city is only now beginning to be gathered. As yet we but modestly perceive how the automobile divides and isolates urban activities and then makes access to such activities cumbersome and costly (although the costs are widely dispersed and highly disguised). We are also slowly learning that the automobile's once undoubted efficiency, convenience, and flexibility are myths set into asphalt and concrete by the auto's transformation of the city.

The sheer quantities of urban land used for garages, driveways, streets, alleys, parking lots, boulevards, freeways, trucking terminals, and automotive commerce, make a good case for the assertion that half or more of the American city has been given over to the car, particularly if we count the automobile's role in creating unusable spaces and inducing abandonment and sprawl.

Society never decided to give the automobile such priority in the city, of course. Why did it happen? First, the process was self-feeding: Every road or parking expansion induced more traffic, which in turn prompted more road improvements. Second, the process was self-reinforcing: Each step of automotive "progress" had the dual effect of reducing the viability of walking and all forms of public transit on the one hand and of promoting suburban sprawl on the other. Third, the process was catalytic: The rising tide of support for the automobile after 1910 occurred as an interplay between corporate, public, and private sources. Investment in one promoted and often required action by the other. The interplay acted out the rural myths on the suburban lot and figured in the elusive struggle for privacy and individual ownership.

The powerful interplay succeeded in completely remaking the city. Yet it operated fragmentally and without a perception of consequences. Corporate, governmental, and private actions built on each other without focus except to serve growing traffic. An auto determinism—not unlike that of economic determinism—arose in a context of enormous profit, penetrating advertising, and powerful lobbying. The result today is a gargantuan system of enforced and incessant movement that should be sobering even to the most ardent automobilist.

The automobile, like the economy, grows indirectly on urban debilitations: Separations or urban activity are made in a struggle for mobility. Very little desirable open space remains while fantastic expanses of land are consumed to make that space accessible. Journeys of escape are a part of the process of urban deterioration. Dispersed and less efficient urban patterns are idealized as wealth and convenience. Endless freeways and boulevards are built at costs that would shock a legion of Arab oil emirates.

Although most auto expenditures revolve around the vehicle itself, freeway costs alone illustrate how urban development might have followed a more constructive course. Urban freeways cost roughly ten million dollars per mile. In Fresno, the sixty million dollars that would build only *six miles* of freeway could construct a million-dollar community center at every one of the sixty-odd elementary schools in the metropolitan area. Combined with existing school facilities, the new gyms, pools, club rooms, and libraries afforded would provide a magnificent service to every neighborhood. Yet more than fifty urban miles of freeway were planned in Fresno in the heady freeway years of the early 1960s. And freeways merely cap complete systems of boulevards, local streets, and parking.

But it is the automobile itself that entails the greatest cost burden. The steep costs of automobility highlight society's inability to examine the basic alternatives of urban development. It is instructive, for example, to examine our emotional readiness to spend money for automobiles rather than public transit. We well know that there would be a domestic revolution if families were "arbitrarily" assessed an extra forty dollars per year to sustain a viable transit system. But how many times each year are we just as arbitrarily assessed forty or eighty or a hundred dollars for tires, insurance, and repairs? How often must we pay five hundred dollars for an overhaul or three thousand dollars (with trade-in) for a new vehicle, often a second or third car made necessary by the disintegrated nature of the city?

The Strategy of Urban Defeat

The car's daily inconveniences are tolerated with the same willing bias, whether it means getting the car across town for repairs, being delayed by congestion, having to make frequent long trips for nearly every urban service, searching for convenient parking places, or walking through dreary parking lots. The journey to work—usually through ugly environments—averages between twenty and thirty minutes in the larger metropolitan areas, but it often exceeds an hour.

Our tolerance of great costs and inconveniences, although difficult to understand, pales beside our readiness to accept death and injury. Until 1973, death on wheels had grown to 56,600 per year and injuries to 5,190,000. How long would we tolerate these if the injuries had occurred in 25,000 train accidents (injuring two hundred apiece) and the deaths had occurred in 560 air accidents (killing one hundred each in ten air crashes per week)?

The urban paradoxes seem to revolve most acutely around the automobile. The irony is deep because the automobile can never be truly universal—even if it could be ecologically sustained. Today only half of the American population carry driver's licenses. The poor, elderly, handicapped, and youth are either exceptionally deprived of mobility and access to the city or must be personally chauffeured.

If we reflect on the consequences of the one-family transit vehicle and the one-family house dominating urban development, it becomes powerfully evident that an efficient pattern of urban technology has failed to appear. Transit technology and development had come to a virtual halt by 1920. In retrospect, we know that buses were regressive, acting to prevent the evolution of permanent, flexible, automated, and highly efficient systems of rapid transit that could have given spine and form to urban development. Building technology and architecture became stunted where they should have become most dynamic: in developing dwelling environments. Both office and factory buildings were constructed as isolated and unrelated machines rather than as integral elements of a human ecology. Utilities were built in a manner that subsidized sprawl rather than promoted quality, efficiency, conservation, and stability of the whole urban system.

The spread-out city resulting from the one-family house and car also acted regressively on the urban institutions that might have ameliorated the social condition of massive urbanizing populations. But rather than creating locally based organizations through which people could evolve self-reliant capacities to advance their own well-being, distinctive styles of life, and vigorous grass-roots social democracy, we developed instead a pattern of massive, rigid, and alienating institutions that brought uniformity and sterility to marketing, education, health, housing, urban renewal, and socioeconomic assistance.

Commerce and Industry

Nevertheless, the house and car alone do not tell the whole story. Promoting raw consumption of valuable urban space penetrates the whole city, not the least commerce and industry.

Consider how the space demands of a small, thousand-square-foot shop (such as a shoe, book, or stationary shop) have exploded. Although this store in a downtown area of 1920 or 1930 might have the same interior space as one in a shopping center, the gross space requirements have skyrocketed, as Table 7 illustrates.

Table 7. Retail Store Space Requirements
(In Square Feet)

	Traditional Downtown	*Current in Shopping Center*
Retail	1000	1000
Parking	160	4000
Street	240	8000
Alley	200	(With Parking)
Pedestrian	200	200
	1800	13,200

The low requirements downtown resulted because most people walked or rode public transit. The shop, say twenty by fifty feet, had slightly more than one on-street parking space. Curb parking occupied only about 160 square feet on a two-lane, forty-foot-wide street because street and parking access were the same. In small cities many cars were parked in front of nearby residences. Today the same store requires about eight parking spaces and part of a truck loading space.

The Strategy of Urban Defeat

The major new space demand, however, involves the wider suburban boulevards. Whereas the older narrow streets were fronted by stores or residences, the new and expansive boulevards and freeways no longer provide direct access to parking spaces. Those access ways are built in addition to local streets; they are the interior "streets" of parking lots. In other words, access and movement are increasingly separated, complex and consumptive. The old pattern was undesirable, to be sure, but it had the virtue of requiring only a fraction of the space in today's shopping centers.

The old downtown clustering of stores, repair services, offices, hotels, and other establishments also promoted the efficient use of space. An office worker was also a shopper. Every separate activity downtown did not require another auto trip, parking space, or even an automobile. When specialization and separation of activities occurred, more parking spaces became necessary to cover the more frequent parking stops and the more localized peak demands for parking. Parking lots now empty immediately at closing time. Moreover, the reduced proximity of many establishments diminishes access between activities and the varied sharing that is the life of a city center.

Yet a third stage of commercial decentralization and dispersion has appeared, following the onset of strip commerce in the 1920s and the appearance of shopping centers in the 1930s. The new stage completely isolates commerce, systematically separating every establishment from every other. Particularly noticeable in restaurants, banks, and discount stores, the new pattern enlarges on earlier precedents of motels, automobile dealers, and drive-ins.

An example is a new branch of the Bank of America in Fresno, appropriately called the Autobank. The building, about nine thousand square feet, is the sole structure of a complete block of 81,500 square feet and covers one ninth of the land (rather than the one-fourth that is normal for a shopping center). Although most of the land is given to customer parking, some is devoted to four drive-up teller stations, some to landscaping, and a great deal to employee parking. Space is reserved for two future teller stations to be equipped with vacuum tubes and television, indicating another result of massive space consumption: the high-cost of capital installations.

The block on which the Autobank stands so austerely, which as late as 1940 might have been occupied by twenty or thirty businesses with offices or dwellings over them, now announces an ultimate urban separation and level of consumptiveness. Carried to its logical outcome, every business would comprise its own shopping "center," a block surrounded first by parking and then by wide thoroughfares. Such a degree of urban deconcentration would compel the use of a car for *every* transaction one makes. Can any demonstration of society's misunderstanding and misuse of the city, illustrated by the Autobank, be more poignant than the picture of barrenness, disfigurement, forced mobility, and compelled waste imposed by every activity set alone in a sea of parked and moving vehicles?

Offices have followed a similar trend toward dispersion of location, isolation of site, and specialization of urban space, especially in the middle range of cities (from 50,000 to 500,000 people). The pattern varies from buildings scattered along commercial boulevards to very large concentrations of office buildings, such as El Segundo and Westwood Village in Los Angeles. Highly prestigious are the one-story offices located along a fashionable avenue, affluently landscaped and set especially close to personalized parking spaces. The highest premium, which is most often associated with corporate home offices and research laboratories, are the complexes sited on their own "rural" campuses, such as the opinion research, educational testing, and science laboratories (electronic, atomic, petrochemical, pharmaceutical) scattered around the countryside near Princeton, New Jersey.

The dispersal is equally powerful in industry. Manufacturing is needlessly separated into large industrial zones connected only by their industrial classification. Functional integration among the segregated industries is rare. Each plant is likely to be isolated from railheads, supplies, repairs, banking, and restaurants. Enforced, frequent, long-distant, and yet dispersed commuting forecloses transit and demands parking lots often exceeding the producing spaces themselves. Elite industrial parks, such as the terraced sites on Stanford University lands in Palo Alto, then allocate nearly as much land to grass, shrubs, and trees, another backhanded and wasteful gesture of spacious urbanity.

We have yet to understand the ecological significance of this new giantism. Conquering and occupying vast land areas involves not only the machines of conquest themselves—automobiles—but also the machines that sweep, scrape, plow, mow, and manicure the large parking and landscaped areas. The collectively vast areas these machines tend are either asphalted wastelands or landscaped decorations. The sole function of the landscaped areas is corporate status; these areas are but rarely accessible or suitable for walking, picnicking, or playing.

Another feature of the isolation of commerce and industry is the support systems it necessitates. The levels of technology, complexity, and cost of the bank tellers' drive-in station (consisting of a bullet-proof cage, the money exchange trays or tubes, and closed-circuit television) highlight the less obvious requirements for the conquest of space demanded by isolation. So do the otherwise unnecessary in-house lunchrooms and cafeterias, as well as the installation of special equipment, such as copiers and printers, that might be shared and improved through central service organizations.

The building of discreet facilities on large sites in isolated locations with huge parking areas along major boulevards or near freeway interchanges is the essence of our misconception of the city. Everything is organized for intricate, massive, and ruthless control of access and function by great machines while efficiency, access, and exchange are grossly diminished. "The right to have access to every building in the city by the private motor-car," states Lewis Mumford (1970), "is actually a right to destroy the city." The destruction of the city is a consequence, at least in part, of industries or services locating at the centers of traffic rather than at the centers of population, causing traffic volumes to become ever more chaotic and massively dispersed.

City Center

Nowhere has the damage to our urban ecology—that is, the efficiency, balance, stability, and quality of environment—been greater than in the general decline and debilitation of the urban center. The aggravated decline of the metropolitan core is the exact counterpart of urban dispersion to the distant suburbs. It reflects the same forces of disintegration, random location, and increasing separation. However, the degeneration at the center is more serious because it is, truly, the heart of the metropolis.

Many persons do not care whether central areas decline or disappear, just as many are unconcerned about the decline of whole cities. Nevertheless, the city and particularly the urban center is acutely vital to them, no less than the effectiveness of government or the vigor of the economy.

The critical fact is that *urban centers are necessary to integrate the functions of the metropolis,* just as the whole city integrates the functions of a district, region, or continental area. It is the precipitous decline of the city's ability to integrate that most seriously afflicts the city's performance in contemporary society. City centers traditionally weave together the vital roles and activities that comprise civilization: living and working, working and producing, producing and consuming, consuming and relaxing, relaxing and creating. Or, to put it differently, the city integrates mundane functionalism, trade and wealth, communication and transport, religion and education, science and technology, public and private affairs, social classes and political power.

The vitality of the city center derives from joining human activities freely and dynamically into an organic whole. Each contributes variety and interest. All support and complement each other: rest no less than work, beauty no less than function, and the new no less than the old. If a city as a whole is a concentration of human activities organized for the most varied human interests, the city center embodies the most intense and exquisite of these values and is formed most precisely to excite the human spirit. San Francisco and New York are commonly accepted as the leading city centers in North America, although they display but part of what we know is achievable and are primitive if considered against the horizons of urban form. Europe inherits a much richer legacy of urban centers from a time that necessitated the intensity of urban development (producing urban efficiency) and also prided itself on building outstanding permanent structures (by people who would scoff at sharp calculations of return on investment for every square foot).

Although European city centers were well established before

technical capacities (such as high-rise construction, electric lighting, improved plumbing, air conditioning, elevators, and escalators) could underwrite a theoretically optimum scale and pattern for urban living, they did achieve a high urban efficiency with high architectural hospitality, albeit necessarily at a relatively low order of magnitude. Unfortunately, both Europe's rich heritage and the fuller potential of new building systems failed to appear in the much newer American city centers.

Alas, technology in American city centers has been badly misused. In the few urban centers that did not directly decline, the large, new, single-purpose buildings stand in a rigid marching order—cold glass, concrete, and steel boxes filled with disciplined people who pass paper and do the massive organizational work that sustains the massive urban functionalism. Like the machinery of transportation, the technology of buildings has had the effect of destroying the beneficial proximities of the human scale that could facilitate human contacts, create personal spaces, eliminate costly consumption, and advance the overall efficiency of the city.

There were creative explorations, particularly the three-dimensional dynamics of Eugene Henard and possibly Antonio Sant Elia's ideas of horizontal and vertical movement, both before World War I. They were all but ignored, primarily because of the fragmented initiative that underlays urban development. Given the completely passive role of government and the almost sacred position of streets, any line of evolution beyond what one owner could do on a single parcel with exclusive zones under rigid building codes was precluded and largely unimagined. Grand Central Station and Rockefeller Center were the only solidly innovative structures built in the United States between 1900 and 1950.

If in 1920 the American urban center lacked a high degree of conscious integration and internal efficiency, it was at least nearly complete in the functions it harbored and therefore reasonably able to unify the life of the whole metropolis. Manufacturing, the least desirable occupant, was nevertheless a part, and useful because of the many linkages it helped maintain. The next five decades, however, saw this completeness and supremely important interdependence largely evaporate.

Industry, never the mainstay of downtown, steadily diminished. Most of the output that the center had housed in 1920 moved out. Industry's mushrooming scale demanded larger sites, and the motor vehicle made them accessible. Then, with increasing momentum, retail commerce, corporate offices, entertainment, and housing also left the city center. Only government seemed to be a loyal downtown tenant. Although some city centers prospered after 1945, they did so mainly in the form of office towers that emphasized the planners' specialized term for downtown, the *central business district*.

Although housing traditionally takes last place in urban locations, stepping aside for commerce and staying out of the path of industry, the vitality, variety, and convenience of living in or near downtown were so compelling that dwellings were historically built over shops, in high-rise apartments, or otherwise huddled in the byways. If the poor crammed into the older tenements, the wealthy flocked to the Park Avenues. However, even these attractions gradually dissipated after 1920, and especially after 1950. The steady exodus of business, the decline of transit, and the decimating effects of the automobile all undermined the qualities of living downtown. With slums, crime, and ghettos, living in or around the core became the least desirable habitat in most metropolitan areas. A broader degeneration was then inevitable, which overwhelmed the pitiable pockets of costly renewal.

If the complex causes and effects of the downtown's decline could be sorted out, transportation would most clearly fall on the side of causes. The strongest indictment would focus on the automobile, especially its pervasive penetration of nearly every land parcel and its redirection of metropolitan growth. Trains, however negative their environmental qualities, at least gave strength to the center, as did rail transit. Now many great stations are empty, and the fifty-year nondevelopment of transit is felt in every metropolis. Transit has virtually been reduced primarily to a last-resort system for the young, poor, handicapped, and elderly and secondarily to a fail-safe mechanism to relieve peak congestion on the minuscule capacities of immense freeways.

The car, no matter how we read it, was disastrous to the heart of the city in three ways. First, it forced many businesses to relocate for parking expansion, street widenings and extensions, and

The Strategy of Urban Defeat

freeway construction. Second, it induced businesses to relocate in outlying shopping, office, and industrial areas through its powers of suburbanization and sprawl (and with the help of heavy subsidization). Third, the debilitated, auto-dominated environment of the downtown consequently reduced the volume, quality, and usefulness of the downtown's essential linkages, not only creating a mood of abandonment but actually reducing the core's ability to perform its economic and social roles.

The dominance of the automobile swept away the genuine urbanity of the city center, including finally its religious and cultural functions and certain of its governmental activities. Once on the periphery, such activities lost their urbanity to misconceived ideas of spaciousness, accessibility, and beauty. The new religious or cultural site is usually far less accessible in real time and thus more isolated from its more dispersed clientele and complementary services than it was downtown. The irony is that exactly the same fate of fragmentation is now befalling what remains downtown. The central core then also becomes more spacious, dispersed, and isolated from its clientele, complementary activities, and back-up services. It, too, is just one more center that is not really a center at all.

Again, the advantages have shifted to the least efficient operation of the least efficient mode of urban transportation. The integration once performed by the downtown through direct proximity of shops and services has been transferred to the creation of enormous transportation capacities—and new levels of congestion—by the automobile. Once more we see why urban activities focus at the concentrations of traffic rather than at the concentrations of people: Movement is literally the new "integration." Yet the movement is really disintegrative, in effect, being massive, dominating, burdensome, debilitating, resource-depleting, and socially alienating.

Where reinvestment in the city center has occurred at moderate levels, as in Kansas City, the emerging pattern resembles the shopping center, with an inner building complex surrounded by oceans of parking, major thoroughfares, and freeways. Sometimes the land area occupied by the inner freeway loop alone approaches the quantity of the nonautomobile land thus framed.

And on this framed land, site debris remains from old buildings, useless streets, alleys, and postage-stamp lots. Given our splintered processes of urban action, developers cannot consolidate land, close streets, or relocate utilities. And federal or local government rarely participates in land development initiative, even after slum clearance. Thus not only do the forces of evacuation and deterioration operate vigorously downtown but the development process by which superior urban environments could be created is stalemated.

The American urban center, reduced in size and capacity, narrowed in function, thinned out and yet congested by automobiles, less accessible to the poor and shunned by the wealthy, deteriorated and unable to find satisfactory foundations for renewal, has tragically lost its ability to give oneness to a city, to make it work, and to give economic, social, and cultural stimulation. Thus, in short, the vigorous urban centers that once optimized urban benefits in a time of limited technical capacities have now fallen prey to vast and ecologically precarious technical capacities.

The accumulating losses were not noticed heretofore because they were associated with the growth of personal wealth. But with rising problems that cannot be bought off, a new awareness is beginning to appear. A growing number of people, recognizing the urban cardiac failure in our city centers, realize that a radical impasse is upon us.

Land and Nature

Land is literally the foundation for cities. Its urban meaning, however, is interwoven with degenerative myth. Land is our basis for orientation in the world, to space, to place, and to travel. It is also our basis for food and shelter, our claim to resources, our entrée to natural beauty. Our rural tradition identifies land with income, power, even subsistence, and customary belief makes land almost inseparable from home, personal security, and status.

Land underlying human tradition becomes a matter of increasing paradox as we congregate into massive and complex urban systems.

In cities there can be too much land, just as there can be too little. American cities physically consume too much land. Using too much land directly produces intense congestion—a congestion of movement to overcome the vast spaces and deadly distances. Using too much land means that we must use too much transportation. Too much transportation paradoxically results, as we have seen, in too little accessibility to the benefits of the city. For almost the same reasons, we can say that we have too much city and too little urbanity, just as we have too much land and too little nature.

There is, of course, no direct shortage of raw land for cities. Observers point out that 75 percent of the American population lives on only 1.5 percent of our land area. Then, in masterful confusion, they assert that there is a maldistribution of population. Can we imagine a more perfect way to brutalize human relationships or more completely defeat nature than to redistribute the urban population to physically dominate as much as ten percent of our land, let alone thirty or fifty percent? The basis for both natural and human diversity would be completely undermined by the struggle to maintain any degree of civilized contact between people. Already the frayed and strained ligaments of transportation challenge the capacities of our vast technology. Over 20 percent of our economy, more than $250 billion per year, is allocated merely to automobility and its auxiliary enterprises.

Yet, strangely as the paradox operates, land is very scarce in cities. This scarcity results from pressures built up by our systems of land tenure, real estate marketing, enterprise organization, rural values, and individualized transportation—all of which promote excessive land consumption. How does our land system operate to contribute so profoundly to the problems of cities?

First, our tradition of urban land development is based on *sub-dividing* land, fracturing it down to the lowest common denominator of use for separate and discrete activities. Dividing to discrete minimums denies a larger urban unity, except insofar as some complementary activities continue to congregate in common areas. Even these congregations lose their proximities by larger sites with expansive parking that prevent foot access between enterprises and homes. An underlying chaos is thus organized deeply into urban land management.

Second, urban location is a factor of land value. (Zoning must be dismissed as but a minor qualifying agent, and at best tidies up what would have occurred without it). Blue-chip commerce pays most per front or square foot and moves to the most desired locations (for example, shopping centers). Other commerce cannot pay the high prices. Service establishments, lower-class stores and restaurants, and the unnamed variety of establishments that formerly occupied the fringes of downtown, although functioning smoothly with it, are completely excluded from shopping centers. They scatter haphazardly along boulevards or hang on in cheap, declining parts of downtown. The result is both a dispersion and segregation that denies the vital proximities that make cities work.

The increased chaos of location and the multiplication of space consumption increase the pressure on the land market, producing a sharper hierarchy of desirable and profitable business locations. The number of good locations proportionately diminishes, which puts greater emphasis and premium on obtaining the better ones. Segregation of commerce is then extended on a new scale. Consequently, location and land costs become more critical for every business and more profitable for real estate operators. The result is a self-feeding irrationality of urban form.

Third, the nature of urban land markets assures that land prices inevitably press on the ability to pay. For wealthy people or prosperous businesses, the essential matter is status or advantage, and the site costs are relatively unimportant. However, the wealthy determine the willingness to pay and set the upper price range. For those in the middle ranges, the cost of a business site or residential lot is critical but manageable, a struggle between cost on the one side and benefit and status on the other. For the weak businesses and the poor, there is a desperate marginality. Any increased shop rent or removal for redevelopment or freeway construction often wipes out a business. A similar event for a family means depriving the members of essential food, clothing, and medical care, or a move to the lowest standard of housing and more intense crowding.

These actions of the market are taken largely for granted since they are seen to operate according to immutable real estate laws. What is not recognized is that the abounding chaos assures a sharp hierarchy of real estate advantages for the most powerful while diminishing the human benefits for everyone. The chaos also assures a maximum pressure on all land resources, despite many vacant properties. The cruel truth is that every new increment of wealth that appears in society through technological advancement

The Strategy of Urban Defeat

merely escalates the demand for and prices of land in close proportion to the dollar gain in business and per-capita income.

Fourth, given the penetrating chaos and exceptional pressure on land on the one hand, and the conventional attitudes assuring public poverty in a sea of private wealth on the other, it is quite understandable that so little urban land is devoted to well-located, varied, and articulated parks, preserves, and playgrounds or that *urban* forests and farms—special environments that serve elemental urban purposes—are not developed.

Fifth, quite suddenly we also find that good agricultural land is no longer abundant. The rapid world disappearance of cheap energy and the serious decline of world food stocks abruptly put an unprecedented importance onto American agriculture, both as a world food granary and as a critical earner of foreign exchange. But American farming is energy-intensive and totally dependent on huge supplies of petroleum. Hence, every acre of the most productive land now takes on an entirely new significance.

At first glance, cities do not appear to threaten significant quantities of farmland because they occupy no more than 5 percent of all farmland. Also, much existing urban land was never on high-yield soils. However, when the matter is examined closely, the urban threat to productive agricultural land is very serious.

The most critical case is in California, the nation's largest and most diverse food producer, which depends on about seven million acres (only 7 percent of its land area) of grades I and II soils for most of its nuts, grapes, citrus and other fruits, cotton, vegetables, and field crops. However, three of its most fertile valleys, Santa Clara, San Fernando, and San Gabriel, have been largely lost to agriculture by postwar suburbanization spilling out from the San Francisco and Los Angeles metropolitan areas. Other serious losses of scarce rich soils have occurred in the valleys of Napa, Sonoma, Monterey, San Luis Obispo, Santa Barbara, Ventura, San Bernardino, Riverside, and San Diego counties. Orange County has lost most of its orange growing to the southern part of California's great Central Valley.

Nor are the Central Valley's excellent lands immune from the urban bulldozer. The Valley's good soils exist in strips and pockets. It is precisely at the centers of these areas that the most vigorous towns originally took shape and grew most rapidly. Today nearly all of the Valley's large cities, notably Sacramento, Modesto, Fresno, and Bakersfield, spread out onto some of the most productive lands in the world.

Agriculture, which was the reason for the existence and location of hundreds of cities and towns, is now being permanently diminished by the continued mushrooming of these and other cities. The newer urban growth has less and less to do with agriculture and more to do with the expansion of carpet, tire, or machinery manufacturing, plus the larger acreage demands for workers' housing, which steadily replaces rows of walnut, peach, grape, and cotton plands.

California legislator Charles Warren reports in an October 1974 issue of *California Today* that "Each year 64,000 acres of prime agricultural land are lost to residential or industrial development." The state's Division of Soil Conservation reports that, aside from the permanent loss of this land from farming, the annual loss of capital improvements (for example, reclamation, leveling, irrigation, buildings) amounts to $207 million. Although new acreage is being added to agriculture, that land generally has inferior soils and requires proportionately greater capital investments to put it in production.

A fundamental social shortsightedness is evident, and it can be traced to a confusion about the nature and use of urban and rural land.

The most important rural-urban distinction to be made is between *land* and *space*. Land is essentially rural, usable primarily as a two-dimensional interface between soil and sun, as an access to earth resources, and as the preserve of the wonder and beauty of nature. Space, however, is dynamically urban, used to organize human exchange, to afford a congenial man-made physical and social habitat, and to preserve a large volume and variety of natural habitats—or "land"—in the city.

The critical role of urban land, therefore, is to afford the creation of urban space that can be shaped to maximize all functional, environmental, economic, and social benefits of urban life. Urban space is capable of becoming a quantifiable and precise tool of vast importance in defining, shaping, and evaluating urban form.

Even without a theoretical basis to create truly dynamic urban space from rural land, society cannot long avoid urban land reforms. The present destruction is too profound, too powerful, and too imminently disastrous to allow speculative profits to rule. The best solutions, I would argue, are founded on new creative potentials. An articulated concept of land and space has an important creative potential and is necessary to any reasonably complete approach to urban development.

Density

Density is shrouded in myth to almost the same degree that land is. But this myth is especially powerful among the design professions. Professional urban planners are unable, despite their training, to detect the underlying contradictions. Throughout their plans and documents we find an emphasis on large lots, huge parking requirements, wide streets, and land-eating freeways. These are precisely the conditions that deny urbanity, variety, and real spaciousness, although they are identified with the highest "standards" of urban development.

Both high and low density pose serious but very different urban problems. A review of each can highlight some of the more critical errors we make in urban geometry.

The historic problems associated with high density are largely related to inadequate building technologies and severe poverty: crowding, dilapidation, and lack of essential plumbing, lighting, and ventilation, as well as acute deficiencies of open space and vegetation. High density is too readily identified in most people's minds with slum tenements, which call forth visions of disease, crime, deprivation, and mental and social aberrations. From the 1830s on, tenements were either constructed as an urban barracking for the poor, as in New York City, or gradually appeared through a partitioning and crowding of once desirable dwellings. Foreigners, rural migrants, and minorities traditionally occupied tenements in waves. The sometimes unbelievably crowded conditions were always situations to escape. Success and status demanded that one leave at the earliest possible time. Hence, we have the image that the poor live in high density, the rich in low density.

This image and tradition is what allowed a medical doctor to write of the "disease of high density." Often the crowding—which is not at all the same thing as high density—occurred simultaneously with degenerative street commerce, pushcart drudgery, teeming confusion, rotting vegetable smells, and the unrelenting congestion of every foot of street space. That was the picture of New York's Lower East Side in 1900. In other cities the tenements were a part of or in the shadows of sooty, noisy industry, sweatshops, barren warehousing and shipping, or bars and brothels. Visibly and undeniably, everything imaginable was wrong. And what was most wrong, it seemed, was the visible mass crowding that was and remains falsely associated with high density.

Wealthier people inevitably conceived their ideal as a large house on its own park-like estate, even when they continued to choose to live in apartments close to work and cultural and social opportunities. Although preautomobile practical limits of commuting time from large-lot homes began to be reached in the larger cities in the early 1900s, and postautomobile limits were reached in the 1960s, a counter-ideal to the single-family house never appeared.

The consequence of this limited view was that many profound and varied possibilities of multiple dwellings have not been conceived, investigated, or developed. Apartments evolved on an exceptionally barren format, even though abounding in opportunities vastly exceeding the possibilities of isolated dwellings segregated by fences and distances. The innovations that did occur, such as the penthouse, garden apartment, common laundry rooms, and community rooms, usually responded to narrow real estate appeals, zoning limits of dwelling units per acre, or percentage limits on land coverage by buildings. In reaction to tenement life, the apartments were sterilized of diverse public life. They were removed from the intimate diversities and conveniences of shops and entertainment, and from schools and churches to a degree, all the more when put in a "spacious" parklike setting. In response to real estate profit calculations, apartments became stacked single-family houses, organizationally little better than the old tenements.

Yet there is a more profound and more fallacious basis for our negative reactions to high density. High building coverage of land in the older pattern of apartments removes one from vital contacts with nature, a removal often unnoticed but rarely unfelt. The enormous waste of land associated with blocks, lots, and streets, combined with speculative land-pricing, assured that the land would be overbuilt. The only reliable open spaces were the cobblestone, concrete, or asphalt streets. The hard ground surfaces, the rigid vertical lines, and the woefully barren apartment designs were enough to depress all but the least sensitive urban residents.

Reflecting on the multiple dwellings built during the last hundred years, it is difficult to find a valid social basis for the manner in which they were developed, other than basic shelter in a market rarely made competitive by innovation. The city thrives on a variety of natural and built environments responding to the diversity of human sentiments. But neither the degraded, raucous, and internecine tenements nor the bleak, sterile isolation of the more contemporary apartments, which are built primarily to provide the highest return in the shortest span of amortization, create an environment suitable to the social and cultural aspirations of people in an affluent land.

Hence, a critical reason why Americans prefer low-density, one-family living is their unfortunate experiences with tenements and more contemporary apartment complexes. One regrettable consequence is that the free-standing family house, which benefited by a rebound from the obvious evils of the crowded central city, provides a perfect complement to the aggrandizing automobile.

Density offers an important basis for considering the geometry and logistics of urban living. Stated succinctly, low density contradicts the very nature of a city—what it is and must be to serve people with reasonable efficiency, amenity and spaciousness. Despite the popularity of private uses of land (which are injurious to the whole community), low density—the wide distribution of people across the landscape—scores abysmally in almost every department of urban performance.

Homesites of four or five acres may satisfy the desire for a rural setting but they also create a "no man's land" that is neither urban nor rural and that defeats both. Consider whether fifty five-acre parcels in a rural setting could be as productive as one 250-acre farm. Only larger acreages are likely to be seriously utilized, competently managed, or make optimum use of expensive farm machinery. The small plots waste land in fields (for example, in tractor turnaround spaces), buildings, grounds, and roads.

In an urban setting, five-acre parcels multiply the acute burdens already present in the suburbanized metropolis. Both spouses are likely to work, usually in different directions and sometimes in different cities. Their trips are frequent and much longer than their suburban counterparts. The house is severed from efficient water, sewer, and gas lines. It is subsidized by electricity rate structures created for electrification of economically efficient farms and by repair and delivery services similarly designed. All urban parcels over a quarter acre will pose a yet inconceivable nightmare of urban logistics should they involve any large part of a metropolitan population.

We occupy urban land as if we had never learned the most fundamental lesson of urbanity: that sharing land and exchanging skills, wealth, resources, creativity, and human warmth enormously enlarge the skills, wealth, resources, and humanity of everyone. The modern success in production demonstrates the high potential of sharing, yet we cling to a kind of private possessiveness of land that defeats our urban humanity. When will we learn, for example, that, in a metropolis, it is all but impossible to sustain large public open spaces if private minispaces grow to such a scale and volume that substantial burdens are created in overcoming the increased distances and spaces?

Low density means separation. Separation prevents us from walking; we must drive to every store, service, or event. The trip by car is not laced with the character of human faces, not stimulated by flowers or window displays, and not conducive to physical exercise or reflective thought. Rather, the drive rigorizes the senses and tenses the nerves. Human association does not occur spontaneously through chance meetings, only through appointments made for specific purposes.

What I am talking about here is urbanity. Urbanity arises from a geometry that places the things of urban life into beneficial proximities and an attractive whole. With low density, proximities are lost in a sea of traffic, dead spaces, steel, and asphalt. Human relations are rigidified; learning is narrowed down to the vicarious specialties of the classroom; arts and humanities are abdicated to

The Strategy of Urban Defeat

the professional; politics shift toward the media and corporate interests. The citizen then withdraws into cynical self-interest and, in the extreme, slips into social backlash.

I repeat: the city is inherently a concentration of people, structures, and activities. To the extent that varied linkages become strained, then useless overburdens are added to people's lives. With high land consumption demanding consumptive machines, people become more "practical" and yet more wasteful, thus losing many dimensions of the urban humanity open to them.

If dispersion were carried out for whole cities to the extremely low densities now being introduced, the city simply would cease to function. The logistics of space and machines would guarantee a new Dark Ages by rapidly accelerating the exhaustion of resources and by prompting a form of collapse like that projected in the Club of Rome's *The Limits to Growth* (Meadows and others, 1972). The most powerful force in urban development today is the increasing distances between people—the so-called "higher standards" of low density that make "higher standards" of individual mobility an absolute and tragic necessity.

In the 1960s the multiple dwelling began to reassert itself. However, the new apartments are completely wedded to the automobile and the waste of urban space, built predominantly on large new sites around the urban periphery and served by space-devouring freeways, boulevards, and parking. Transit connections are weak or nonexistent. Services are scattered.

Whereas the traditional justification for compact urban development was its immediate access to the employment, services, and varied amenities of urban living, what we now foresee is a scattered high-density essentially unconnected to factory, office, shopping, entertainment, recreation, open spaces, or other urban amenities—except, of course, via the ubiquitous roadways. Therefore, despite a new compactness of urban development, the suburban isolation, sterility, and gross inefficiencies continue on their inexorable course.

Passage Versus Place

Urban history may be portrayed in terms of human movement, from nomads who had no settled communities and were sustained by animals to peasant villagers who lived out their lives in one dwelling and were supported by what they grew in one place. Most peoples prior to the industrial age emphasized place in their lives. The difficulty of travel virtually required that each person remain within a constricted radius. The distance from farm to village was not generally more than a couple miles.

Within a village or town, every extra yard to market, drinking water, or washing center demanded grueling work. Both movement within the village and the spaces devoted to passage were necessarily minimized. People simply had to build settlements that could operate within the physical capacities of their bodies. Wind, water, and animal power but marginally eased the burdens of space and distance. Both structures and the spaces around them had to be fashioned to the human scale, usually on the tight side.

Fortunately, the body or work scale of the individual and the buildings he occupied also coincided with a human scale of social interaction and an aesthetic sense of urban space. This common human scale underscored the fact that *place* meant personal identity and was connected with security, association, and celebration—community in the fullest sense. And it was this "placeness" that shaped economics and politics, from the simplest bartering to broad theories of the state, until the emergence of modern nationalism.

The interwoven revolution that multiplied production, movement, and exchange also revolutionized urban development. Movement *within* urban settlements began to be emphasized, especially in America, where seemingly unlimited land, lumber, and working animals had affected a looser pattern of dwellings from the outset of colonization. In place of common walls between buildings, which minimized the need to move, emphasis shifted to common and complete access to every property that would assist, as well as demand, movement. In this first subtle shift is a profound transformation ultimately affecting every fibre of the urban anatomy, a course of action that has not yet crested with the automobile. Not only was there an unprecedented realignment of all urban tissue for the advantages of mobility, but subtler shifts occurred simultaneously. In urban terms, emphasis shifted from activities in and around buildings to activities involving the use of land, from continuity and permanence to expendability and change, and from decisions based on pride and tradition to those based on return and profit.

The Strategy of Urban Defeat

A kind of equilibrium, however, took place between passage and place in the nineteenth-century grid city of lots, blocks, and streets. A moderate compactness creating the proximities of a reasonable urban efficiency in the larger towns appeared with the universal access of the wide American street. But then, as transport technologies radically changed with the automobile, the resulting expansion of boulevards, creation of freeways, and implosion of parking into every urban parcel completely broke this equilibrium in the decades between 1920 and 1970.

The old village equilibrium seemed to favor living places and to approach ecological stability. A new ecological validity or stability, however, has failed to appear. Today we have lost not only our sense of place in the city but also an equally fundamental equilibrium between place and transportation. The resulting material and human losses are disguised by the flux of explosive change and mollified by the capacities of production.

The imbalance is twofold. First, what planners refer to as coordination of land use and transportation in reality formalizes a degenerative interplay: the large sites, then the mass movement, and finally the large areas required for movement and parking. "Dead spaces," such as dwelling setbacks or freeway shoulders and interchange spaces, are necessary to separate dangerous movement from in-place activities. That these spaces are dead has been covered and disguised by landscaping. This interplay between land use (place) and transportation (passage) has few limits if privately supported, officially sanctioned, and fed by the dispersed and interlocking investments.

The second interplay, between roadways and parking, is pursued by the transportation experts who chose to ignore the natural roles and efficiencies of walking and transit. They have worked almost exclusively for the automobile when they know or should know that (1) massive parking lots alone demand as much walking as a theoretically efficient city, and (2) automobiles are necessarily limited to relatively affluent and healthy people in the prime ages from sixteen to about seventy-five. In place of articulated modes of transport *united* into the design of cities, they have pursued a futile "balance" among local streets, boulevards, and freeways on the one hand and movement and parking on the other.

This balance is supposedly created in response to "what the

people want" or to what the traffic engineers call demand. They measure traffic, make projections, do origin-destination surveys, and evaluate congestion and accidents. They then estimate roadway deficiencies and project corrections over a ten- to twenty-year period. They do not seem to be dismayed, despite continuous escalations of budgets over the decades, that the scale of deficiencies rises to entirely new orders of magnitude with each major assessment. Only in the most recent years has this trend shown its first encouraging signs of reversal.

The American city became visibly less localized and more mobilized each decade after 1900 and became dominated by the automobile after 1945. To meet the car's voracious demands and to expand the number and size of isolated properties with separate buildings serving unrelated functions—that is, to minimize placeness in place activities—the entire range of the urban anatomy and function, from the whole transport network to the behavior of the individual, was revolutionized in less than a century. Urban borders spread outward to nothingness. Central areas lost their ability to perform their minimal integrative functions for the metropolis. The new urbanism was workable only because the exploded functionalism could absorb a large part of the rising productive wealth. Place became a function of transportation, rather than the reverse (which had been theorized by planners). Place consequently lost most of its importance, which, as we are beginning to see, is ecologically and socially disastrous.

The roots of our urban crises today are the same forces that made us modern. They operate on a degenerative interplay that reversed what should be the primary values of place and the secondary values of passage. If village people in the past were highly constricted in travel and its experience of novelty, urban people today have been forced into an incessant and deadening movement. A paramount role of the renewed city will be the restoration of a balance between passage and place that can do justice to the rightful roles and experiences of both.

Zoning

Although zoning, a police power, came into being to protect private property, it became local government's chief tool to shape

The Strategy of Urban Defeat 103

urban society for the twentieth century. The endless nuisances and incongruous relationships appearing in the city of 1900 or 1920—smelters, canneries, dairies, machine shops or warehouses mixed with houses and stores—were intolerable to homeowners, who lost all semblance of tranquility, or to merchants, who saw their businesses crumble around them. For municipalities, the mixed land use was assessed as one of the most critical factors inducing urban decay. Zoning was also perceived as protecting both public and private values. Consequently, in many minds zoning became almost synonymous with the entire planning process.

It is therefore not surprising that when New York City introduced the first comprehensive zoning ordinance in 1916, the act was hailed as the beginnnig of a new era of rational urban development. Most cities followed New York's lead by adopting zoning ordinances within thirty years. General plans were later composed in large part to provide a justification for the application of zones to a whole city.

Zones not only separate the general land uses—residential, commercial, and industrial—but divide each into three to six densities, scales, or special characteristics (for example, C-1, neighborhood shopping; C-3, regional shopping; C-M, commercial-industrial). Such scaling is consistent with scientific classification and technical specialization but ignores equally important models in industry—models that demonstrate the intimate and organic integration of specializations to produce a telephone, a house, or an aircraft.

Zoning poses serious theoretical and practical difficulties. Built into it are severe contradictions that not only undermine its purposes but also contribute to forces that are destroying the roots of urban viability. The essence of the contradictions, as I have suggested, is that zoning *segregates* urban activities that need to be close to one another. Rather than integrating varied functions into rational proximities, zoning separates them, reduces their common (urban) efficiency and deprives individuals of rich cosmopolitan interaction. As practiced, zoning is quite simply an overreaction to the urban chaos prompted by randomly industrializing the gridiron layout. Zoning was also a reaction against the early, primitive environmental qualities of industry. And although the chaos and debilitations were real, zoning was a poorly conceived response.

Functionally, zoning puts similar activities together, even though such activities often do not serve and need each other. Manufacturers require processed materials, technical and financial services, and workers. Commerce requires finished goods, supplies, repairs, a complementary range of establishments, and workers. Residential areas require goods, services, and employment; and they begin to come to life with churches and cultural institutions. These interactions are denied or discouraged by zoning.

At least three contradictions are inherent in zoning. The first is the sanctification and enforcement through law of the degenerative interplay of increasing spaces, distances, and mobility. Segregation of functions into classified zones (combined with requirements for large parcels and extensive parking) separates complementary activities and increases requirements for mechanical travel. This separation encourages the automobile, and together they detonate the demand for land.

The second contradiction is that zoning allows the automobile, promoted by the huge zones, to create a chaos as great as that which zoning was intended to eliminate. One result is simply urban sprawl, which creates urban-rural conflicts ranging from irrigation difficulties and crop damage to chemical spray complaints and urban tax assessments on farm land. Many farmers zoned and taxed as urban are forced to sell their land into the speculative real estate market because they can no longer compete with farmers having lower assessed values.

The chaos is also found in the commercial strip, created in response to the automobile—a paradigm of urban chaos, inefficiency, ugliness, and the very conflicts that zoning should have helped us to avoid. Yet the strip is firmly set onto zoning maps, and much of the strip is made up of automotive services made necessary by the zoned urban dispersion. The foul air, the raucous noises, the massive pavements, and the traffic dangers promoted by zoning probably equal the nuisances of the prezoned city. Relatively few residences, schools, or parks are out of range of the heavy traffic noise. No one escapes the pollution. All of us play the random game of accident and death.

The sharpest attacks on zoning today focus on its use as a tool of class privilege. This third contradiction within zoning is also inherent where social power is unevenly distributed. Upper-income, low-density suburban governments in metropolitan areas apply the police power to zone acre-size lots with building restrictions that effectively exclude lower-income groups and affect a de facto segregation of minorities. Few people any longer deny that this has been one of the most powerful results of zoning.

As I have noted, class privilege also operates in commercial zoning. If retail commerce is redistributed into blue-chip shopping centers, to old greying commercial districts, and to decaying downtown areas, or if it is spread endlessly along commercial strips, a social segregation of shopping and commerce inevitably results.

When the segregation involves private ownership of shopping malls, a harsher social exclusiveness appears. Because shopping malls harbor stores and shops that respond only to hard money, and because mall doors are locked at 6 or 10 P.M., any form of free socializing, let alone loitering, is automatically eliminated. As a consequence, retailers are able to organize the entire environment for the best of the hard and soft sell, and the moneyed and the class conscious can pursue their interests without having to rub shoulders with "undesirable" segments of society.

Can we not seriously question a fundamental methodology resting on a negative principle of preventing the worst rather than striving for the best? Unfortunately, preventing the worst has characterized urban development since the city-beautiful movement faded after 1900.

The existence of zoning is based on political decision, making zoning an arena in which sharp business competition inevitably favors the powerful. Although a planning commission or city council may resist the henpecking at established zones by small operators, it lays prostrate before the power of commercial eagles. A zone change for one parcel might be easily denied when the result would infringe on a stable neighborhood. But a zone change to accommodate a regional shopping center is a different matter. When a team of architects, planners, and attorneys descend on a city commission or council with millions of dollars as bait, the temptations are as powerful as the politics, despite the demonstrable fact that many such centers upset the established pattern of metropolitan retailing and undermine the viability of the downtown, disrupting huge existing investments and accelerating decay in large areas of the city.

This was the case in Fresno when a regional shopping center

was proposed in 1964 at a strategic location five miles from the city center near the intersection of the two most important commercial strips, close to a proposed freeway interchange, and in the center of largest population growth. There was serious controversy, since the proposal was completely contrary both to adopted plans and to existing zoning. But the politics worked smoothly after a first denial, and the change was accepted through a combination of quiet work with the politicians, idle promises of development in the downtown, and a threat either to move the proposed center to a suburban municipality or not to make an investment at all. Hence, today the Fashion Fair shopping center flourishes with its three department stores while only two remain downtown.

Many of the shortcomings of zoning have been recognized for several decades. Imaginative efforts have given zoning something of a more positive role. Jonathon Barnett has described in *Urban Design as Public Policy* (1974) how a team of former New York Mayor John Lindsay's administration developed incentive zoning in special design districts to achieve specific public objectives. Theaters on Broadway and retail stores on Fifth Avenue were not holding their own economically and were in danger of continuous decline. Yet each was essential to the health of the areas in which they existed. The simplest answer was to provide zoning benefits (height, bulk, form) to owners who included theaters or retail outlets at appropriate ground levels, as well as to adopt design criteria suitable to those districts.

Earlier, a similar procedure was developed in the planned unit development, a method designed to eliminate many detailed and restrictive zoning provisions (such as wasteful setbacks and side yards) where important benefits of large-scale and comprehensive design were possible. Again, incentive arrangements were central.

Both approaches dramatically depart from the old concept of zoning as segregation. Indeed, in some respects both are antizoning provisions incorporated within the zoning ordinance. Or, to put it differently, they shift zoning toward an integrative methodology in urban development. These approaches, no doubt, will be highly useful, but they rest on a cumbersome yet fragile and still basically negative approach to quality in the urban development.

One wonders whether zoning is not another DDT. Both DDT and zoning are undoubtedly desirable instruments for certain specific and limited purposes. But when seen in the long term, when all consequences are evaluated and the general human condition is brought into perspective, perhaps we may have to judge zoning as we did DDT, and either radically change its methodology as a controlling feature of urban development or limit its uses to those few matters where its impact is entirely positive.

The strongest case for zoning, it appears, lies in an area where it has been used least: to control regional development, especially to channel urban development into its most desirable form, on the one hand, and to protect nature and agriculture, on the other. If zoning is basically protective, it can do no better than to protect the physical setting in which our human nature originally evolved or to secure the stability of the human ecology of each region.

A similar case for zoning can be made in the area of *conserving* the more valuable existing urban habitats through the use of special districts, such as those described by Jonathon Barnett. Otherwise, where the objective is widespread renewal or the *creation* of new environments, it is doubtful whether zoning has anything of value to offer. A new, more positive and integrative methodology is called for.

Limited space prevents reviewing here other development controls, the most important being subdivision regulations. Here it is sufficient to say that subdividing land fractures it into the lowest denominator of urban design, to the use of land by a discrete structure that lodges a single-purpose activity. Like zoning, subdividing denies integration of the urban activities, structures, landscape, and even transport. The questions that have yet to be asked about subdividing are, first, its rural-inherited emphasis on land as against the more dynamic potential of urban space and, second, its all but complete domination by vehicular traffic and access to property.

Taxation

Municipal government, initially conceived simply to protect civil order, was thrust into the provision of innumerable services during the nineteenth century. Now local government has also been forced into a role it has hardly recognized: giving civilized form to the new kind of society created by urbanization on a large scale. Today every city and urbanized county government demonstrates that it is unprepared for such a role by tradition, temperament, and organization. Consequently, the tools available to cities are inchoately conceived and badly applied.

One tool is taxes, the charges for services in the public sector of the economy. Taxes powerfully shape urban life, nearly as much in how they are assessed as in how they are expended by government.

In America we are moderately alert to a democratic expenditure of tax revenues but blithely errant about using the assessment and capital expenditures processes to constructively shape human environments. We do not require the advice of tax shelter experts to know that every dollar collected in taxes is an invisible hand influencing how and where five or ten private dollars will be invested. If both ends of the tax tool were used with even minimal imagination and consistency, they could in time result in major savings for utilities, public works, police, and fire protection. Here our attention will focus briefly on tax assessment and its corollary, utility rate structures.

The debilitating effects of urban property taxes are well known. Taxing both land and improvements throws a depressive weight on the improvements. All improvements without a sharp visible dollar return—better and more permanent designs; detail, trim and finish; and works of art—are discouraged. Then, on the other end of the scale, slumlords make windfall profits by providing minimum quality, low-assessed housing while permitting crowding and deterioration.

The relatively low taxes on land permit thousands of properties to remain vacant and unused for long periods of time, thus simultaneously encouraging higher overall land prices and real estate speculation. The high assessments in central areas encourage dispersion of development to the less costly, lower assessed, and larger sites on the urban periphery, thus encouraging downtown decay as well as urban sprawl.

The undermining effect of taxation is reinforced when property taxes are compared with fuel and motor vehicle taxes. Property taxes support general government. Very little of that money is used to encourage property development or renewal. Motor vehicle taxes, however, are reserved almost exclusively to promote this overbuilt form of urban transportation, despite the fact that most street and highway monies came from the general funds in the car's early developmental decades.

Utility charges are like taxes, except that they are tied to specific services and most of them are operated by corporations. They also have effects similar to the effects of taxes. Electricity, for example, is charged by urban and rural rate zones. The urban rate boundaries are customarily generous, extending to many large acreages to encourage early—or sprawled—development. And in most cities no rate differentials exist between the efficient high-density areas and the costly areas of sprawl. Intensive and central uses clearly subsidize the inefficiencies occurring in urban development. The centrally located office subsidizes the decentralized office. The apartment subsidizes the single-family house, especially the house situated on the large lot of the wealthy.

The observation has been made that we use our wealth to undermine the good life. If movement is becoming paramount in the city (as it is), and if our places of life are becoming temporary, expendable, and degradable (as they are), then our powers of taxation and utility rate making cannot escape the charge of being powerful contributors.

Taxes so decisively influence decisions on the form and use of property that one must question whether any tax should ever be assessed unless its direct and indirect influences are determined to be beneficial. There are no neutral taxes, yet we have hardly considered urban performance standards for tax assessment.

Public Services

Among the powers of government that can give positive direction to urban development, the power of the purse is more direct than taxation, more creative than regulation, and probably more critical than both. Given the historic lack of a comprehensive concept of local government applicable to our urban age and the traditional reticence of Americans in matters of government, we should not be surprised to learn that public money is generally noninfluential, frequently contradictory, sometimes destructive, and only occasionally beneficial in positively shaping urban environments.

Such a situation is to be expected when schools, transportation, and utilities are built or when police, fire, waste disposal, and postal services are provided mainly by semiindependent agencies or departments of different levels of government only in response to new demand. Despite zoning and subdivision controls, the demand for urban services can be created virtually anywhere, at any time, in any form, and by any private interest; public bodies then become obliged to provide those services. The more dispersed and antiurban a project is, the more it is likely to entail higher public expenses and to be favored by these direct but unaccounted-for public subsidies.

Many thousands of square miles of California's Mojave Desert and foothills have thus been blandly peddled into a ghostly urbanism. Few people have considered how they have become the medium the inefficient expenditure of billions of dollars in public facilities and services. This kind of urban development stretches limited services and increases their costs, whether for long-distance school busing or for police and fire protection. The hillsides of New Jersey and Connecticut are similarly spotted with houses. If housing in a city is dilapidated, we know that the problem one day will fall on government. If housing is on two-acre plots, however, we do not yet recognize that it is a huge hurdle and a threat to municipal solvency.

Responding to physical sprawl is but the most obvious misuse of public services in undermining any clear and purposive urban form. Another "sprawl" is found in the specific location and relationships of the public services themselves. Any public capital-improvement map of a large city reveals that schools, libraries, playgrounds, parks, fire stations, transit lines, and utility yards appear as if they were built according to a random game theory. A few cities have put schools and neighborhood parks on adjoining sites, and frequent ad hoc arrangements between education and recreation departments are found. As a rule, however, each municipal department builds its facilities as if it were an independent land developer.

Examine any typical elementary school and its grounds: ten acres, fenced and locked after 4:30 P.M.; isolated, unrelated, and aloof from the vital happenings of society; removed from the diver-

The Strategy of Urban Defeat 111

sities and experiences of nature; partitioned to a maximum span of teacher control; segregated by age and rigidified by roles of teacher and learner; dependent on vicarious learning at an inexperienced age; and structurally devoid of a responsiveness to individual curiosity. The bulk of what develops a mature person is purged from this costly but vacuous setting of education. The same isolation producing both social sterility and chaos in the city is found in the school.

Although schools and recreation work well together on school playgrounds, the relationship of gyms, pools, and craft rooms is uneasy. Although libraries and fire stations might be profitably joined with schools and recreation centers to form small community centers, each agency fears a subordination of its role and a limitation on its basic service if moved into a facility of another. As things stand, they may be justified. But few efforts have been made to design public centers to provide equal advantage for each service and to enlarge the public advantages.

A movement to design and build "community schools" operating simultaneously as community centers and as schools has been promoted by the Mott Foundation of Flint, Michigan. Although a number of good examples are found across the country, the movement has not taken hold. One reason stems from the apparent lack of community tradition in this country and therefore the lack of a clientele to give this movement a political base. In addition, because such centers are tied to school sites, they must operate without broad public support.

And so each public service remains essentially alone and unrelated. Each uses sophisticated analytical techniques to determine best sites and optimum levels of service but actually operates crudely within a shifting, unstable, unpredictable urban scene. The services neither correlate with each other nor have a useful impact on growth patterns. The chaos of urban development is thus perpetuated. Aside from crises, cross-jurisdictional innovative programs are not possible because most agencies carry effective veto powers.

Unlike the highly unified, sociotechnical systems of the military, space exploration, and manufacturing arenas, the whole city can find neither a unifying purpose nor a basis to judge the highest contribution and best integrative role of each service. Since both urban environments and municipal services are intimately interwoven into people's lives, a common form and pattern of public agencies, their services and facilities, are necessary to approach optimum living conditions. Nothing less than a coherently conceived system is capable of serving the diversity of human aspirations. And the diversity born of disunity or general inefficiency of the whole public service is self-limiting, debilitating, and threatening to every individual.

Institutions

The location of significant urban institutions becomes the anchor point on which much of the direction, character, and quality of urban development is determined. Only transportation generally exceeds the impact of major institutions in shaping the city. Fresno, California, built on flat farmland, clearly illustrates the point.

The most important single event determining the future of Fresno was the building of a station on the northeast side of the newly constructed Southern Pacific railroad in 1872. That site located the city. The next most important event was the decision in 1949 to relocate California State University, Fresno (then Fresno State College) to a site seven miles northeast of the now unused passenger station. That decision figured into most of the acute problems arising from rapid growth, change, and deterioration in the next twenty-five years.

The new campus site was selected because the new School of Agriculture required a demonstration farm. Today about 6 percent of the university's fourteen thousand students study agriculture, of which about seventy regularly work farm plots in cotton, grapes, and other crops. However, most students are required by the great distances and poor bus service to own a car. Most professors were obliged to buy a second car. The academic campus thus became an educational shopping center surrounded by huge parking lots. All university programs are implicitly based on the logistics of who can get to the campus at what times by auto.

But the most telling impact was on the city. The site, since expanded to fourteen hundred acres, gave official sanction, clear status, and physical momentum to the same extreme northward im-

The Strategy of Urban Defeat

balance of urban growth that the university's earlier campus had helped propel in 1911. Almost from the first settlement, Fresno's growth favored the north: first the station, then the court house and downtown shopping, then the better housing, and finally the institutions.

Meanwhile, West Fresno, whose health and growth is essential to a well-developed metropolis, attracted, in succession, ethnic migrants, poorer housing, thirteen wrecking yards, and three dumps. As late as World War II, a quarter of Fresno's population resided in West Fresno. By 1956, when the new campus was coming into its own way across town, the percentage had dropped to 18 percent. Now it is below 10 percent and predominantly black.

Cotton now grows but two miles to the southwest of Fresno's heart. One must travel eight or nine miles north to find comparable open fields or orchards. The university's new campus assured this imbalance directly by weakening access to and undermining the downtown, promoting excessive strip commerce, and inducing all major shopping centers to locate in the north, and indirectly by encouraging a segregation of the ethnic poor. Inevitably the problems of West Fresno were unattended to and grew.

Had the university campus been located close-in (and a relatively close-in site was actually planned until the university's farm came into the picture) or in West Fresno, there would have been at least a partial correction of the unbalanced growth. From 1950 to 1975, Fresno more than doubled its population; an astute location and campus plan might have produced a radically different urban area during this period.

Comparable situations exist in other San Joaquin Valley towns. A new state college was recently located southwest of Bakersfield and immediately helped prompt excellent housing in the vicinity, although prestigious housing and the junior college already existed to the northeast. Especially in a fast-growing city, the city's economics, politics, and development all respond very delicately to the major precedents. In Fresno's case, conditions in 1950 assured that a growing campus would have a dramatic effect on future development as well as on its obverse, urban deterioration.

The root issue is that a major institution's incomparable effect on the physical, economic, and social conditions of a rapidly changing American city is hardly recognized, not at least beyond the special interests and narrow perspective of the institution itself. In the case of the relocation of Fresno's university, the radical and foreseeable effects on the downtown, transportation, deterioration, social and cultural vitality, and parks and open space, not to mention student lives, were ignored. What was actually uppermost in the early campus planning was the need for a demonstration farm and lower land prices. Thus building oversized, specialized, and nonrelated campuses is identical to building oversized and nonrelated house lots, factory sites, and strip commerce.

The sprawl created by huge, isolated and specialized sites is also revealed in the campus design. In such designs, each building is set unto itself, virtually barracking the land. Under such conditions, the landscaping, although pleasant to view, simply fills space and creates distances.

Rather than respecting, optimizing, and benefiting from its own power of city-making, the university chose to unite its teaching with the demonstration farm while ignoring the illimitable learning possibilities of the city: all social sciences and social professions, all arts and humanities, as well as all student, faculty, and staff services. In other words, it turned its back on urbanity, the vital mutual stimulus between city and university that for centuries has contributed so much to urbane intelligence, and a process through which medieval scholasticism evolved into the modern university.

We can admire the interweaving of the universities of Paris and London into their respective cities without denying that the university campus should have an internal integrity of its own. Yet the two entities are interdependent in both function and spirit. Efforts to isolate them rebound negatively for everyone.

Other institutions also powerfully influence the form, function, and spirit of the city. In 1972 the Internal Revenue Service built its western regional service center on forty acres of walnut and grape land three miles east of downtown Fresno. The one-story office structure was built for two thousand permanent and two thousand seasonal employees on eleven acres. The rest of the land is devoted to parking, except a few front acres of landscaping.

The nearly windowless building, looking like an automobile factory by day and a maximum security prison by night, is beyond walking distance of commercial services and homes. Had it been located in a high-rise building in the depleted and underdeveloped downtown, employees could choose to use transit, could choose from a mixed fare for lunch, and could shop at noon or after work on the Fulton Mall, one of the nation's most attractive downtown environments. Instead, employees must depend completely on the automobile.

The downtown was not even considered for the IRS service center. The irony is that the isolated IRS location helps defeat the $30-odd million that federal and local governments have spent on rejuvenating downtown Fresno. It also helps defeat the heavy annual subsidy of the weakened public transit. Moreover, the low cost of land and construction at the center site is offset by the costs of huge parking areas (fully lighted); of heavier traffic volumes; and of transporting mail, supplies, equipment, repairmen, and other services to and from the center. Every employee also subsidizes the location in effect because of the extra driving made necessary and by the second automobile that many IRS employees had to purchase or keep.

The IRS example is matched by the 1974 relocation of Saint Anges Hospital from a site two miles to a site eight miles north of downtown and from a ten-acre to a thirty-acre plot. The new six-story building, however, covers hardly more than two acres; most of the remaining twenty-eight acres responds to and promotes parking demands (as well as current expansion). It thus follows the usual pattern of filling space, creating distance, and generating traffic. Saint Agnes is not a government entity, and the hospital stressed this fact in the process of securing local approvals and facing a court test. Yet the bulk of the construction money was federal and public. And regardless of whether or not most of its money is private, the hospital is vital to the pubic and has widespread influence on future growth.

Such isolationist thinking influences the location of other public institutions as well. Increasingly, for example, the postal service locates both "central" and branch post offices at sites that few can walk to and that are isolated from homes, stores, and other activities. This process, self-fulfilling and self-feeding, now afflicts the great public establishments of the city. They, too, destroy space, promote useless motion, and undermine both the healthy city and, ultimately, their own effectiveness.

Degeneration

When the thought first occurred to me many years ago that the American city might be inducing its own decay, it seemed illogical, almost culturally subversive. After all, we are a rational society based on empirical science, sound economics, and systematic management. But after many years of observation, a more damning conclusion has become evident: The American city is self-destructive.

The conclusion is heavily supported by fact. Most important is that healthy, congenial, and stable cities are not thought to be in the best interests of a "dynamic" society. Our individuality, technology, economy, and dominant institutions seem to be antiurban, even as they are products of, and depend on, urban environments. An almost conscious destructiveness operates in a wide range of arenas: the consumptive house, the promotions of commerce and industry, the endless expansion of the least efficient transportation, the needless and self-contradictory occupation of land, the segregative force of zoning, the sprawl effects of property taxation, the public service subsidies to sprawl, the scattering and isolating effects of major institutions. We could add to this list impermanence of building design and construction, amortization and tax write-off practices, and government and bank loan practices.

As independently wasteful as each element is, the truly destructive impact occurs through the interplay among them all. It is this combined force that we must examine in asking why degeneration penetrates so deeply and operates so powerfully in our cities.

A description of the interacting forces of decay may start at many points and follow different trails of interactions that reverberate cause and effect. Whatever path we take, it inevitably reveals the virulent internecine processes of the city as a whole that undermine the content of affluence and the inner value of democracy.

I have variously described how the consumptive process tends to grow unendingly. If land is used consumptively, for ex-

The Strategy of Urban Defeat

ample, huge burdens are then thrown on transportation. In our system, that means the automobile, itself an independent force of consumption that closes the cycle. Then the race is on: as the need grows for more vehicles, more parking, more boulevards and freeways, we also propel the need for more land, more buildings, and more facilities. Commerce and industry respond vigorously and happily, multiplying the machines and products required by the urban functionalism.

This cycle of consumption is the mainspring of degeneration, the wild accelerator wasting fuels, other resources, land, and time. But it represents only one side of degeneration; on the other side is an opposite and almost equal accelerator: degradation.

We start here with transportation. Inevitably, the good driving environment is a bad human environment. Streets, highways, parking lots, and garages are to the person hardly less than destroyed environments: barricaded, barren, forbidding, and conducive to mugging and rape. Traffic rasps upon all that it borders, defeating the front porch and the storefront as we once knew them, as well as their companion joys of walking. The great American strip created by the car is outsize in scale, illogical in function, and inhuman in performance. Its signs and billboards compete in boastful distaste to capture one's attention at great distances.

The debasing environments create a compelling desire to escape for all who can afford to do so. We insulate ourselves in hard, fast, powerful, air-conditioned cars and in increasingly barricaded and isolated houses. We use much of our precious unroofed and unpaved urban land for protective insulation, which we call landscaping. More and more resources are given to escape, protection, insulation, and defensive privacy. And then, in reaction to these, we exaggerate the prerogatives of individuality, status, and power, however shallow and abrasive their rewards have become.

Given the interwoven destructiveness of the city and our tendency to relocate rather than to renew, the city is condemned to unrelenting decay. Those who can escape to the new areas and can demand construction of the freeways and other paraphernalia of massive functionalism form a subsidized upper class. Those who must live in old areas, which cannot perform at the high level required by urban functionalism, form the lower class. The middle class struggles in marginality, occasionally escaping from and occasionally stumbling in the fast-changing, trade-in, throw-away city.

The old areas, ripped apart by the many debilitations of traffic, can neither move all the cars nor park them without completely altering in character. Since automobiles are the precondition of urban subsidy and investment, renewal is impossible, almost a contradiction. Full maintenance is impractical. Only the slumlord can profit. And only a few fortunate living areas have seen the process reverse.

The question must be asked whether the rapid technological changes in housing—in heating, lighting, electricity, plumbing, space, and storage—have made sturdy, permanent structures as obsolescent as the stick-built house. One would think so. Yet it is precisely the older, solidly built Georgetown in Washington and Society Hill in Philadelphia that have been renewed so dramatically since World War II. The practice is far more common in Europe, where buildings centuries old are regularly renovated and given modern kitchens, bathrooms, and other creature comforts. Whole neighborhoods pass through such transformations while their character is preserved and traditions are unbroken. Deterioration in Europe as we know it in America is relatively rare.

An epic irony it is that American cities, built to the world's highest standards of mechanical installation and spaciousness, are subject to the most rapid and intense decay found in the world. In most countries the issues of cities revolve around finding the means to make both public and private improvements. In poorer countries the problem is the uncontrolled squatter settlements, which sometimes grow to the hundreds of thousands in a few years. But in the United States the question is reversed: How can we avoid deterioration of neighborhoods that would seem heavenly to an Indian, Egyptian, or Ecuadorian? As it is, we build neighborhoods as if their vitality were limited to thirty or fifty years.

No society can build its cities anew every half century. To abandon and rebuild imposes chaos in the social system, denies roots to local institutions, and robs precious identity and stability from the individual. No society can build so as to constantly demand more consumption. The newer homes, built on an acre or two, designed for four cars, and located miles from urban essentials, impose giant

The Strategy of Urban Defeat

ecological burdens unsustainable in a world of finite iron, oil, and copper.

The city cannot grow like a formless amoeba. What appears to be freedom is but brutal incapacity. Both natural evolution and civilized change demonstrate that the capacity to act is dependent on an astute economy of structure. Similarly, freedom rests on clear and simple order. A precise, logical, balanced form is the essence of any capacity, that of the city no less than that of the body. A balanced leanness of body mass underlies the fish's ability to swim and the bird's ability to fly. Unstructured massiveness is the condition of incapacity, which biologically means decay.

Such a statement seems contrary to the obvious technological powers of the United States. Indeed, those powers are rooted in cities. But it is precisely the brilliant power of our technology that blinds us to the underlying debasement and decay where that power originates. The unarticulated relationship between industrial technology and the city now brings man close to burning out the resource foundations of technology, heightening the possibility of ecological disaster within the lifespan of most children today.

The disorder and degeneration so uniquely afflicting American cities are hardest on the poor and the disadvantaged. Indeed, urban disorder and degeneration have become a large part of their handicap. The turbulence in real estate, retail marketing, transportation, and manufacturing gives powerful advantage to the wealthy and vigorous. Profits do amass to those who can act fast, expediently, and exploitatively. Benefits just as decidedly are denied to those without the preparation, inheritance, inclination, and opportunity to follow the maneuvers of urban chaos.

But we need to be wary of making urban development a product of advocacy. Advocacy planning may have a limited role to play, but it can never build good cities. Niccolo Machiavelli and Saul Alinsky are both prophets of advocacy; they would be dangerous prophets of urban form. Their cities could be little better than armed and barricaded urban encampments.

Deeply rooted in American city-making is an obsolescence and dynamic decay more profound than that of most consumer products. A toaster, lawn mower, or car is easy to replace, involving primarily the energy, cost, and effort of recycling and remanufacture. But the house is not easy to replace. The house is part of an organic city. The delapidated condition of some dwellings has an impact on a whole neighborhood, discouraging repair of all houses. Obsolescence of the house means obsolescence of the neighborhood. The great investment and dynamism of American cities do not protect against urban decay. On the contrary, decay seems to have become part of the economic process.

Renewal

Urban slums are as old as cities. However, official urban renewal did not take place until the uniquely modern forces of degeneration were fully operating in cities.

Traditional slums are associated with the inability of people to improve their living condition. Urban degeneration as we know it in the United States arises mainly from a misuse of technology and wealth. Although much bad housing remains from poorer times, the powerful problem of renewal in the United States rests most acutely on the complexity and dynamics of urban degeneration.

A serious confusion has arisen between these two very different but closely related problems. Modern programs of renewal were *created* largely in response to urban degeneration but were *organized* mainly in response to the traditional problem of slum housing. The confusion is typified by Martin Anderson in his attack on urban renewal, *The Federal Bulldozer* (1964). He first quotes Walter Blucher, a prominent planning official: "The *slums and blighted areas* of America are growing faster than they are being destroyed, and nobody seems seriously distressed about this fact" (italics added). Anderson challenges this statement: "This is not true. By any objective, consistent measure, the decade from 1950 to 1960 witnessed what was probably the greatest improvement in over-all *housing* quality ever shown in the United States, especially in cities" (p. 6, italics added). Anderson, like many persons in planning and renewal, confuses bad housing with deteriorating cities and does not recognize the structural problems of cities that underlie the deterioration and much of the bad housing.

Housing and slum clearance was mandated in the Housing Act of 1937. Building housing took precedence; redevelopment was

The Strategy of Urban Defeat

not separately instituted until the Housing Act of 1949. Local housing authorities today reflect the 1937 law, redevelopment agencies the 1949 act. But still the confusion remains.

In the Housing Act of 1954 renewal was expanded to include rehabilitation and conservation, as well as redevelopment. A "workable program" was required that emphasized planning, improved relocation procedures, and citizen participation. What appeared to be a soundly evolving redevelopment program, however, was narrowed to production-like clearance projects. "Well planned" and "integrated" neighborhoods mandated in the 1949 act could be reduced to the resolution of traffic, utility, and zoning problems. "Neighborhood" and "community" were easily construed to mean housing projects. Any urban ideal beyond eliminating obvious delapidation found no serious place in the programs of the 1950s or 1960s.

Today's urban renewal process can be characterized in four ways.

1. Rehabilitation and conservation have become almost insignificant efforts in the overall expenditure of renewal funds.
2. Discrete projects are emphasized, planned in sharply defined local areas and carried out in one broad phase normally covering five to ten years.
3. Land is purchased, assembled and resubdivided within the project to create new streets, blocks, and parcels based on rezoning and on meeting the demands of traffic and the real estate market.
4. Project areas are cleared of structures, normally wiping the slate clean, and resold to developers.

Accordingly, redevelopment recycling of small parts of the American city is not essentially different from that now normally initiated by developers acting on their own on the urban fringes. Projects are brought to completion at high technical standards. Then both the redevelopment agency—the real estate recycler—and the new developers abandon the project for another fifty-year downhill ride. The parcels and blocks are larger, according to current demand. Similarly, although streets are fewer, they are wider, and parking is enormously expanded, meeting all specifications of urban functionalism.

Families are now treated with kid gloves and given substantial funds for relocation. Yet there is little recognition that every neighborhood, even those with little externally observable virtue or security, provides some wholesome benefits to its inhabitants, perhaps the poorest inhabitants most of all. A social integrity of either the cleared or the relocated neighborhood is virtually absent.

Redevelopment thus emphasizes what is removed more than what is eventually redeveloped. What is to be removed defines the project site boundaries, not the prospects for an integrated development. Comprehensive approaches to the physical, economic, and social development of a living community are lacking, except as required in process. New towns in-town reveal more comprehensiveness of concept and cohesiveness of form, but their existence is still infrequent (notably Cedar Riverside in Minneapolis and Roosevelt Island in New York City).

By comparison with the scale of cities, the scale of funds devoted to the struggle of renewal resembles playing penny ante in Monte Carlo. Only about one dollar was spent on renewal in the 1960s for every $120 spent by the private building industry. In over twenty years of effort, New York City redeveloped hardly more than two square miles. Scott Greer likens this to "controlling an elephant with a toothpick."

But the poverty of the purse is matched by the poverty of concepts under which the programs are undertaken. When some downtown areas, for example, have been cleared of dozens or hundreds of stores and the land remains unused, the urban surgery has evidently shocked the already weakened central area. Renewal itself then apparently contributes to urban sprawl.

Consider a few basic questions about renewal practices:

1. Why have we not based the urban renewal process on a comprehensive urban strategy covering the *whole* city and pursued as an integral and permanent part of urban development? With social equity carefully evaluated, renewal could assist in improving healthy as well as poor living areas, leading toward better environments throughout a city.

The Strategy of Urban Defeat 123

2. Why have we not carried renewal forward according to models of overall urban efficiency, amenity, environment, and community? Why have we not allocated renewal funds to wide-ranging research and program innovation? Why not design every renewal project as an experiment?
3. Why is there no *constructive social dimension* of urban renewal? If redevelopment cuts into the raw flesh of urban life, why do we not incorporate the companion questions of family, employment, welfare, health, and education into a complete process of community development? The efforts of Model Cities and the Office of Economic Opportunity moved in this direction, to be sure, but they were created as separate programs, lacked incisive methodology, misused citizen participation, and bogged down in local and national politics.

Part of the answer to these questions is that renewal is viewed as outside the mainstream of city life, just as cities are perceived as outside the mainstream of national life. Neither renewal nor cities are certified as truly American or democratic. They are hardly the objects for a commitment of wealth, technology, or national leadership. Were renewal in the mainstream, consider some of the creative possibilities, outlined below, that might have been pursued in the first century of metropolitan development.

In-place renewal. Redevelopment need not disperse residents across the urban map. A neighborhood structure can be completely transformed in three or four stages without families having to be permanently relocated. Values and traditions of new vigorous community can evolve from old foundations, regardless of former weaknesses.

Renewal with preservation. Fortunately, a sense of the past is beginning to penetrate official civic action. No matter how bad an area may be, there are usually some structures or features that deserve preservation and reuse and that offer a basis to build anew from the past.

Functional renewal. One of the more creative possibilities is the redevelopment of particular urban functions. For example, scattered auto wrecking yards might be relocated into one well-designed center and joined with a scrap metal processor, improving the industry's effectiveness and removing their blighting effects. In West Fresno about a dozen wreckers hold, in effect, a vice-like grip on all directions of potential urban expansion. The local Redevelopment Agency and Model Cities program eliminated many difficult problems in the existing built-up area. But until the wrecker's ring of blight is removed, there is little hope of attracting to West Fresno its share of private capital or of achieving a balance of middle- and upper-income housing. Similar redevelopment projects could be creatively directed to automotive services, building materials and construction, office equipment and furnishings, and any other activities that benefit from common locations or integration.

Renewal from strength. Urban renewal will always be limited in usefulness if it concentrates only on decay. Many declining areas have strong features—fine old homes, a park or parkway, excellent churches, schools or hospitals—that provide a good foundation to renew from strength. In West Fresno, again, the multiple rows of palm and eucalyptus trees along stately Kearney Boulevard provide an unsurpassed opportunity to renew that problem area by encouraging the better quality housing it needs for a balanced community. Unfortunately, the American tradition of government excludes itself from actively creating the kind of city it must govern, tax, provide with services, and, perhaps, completely redevelop.

Renewal to achieve critical design objectives. More than any other component of urban development, renewal can and should strive for the large urban efficiencies, the dynamic possibilities of building systems with large integral parks and natural areas, the wide range of potential amenities, and the neighborhood unity that could give people the ability to perceive their local possibilities and act coherently on their own behalf.

Renewal of transit and walking. Transportation has a powerful effect on the viability of all urban areas, both positively and negatively. But other than reorganizing streets, urban renewal and transportation operate from independent agencies and are joined only incidentally. Building for permanence necessarily involves superior transportation. Permanent, reliable transit and useful, pleasant walking environments are necessary for stable business and housing and for providing a definite shape to the urban anatomy.

These observations merely broach the renewal possibilities.

The Strategy of Urban Defeat

We will not be prepared to explore the larger urban dynamics until our conception of cities changes, until we recognize that imaginative urban development determines the good life no less than that of science and industry.

Recreation: The Last Escape

The city's accumulating spectrum of handicaps has now begun to promote urban escape in a new and threatening form. We have seen how escape to the suburbs by industry and commerce, as well as by residents, debilitates older central cities while promoting an unrelenting and unrewarding consumptiveness in suburban areas. Now the escape is spreading into the distant sanctuaries of nature with new tools and new power: recreation vehicles and subdivisions.

A relatively new, potent escape from the sordid conditions of urban life is provided by recreation vehicles. A growth phenomena of the 1960s, recreation vehicles grew almost as dramatically as the auto during the latter's fantastic expansion between 1907 and 1917. Shipments of travel trailers, camping trailers, truck campers, motor homes, and pickup covers leaped from 80,000 in 1962 to 747,000 in 1972. Motor home sales alone exploded from 4710 in 1965 to 116,800 in 1972.

Although we may all wish to travel to and "camp" with ease at Grand Canyon or the Great Smokies, we must also become aware of the clear consequences of vehicular camping, such as the huge quantities of fuel that are depleted in order to build and operate the plug-in homes and to build the costly highways into the forests, lakes, and seashores. In 1974 forty-six experts in California concluded that a rationing system for admission to parks was imminent. Such rationing would cover most parks for most of the year, not merely, for example, Yosemite on the Fourth of July weekend (where in fact visitors range into the hundreds of thousands on ordinary weekends). The motorized campers also inundate Pinacles, Arches, Shenandoah—or any attractive, peaceful site—throughout the summer. What perhaps was attractive and peaceful has been destroyed by congestion, signaling a new self-defeat by vehicles and the attending roads, parking lots, service stations, and campsites (most of which are designed only for vehicles).

If the city's unattractive environment pushes people to visit nature hundreds of miles away or fails to provide many natural attractions close to home, then the metropolitan millions will inevitably tramp on wheels and eventually desolate every attractive shore, forest, lake, or mountain retreat in the same way that they have desolated the cities. Many natural environments are destroyed or defeated for human pleasure more easily than cities. The danger arises from the same motorized recklessness.

Recreation properties, stemming from the same great wealth and bad cities as the recreation vehicles, became prominent in the late 1960s. While mountain and lake cabins and cottages have long been a part of the American ethic, carrying historic images of mountain men, homesteading, and frontier individualism, recent trends portend a scale of escape, a variety of environmental chaos, and a volume of physical depletion not yet seen in North America.

In 1970, 2,143,000 leisure homes, concentrated in the northeast and in Michigan, Wisconsin, Minnesota, Texas, and California, accounted for a mere 3 percent of all housing units. In 1973 the U.S. Office of Interstate Land Sales reported 2128 projects selling 1,655,894 new recreational properties. These covered 1,747,000 acres, an area equal to all land occupied by California's urban population of eighteen million. This land, however, is being developed at a density of less than a third of California's already sprawled cities. Moreover, many land projects are not reported for interstate sales. Additional millions of acres are reportedly being held for development by large operators, especially in Florida, New Mexico, and California. And many of the 130-odd new towns in the United States are in reality recreation land developments.

Much of the desert of the Southwest, for example, has become pockmarked with road grids scratched onto vast sagebrush expanses, with only an occasional house to indicate a serious intention to occupy the land. Many of the projects arose in the 1950s and early 1960s, when the tide of metropolitan growth in such cities as Los Angeles, Las Vegas, Phoenix, and Tucson spilled over onto the desert expanses ten to seventy miles out. It seemed then that the vast Mojave Desert might become a suburb of Los Angeles. Over ten million people were projected for Arizona within a matter of decades, creating, if true, an ominous prospect of urban sprawl throughout the state. Through the disastrous Small Tract Act of

1938 the government became a desert developer itself; hundreds of thousands of two-and-a-half-acre parcels were "homesteaded" for a three-hundred-dollar "improvement."

The one-acre parcel—itself a consumptive vastness—nevertheless remains the norm for recreational parcels. When projects exceed five hundred parcels—and projects of ten thousand parcels are common, some surpassing fifty thousand—they cannot avoid a suburban character, emphasizing traffic, garish commercial strips, and all of the acute problems of the spread city. Yet, despite their suburban character, recreational projects provide an astonishingly low level of urban facilities and amenities. A survey by the American Land Development Association in 1973 revealed that only 56 percent of the recreational land projects had central water systems, only 42 percent had central sewage systems, only 17 percent had garbage collection, and only 44 percent had paved streets. Electricity (88 percent) and telephone (80 percent) were the only facilities that could be considered to be in general use. Only 13 percent of the projects had a shopping center available. And the provision of facilities is not likely to be greatly expanded because of the high costs connected with serving large lots and low-level occupancy (only 40 percent of the dwellings are occupied more than sixty days per year).

Many people convert their recreational structures into permanent residences. Given the excess quantity of parcels put on the market, a very mixed condition of seasonal homes, permanent homes, and empty lots inevitably results. A government report has already suggested that these developments could create more serious environmental problems than those we witness in most cities. The personal and financial commitments are too weak, the market is too sensitive, and the conditions of deterioration are too ripe for anyone to be sanguine about what will result when these projects meet the inevitable problems connected with consumptive, underorganized, underbuilt, ruralized urbanization.

The typical projects now available amount to desert, mountain, and shore suburbs that are fifty to two hundred miles removed from primary residences or that entail a very long daily commute for many of those who make the recreation site their permanent dwelling. Most projects are low-quality suburbs by any critical accounting, despite the fact that they are usually located in choice sites along rivers and lakes, in forests, or beside the sea. Their suburban form demands suburban services. Their exceptionally low density creates a dependency on the automobile to provide access to water activities, golf, tennis, clubhouses, equestrian sports, commercial services, and even schools. The serious lack of central water and sewer facilities and the unpaved roads, combined with the pioneer construction and add-on character of so many vacation homes, suggest a rapid deterioration.

Decline is already evident in some locations. The possibility of gasoline rationing, now widely predicted as inevitable, enlarges this prospect. A burdensome price for fuel could have the same effect. Since 46 percent of the recreation homes are more than one hundred miles from their owners' primary home, and half of these are over two hundred miles, the threat is real enough. It is possible, perhaps inevitable, that we will soon see recreational slums in some of the world's most inspiring settings. The dismal urbanity surrounding much of Lake Tahoe forces one to wonder why such natural beauty engenders such despoliation.

Motives are one of the more disturbing features of the consumptive retreats. Many motives—living in a peaceful setting, having an abundance of recreational opportunities, meeting new people in new circumstances, and finding a sense of community—are exactly the qualities we could and should have been building into our cities. It is precisely the dispersion, transiency, and pervasive division of land that directly prevent such things from occurring. But rather than building these qualities into our cities—and such goals are all feasible, with vision—we build and bind ourselves to undesirable urban environments for the wealth they produce. Now we are beginning to use that wealth to build what in many respects are even less desirable human abodes of escape in exquisite natural areas.

The portent of human defeat could hardly be more complete: undermining of the land, of energy, of natural beauty, and, ultimately, of humanity. The aspiration for deeper human association and the feeling of community stand high on the recreation land industry's estimate of its appeals, but a momentary exuberance during an early development stage is the best that can be expected. Community, after all, rests on a reasonable contiguity of interaction, continuity of association, and "centering" of social behavior, all of which are denied or minimized by the low density, the random and intermittant occupancy, and the lack of unifying facilities and organizations. Still, "many buyers," observes a report produced for the federal government "view these locations as places where such informal interaction can once again take place" (Ragatz and Associates, 1974, p. 25).

Clearly, we are witnessing an elementary self-deception. Fueled by parcel peddling, we are starting the last run on dividable lands on the continent. Instead of creating constructive lifestyles and a medium for varied communion with nature, recreation land developments are promoting a more basic environmental treachery than we built in the city. There are unmistakable signs that the most degenerative qualities of the cities are simply being transferred to many of our nation's most spectacular geographies, climates, and settings. The few million existing recreation homes could explode to twenty or thirty million within a few fecades, even as serious deterioration sets in on the older projects.

These observations should not be construed as those of a purest determined to protect every wildflower. Human settlements within prize environments are desirable. The question, as in cities, is what kind of settlement is appropriate—what is ecologically sound and socially creative? How shall we guard the prizes rather than defeat them? Imagination, careful analyses, projections of consequences, and acute judgments are paramount—not ownership, markets, and profits. Our natural trust has worn thin, but it cannot be forsaken.

What most concerns us today is, first, how much of our rush on the remaining wildness of our earth is the *push* of the deathly cities we build and, second, how destructive is the unselective tidal force of that exodus. One day, perhaps, when citites are joyously attractive, we may be able to assess the genuine *pull* of the outdoors. Given the present aggressiveness of our technological society, the danger is as serious for nature as it is for the cities from which we escape.

5

The Environmental Toll

I have outlined a picture of cities not unlike that of cities destroyed by war or by natural disaster. Such a view is corroborated by Adolf Ciborowski, probably the world's most experienced rebuilder of cities ravaged by man (for example, Warsaw) and by nature (for example, Skopje). Ciborowski (in Schneider, 1971), a long-time United Nations expert, concedes that a third and completely new force of urban destruction has now appeared in the modern world.

The many facets of this new urban destruction are imbedded directly within the pattern of construction of cities. A nearly complete and predictable system of defeat is thus incorpo-

The Environmental Toll

rated into the anatomy of the twentieth-century metropolis. This system of defeat is directly correlated with the dramatic advances of the world's most productive economy. Indeed, such gross destructiveness could neither occur without the barrage of industrial artillery nor be survived without the industrial refabrications.

We build industry compulsively, and we build our cities for industry and input-output affluence without considering the consequences. Then, when we find that the cities work badly, we build more industry to overcome their ill effects, permitting us to abandon the inner city, escape to outer suburbia, become more environmentally destructive, and withdraw to our privatine strongholds. Spaces, distances, mobility, and isolation build on each other to create and then compound a larger chaos.

If profligacy were somehow necessary to achieve congenial living conditions, we could possibly justify the huge, raw output. But in fact no such justification exists, certainly not in terms of resource demands, use and consumption, or the final disposal of what we make. Yet in the consumption-demanding environments we have built, the immense input-output associated with a growing "standard of living" remains the dominant force of institutions.

The hard and ironic fact rebounds on all of us every day: *The creation and destruction of cities are the same thing.* Here is the ultimate paradox of modern urbanism and environmentalism.

The elements of this paradox are largely known, nevertheless. They are called the urban and environmental crises. And the results in death, destruction, pollution, and resource depletion now strike us hardly less powerfully than shooting wars. And, like war, the fuller costs, deeper sorrows, and greater human depression can never be adequately assessed. Still we build destructive environments deeply into our habits of thought and action, no less than our conditioning for war. "All of us are cripples," said Ivan Illich in a speech, "some physically, some mentally, some emotionally." And it is the crippled, demented city that perpetuates the crippling of individuals.

Here in the creation of cities are raised, I believe, the most ominous problems and also the most brilliant possibilities of advanced society.

This and the two following chapters describe in broad terms

the toll on all of us—and on our children and their children for generations to come—for overstepping the trust of Mother Nature and for disregarding the inner signals of our humanity. We are haltingly learning the first rudiments of a humane accounting of environments and institutions. We must become aware, however, that a far more rigorous accounting is urgently due.

Dangerous Environments

How is the physical health of the individual adversely affected by the environments we make or modify? In a large country we may discount the fact that 1547 people were killed in aircraft and 1437 were killed in boats during 1972. More serious is the fact that 14,100 were killed on the job, many of them in farming, mining, and logging jobs. Fire, a more urban hazard, caused 11,900 deaths in 1972. The real killer was the automobile, the most urban form of violent death, which claimed nearly five times as many deaths as fire and more than three times as many victims as murder. In 1972, just prior to the "energy saving" speed limit of fifty-five miles per hour, we killed 56,600 and injured 5,190,000 people in 24,850,000 traffic accidents. The cost was nineteen billion dollars, almost one hundred dollars per capita, discounting the additional billions expended for safety engineering and construction, highway patrols, and driver training.

Injuries are always a disputable statistic. But if only one tenth of the reported injuries have a lasting effect, nearly twenty million living Americans have suffered extensively from auto accidents. At present rates, our entire existing population will suffer some auto injury within the next fifty years. Auto deaths, now well into their third million, have surpassed all American battle deaths since the Revolution. Only on a few bad days during our many years in Vietnam did American battle deaths exceed the carnage on the streets and highways at home. Yet neither our government, our vaunted array of free institutions, nor the people themselves have awakened to the deeper human suffering and loss.

And accidents and death are but a small part of the unintended results of our environmental pattern. According to a report

The Environmental Toll

to the 88th Congress, our built environments, which we alter to make machines minimally workable, directly contribute to a wide variety of respiratory diseases, including bronchitis, constrictive ventilator disease, pulmonary emphysema, bronchial asthma, lung cancer, and nonspecific infectious upper respiratory disease. The first annual report of the Council on Environmental Quality states that the tie of air pollution "to emphysema and chronic bronchitis is becoming more evident. . . . physicians have traced 18,000 more deaths in the United States to these two causes in 1966 than 10 years earlier—an increase of five and a half times. . . . the frequency of these diseases is much higher in cities than in nonurban environments" (1970, p. 17). The Department of Health, Education and Welfare suspects that a number of other ill effects are related to air pollution, including genetic mutations, congenital malformations, metabolic and biochemical changes, impaired perception or behavior, diseases of the central nervous system, stroke, hypertension, and cardiovascular diseases.

A team at the Medical College of Wisconsin reported in the *Journal of the American Medical Association* the "astounding observation" that 45 percent of nonsmoking persons surveyed from twenty-nine thousand blood donors had dangerously high levels of carbon monoxide in their blood, a condition especially harmful to the elderly, infants, and heart patients. Urban people carried higher average levels than rural residents. Overall, the highest concentrations of carbon monoxide in the blood were found in Denver, Los Angeles, and Chicago (Stewart and others, 1974, p. 1194).

Noise is a direct auditory reflection of urban friction and a misapplication of machines in cities. If our urban systems were more efficient, we would employ fewer machines, and they would stay in the background. Noises would be predominantly human— voices, feet, ballgames, music, hand tools—and would remain at a human scale.

Sometimes called the slow agent of death, noise is reported to have doubled each decade, although widespread concern and recent official action have begun to slow the growth. Nevertheless, noise reportedly affects eighty million Americans. Compensation claims have mushroomed as the decibels continue to peal ever more damagingly. Still, most people quietly suffer their loss under the auditory bombardment.

Environmental Degradation

Pollution is the most widely recognized environmental problem. Since it has been widely considered, I will deal with it only briefly.

The Environmental Protection Agency estimated that air pollution accounted for sixteen billion dollars in damage to health, crops, materials, and property values in 1968 and that without controls this figure would have risen to twenty-five billion in 1977.

Water pollution, especially as it relates to water-born diseases, has been a source of concern for a longer period of time. Water is also a more strictly public or industrial matter, and both the decision-making and the blame are more centralized. Consequently, when programs are undertaken, such as that along Oregon's Willamette River, the positive results verge on the spectacular. When domestic and industrial effluents were effectively treated along the Willamette, fish regenerated, fishermen returned, and hundreds of miles of river shoreline became attractive recreation grounds for hundreds of thousands of people. Simultaneously, five major new parks were developed, one in every county along the Willamette River.

Unfortunately, other problems are not as close to solution. Water runoff and flooding increase measurably with the expanded hard surfaces of streets, driveways, and roofs. Flood danger increases rather than diminishes in low-density cities, according to the United States Geological Survey. Citing Riverside, California as an example of a low-density city, the survey reports that in one third of the urban area, 90 percent of the surface is impervious, and that in the built-up area, 60 percent of the surface is impervious. Wider streets, larger parking areas, and broader buildings more than compensated for the lower density of development. The survey estimates that if an urban area is 80 percent sewered and 60 percent covered by pavements or buildings, the water runoff in an average one-year flood will be more than four times greater than if left in a natural state. Quite expectedly, this problem continues to escalate.

Solid waste in the United States, mushroomed by the growing consumptiveness of cities, exceeds five billion tons each year. The disposal cost for residential, commercial, and institutional wastes alone is four billion dollars. Anyone who visits any large-city dump and watches the lineup of trucks emptying refuse in long, deep trenches may well wonder if the major product of this country is not garbage. Yet waste output of Americans continues to grow. The number of glass containers, for instance, increased from nineteen billion in 1955 to about forty-three billion in 1975—and glass is but 18 percent of the solid waste derived from packaging materials.

Pollution now concerns many people, of course. A growing number are equally concerned about the self-propelling malfunctioning of cities. Yet to be understood is the connection between malfunctioning cities and society's rapacious attack on nature.

Pollution of air and water, for example, is understood as a fact of industrialization at this stage of technology, almost a necessary fact of city life. Eliminating pollution is perceived, with almost religious faith, to be a technical question. However, technical or specialized solutions alone are self-defeating because they transfer the problems to the larger setting of life, often enlarging those problems in doing so.

The mechanical suppression of pollution requires additional industry and energy, thereby demanding more resources and raising the level of pollution. What is most crucial today is the whole setting—especially the whole city—we have created within which industrial technology operates.

Society has not yet grasped the fundamental conditions of industrialization and urbanization, particularly the relationships between them. Instead, we have tended to put blame for our urban and environmental crises on population growth, a significant but demonstrably nonbasic cause of our urban and environmental problems.

It is common, almost universal, in the literature of family planning to speak about congestion, pollution, and environmental problems as the direct evils of population growth. Although limiting the population on earth has now become an elementary necessity—especially in the crowded, poor countries where problems of people, industry, and cities are in many respects the obverse of those in the advanced industrial and urban countries—the crunching issue is the urban industrial pattern created in the human environment. Whereas the American population did not quite double between 1920 and 1972, the index of manufacturing production grew almost tenfold and cities tripled in size.

Clearly, modern pollution derives from production and product use, not from people as such. People are ultimately responsible, of course, but far more because of their industrial power and environmental behavior than because of their sheer numbers. The specific sources of pollution and the vast related problems derive from the urban form and the technological presence that we have created so recently and that we have used to transform the planet so dramatically. In our frustrations, nevertheless, we reenact the old Malthusian nightmare while largely ignoring the radically more dynamic urban industrial developments hitting us fully only within recent decades.

Unfortunately, family planning, although absolutely essential, treats population growth in terms that dangerously blind us to the more biting questions of cities and industries. Clouded are the more immediately urgent issues of vast urban inefficiencies gathering force and of the great industrial capacities that promote and force-feed those inefficiencies. The destructive setting has quite literally converted human amenities to burdensome necessities. More directly challenging to our way of life than population growth is the compulsive multiplication of machines in urban environments. Good cities require fewer machines than we realize and cannot tolerate as many machines as we are forcing onto them.

Deprivation Environments

Although people now express an unprecedented concern for pure air and water and for reducing noise, society has not yet focused attention on the accompanying physical and social restrictions that have crept into city life. Pollution of the natural elements has raised vital new questions of health; the parallel urban

The Environmental Toll

constriction raises equally vital new questions of human freedom. In this arena, critical abridgements of human life now occur.

Although everyone is affected by urban constrictions, those most seriously afflicted are, as noted earlier, the young, the old, the handicapped, and the poor. These groups comprise the majority of shut-ins and suffer most the exploded distances that require the automobiles that they cannot own or operate. Members of these groups are, in many cases, the same people—comprising half of the population—who do not carry drivers licenses and who are deprived of vital access to work, school, doctor's office, grocery store, entertainment, and friends, unless relatives and friends make special sacrifices to accommodate them. Some elderly people use a triwheel bike, but the risk in traffic is great.

Shut-in is a peculiarly modern term, since anyone who could hobble in the villages and towns of time past could at least appear at the market or church. Our shut-ins cannot drive and are locked to the television set. Strangely, avoiding becoming a shut-in is a struggle facing all of us. It forces us to buy the second or third family car. Even then we never completely eradicate the threat.

If amenities in the spread city—from museums and universities to parks, churches, and lodges—mean a drive of fifteen minutes to an hour each way, then we tend to exclude all those activities for which the travel requirements exceed our personal threshold of motivation, energy, time, and money. Ultimately, the reduced levels of participation that result lead to lower levels of facilities, even as many specialized and isolated facilities remain unused much of the time. Our capacity to participate, to build and organize for what we want, is seriously diluted in consumptive distances. The more unique interests, associations, and hobbies—those most likely to broaden our cultural horizons—suffer most. All too often they are not pursued and cannot be activated at all.

Hence we experience a huge and largely unrecognized personal and social loss in our present organization of the privatine city. Although we have pressed into being a fantastic variety of means for all kinds of action, these means lack an organic wholeness, seriously cancel each other out, and therefore deny us much of the real human potential. Our choices are much more limited than they need be, and our freedom is more constricted than it should be. All of us are shut-ins in a sense, regardless of money and energy.

Loss of Time and Space

One of the greatest environmental losses we suffer is time, which we value so highly at work and use so badly at leisure. Some persons consider time to be our scarcest resource, and indeed it is becoming just that through gross wastage. As Robert Kleemeier has noted, civilization can be measured by "the degree that men perceive the use of time to be a problem" (in Fabun, 1970, Part 5, p. 8). Clearly the achievements of our civilization derive from our discipline of work time, in contrast with the Greeks, who understood the creative uses of leisure time.

Yet for all of our concern for the productive uses of time, we lose the best of it in what Ivan Illich calls a "rain dance of time-consuming acceleration." The point about time and speed that our civilization has yet to understand is that both can annihilate experience, that is, rob experience of absorption, reflection, inner organization, reformulation of thought and behavior, and, ultimately, human meaning. Behavior that is rushed, rigidly paced, or constantly pressed for greater output easily becomes barren of social worth or robbed of interpersonal feeling. The constant traveler blurs his impressions of places, dates, and events. The compulsive goer loses touch with the reasons for going, the doer with the reasons for doing. The disciplined, time-conscious worker too easily loses his ability to relax, divert, reexamine, and recreate, which deprives him of the wholeness of the human experience. The commuter who countlessly repeats his journey in utter monotony sees places only as lifeless milestones in the deadened sequences of time, not as settings for significant events or associations. He becomes numbed to what he passes through.

This dead time is no minor consideration. In the country that invented time-and-motion studies, an adult rarely considers the entire time and motion demanded for his mobility. Without too much exaggeration, Ivan Illich illustrates: "The model American male spends more than 1,500 hours per year on his car; driving or sitting in it, parking or searching for it; earning enough to pay for

The Environmental Toll

the vehicle, the tolls, the tires, the insurance or the highway taxes. These four hours per day . . . do not include his transport-related dallying in hospitals, traffic courts, and garages, [or] his sitting time before the TV to be sold a new model" (1974, p. 51).

If we consider only the time spent directly behind the wheel, a little more than an hour per day, the American driver will be incarcerated for some twenty to thirty thousand hours during his fifty years of compelled driving. Translated into extremely scarce free time, between ten and fifteen years of leisure are sacrificed in tedious, dangerous, costly, and largely unnecessary movement. We might ask what new ranges of humanism could flourish if tens of millions of people were to have an additional thirty thousand hours to spend creatively in their lifetimes.

The counterpart of time is space, and our loss of space is as telling as our loss of time. If we measure the spaces and facilities available to the individual in the city by quantity and variety, we find that they are pitifully meager, minimally usable, and marginally accessible. The only space a person can use flexibly is his own lot and house—a fact that helps explain why the one-family house is coveted so dearly. In nearly all other spaces the individual is a guest, an onlooker, a worker, or a buyer—restricted to particular behavior at particular times under circumstances he or she cannot control.

The largest quantity of space available to individuals comes in the form of streets, and this space is only available when one is impounded in a car. Sidewalks in the motorized city are not only forbidding, they are all but useless. The roadway spaces are usable only to escape to other one-use fragments of the city, and that escape requires costly vehicles, licenses, and discipline. The spaces one goes to are available only for qualified entry. Shopping centers are open during hours convenient to selling; they are designed to avoid other kinds of association or organization. Schools are open from 9:00 to 4:00, and the student is pinned to his or her seat.

Parks are mainly distant, unresponsive, and uncreative. Citizens cannot actively involve themselves in how parks are used or developed. The park's natural spaciousness is infringed on by the same space-destroying methods used throughout the city. Paul Brooks cogently observes that a park's size is directly related to the way you use it: "Every road that replaces a footpath . . . shrinks the area of the park."

Today's city is fragmented into thousands of mutually exclusive enclaves, so organized around privacy that individuality is reduced by isolation to individuation, or loss of social personality, and yet so built around special interests that organizational purposes prevail over those of the individual. The person is largely deprived of varied public and semipublic spaces and facilities in which he or she can actively participate and feel at home.

Deprivation of time and space continues to grow. Initially, the pedestrian gave way to the auto; then the street gave way to boulevards, freeways, and massive parking facilities; finally every space and facility became separated from every other. As the city becomes more fragmented, as private cloistering dominates individual behavior, and as the efforts to overcome the dispersed fragmentation dominate human energies, both free time and usable space measurably decline. Choice, opportunity, and a very basic freedom—movement in the environment—wither, even as the propaganda of increased wealth, spaciousness, mobility, and leisure continues unchallenged. Once more we face another dimension of the urban paradox: The person is alienated from time and place in city life by another great "tragedy of the common"—reducing a shared value by the methods used to seek it.

Resources

The cyclical expansion of urban spaces and distances dramatically accelerates our demand for all resources. Motor fuel use multiplied tenfold between 1920 and 1970. Aluminum output exploded sixtyfold and steel output tripled in the same period.

The cost of exploiting resources is the future. The vital question about our mineral and fossil resources is their rate of depletion. Other questions, such as grade and distribution of ores and their accessibility, are appendages to the rate of depletion. Even a large reserve is not important if exhaustion is rapid.

On that awesome date when accessible, high-grade resources give way to minimally accessible or marginally workable finds, or when possibilities of synthetics or substitutions of one

The Environmental Toll

resource for another drop precipitously, society will then have written the final tragic denouement of progress (if not, indeed, of civilization).

In 1969 the Chairman of the Committee on Resources and Man, Preston Cloud, concluded that "although there is disagreement . . . as to the magnitude and specifics of our resource problems . . . there is no disagreement . . . about either their urgency or their long-range aspects. Complacency, delay, and short-range views jeopardize our chances of finding satisfactory solutions" (Committee on Resources and Man, 1969, p. x). Kenneth Boulding, quoted in the same report, was more graphic: "Our desire to conquer nature often means simply that we diminish the probability of small inconveniences at the cost of increasing the probability of very large disasters" (1969, p. 21).

A new class of warning was raised in the now classic study by the Club of Rome (Meadows and others, 1972). Although shortcomings are to be expected in such ground-breaking studies, the general foundations and powerful conclusions of this study cannot easily be set aside. The authors recognized the tentativeness of their methods and incompleteness of their data; for example, they included no social factors at all. Their intention was to demonstrate what would likely result if certain trends were followed for a century or longer. We cannot lose sight of some of their major findings:

"If the present growth trends in world population, industrialization, pollution, food production, and resource depletion continue unchanged, the limits to growth on this planet will be reached sometime within the next one hundred years. The most probable result will be a rather sudden and uncontrollable decline in both population and industrial capacity.

"It is possible to alter these growth trends and to establish a condition of ecological and economic stability that is sustainable far into the future. . . .

"If the world's people decide to strive for [ecological stability] the sooner they begin working to attain it, the greater will be their chances of success" (Meadows and others, 1972, pp. 23–24).

This last judgment—time—is particularly critical, for "the closer any human activity comes to the limit of the earth's ability to support that activity, the more apparent and unresolvable the trade-offs become" (1972, p. 86). *The Limits to Growth* thus challenges one of the world's most trusted and time-worn security responses: *Do nothing.* "Taking no action to solve these problems is equivalent," stress the authors, "to taking strong action" (p. 183).

Doing nothing, of course, means a growing exploitation of resources under a system that takes no heed of resources until the shortages appear within the short time span. The threat of resource exhaustion is new in the world, presenting itself at a time when world society is in the midst of what must be counted as its major phase of universal industrial development. Many countries are only now beginning to make serious demands on nonrenewable resources. This drive for industrialization, seemingly irresistible, gathers force while the material base for production falls steeply. Given such a perspective of our time in history, the judgment of Kenneth Boulding that "our existing economy is essentially suicidal" appears eminently justified.

The lessons we have learned to date do not seem to help us. Our tradition is largely confined to the creation of capacities. We depend utterly on technological momentum. Technology "has been so successful in the past," warns *The Limits to Growth,* "that a whole culture has evolved around the principle of fighting against limits rather than learning to live with them" (Meadows and others, 1972, p. 150). Our trust in science is a faith born during a very short, fruitful, and possibly unrepeatable historic period of discovery.

The time the world may have sufficient resources is illustrated again in *The Limits to Growth* if the true picture falls somewhere between the known quantities of resources and five times that volume, the exhaustion of many important resources will occur closer to fifty than to one hundred years from now if we continue exponential growth. Only coal, iron, and some less important minerals appear to give us a secure century for uninhibited growth. Some metals, such as copper, lead, mercury, and tin show an early demise, even should a nearly impossible no-growth situation appear in the next decade or two (Table 8).

It is unimportant here to debate when the resource crisis will strike. We know under exponential growth that the differences

Table 8. Years Available Under Exponential Growth of Nonrenewable Resources

Resource	Known Reserves	Five Times Known Reserves
Aluminum	31	55
Coal	111	150
Iron	93	173
Copper	21	48
Lead	21	64
Mercury	13	41
Natural Gas	22	49
Nickel	53	96
Petroleum	20	50
Tin	15	61

are only a few decades in most cases. What is now critical is that more than a third of the world's resource consumption is American. This very lopsided condition challenges American industrialization more than that of any other country. Table 9, which gives the percentage of major industrial materials imported into the United States, reveals our rapid depletion of domestic resources and, further, how rapidly the form of industrialization we have experienced, if spread to the whole world, can deplete the earth's resources.

Table 9. Percent of Industrial Raw Materials Imported to the United States

Raw Material	1950	2000
Aluminum	64	98
Copper	31	56
Iron	8	67
Lead	39	67
Nickel	94	89
Tin	77	100

Source: U.S. Department of the Interior, 1972.

If I am correct, the resource problem of industrialization lies squarely in our pattern of urbanization. Both of these fundamental conditions of modernity emerged together and shaped each other. Both were organized to promote production and consumption. If the American model is followed throughout the world, the planet is headed for ecocatastrophe.

Originally, ecocatastrophe was defined as the massive effects resulting from accelerating demands on a declining resource. Now, as Harvey Wheeler has noted, in advanced technological orders we find a process in which nearly all departments of the environment—including the environment itself—become marginal.

In the United States we are approaching the point, argues Kenneth Watt, in which the energy required to keep the system going will be greater than that used productively. Yet, despite the losing ratio of input to output and the grim outlook for resources, the system continues to accelerate waste consumption each year. This economic squirrel wheel, with its ominously increasing overhead, does not ameliorate the conditions of the poor classes or of poor societies. Most of the added consumption is forced on those who are already highly consumptive.

Once again we find that two fundamental problems feed on each other. Resource exhaustion now confronts us on the one side, and urban consumptiveness largely defeats creative living on the other.

One resource, timber, poses an enigma in the United States. It is renewable and its consumption rises more slowly than does the consumption of most materials. Yet American consumption surpassed domestic production before 1925, despite a spacious continent and major substitutions of other materials. Again, the problem is closely linked with the urban environment. The postwar suburban city remains a city of wood. As long as it is, can we expect it to achieve a stability of form and function? Or can we expect the forests to maintain a stable timber supply?

Commercial timberland in the United States decreased more than a million acres per year between 1962 and 1970, leaving approximately five hundred million acres in productive forests. The Forest Service anticipates that five million acres will be lost in each of the coming decades. Hence, the foundation to sustain an ample and permanent timber supply slowly dwindles, while the market for woods continues its historic growth.

The Environmental Toll

Given the unstable conditions of cities and the dwindling timber supply, it would seem clear that building the city more permanently and using less timber are mutually supporting cases.

Energy Waste

Essential in moderation but dangerous in excess, energy is promoted endlessly in the United States. Although energy is constantly and abundantly renewed from the sun, we concentrate our exploitations on the scarce residual deposits of that energy, the fossil fuels.

Energy consumption increased nearly three times as rapidly as the population between 1920 and 1970 in the United States, from fifteen to eighty quadrillion BTUs. In 1920, 78 percent of our energy consumption was derived from coal. Roughly the same quantity of coal was mined in 1970, but it then constituted only 18 percent of consumption. The growth fuels were petroleum, which expanded from 14 to 46 percent of our total energy consumption, and natural gas, which rose from 4 to 31 percent. Hydropower remained in the range of 4 to 5 percent throughout the period. Nuclear power was still relatively unimportant, although rising.

The energy growth rate has recently accelerated. Between 1950 and 1965, energy use grew at 3.5 percent annually. After 1965 the rate increased to 4.5 percent. Until very recently, about 95 percent of all energy was derived from the nonrenewable fossil fuels, predominantly the inexpensively extracted, refined, and used petroleum and natural gas—the energy resources with least national and international reserves. If all the world used petroleum at the rate of the developed countries, the world's presently known reserves would be exhausted in little more than a decade.

By comparison with other countries, the American use of energy is profligate. In 1969, the United States consumed 300 million BTUs of energy, compared to 165 million BTUs for Sweden, 101 for France, 81 for Japan, 5.5 for India, and .7 million BTUs for Ethiopia. Two simple but thundering facts of energy are therefore beginning to be realized in the exponential mind of modern man: (1) society, especially American society, is making a "run on the bank" of nonrenewable fossil fuels; (2) compound growth of energy consumption cannot continue in industrialized societies, not even at a rate of 1 percent annually, when added to an already high consumption rate.

Americans use two and a half times the average energy consumed by West Europeans, ten times that of the Latin Americans, thirty times that of the Africans. Although we have only 6 percent of the world's population, we account for 33 percent of the world's entire energy consumption. Assuredly, world society is approaching an energy breaking point within a few brief decades at which normal social functions can no longer be maintained.

By commanding such a high proportion of such a rapidly declining world resource, the United States puts itself in an extremely precarious, almost suicidal, dependency, as well as in a very serious moral position. How can we justify nearly double the energy consumption of Sweden or triple that of Japan, especially when we know that we burn irreplaceable resources mainly to maintain degenerative cities? If we cannot predict the particular events of breakdown—war, regional and national isolationism, economic crises and decline, political blackmail—we can be certain that they are being rapidly precipitated by the way we build our environment.

We do not know how much energy we could save and still live comfortably and freely. We do know that we could save a great deal of energy. The car and the one-family house are simple examples of enormously debilitating social gluttony. By merely changing the design of the car and the house we could reduce their energy consumption by roughly a third. If we redesigned the city to save energy, as well as to achieve many other objectives, we could save up to two thirds of our per-capita use of energy, especially if we also eliminated the industrial and commercial support required for producing and maintaining the car and house. Much of the remaining energy demand could be met by direct solar sources.

I speak hypothetically, of course. But when we see how energy demand so easily quadruples without noticeable benefit, we must realize that there are great possibilities of conservation. Yet the economy continues to promote gross energy growth, despite some recent moderation, and growth remains the policy of government.

Project Independence remains in effect America's answer to our first energy crisis. This program of domestic energy "develop-

The Environmental Toll

ment," begun by Nixon, assures a rising rate of consumption and postpones a reckoning in establishing a permanent accommodation to nature's finite store. The longer this policy lasts, the closer we come to total human capitulation. And while it lasts, it puts on blinders to protect the exponential tradition.

The Ford Foundation's Energy Policy Project (1974) illustrates the impossibility of continuing the development policy. The project estimated that an annual growth rate as low as 1.7 percent—hardly more than a third of the recent rate of 4.5 percent—would triple American consumption between 1975 and 2050, the life expectancy of a person born in the 1970s. Should high historic growth trends continue, energy consumption would double every fifteen years, and the next seventy-five years would see a thirty-two fold increase in energy consumption.

The Ford Foundation report makes clear that maintaining recent growth trends as long as twenty-five years will require rapid development of every major source of energy: petroleum, gas, coal, and nuclear. Every source of energy poses major hurdles and serious unanswered questions. The case of gas and oil, which have extremely limited known reserves, is perhaps most serious. Coal development is plagued with underground mine safety, open-pit environmental damage or restoration, and unresolved air-pollution problems (for example, harmful trace elements not removed by current pollution-control technologies). Nuclear power is increasingly controversial because of reactor safety, radioactive waste management, nuclear theft or sabotage, thermal pollution, and cancer-producing radiation in uranium mines. Oil shale and tar sands are expensive, require high levels of energy for extraction, and raise enormous environmental questions in the producing regions. Hydropower has reached, if not overstepped, its optimal development in most areas.

Today other sources of power—geothermal, wind, tidal, recycled waste material, and especially solar—are very promising. But these, too, have strict limits, if we are not to build forests of windmills or plate over the landscape with solar receptacles, as well as escalate resource and energy demands to produce them. The new and the conventional power sources have clear benefit when developed with restraint. Every aggressive step toward "complete development" increases the overhead—technological, natural, economic—required to exploit the lower grade or marginal energy resources.

Energy Damage

Were energy waste the whole story we might throw our confidence into the furnace of science and steam ahead. But another complex side of the energy issue, which society has hardly begun to consider, is equally important: At what point does the quantity of energy increase economic and social—as well as environmental—disruption? No longer can we ignore the possibility that the sheer amount of energy used per capita—for frenzied movement, redundant industries, and inappropriate consumption—may pollute social relations as badly as it depletes resources and degrades environments.

Ivan Illich, writing in the February 1974 issue of the *Ecologist,* postulates that "a people can be just as dangerously overpowered by the wattage of its tools as by the caloric content of its foods. . . . For the primitive, the elimination of slavery and drudgery depends on the introduction of appropriate modern technology, and for the rich, the avoidance of an even more horrible degradation depends on the effective recognition of a threshold in energy consumption beyond which technological processes begin to dictate social relations." Beyond a certain level of GNP, Illich argues, "the cost of social control must rise faster than total output and become the major institutional activity within the economy. Therapy administered by educators, psychiatrists, and social workers must converge with the designs of planners, managers, and salesmen" (p. 50). Here a classic case of social entropy is set beside environmental entropy. Both nature and man become marginal to the degree that industrial growth (that is, energy) surpasses strict limits of sufficiency.

If, as Illich says, the appropriate level of per-capita energy use is knowable and measurable, that level must necessarily be the minimum by which society can secure the goods and services that are genuinely beneficial. All else is an unnecessary burden, a waste, a degradation, and a run on the bank of scarce resources. To argue that predicted increases of energy demand are necessary for human

The Environmental Toll

welfare ignores the fact that a very high proportion of today's energy consumption is required by the disastrous human settlements we have constructed, including the promotions and built-in energy waste of so many machines that are, in the end, counterproductive. The vast web of waste built into our housing, transportation, industry, commerce, and everyday products is a tragic history we have yet fully to discover. The issue is especially anguishing because we have not seriously examined the positive human opportunities and permanent solutions open to society through avoidance of environmental excesses.

Nowhere in industrialized society, therefore, do we find a greater virtue of necessity than in solving the clutch of energy problems through policies of conservation that will halt the race of energy development and consumption. And the greatest possibilities of constructive conservation are within the cities.

Instructive but limited clues to some dramatic energy possibilities exist in varied per-capita energy use in different parts of cities. A report of the Regional Plan Association and Resources for the Future, *Regional Energy Consumption* (1974), revealed that energy savings in New York increased as the density of population increased. When the region's thirty-one counties were arrayed by population density, the energy consumption dropped nearly one third as the population density increased from one hundred to forty-thousand people per square mile. Manhattan, with seventy thousand people per square mile, had a relatively higher consumption rate because of its concentration of offices, shopping, and entertainment. The report concluded however, that in reality *"Manhattan has the lowest per-capita consumption of any county in the Region"* (p. 8, italics in original).

Transportation energy was not directly affected by density, dropping nearly 75 percent in the dense center of the region. Significantly, transportation was also the fastest growing user of energy in the fast-growing energy field, having increased its share of total energy consumption in the New York region from 28 to 34 percent between 1960 and 1970. Between 1950 and 1970, the region's passenger-miles of travel increased 63 percent. However, gross transportation energy use increased 146 percent. While transit energy consumption actually fell slightly, along with its ridership, auto energy consumption grew steeply because of wider ownership, more trips, and longer distances. Furthermore, projections indicate that transportation's share of total energy consumption will rise again to 39 percent by 1985.

These figures are corroborated by another pioneering report, *The Costs of Sprawl* (Real Estate Research Corporation, 1974), which indicates that the number of miles driven in automobiles is likely to double in a low-density sprawled development compared with a high-density planned community. Similarly, the energy consumption per dwelling (including family transportation) in low-density sprawl is nearly double that of high-density planned development.

It is appropriate here to remind ourselves how energy requirements radically vary by different modes of travel. In terms of BTUs per passenger mile required, various modes rank as follows: bicycles, 200 BTUs; walking, 300; moving sidewalk, 400; buses, 1200; railroads, 1700; automobiles, 4500; and aircraft, 9700. Although walking is fifteen times more energy efficient than driving, walking is plainly not a feasible alternative—although it is a necessary supplement—to the automobile in our present cities. However, if we project a city in which some 80 percent of today's personal travel miles become unnecessary, and if we assume that energy-efficient transit will be most effective and flexible for some part of the remaining travel miles, then we can also imagine that walking might be as convenient and pleasurable as it would be effective in saving energy.

Many persons will question our ability to reduce the requirements for urban travel by 80 percent. Here I will merely state that such a reduction is possible, is feasible by current measures of feasibility, and is imperative for both energy conservation and good cities.

Toll of Rationality

People have anguished about the military frame of mind and the institutional biases that compelled America to participate in the Vietnam catastrophe. Is it not time now to ask whether a parallel frame of mind is not carrying world society into disasters of

The Environmental Toll

cities and the natural environment, both exhausting resources and undermining social stability? How much longer can we ignore the need for achieving environmental peace and social grace?

Perhaps there is a pervasive irresponsibility in society that is deeper than Watergate, CIA, and corporate bribery. Ralph Nader has observed a phenomenon in bureaucracy he calls "official insanity." Such an insanity would appear to be an integral part of an organizational logic and power that takes leave of its human constituents. Is not growth the penetrating assumption of bureaucratic organization, and is not growth another word for power over both nature and people?

In corparate production, the question is no longer the meeting of demand; it is the creation of demand. In government, policy responds smoothly to the industrial clientele in the wings. And this response has become the clearest manifestation of what is called a *corporate society*. Note a few examples:

The Bureau of Mines can blithely project up to a fivefold increase in the American consumption of aluminum between 1968 and 2000 (U.S. Bureau of Mines, 1970). Although growing aluminum markets are thoroughly enumerated and the economics are carefully weighed, discussion of "apparent resources" is cursory and without analysis. The client is the mining industry, not the public. The approach reveals a psychology of exploitation, covered by an objectivity of facts but ruled specifically by special interests.

The Forest Service similarly projects the demand for timber to expand from 12.7 billion cubic feet in 1970 to 23 billion in 2000 (U.S. Forest Service, 1973). A lower estimate of 19 billion cubic feet is also projected, not on the basis of sound public policy but on the possibility of higher relative costs that might affect timber sales.

One of the most astonishing documents is *The U.S. Energy Problem* (Vol. II, Part A), produced for the National Science Foundation by Intertechnology Corporation in 1972. Compiled from a survey of fifty-six separate forecasts of energy demand, electrical energy is projected to increase thirty-eight times between 1970 and 2040, a rate of 5.4 percent per annum, or to double every thirteen years. The mischief of such a projection is that it supports programs that would increase *per-capita consumption of electricity twenty times* in that seventy years.

How is this rise in consumption possible? How would this increased amount of electricity be used? What good purpose would it serve? We have already experienced a comparable order of growth in the past seventy years, but expanding exponential growth infinitely is dangerous. Will electricity radiate from the walls and make it unnecessary to bother with plugs?

What about the means? The Federal Energy Administration (FEA) estimated in a background paper in August 1974 that investments required for Project Independence between 1970 and 1985 range from $450 billion to $700 billion. The FEA predicts that the required capital "could be as high as 35 percent of total U.S. investments." The FEA agrees that "all of the questions" in obtaining the capital necessary for Project Independence "have far-reaching political, social and economic consequences." And, as if admitting that those consequences will not be completely positive, the FEA background statement of August 1974 concedes that "difficult decisions must be made."

Such thinking lies deeply within the expansive belief systems permeating all government and business bureaucracy. That belief system, having shifted from raw continental resources a few decades ago to scientific momentum, is now losing credibility.

A classic statement—revealing more faith than logic—was made by Julian W. Feiss of the U.S. Geological Survey some years ago: "In spite of the accelerating drain of the world's mineral resources, it is now recognized that they will never really be exhausted. Just as advances in technology have made it possible to exploit today ores so lean they would have been considered worthless only fifty years ago, new advances will make it possible to extract metals from still leaner ores in the future. In fact, technology keeps creating new resources" (Fabun, 1970, Pt. II, p. 11).

Joseph L. Fisher stated the megatechnic faith in more operative terms, saying that "the age-old concern for resource shortages seems to have boiled away to a scientific-technological-economic-management problem. . . . The essential thing is to enlarge our capacity in science, engineering, and management" (in Darling and Milton, 1966, p. 275). Put another way, Fisher, who was president of Resources for the Future for many years, commits society to an ever accelerating race for ever diminishing resources. How long can we win such a race? Are we winning even now?

Another demonstration is provided by Nobel prizewinning physicist Hans Blethe, who states the case for nuclear power plants in almost desperate terms, announcing—quite erroneously—that there is "no reasonable alternative" to the increased use of nuclear power.

Garrett Hardin, whom we can thank for giving us the rationale for "The Tragedy of the Common," challenges the core of this kind of thinking. He began that article (1968, p. 1243) by discussing the arms race and quoting an arms authority: "Both sides of the arms race are . . . confronted by the dilemma of increasing military power and decreasing national security. *It is our considered professional judgment that this dilemma has no technical solution,*" stressed the defense authority. Hardin then proceeds to apply the same conclusion to our environmental and resource problems. The result has stirred a new insight and a profound concern.

To cast doubt on our prevalent foundations of thought and action—science, technology, and bureaucracy—is also, admittedly, to cast doubt on the most brilliant achievements of recent centuries. Nevertheless, there is no proof and there can be no proof that increased support of science and management will resolve the resource questions—or any other questions. Both science and management are methods. Methods always have limitations, and these are least apparent when successes are most strident. To transform a method into a faith is the ultimate form of both official insanity and organizational inhumanity.

Our environmental toll did not appear without an apparent conditioning of the mind behind it. On one level, the conditioning rides on the astounding accomplishments of our age. On another level, it rides with the blindness and bias we have brought from the past and merged with our new powers. The city is perhaps the greatest manifestation of our conditioning and our accomplishment. But the city is also a silent partner we do not see, a medium so much with us that we do not know it, a condition we are not able to feel. As such, the city has become a dangerous environment, powerful for the special interests who built it, but not yet within the grasp of the whole society.

6

The Economic Toll

If management and technology are the parents of industrialization, economics is its godfather. Just as clearly, economics is also the godfather of urbanization, for the laissez-faire market forces have as effectively determined the nature of urban land, mobility, services, and daily routine as they have brought us store bread, TV programs, and auto styling.

The role of economics, however, is now being severely tested. No longer is economic behavior explainable in classic economic terms, if it ever was. Despite the vaunted "science" in economics and the "fine tuning" economists thought they were giving the economy two decades ago, a startling economic chaos has appeared. Inflation combined with severe unemployment, great trade gaps, the existence of an income spread amidst affluence, and new ecological burdens reveal an unexpected hole in economic practice.

The Economic Toll

At first view, the city would seem to have little to do with the present economic disarray. Historically, cities have figured little in economic thought. But urban thought, we are compelled to admit, has not been advanced enough to have much at all to say about economics. However, the powerful leverage employed by the oil-rich countries in 1973 and 1974 dramatically underscored the high levels of mandatory consumption associated with urbanization in the industrial countries. The Arab oil embargo also suddenly refocused attention on the *political* economy. We do not require a new general theory of economics to realize that there may be a close connection between the urban chaos and the new economic chaos.

Counterproductive Affluence

The economic undermining of the city—and, in turn, the urban debilitation of economics—is far more challenging to economics than economists are ready to admit. As we suggested earlier, the historic drive to high productivity has transformed itself into a drive to promote consumption; the corollary development is that unbearable demands are built up against resources, not only the fossil fuels but also the ordinarily plentiful land and water. In the city, for example, these demands are built up around transportation, then construction, then industry and commerce, and ultimately the uglier forms of economic expansion: pollution, debilitation, escape and abandonment.

The ideology of endless monetary growth inevitably drains resources and puts continuous strain on family and governmental budgets, often threatening to overwhelm both. When social behavior, where human purpose is lodged, is subordinated to the means sustaining life, we can, I believe, legitimately speak of determinism. When economics, which has attained a powerful determinism, works as if people were units of maximization, we can fairly expect that pressures and counter pressures will result in unpredictable behavior, sometimes irrational in the context of the classic economic models.

A bias that economic philosophers left uncorrected rests in the nature of money itself, which mistakenly grew into a measure not only of the value of goods but of human worth as well. Society could not, of course, function without this lubricant of exchange. But, as money extended itself more forcefully to labor, land, education, health, recreation, and entertainment, each previously organized by nonmonetary arrangements, money became the nexus for our sense of social legitimacy. Consequently, society, having made money itself the chief good—or, to put it the other way around, having made humanity itself the chief salable good—is now unable to take critical account of the most human elements of civilization: informal institutions, casual interpersonal relations, and the sense of place, beauty, nature, human tradition and greatness. These and many other values are not obliterated, but they are withered, diminished, discounted, and denied a place in social reality. Only through paying customers do they figure into the feasibility of most urban projects, precisely in the way that Tocqueville spoke of the slow, subtle appearance of political tyranny in society.

Money is a linear measure of value. When human values are transferred to it, they are too easily reduced to a series of items to be acquired. Then, as the diverse joys of work, association, community, security, common enterprise, and spontaneity of interaction fade, ever more importance is placed on money. Like the city that continuously expands mobility to prevent the collapse of essential mobility, men become increasingly enamored of money as common joys are lost in the struggle for financial survival.

Consequently, money now compensates not only for work but also for social deprivation. We have passed through a century of unparalleled economic growth and a concomitant loss of power by the individual. As a result, most people now compensate by increasing their supply of money to buy the diversities and securities they have lost elsewhere. This compensating has made economics both incestuous and profoundly unjust. E. F. Schumacher (1975, p. 14) poignantly reminds us that "Until we concern ourselves seriously with social and economic justice, we shall find it impossible to conquer inflation." What better mechanism can we develop for rising consumptiveness, resource depletion, and urban disorder than an increased dependence on income for one's satisfactions?

No other course is possible when economics becomes obsessed only with means and yet also dominates social ends. How could it do otherwise? Economics is a "put-through" process—it

The Economic Toll

aggressively processes both resources and people, multiplies waste, and minimizes all noncost human satisfactions.

Some years ago the federal government projected that per-capita income would rise from about four thousand dollars in 1970 to thirteen thousand dollars in 2020. Although the projection was made for important planning decisions in the northeastern United States, no one asked whether tripling income was the right thing to do or whether such a rise in income would genuinely serve human purposes in a mass society. Might such a prediction simply measure a deadly kind of inflation in which the real losses are the environment and resources—and possibly our humanity?

Such a projection is revolutionary—no less so for being a linear extrapolation of a past trend—and poses a number of vital issues. How is such a level of production and service to be earned? What are the resource, environmental, and social costs? How is such a high level of income to be spent? How much will be forced expenditure? Could such an income level diminish rather than expand social and environmental freedom? Finally, how much human insight does such an income projection represent? Because of our emphasis on producing and consuming, according to Sanford Farness (1964), we now view "nature and ourselves in terms of exchange value. . . . Such thought habits . . . have created the impression that . . . we are somewhat helpless in dealing with technological change and urbanism because they are similar to the relentless, impersonal, and autonomous forces of nature." If we accept this relationship to technology and urbanism, then we surrender ourselves to the blind forces we have created—an antithesis of civilized life.

Economics has emulated the physical sciences more than any other discipline. It has reached a status in government second only to law. And its success, measured by influence, prestige, and raw economic growth, is today supreme. Yet many of the sages of supply and demand know that the most basic tools of their trade are in trouble. The money measure they depend on so completely runs headlong into human values, environment, resources, and the city. As the basis for organizing all social resources, money itself stands mute, as inhuman as the mathematics its superlative power is built on, even as it ignites infinite ambition and work. As our trusted science of the commonwealth, economics nevertheless works as if there could be no tragedy of the common.

Whether our danger derives from economic surfeit and the exhaustion of the earth that will assuredly accompany it or from economic domination of both the means and ends in society, it is certain that we are moving into a time of storms. As yet we have not learned to read the gross passage of the seasons, let alone the complexities of weather. Perhaps many of the storms could be avoided if, as E. F. Schumacher suggests, our economic masters did not "suffer from a kind of metaphysical blindness."

The point is critical for cities. American urban environments have become direct physical representatives of economic organization and philosophy. Despite the rise of development controls, cities are designed for infinite marketability. Exchange, it seems, is built into the lot and one-family dwelling, especially when one considers their social isolation and sterility. Exchange is also part of the design of private transportation, streets, and parking spaces (which promote mobility and purchase). Where are the urban places designed for true celebration of life and free interpersonal involvement? Even today's best civic assets are seen not so much for what they are as for their attraction of industry and commerce.

In building the city this way we damage the environment and our inner well-being. Good urban forms cannot accommodate themselves to infinite growth or be reduced to the lowest common denominator of exchange. Environments and people eventually rebound on economics in very illogical (that is, uneconomic) ways. Just this kind of rebounding I believe, is happening today.

The city cannot, at its innermost level of organization, become a medium designed to infinitely accelerate exchange and current income. When a city is so designed, it overruns the finite environment and undermines the delicate social matrix in which human personality and sensibilities are fashioned. Then both the means and the purposes of economics are defeated.

Sprawl Economics

New and powerful clues of our unprecedented urban waste are beginning to be found. If the important study, *The Costs of*

The Economic Toll

Sprawl, is indicative, economics may yet become effectively engaged in building better cities—especially in pursuing economics as an economy of means—and may yet help establish a firm, practical basis to discover the wider reaches of the human potential of cities.

The Costs of Sprawl (1974) is urban drama portrayed in cold numbers. Prepared by the Real Estate Research Corporation for the Council of Environmental Quality, the Department of Housing and Urban Development, and the Environmental Protection Agency, the report thoroughly demonstrates the utterly dismal cost and resource structure of our conventional suburban sprawl of one-family dwellings. The report exposes the results of numerous and often unrecognized sprawl subsidies, ranging from roads and mail delivery to groceries and utilities, and the unstated but deep operational biases working against the poor throughout public and private affairs and in urban form: taxation, capital expenditures, public services, loan practices, accessibility to goods and services, and even prices (that is, the costs of sprawl that are buried within the price of a shirt, a carton of milk, or an appliance).

Table 10 gives a summary of the report's findings. The major finding is simple and dramatic: planned high density development saves at least 44 percent of the development costs associated with conventional housing in unplanned sprawl. No less than $227.5 million can be saved in a community of 33,000 people through contemporary and very ordinary high-density developments.

The major savings occur throughout the ledger. All elements of the structure (foundation, shell, plumbing, heating, electric) are more costly in sprawl, with the exception of air conditioning. Paving, parking, and landscaping are three times as expensive. Utility connections are nearly nine times as great. Community improvements reveal similar advantages for high-density. Street and road costs drop 40 percent, utilities 46 percent, and land 43 percent. Moderate operation and maintenance savings (11 percent) are achieved each year. Only open space and recreation, very minor costs overall, rise with high density.

The powerful balance sheet also demonstrates that most environmental and personal considerations favor high density. The demand for energy (electricity, natural gas, and gasoline) drops 44 percent. Water needs drop by a third. Auto emissions are reduced 50 percent, while those from natural gas drop 43 percent. Water pollution falls 40 percent. Significant savings are reported in police and fire protection.

Despite the generally mediocre and unimaginative urban design of apartment development, the study finds that ordinary apartments in a well-organized community are responsible for a 48 percent decline in auto travel and a 53 percent drop in auto accidents. High density eliminates six hours of housekeeping, repair, and maintenance each week for both husband and wife. The report attributes significant advantages for high density in retaining or achieving better visual effects and in preserving vegetation and wildlife, inasmuch as a smaller portion of the land is covered by buildings. For the same reason, unusual or difficult sites can achieve better design advantage.

What are the disadvantages of high density found in the study? Traffic noise, they report, is likely to be greater because traffic is more concentrated on fewer roads and requires compensatory buffers or setbacks. Crime is about one-fifth higher than in sprawled developments unless special design precautions are made. Personal costs associated with privacy, personal ownership, status, and authority are higher in more concentrated development. As the authors note, however, improved apartment design and condominium ownership are increasingly identified with the improvement of these same personal values. They say that in apartment living, "independence, freedom, and less responsibility" are more commonly achieved.

The Costs of Sprawl is a fundamental indictment of sprawl and of the interlocking arrangements that brought it into being and continue to give it the "preferred" stamp of approval. The report demands attention by all who influence urban development. When the authors (Real Estate Research Corporation, 1974, p. 93) say that "the most expensive community to create and to operate is low-density sprawl—the most common type of development at the urban fringe," they are, without saying so, providing an important, although limited, first answer to the challenge set in *The Limits to Growth,* as well as to the more immediate energy, transportation, and environmental crises.

When they say that "total capital costs (exclusive of land and financing charges) average $48,502 per housing unit in [low-density sprawl] compared to $27,025 for the high-density planned community," they are also providing a limited but important answer to some of the critical problems of human poverty, especially the environmental burdens on the poor (p. 93)'.

Here it is the quality of the urban environment that most concerns us. The thinking found in the report is firmly stabilizing rather than exploitive in its economic and ecological implications. As prosaic and unattractive as the terms *high density* and *apartment* are today in the United States, only by these means can the city be anything but consumptive, wasteful, and unstable. The lesson that America must learn from the last half century of unfortunate urban experience is that the city is necessarily and inevitably a fact of high density.

The Costs of Sprawl stresses that any distortions that appear in the study "more or less uniformly understate the level of costs and the differences between development patterns" (p. 7). For example, the low density figure the authors use—three dwellings per net acre—is not very low; in many areas one dwelling per acre or more is common. Nor does the sprawl the authors describe indicate the true quantities of vacant land—much that is neither urban nor rural—existing in thousands of exploded urban fringes. Similarly, the high-density model used in the analysis assumes that only 40 percent of the dwellings are high-rise buildings, and these buildings are calculated at only six stories. The balance of the "high" density consists of walk-up apartments (30 percent), town houses (20 percent), and single-family clustered developments (10 percent). Hence, the 44 percent cost benefit of planned high-density over low-density sprawl is understated merely by the assumptions that were used.

One day, when we go beyond pure economic comparisons or the elimination of gross environmental waste and begin imaginative and equally incisive studies on the human potential of compact urban development, we will begin to explore the broader reaches of urban design. Raw calculations of density will become supportive, not central. We will likely attribute as many environmental and social advantages to good *design* of compact development as

Table 10. The Box Score: Costs of Sprawl

			Low-Density Sprawl	High-Density Planned
Prototypes				
Dwelling units			10,000	10,000
Housing types				
A Single-family, conventional			75%	
B Single-family, clustered			25%	10%
C Town houses, clustered				20%
D Walk-up apartments				30%
E High-rise apartments (6-story)				40%
Community population			33,000	33,000
School children			11,000	11,000
Community land budget (acres)				
		Units/acre		
Residential				
	A	3.0	2,500	
	B	5.0	500	200
	C	10.0		200
	D	15.0		200
	E	30.0		133
Open space/recreation			400	660
Schools			260	260
Other public facilities			140	140
Transportation				
Neighborhood ROW			710	300
Expressway			80	80
Total developed acres			4,590	2,173
Vacant land			1,410	3,827
Total community acreage			6,000	6,000
Community requirements and results				
1. Street lengths				
Local (50' ROW)			432,149 Ft.	65,445 Ft. (60' ROW)
Collector (60' ROW)			101,350 Ft.	95,460 Ft. (70' ROW)
Arterial (100' ROW)			64,100 Ft.	38,558 Ft. (100' ROW)
Freeway (250' ROW)			3 Miles	3 Miles (250' ROW)
2. Utility pipe and cable lengths				
Neighborhoods			494,500 Ft.	154,443 Ft.
Improved vacant areas			48,060 Ft.	8,936 Ft.
Semiimproved vacant areas			20,909 Ft.	6,970 Ft.
3. Water consumption				
Gallons per year			1,168,000,000	762,850,000

The Economic Toll

	Low-Density Sprawl	High-Density Planned
4. Energy consumption		
Natural gas, billion BTUs per year	1,347.090	795.177
Electricity, billion BTUs per year	1,007.610	604.960
Gasoline, billion BTUs per year	1,705.037	857.263
5. Vehicle miles per day	539,000	271,000
6. Auto travel time per individual (hours)		
Head of household	1.02	.63
Spouse	1.30	.62
Children, other	.45	.19
Total	2.77	1.44
7. Police services		
Number of vehicles	12	8
Employees	60	45
8. Fire services		
Stations	2	1
Fire trucks	6	5
Employees	76	62
9. Air pollution, pounds per day		
Private automobiles		
CO	4,040.21	2,031.35
HC	487.20	244.96
NO_x	475.32	238.98
Residential natural gas		
Particulates	142.74	81.57
SO_x	4.76	2.75
CO	3.17	1.68
HC	317.20	181.24
NO_x	951.60	543.72
Total	6,422.20	3,426.23
10. Household work, hours/week		
Not employed wife	40	24
Head of household	12	6
Total	52	30
11. Traffic accidents per year		
Local, collector and arterial (2-lane)	461	200
Arterial (4-lane)	225	101
Freeway	57	50
Total	743	351
12. Crimes per year		
Crimes to persons	70	86
Crimes to property	1,230	1,474
Total	1,300	1,560

Neighborhood costs per dwelling unit

	A Single-Family, Conventional	B High-Rise Apartment	B as % of A
1. By constant population (3300 persons)			
Residential	$32,146	$15,188	47%
Schools	4,538	4,538	100
Other costs	8,783	1,962	22
Total	$45,466	$21,689	48
2. By constant floor area (1200 square feet)			
Residential	$24,720	$20,103	81%
Schools	5,354	1,646	31
Other costs	8,783	1,962	22
Total	$38,857	$23,731	61
3. Structure cost per square foot (constant 1200 sq. ft.)	$18.58	$16.36	88%

Community costs: summary

	A	B	B as % of A
1. Capital costs per 10,000 units			
Open space/recreational	$ 2,684	$ 2,978	111%
Schools	45,382	45,382	100
Public facilities	16,615	16,304	98
Transportation/streets	37,965	22,862	60
Utilities	61,974	22,432	36
Residential	320,400	160,300	50
Land (developed and vacant)	29,539	16,814	57
Total	$514,559	$287,062	56%
2. Operating and maintenance costs per 10,000 units (annual)			
Open space/recreational	$ 260	$ 380	146%
Schools	9,737	9,737	100
Public services	5,575	5,164	93
Transportation/streets	396	209	53
Utilities	5,141	3,335	65
Total	21,109	$ 18,731	89%

The big savers of high density

	A	B	B as % of A
1. Capital costs			
Residential	$320,400	$160,300	50%
Streets and roads	37,964	22,862	60
Land	29,539	16,814	57
Water supply	27,236	9,607	35
Storm Drainage	16,823	5,346	32

	A Low-Density Sprawl	B High-Density Planned	B as % of A
Sanitary sewage	11,771	5,153	44
Telephone	2,731	870	32
Electricity	1,706	885	52
Gas	1,703	568	33
2. Operating and maintenance costs (annual)			
Electricity	$ 2,361	$ 1,418	60%
Gas	2,174	1,345	62

Source: Real Estate Research Corporation (1974) (Detailed Cost Analysis). The analysis compared various development forms for a hypothetic community of 10,000 dwelling units and 33,000 people on 6,000 acres, and a varied housing type for a neighborhood of 1,000 dwelling units with a varying population and acreage.

to high density in economic evaluation. The economic toll is simply the easiest place to begin the documentation. In the end, I suspect, we may find that the form of the city is the most regressive element in our economy. *The Costs of Sprawl* serves as an excellent wedge to widen our understanding.

Disservice Economics

The spectacular fact of modern economics is that the self-defeat implanted in its most fundamental processes now grows, across the board, almost in proportion to the degree to which specialized developments succeed.

The roots of impending disaster are not difficult to see. An increasing part of our energy supply is directed to the production of energy. An increasing part of our transportation operates in the service of transportation. An increasing part of our industrial output serves and promotes increased consumption of land, resources, and time. Industry requires more energy and more transportation to move lower-grade ores greater distances for more difficult processing than ever before.

Unhappily, as I have described in earlier chapters, the city's ill-begotten form demands massive input and then continues its deterioration under the impact of waste production. National input-output accounts in effect define a healthy economy as the antithesis of both a valid natural ecology and a satisfactory human environment.

Realization of the utter contradiction is delayed because depletion, pollution, and other forms of environmental degradation rarely affect the specific people who perpetrate and accelerate the damaging effects. Nature's retaliation is usually generalized and removed in time and place from particular damaging occurrences. Recognition of economic externalities and regressions remains primitive. Otherwise we would not count massive levels of auto accidents, refuse disposal, and long-distance commuting as part of the GNP. Nor would we give depletion allowances to promote resource consumption or tax write-offs for abandoning major parts of our cities.

We live in the first period of history in which responsibility is becoming completely collective, nearly absolute, and, as we are often reminded, the effects are essentially uncorrectable.

Unfortunately, although the simple despoliation of our physical assets on earth is beginning to be appreciated, the accompanying social degradations have not been recognized as anything like a common "environmental" problem. The many social crises that are recognized are treated as special problems for judges, psychiatrists, welfare workers, and counselors, not environmentalists or economists. Economists do not look at crime or insanity except in terms of dollar costs.

We await new and penetrating studies, like *The Costs of Sprawl*, that get to the taproots of the modern malaise. Even as we wait, however, fragmented and partial insights give us clues to the burdens of undirected economic development. *The Costs of Sprawl* itself noted that planned, high-density development permits the police to reduce their patrol officers and vehicles by one third compared to unplanned, sprawl development. Fire departments can eliminate one sixth of their trucks and personnel and half of their stations—the sprawled substations.

Kenneth Watt, a noneconomist concerned with the *size* of a city rather than its form or degree of concentration, found important savings for police and public works budgets in the smaller California cities. Table 11 summarizes his findings.

Some years ago a group of Russian city planners visited the

The Economic Toll

Table 11. Revenues and Expenses by Urban Population

City: Mean Size	Number of Cities in Sample	Local Revenue Per capita	Public Works Expenditures Per capita	Police Expenditures Per capita
2,799,500	1	$126.59	$32.34	$22.39
179,831	4	$102.85	$27.83	$17.08
96,929	10	$ 83.92	$24.91	$13.87

Source: K. Watt (in Fadiman and White, 1971, p. 115).

United States and were dismayed when they discovered that we were not at all concerned about the upper limits of city populations. To them, the question of size was a paramount consideration in determining the efficiency and livability of their cities. Since the 1920s, the Soviets have built hundreds of new towns and have effectively reduced the growth rate of Moscow. We have not debated urban size because we have not seriously debated the ideals or efficiency of urban form. Until economics and many other fields do become profoundly engaged in these questions, rather than being swept up in the exponentialities of input-output, gross product, and profit, the roots of our epic debacle will not be grasped.

There is some hope in the late-developing field of urban economics. One of its early practitioners has hypothesized that the quality of life varies inversely with the city's size. Through detailed analyses of wages and cost of living in cities of various sizes, Irving Hoch suggests that as much as 13 percent of personal income may act as compensatory payments for the disutility of living in large metropolitan areas. Since his base of evaluation was large and small metropolitan areas that do not vary significantly in the kind, spacing, or design of living conditions, the 13 percent disutility figure may be considered a mere opener on the subject, one lacking a practical measure of potential or ideal urban environments.

But ideals in urban environments do have their effects, sometimes even when the conscious appreciation is low. A property value study in the vicinity of Philadelphia's 1,294-acre Pennypack Park supports what we know intuitively: people like living near parks. Despite the report that nearby residents do not consider natural amenities to be important, the study indicated that location rent reflected by the park amounted to $1,171 for a dwelling forty feet from the park to $104 for a dwelling twenty-five hundred feet away—or one third of the land value adjacent and 4 percent a half mile away from the park. The authors concluded that each acre of the large park "may be said to generate $2600 in location rent (Hammer, Coughlin, and Horn, 1974, pp. 274–277). Considering the entire range of uses and values associated with parks, this study seems to suggest that many parks represent, like New York's Central Park, a city's most valuable land.

Time values are similar to those of space. Bertrand de Jouvenel notes that when housing is designed for a rent that an occupant can afford *now*, it is built in a manner that is inconsistent with his future income. "Cheap building," says Jouvenel (in Smithsonian Institution, 1968, p. 112), "is associated with rapid obsolescence, itself a cause of high cost." When we observe the catalytic depressiveness of cheap construction, obsolescence, and nonrepair in a city, respecting too closely a group's present ability to pay becomes a travesty on the human struggle for improvement. The whole society must pay an outrageous price for the debilitating economics, depressing social effects, and bloody redevelopment surgery.

Not understanding Jouvenel's principle is equivalent to not understanding the social utility of lending, interest, and capital markets, or of good plans, foundations, and improvable structures. When all economic and social costs are considered, building strictly according to a consumer group's present ability to pay may put a future charge on society on the order of ten times what an original substantial subsidy might have been. Such a subsidy need only be sufficient to guarantee permanence and encourage continuous improvement. Jouvenel (in Smithsonian Institution, 1968, p. 112) says that social utility is better served by building for a long term. As yet such reasoning does not penetrate our system of city-making or the economics behind it. The throw-away city is the result, and it suggests that the people, too, are expendable.

Nevertheless, we continue to measure our wealth only by current income, by naked production that promotes nonrewarding consumption. Accompanying the emphasis on sheer output is an emphasis on decay. Yet throw-away cities are not easily disposable and replaceable. Instead of rebuilding and renewing, we escape to outer suburbia and, as often as we can, to mountain and shore retreats, leaving the central city to pass away. We cannot escape, however, the peculiar affinity between high current income and high permanent waste.

The antithesis of an excessive emphasis on production was described by John Galbraith in *The Affluent Society* (1958, p. 124). Economic security, he said, has come to be associated with a high level of production, but this level is built on an ingenious defense with a profound flaw. "If the individual's wants are to be urgent they must be original with himself. They cannot be urgent if they must be contrived for him. And above all they must not be contrived by the process by which they are satisfied. . . . One cannot defend production as satisfying wants if that production creates the wants."

Similarly, Galbraith (1958, p. 128) considers that "the final problem of the productive society is what it produces. This manifests itself in an implacable tendency to provide an opulent supply of some things and a niggardly yield of others. . . . The line which divides our area of wealth from our area of poverty is roughly that which divides privately produced and marketed goods and services from publicly rendered services. . . . our wealth in privately produced goods is, to a marked degree, the cause of crisis in the supply of public services."

The city vividly demonstrates the dichotomy between private and public wealth. The city also establishes conditions on which excessive production of goods are sought as a surrogate for security. Yet it is the production of excessive goods for contrived wants, on the one side, and the public poverty, on the other, that undermine not only our age-old concern for security but also the liberal ideal of equality. The bad city, although hurting everyone, is most damaging to the powerless. Ironically, it is our striving for security and equality that leads us to champion rude production as the panacea for distorted conditions of life.

Until economics can effectively rid itself of what Mumford calls "inflation of the money motive," we will be unable to build livable cities that are truly congenial to human beings. That is because, as Mumford says, "the peculiarity of money is that it knows no biological limits or ecological restrictions" (1970, pp. 165, 167).

It is mainly the ecologists and the humanists, not the economists, who decry the inefficiencies, inequalities, and instabilities within our present economic structure. Economics rests its gigantic power almost solely on raw productivity. And high productivity it can claim. The question for us, however, is broader, deeper, more urgent. The powerful input-output cycle of production—without the former direct restraints and balances of nature—is becoming a regressive cycle of waste that eventually guarantees a wasteland.

The Galbraiths, Jouvenels, Bouldings, and Schumachers are too few. They carry prestige but little power. E. F. Schumacher (1973, p. 98), a credentialed but lonely figure outside the close-marching lines of economists, highlights a massive weakness. "The economists have an easy way of dealing with [human activities]: They divide all . . . between 'production' and 'consumption.' Anything we do under the heading of 'production' is subject to the economic calculus, and anything we do under the heading of 'consumption' is not."

Consumption is not merely a simple end result of production. Rather, it is an economic process as complex and critical as production. Consumption is the other side of the economic coin and deserves the same critical concern for inflow-outflow as the input-output of production. The efficiency of consumption—the minimization of waste—has now become the biting question of society, occupying the position held by production until this century. And the question of consumptive efficiency rests mainly on arrangements of the urban environment.

If cities before production began to soar had to be efficient for all of life's struggles, they lost that efficiency in the contrived consumption that arose about the time Henry Ford began to produce the Model T for less than four hundred dollars while more than doubling the day wage of workers to an astounding five dollars. In one short era Ford created a huge and costly new product with unprecedented industrial efficiency and then promoted its mass market with the higher wages that efficiency made possible. Decades later the car became a mass necessity because it helped set the city on a tragic course of mobilized frenzy, inefficiency, and decay.

The Economic Toll

When we begin to learn that consumption, like production, deserves its own philosophy and methodology, and when we learn that it is the economics of consumption that determines the economics of production, not the other way around, we will then help bring economics closer to ecology while also bringing public wealth into better balance with private wealth. A valid consumer economics will guide production in choices of product, design, quality, and volume. Simultaneously, an economics of consumption will teach us how to create immensely better urban environments.

Meanwhile, perhaps we should recall Peter Drucker's dictum that society produces, not individuals. Individuals in an industrial system can only work, only make a fractional contribution to production. Their role is partial and entirely dependent on teams, divisions, contracts, and specialized support for the creation of a modern product. Output is therefore collective and organizational. So too, consumption is becoming collectively determined. Individuals can no longer choose a large part of their consumption but rather, of necessity, heavily reflect the institutional arrangements and environmental forms that in truth guide what and how we consume.

We have so structured both products and the physical environments that if one is to benefit from advanced technology at all, he normally *must own* all that he uses: houses, cars, appliances, yard equipment, boats, recreation vehicles. Each year more money is demanded to stay above the rising inflationary levels on which poverty must be defined. This cycle is a tyranny on family budgets and a tragedy of the poor in a wealthy land.

Individual production and consumption are important for freedom. To produce is to create. Losing one's ability to produce means losing one's ability to create. Creativity depends on the freedom to bring a concept into physical or social reality, be it a pot, a play, or a moziac. It also depends on an interpersonal sharing with others. Eliminate the ability to produce and directly sell at least some goods to others and we lose the vital social nexus of both production and consumption, as well as the appreciation of craftsmanship, the pride of ownership, and, with these, prized identity and trust. Yet, like the loss of walking in the city, the loss of creativity is too often not missed and frequently becomes ridiculed as well.

Market Imperialism

It is astounding how we accept as normal, indeed imperative, that the fate of cities lies buried within market economics. Today's struggles of the drop-out society and the ecological and humanistic movements constitute a moral and philosophical rebellion against the economic determinism that got its hold on Western society only in the nineteenth century and now dominates human behavior approximately to the degree that society has become urbanized.

The economic historian Karl Polanyi ([1947], 1974) anticipated much of today's ecological way of thinking in a brilliant essay written over thirty years ago.* He observed how the market economy as we know it appeared mainly in the second quarter of the nineteenth century and how a different society emerged with a very different motivational springboard for human energy and organization. The crucial step, Polanyi said, was that "land and labor were made into commodities . . . treated *as if* produced for sale. Of course, they were not actually commodities. . . . Yet no more thoroughly effective fiction was ever devised. By buying and selling labor and land freely, the mechanism of the market was made to apply to them. . . . The true scope of such a step can be gauged if we remember that labor is only another name for man, and land for nature. The commodity fiction handed over the fate of man to the play of an automaton running in its own grooves and governed by its own laws."

Although markets have existed as long as the world has known traders, they were generally imbedded *within* a social matrix that was powerfully confined by custom, religion, and even the arts. Land and labor remained largely outside the commodity supply and price structure, except through highly guarded and closely governed circumstances. But when land and labor did become "free" in the market, Polanyi says, "the market mechanism became

*The following quotations were extracted from "Our Obsolete Market Economy, by Karl Polanyi, *Commentary,* February 1947. By permission of *Commentary.* (Reprinted in *Ecologist,* July 1974, pp. 212–220).

determinative for the life of the body social. . . . Such a forced conversion of a utilitarian outlook fatefully warped Western man's understanding of himself."

Polanyi refutes the orthodox view of inherent economic motives residing within man: the avoidance of hunger and the hope of gain. Quoting five anthropologists, he notes first that both hunger and gain play insignificant roles for primitive man and observes the "absence of individual destitution [by contrast to destitution of the community] that makes primitive society, in a sense, more humane than nineteenth-century society, and at the same time less 'economic.' . . . Secondly, there is no difference between primitive and civilized society. . . . Whether . . . ancient city-state, despotic empire, feudalism, thirteenth-century urban life, sixteenth-century regulationism—invariably the economic system is found to be merged in the social. . . . Thirdly, there was the startling abruptness of the change" to the market economy and economic determinism so powerfully with us today. In England, Polanyi cites the Poor Law Reform (1834), which made "starvation or work . . . the alternative left to the poor." The Bank Act (1844) removed the making of money from the government, regardless of the need at times to raise employment. The land reform laws opened land to the free market and the repeal of the Corn Laws (1846) created a pool for grain. Thus land and labor reform, the gold standard, and free trade created the conditions in "which the formerly harmless market pattern expanded into a sociological enormity."

For Polanyi, the pervasive expansion of the market, combined with the rising division of labor and the demise of local subsistence, "created the delusion of economic determinism" whereby the "economic system . . . not only 'influences' the rest of society but determines it. . . . *instead of the economic system being imbedded in social relationships,* these relationships were now imbedded in the economic system. . . . State and government, marriage and rearing of children, the organization of science and education, of religion and the arts, the choice of profession, the forms of habitation, the shape of settlements, the very aesthetics of private life—everything had to comply with the utilitarian pattern. . . . But since very few human activities can be carried on in the void

... the indirect effect of the market system came very near to determining the whole of society. It was almost impossible to avoid the erroneous conclusion that as 'economic' man was the 'real' man, so the economic system was 'really' society."

If the conclusions of Karl Polanyi were somber in 1947, humankind today lives in a far deeper shadow than the society he described but three decades ago: "No wonder," he said, "that [man's] social imagination shows signs of fatigue. . . . Our humiliating enslavement to the 'material,' which all human culture is designed to mitigate, was deliberately made more rigorous."

Dismal and Subversive Sciences

Market economics, although reigning for a century and a half and now more penetrating than ever, nevertheless faces a crisis of confidence. Some of the preliminary elements of a new social Magna Carta are coming into being. Major social enactments (the "welfare state") have been set into law; medical care is likely to be withdrawn from the market mechanism; a guaranteed income and major tax revisions are gathering momentum. A group of environmental laws are placing specific public purposes above the proprietary free market. Perhaps we are beginning to recognize that free markets and human freedom are radically different phenomena.

Although many laws have been enacted to rescue cities, all have skirted or dealt gingerly with the sacrosanct free market for land. Precisely because our land remains a sacredly "free" commodity, fragmentation and functional chaos are guaranteed as the norm in urban development. Environmental freedom steadily narrows itself to what one can privately possess, control, and maintain.

When both labor and land are confined to free markets, both the social imagination and the processes that might generate an unlimited variety of public environments and institutions for human fulfillment are necessarily frustrated. On one side, the individual living in the overbuilt and underdeveloped suburb has only exceptionally meagre foundations to assist him in developing his associations and activities. Outside of technical and professional

The Economic Toll

services for hire, our suburbs are social and cultural wastelands, especially when measured against the wealth, education, and leisure available to American society. On the other side, the dominance of the market presses on public affairs so oppressively that our cultural facilities are increasingly designed as "convention centers" that pay their own way and impose no burden on tax resources. When they can pay their own way they become feasible in the market, which then assures that the market mechanism will dominate their operation. This relationship distorts public activities, twists public purposes, and confines social aspirations.

Simultaneously, the financial stringencies in feasibility thinking, which demand minimum investment for maximum return, automatically rule out works that could inspire many generations of people. One-purpose feasibility thinking obliterates the diversities of value, aspiration, identity, pride, and human challenge that always appear behind civic greatness, from a first humble neighborhood improvement to a metropolitan renaissance involving building and landscape design, art and song, dance and festivity, poetry and play, philosophy and inquiry—the range of creative human impulses.

The proper role of economics is no more and no less than increasing the means to satisfy existing and possible human aspirations. All else is impediment, waste, and decay. But instead of facilitating liberal human purpose, the economy now subdues it. Instead of serving human growth through balanced, diverse development, the economy fosters new and deeper instabilities and fissures.

Current literature on social issues reveals a crisis whose roots go back more than a century. The chief problems today stem from the excesses (or successes) of a truly fantastic expansion of technical capacities. In the words of Jacques Barzun, "Man is *not* flourishing." The human self-image has narrowed precisely at the time when society has achieved its greatest material success. A profound pessimism about the human prospect is descending on the most thoughtful. The unbridled faith accompanying the earlier stages of industrialization is disappearing at the very time that the "progress" we so dearly sought has come to be most fully realized.

Harrison Brown has noted the difficulty of making the

achievement of stability and the maintenance of individual liberty compatible. Robert Heilbroner (1974, p. 110) speaks of "an oppressive anticipation of the future," and moves close to advocating the subordination of liberties to assure the survival of society: "Candor compels me" he says, "to suggest that the passage through the gauntlet ahead may be possible only under governments capable of rallying obedience far more effectively than would be possible in a democratic setting. If the issue for mankind is survival, such governments may be unavoidable, even necessary."

If, as Heilbroner suggests, "it seems beyond dispute that the present orientation of society must change," what kind of Magna Carta is required to establish social stability on the one side and maintain or enlarge human freedom on the other?

Heretofore, Western man has concentrated on developing the means of production, and these have provoked the chief controversies of the last hundred years. However, control of the economy by the political left or right now verges on irrelevance, for the vital issue is no longer the class struggle over who works and who benefits. Today, when many industrial and craft workers earn wages higher than those of many professional people, the strict class question has lost its biting urgency; inequality and poverty both arise more powerfully from economic and social chaos than from class suppression.

The new historic issue that rises with power and suddenness to supreme social urgency exists in the vast chasm between the tradition of economics, the dismal science, and the emergence of ecology, the subversive science. The pressing question today is *the general pattern and effect of our entire industrial and urban system*. Capital and labor have now become subordinate issues, for the effectiveness and benefits of both depend entirely on the environmental and institutional structure that channels ecological and humanistic affairs. In many respects, today's compelling issue is the social and ecological control of the economy—the subordination of economic means to social ends and to the imperatives of nature. For this subordination we need a new central locus of social organization, a new pattern of social initiative and response, and a new system of responding to human values. These reorientations speak not only to survival and dignity but to the heart of freedom and democracy as well.

If, as Heilbroner suggests, the need for a new orientation of society is beyond dispute, the city—as city—must play a central if not dominant role. The city is at once environmental, economic, and social, fully capable of achieving the integrations necessary for both ecological stability and social freedom in society. Despite the loss of its traditional unity, the city can reunify if there is a vision of its wholeness. The city can humanize economic life. It encompasses the critical center of all human ecology, although the environmentalists have yet to understand this fact. The city is society's most positive and complete human creation, at once shaping the human dream and manifesting our progress toward that dream.

Had the city been invested through history with a broad active ideal, and had it served as a major integrator of change rather than as a virtually idealless and passive receptacle, I am confident that our human self-image would now be sharper, more positive. The urban integrations might have moderated and more creatively channeled economic and social change while at the same time reconciling production and consumption with environmental necessities, inspiring social diversities close to the individual, and underwriting security and freedom in self-determining community.

However, in reading today's analysts of political, economic, social, and environmental affairs, one is struck either by the absence of acute perspectives of cities or by the outlook of despair for an urban future. In both cases, the difficulty appears to rest in the assumption deeply penetrating our minds that free markets are fundamental in the creation of urban environments. Consequently, we suppress the creativity that we so readily give to the spheres of technology and enterprise. We simply have never learned to envision the most positive possibilities of our closest surroundings—our urban environments.

In anguish, Robert Heilbroner says that if we ask "whether it is possible to meet the challenges of the future without the payment of a fearful price, the answer must be: No, there is no such hope" (1974, p. 136). Although Heilbroner's thinking is both broad and liberal, his statement is quite characteristic of our time and typifies a blindness about the urban environment within which most of us struggle for worthiness and on which all of us depend for our livelihood and our future. Is not our limited conception of the possible city a constricted conception of modern life?

Heilbroner believes that accumulated misdeeds of many decades are threatening affluence, liberty, and social stability. His responses to our dilemmas are pessimistic and almost totally defensive, for he sees dismal prospects within the confining continuum of economic, technical, and political events. He suggests restricting liberty to maintain social stability. In character with our time, he does not consider the prospects of cities at all.

Today, of course, the dismal prospects are unquestionably real. However, we also know that the complexities, resiliencies, and surprises of human history insult the shrewdest forecasters. Therefore, do we need to be so pessimistic when the dynamics of change have never been more evident? If we are simply pessimistic, we overlook the positive alternatives to the present course of events and the foundations we have established for even greater human creativity.

The world economy now faces runaway inflation, and much of this resides deeply within the frustrated human psyche confronting the increasing intrusions of living only by the money motive. Simultaneously, world society cannot delay the achievement of a rough ecological stability within two or three decades, the span of time, many agree, remaining to assure flexibility in the form society can take.

Today we do not know what ecological stability really means. Certainly it means radical conservation measures in which "zero growth" is but a first way station of the transformation. Human settlements are, of necessity, the essence of achieving a stable world order both ecological and economic, critical for every element and at every stage of reform. More fundamentally, human settlements can achieve the necessary radical conservation while enlarging the human prospect. They can become the catalyst to achieve a broader range of freedom.

Cities cannot achieve creative transformation in a society that is overwhelmingly governed by money exchange, market

The Economic Toll

growth, and the rule of special interest. The clash between ecologically sound environments and the market economy—although the problem is hardly recognized in these terms—is perhaps the most crucial source of our incredibly complex and interwoven difficulties today.*

John Stuart Mill (1885, pp. 514–517) stands out as a lonely giant in building a base for a stable economics on a finite globe. The political economy was not to be viewed in isolation, "but as a fragment of a greater whole; a branch of social philosophy, so interlinked with all the other branches that its conclusions, even in its own peculiar province, are only true conditionally."

What stands out so poignantly today, reflecting on those buoyant and seemingly illimitable times one hundred years ago, is that Mill put forward the idea of a "stationary state" of the economy, not because of resources or pollution or deepening economic chaos but because sooner or later it was necessary and, more importantly, because he found it appealing. He was "not charmed" with the ideal of "those who think that the normal state of human beings is that of struggling to get on . . . trampling, crushing, elbowing, and treading on each other's heels."

The positive value of stationary economics suggested by Mill was that the progress encouraged would be most specifically human. His statement, unacceptable when expansiveness had reached but its first modest stage of explosive power, is fresh and demanding in our day of dangerous gluttony. One hardly need remark, he said, "that a stationary condition of capital and population implies no stationary state of human improvement. There would be as much scope as ever for all kinds of mental culture, and moral and social progress; as much room for improving the Art of living, and much more likelihood of its being improved, when minds ceased to be engrossed by the art of getting on. Even the industrial arts might be as earnestly and as successfully cultivated, with this sole difference, that instead of serving no purpose but the increase of wealth,

* My concern here focuses chiefly on the American economic household, although necessarily within the context of world resources. But, as my observations suggest, the analysis applies universally to all modern economic systems.

industrial improvements would produce their legitimate effect, that of abridging labor."

Today we dare not misunderstand the high human potential of a steady-state economy, particularly as it would give us a freedom from economics. The modern equivalent of freedom from hunger is to free ourselves from the drudgery of maintaining a false, burdensome, and dangerous affluence. To substantially free ourselves from economics is to free ourselves from many degrading means of life and to permit us to pursue life's ends deeply and diversely. Only a small minority of people have ever enjoyed this privilege in the past—and it is mostly to them, at least some of them, that we owe civilization.

Putting limits on economics, that is, deemphasizing economic determinism in society, has been variously advised or implied by many economists, including Marshall, Keynes, Rostow, Galbraith, Schumacher, and Boulding, as well as Mill and Polanyi. Paradoxically, unless we now rapidly expand our freedom from economics in the name of ecology, we may lose the freedom altogether in a burned-out earthly wasteland. Nor can we long suppress the individuals, especially outside economics, who envision the larger dimensions of human freedom, the positive forces of being and becoming, the vital life of human engagement with others, and the dynamic growth of the whole human experience within every individual.

More concretely, freedom from economics means (1) freedom from unnecessary behavioral control of strictly economic organization, (2) opportunity to produce as an individual, and (3) freedom to organize one's kind and level of consumption.

Freedom from the behavioral control of ITT, IBM, GM, or GE requires extracting ourselves from all possible dominance of their plants, employment, processes, politics, and mass persuasions. That is a simple imperative of our age. Unlike political freedom, freedom for the *individual* to produce cannot be protected by statutes and courts. This freedom is found in arrangements built into the city. Being an active rather than a passive right, it becomes an active obligation of the city and society.

Freedom of consumption is similarly founded. It, too, is difficult for us to understand and manage because, until exploding

The Economic Toll

cities demanded more exacting behavior and more consumption, a freedom of consumption could be assumed. That freedom diminished dramatically with the appearance of the second family car and the socially isolated, consumptive, and barren suburbs. Ultimately, all three freedoms are the same freedom, so entwined are they with each other and with the form of the city.

In the past we always assumed that increased output was beneficial. Now we know the gigantic price that must be paid for productive excesses. An endlessly increasing stream of goods is literally counterproductive. Something less than the full ability of society to produce is imperative if we are to preserve life on the planet beyond a number of decades, minimize the human overburdens on time, energy, and creativity, and raise human freedom.

It has been said with justification that the old economics was economics and that the new economics is politics. If, in fact, an oligopoly is beginning to dominate the entire economy, not merely an industry, then market economics is becoming a system of concentrated power. If free markets ever ensured free men, it was only before the market completely enveloped land and labor and before the individual lost his ability to produce and consume independently. Honesty forces us to conclude that such a system must be recognized for all that it is and does and that it be forthrightly reorganized into a political economy that pursues a democratic ideal of social equality and human opportunity.

If markets are to be retained—and they should be for freedom itself—they require constraint and redirection to ensure that they do not trample on the freedoms they ostensibly serve. To serve freedom they require, in part at least, a level of functioning realistic to the scale of the individual and a manner of operation more congenial to human sensitivities and aspirations.

E. F. Schumacher offers an interesting perspective of what he calls Buddhist economics. "The Buddhist point of view takes the function of work to be at least threefold: to give a man a chance to utilize and develop his faculties; to enable him to overcome his ego-centeredness by joining with other people in a common task; and to bring forth the goods and services needed for a becoming existence . . . [To] strive for leisure as an alternative to work would be considered a complete misunderstanding . . . namely that work and leisure are complementary parts of the same living process and cannot be separated without destroying the joy of work and the bliss of leisure" (1973, pp. 51–52).

The Buddhist approach does indeed perceive economics "as a fragment of a greater whole." Another way of perceiving the greater whole within which economics serves the wide span of human purpose is as a part of a unified city. To highlight the possibilities of an economic humanism as affected by the form of cities, four summary observations are appropriate. Their import will become clearer in the chapters that follow.

1. Cities provide a framework to give local and regional unity to both economics and ecology, making possible large benefits without compromising traditional macro economics or economies of scale. Neither economics nor ecology can be valid without reference to the city. To the extent that cities themselves are unified, functionally integrated, and efficient, they offer enormous opportunities to save production, conserve resources, and protect the environment. That is, economic efficiency and ecological stability depend on urban efficiency and stability.

2. Cities are necessary to bring economics into harmony with ecology (a unity suggested by their common Greek root). Ultimately, sound economics (that is, the economy of means) must be identical with a valid and stable human ecology.

3. Except for the smallest cities, the most critical economic efficiencies and ecological stabilities will occur at levels much smaller than the whole—at a genuine human scale—probably in populations of less than ten thousand. Both economic efficiencies and ecological stabilities demand a local or human scale, which is also usually the most effective relationship between man and the environment.

4. Cities, the created organic counterparts of our bodies, are the formats on which a social health becomes achievable. Social health depends on shifting economic processes from a quantitative to a qualitative foundation.

The toll of economics is thus not only a shortfall of what we strive for and envision, it is also the loss of what we have failed to strive for and what we have failed to envision. Modern man has been astoundingly successful, perhaps too successful. With all of the success, there is an abiding hopelessness, often, it seems, infecting even those who stand high on the ladder of economic success. Success with a profound hopelessness characterizes the impact of economics on cities.

7

The Human Toll

When our times are put into the perspective of history, they will no doubt be characterized by terms like *industrialization* and *urbanization,* to which may be added a third and no less pervasive description: *alienation*. Indeed, the taut and fractured nature of our behavior, our bureaucratic depersonalization, and the consequent inner turmoil of our psyches seem inevitable results of the kind of urban and industrial world we make.

Here I use the term *alienation* as a collective concept of causes and effects covering many acute personal and interpersonal problems arising in the unique context of modern times. As a person, each of us is whole and strives for wholeness within our surroundings; alienation is the loss of this wholeness. Randomness, brittle divisions, and social incoherencies that constantly bombard our unity of behavior and personality underwrite the growth of human alienation.

The Human Toll

If both human personality and the city have a common bearing on social wholeness, then there is an especially close affinity between them in the case of alienation. The struggle to comprehend wholes consequently impels us to search for the complex relations between the built environment of the city, the social institutions inhabiting the city, and the deep deprivations of alienation.

The affluent, well-educated American appears to be in a transition between two broad lines of personal development. One line, the "pioneering" ethic behind much of our historic material and technical success, seems to be reaching exhaustion, certainly in its motivational power. Several areas are included in this line of development, most notably colonization and westward movement; science, technology, and industry; bureaucratic and corporate organization; the upward extension of formal education; the institutionalized growth of health and welfare services; the economy of pervasive producing, selling, and consuming; and the massive, socially undifferentiated, urbanization. Most of these arenas have only recently begun to lose their pioneering excitement in real human terms. Although some of these fields will no doubt continue to develop, perhaps profoundly in a few cases, the human esprit within them is diminishing appreciably. These endeavors, encompassing the bulk of our national experience, have sought the *external* conditions of the good life and have emphasized specific results and quantity. Now, in a second and newer line of development, we are beginning to seek out the *internal* or *inherent* qualities of existence, those conditions which give depth and meaning to the external progress. But in this arena the individual seems to flounder in confusion.

Most of the external developments, although often exceptionally beneficial in material terms, have not only diminished in human significance but have also destroyed one's ability to experience many qualities of existence. Bound too closely to producing and consuming, our age has depressed the cultural challenge, the inspiring ethic, the deeper spontaneity, and even the vision that the high productivity itself underwrote. One wonders how such a wellspring of the human spirit, made possible by affluence, leisure, and education, has become so mired and constrictive in deep personal terms. We know or feel, in any case, that the conditions of our assiduous, demanding materialism have estranged us from the city and its higher human potential.

Just as the human potential movement partly arose out of therapy for the sick, our striving to overcome the pervasiveness of alienation in urban life might spark a movement that will lead to a higher level of the human potential. Thus, when we approach alienation, we also explore a genuinely new tack for society and civilization. If the city has brought people into closer physical proximity while at the same time causing deeper social separations, the city can also be the foundation for the creation of a more bountiful union—secure, intimate, free, open, trusting, and outreaching.

Physical Alienation

A simple examination of the city reveals a physical structure of alienation. The classic American house, the one-family dwelling on a one-family lot, is designed to achieve isolation and separation almost to the extent of one's means. The more affluent an individual becomes, the more that person's status and resources impel him or her into social exclusion and defensive isolation. Common spaces, common facilities, mutual-interest organizations, and interpersonal bonds are lacking, almost forbidden, in the channels of social action. Most public association is therefore transferred to pockets of special interest and obliged to become more private, more proprietary. Each interest one has corresponds to a different location and set of associates.

Speaking as a landscape architect but with universal implications, Garrett Eckbo (1969, p. 65) observes that "real estate operations require the subdivision of the unbroken surface of the land . . . into a collection of alienable commodities. . . . Every element which goes into the makeup of the single landscape must be separable from it. . . . This commodity consciousness affects our entire psychology about our landscape, atomizes it, puts merchandise spectacles in our eyes." The alienating process, however, only begins by fragmenting the land. In the end it also isolates behavior itself into facile exchange units.

The idea of the city being constituted mainly of thousands of alienated parcels is pervasive. Public spaces, rather than serving as centers for vigorous exchange and social interaction, act mainly as rights of way to pass between private parcels or as points of specialized service. Most public spaces have thus become the public equivalent of private, special-purpose spaces. Some traditionally public spaces have been taken over by private special interests altogether, such as in the shift from the very public downtown to proprietary shopping centers.

Seen alone, every urban parcel represents isolation. Seen together, they represent fragmentation, or at least specialization of the human relationship, where special functional interests are served and common, nonspecific associational needs are not.

Intensive mobility has an identical separating impact. Frequent travel implies numerous contacts, a brevity of interaction, even when activities are not pressing. The frantic and hurtful pace of our lives exists not only in our mobility or in our work—required in part to maintain mobility and the huge spaces it spans—but also in the hectic, almost brutish style of our interpersonal behavior. When unrelieved by sustained in-depth, multiinterest friendships, the person learns to experience and respond only to shallow, particularized exchange.

When the mode of travel is individual, time consuming, and encased in steel and glass, and when it requires nervous strain for safe arrival, transportation carries with it another set of conditions contributing to alienation. Of all the inhuman environments created by society, the image of thousands of people driving alone and isolated along giant, jammed freeways that can kill at any moment strikes closest to an existential nightmare. Yet the feeling of complete social estrangement may be greater in parking lots and garages, where we get on our feet and use our senses more freely and completely. Nor can we ignore the drivers' anxieties over parking and traffic tickets or their fear of confrontations with police and judges.

The wide street surfaces—paved, barren, and harsh—not

only encourage incessant movement but also act as rasping separators of neighborhood life. A revealing study of residential streets in San Francisco concluded that such aspects of perceived livability as absence of noise, stress, and pollution; levels of social interaction, territorial extent, and environmental awareness; and safety correlated inversely with traffic intensity (Appleyard and Lintell, 1972, p. 84). When conditions force one to drive through other people's neighborhoods, we can expect that the social irrelevance and the social interference will specifically alienate us from friends and from healthy living conditions.

The randomness is more pervasive in commerce, which, in the name of competition, has dispersed itself along strips and to "centers" that defeat centrality. On a map, the individual's daily movement pattern appears as a wild scatter diagram. One's quest for goods and services of reasonable quality and reasonable price is a struggle hardly relieved by an inch of yellow pages. Where, then, are the citizen efficiency and ease, the sense of place, the extended coffee and a chance-met friend, and the environmental beauty?

"The chief quality of commodities is salability, which means alienability," says Garrett Eckbo (1969, p. 65). The question we must ask in appraising our life in the city is whether the alienation of goods—and the alienation created by the goods exchange process—does not also alienate the person who must pass through essentially the same process. Bernard Murchland suggests that it does, with a quantitative world resulting "when the exchange value of commodities replaces their use value." That subtle separation between persons has another effect. The more random and fragmented our physical environment is, the more dispersed and mobile we become; in the same way, the more unsure or dissatisfied a consumer population is, the more susceptible the individual becomes to advertising appeals, promotional maneuvers, and cheap throw-away goods.

Urban chaos is always advantageous for the powerful and best organized. Supermarkets killed the neighborhood grocery stores, ostensibly through improved price and selection. Now, however, new chains have emerged (Stop-Go, Short Stop, Seven-Eleven) that replicate the old neighborhood store in size and selection but no longer serve a recognizable neighborhood. Their locations on boulevards respond to and require both driving and depersonalization.

What may be equally alienating in the form of the city is the lost sense of place. "Placeness," or the significance of a particular place to an individual, has been reassuring to humankind for many millenia. In today's turmoil, places not only change, but they lose their very placeness in the endless randomness of cost-benefit decisions, asphalt desolations, and salability of place itself. Thus, under the chaotic complexity, forced travel, impersonality, and personal strain associated with today's specialized setting of behavior, a severe discontinuity occurs between the places and things one remembers, the challenges one must respond to, and the unknown challenges one must expect. Continual readjustment—or future shock—bears down on every person.

If the city's physical environment constitutes a basically formless, neighborless, and anonymous pattern for the citizen, and assuredly this is increasingly the case, we can readily see that this pattern arises from the bureaucratic and economic organization of life. In the city this pattern appears in urban development practices, tax and subsidy systems, and varied business traditions. Socially and ethically, these practices and traditions mean that the economic organizations and special functions will have unity, integrity, and power, but that the general form of the city reflecting the social values of the individual will not have unity, integrity, or power. A sense of personal helplessness is the direct result.

The economic and bureaucratic ideals have a psychologically devastating influence on architecture and urban design, often in buildings of acclaimed design. Jane Jacobs and Lawrence Halprin have begun to teach us the dismal effect on behavior of dead spaces, large and dull surfaces, repelling walkways, and the lack of public meeting places. Ostensibly built for joy, the Lincoln and Kennedy performing arts centers are attractive at a distance of five hundred yards or more but are barren, almost forbidding, when one is close to their bleak surfaces or within their grossly formed spaces. The Seagram building in New York, for all of its finesse, still depicts what it really is: a massive, cold, steel-and-glass machine produced by the machine arts. Despite its elegant interior decor, the machinelike desks speak of the monolithic purposes, subtle personal disciplines, and penetrating social power of the economic and administrative organization.

Institutional Alienation

Physical alienation is paralleled by alienation built into institutions. If we consider a list of our most important organizations—those housed in offices, factories, schools, hospitals, asylums, reformatories, prisons, homes for the aged—we find a generally demeaning, almost Machiavellian structure of interpersonal relations. If we have perhaps rid our organizations of most of the simple cruelties they displayed two or four centuries ago, we have hardly begun to examine their subtler depravations.

In order to comprehend the debilitating effects of urban institutions on the individual, we must consider the premises on which such institutions are created. Although fundamental differences exist between corporate and governmental agencies, the similarity of their effect on individuals (as employees, customers, or service recipients) is striking. The more important distinction to be made is between the "hard" institutions (those that are solidly economic and bureaucratic) and the "soft" institutions (the volunteer organizations that serve personal, social, and cultural interests and that exist on dues, contributions, and modest earnings).

Hard organizations exist for essentially one special purpose. It does not really matter whether they make a product for profit or provide a service funded by taxation. The special purpose virtually assures that the organization will fail to deal with the individual in a whole and complete way. The individual's role in dealing with the organizations is special, limited, and largely unrelated to one's other memberships, roles, or activities. When these organizations have expanded their role with individuals, as with employee health, retirement, and package vacation programs, the individual tends to become dependent and bound to that one organization.

In the American mythology of success, high expectations too easily reduce themselves to an anxiety in the ladder-climbing exercises in which most people must necessarily "fail" in the system of rewards. The joy and happiness of those who rise in an organization are necessarily dependent on the unhappiness of a larger number who remain in the lower echelons of the hierarchy. Although striving and high expectations are imbedded deeply in our Protestant ethic, a rigid hierarchy confines success to a very small minority. The system demands losers in a game of Social Darwinism, which means that social equality and political democracy are denied at the roots of urban society.

Organizations, it seems, use their specialization to secure maximum control over behavior, not only to provide a more expert service but also for the convenience, benefit, and power of the owners or managers. Health, for example, has traditionally been a field of compassion. Yet its vast expansion and technological developments have made it highly bureaucratic—and more susceptible to the prerogatives of managers and professionals. For instance, hospital design and management minimize family visiting with patients as an interference with health care, despite the critical "human factor" in regaining health. Only small-town hospitals tend to relax rules in favor of the whole patient or the whole family (for example, permitting relatives to stay at bedside overnight at crucial times).

Similarly, schools are planned largely to maintain order with the largest possible enrollments and class sizes; to rigidly exclude all learning except that which can be organized, tested, graded, and credited for everyone in a single approved curriculum; and to march each student through the system as rigidly as a car is assembled in Detroit.

A person's role in these organizations is precisely fixed, standardized and graded. Every participant has his or her assigned seat, bed, work place. Yet nearly every person is expendable, exactly like the places and facilities in the city. In most roles, except that of ownership (typically ownership bears rights not available to non-owners), the individual serves at the pleasure of the institution. As a result, friendships and human attachments are also expendable, dependent as they are on one's role in the specialized institution.

The hard institutions quite openly negate many cherished qualities of the democratic tradition. Antony Jay (1967, p. 16), in his book *Management and Machiavelli,* suggests that employees, as workers, have "no political freedom . . . no freedom to publish

... no freedom of speech ... no right of trial ... no sort of representation in the councils which decide how the firm shall be run." How in this bureaucratic world can either the employee or the service recipient maintain individual uniqueness and independent personality? Both governments and corporations discourage initiative and resourcefulness, deny privacy as irresponsibility, and thereby contribute to the defensive privacy we pursue in "private" life.

A very different picture appears when we shift from the hard to the soft institutions, those that are today most concerned with the human qualities of personal fulfillment. The individual's position is rigidly fixed in the hard institutions; this position becomes very tenuous and indefinite in the soft organizations, especially community and cultural organizations. Rewarding involvement appears to require an extraordinary commitment by the individual, which perhaps helps explain why participation revolves around a narrow strata of the aspiring middle class.

The range of human interests represented by the performing and visual arts, by recreation and hobbies, and by conservation and service organizations is obviously very great. It would seem that the natural tendency of the human-interest groups would be to join their activities in endless ways to stimulate higher levels of interest, to ease participation, and to establish a greater cohesiveness of individual involvement in social action. Yet the voluntary groups in the splintered city generally accommodate themselves to the dominant special-interest organizations and become fragmented special interests themselves. There is little in the structure of the city to encourage them to be otherwise. Their locations are dispersed. There is no organizational framework for cooperation, no clear constituency for mutual involvement and support, and no common time to build a habit of cooperative action. Such organizations lack an urban definition of the boundaries and centers by which people, places, times, and organizations can coalesce for the benefit of all.

The meaning of such a pattern, or lack of it, appears to be twofold: (1) Social and cultural *aspiration* is very low, intimidated in spirit by excessive wage earning, which is made necessary in part to maintain the chaotic city. That is, people are alienated from the social and cultural visions of personal growth and substitute money

The Human Toll

and status for them. (2) The *means* for creative public involvement and personal growth are specialized, fragmented, conditional, confined, and fragile. They, too, are alienated.

Alienation affects the way friendships are formed in the city. Christopher Alexander (1966) has pointed to the lack of closed groups of people in our society. The relationships of friends and acquaintances "forms a semi-lattice, not a tree." As observation, Alexander's view is correct. As an ideal or as a matter of choice, this pattern of friendship—having friends unknown to each other—is a model of diminished human value, lost just as a sense of urban place has been lost. I suspect that unless we find an urban format for continuous, multirole friendship between individuals (without, of course, creating a wholly closed system), we will find, as we are sadly beginning to see, that human association is reduced to random, meaningless events or to a series of negotiations that serve only the naked self-interest that concerned Marx.

Reflecting on Louis Wirth's sociology, Don Martindale and Gertrud Neuwirth (in Weber, 1958, p. 39) describe how "the multiplication of the number of persons in interaction . . . makes full contact of personalities impossible. The result is a 'schizoid' property of urban personality. Contacts are impersonal, superficial, transitory, and segmental, leading to reserve, indifference, a blase outlook and the immunization of one's self against the claims of others. The superficiality, anonymity, and transitory character of urban social relations makes intelligible the sophistication and rationality of city dwellers. Freedom from personal emotional control of intimate groups leaves them in a state of *anomie* (a kind of normlessness) as Durkheim put it. . . . A premium is placed on utility and efficiency and leads automatically to the employment of corporative devices for the organization of enterprise."

When we consider the major urban factors producing alienation, it is difficult not to be impressed with the awesome proportions of the depersonalization, helplessness, and unwarranted organizational subordination of the individual. To summarize:

1. Interpersonal relations continue to shift toward *single-purpose* roles, prompting a high degree of specialization, segregation, and exclusiveness of participation in the relations themselves.

2. Behavior is increasingly *utilitarian* in character, confined by a rigid personal discipline and a standardization of interpersonal contact.
3. Social behavior is *fragmented* because each role is reduced to its utilitarian components; the result is personal isolation.
4. Emphasis on *commodity exchange* throughout society demands that monetary values supplant personal and socially originated values in many otherwise personal or intimate relations, including courtships, dress, recreation, friendship, and education.
5. Socially undifferentiated population masses in cities, combined with the factors just listed, produce a *randomness of interpersonal association,* assuring that friendship will be largely secondary and circumstantial rather than basic and that enduring interpersonal bonds are minimized (or are viewed as burdensome).
6. Institutions demand *dominant-submissive relations* between participants, inducing "games" of power and status in interpersonal relations and personalities.
7. The individual is *expendable* to formal economic institutions despite his or her psychological dependence on them.
8. Every individual is subject to a multitude of *threats, disruptions, inconveniences, confusions, insults, and dangers* that arise from the specific organization of technology, bureaucracy, and large urban environments.

No one or two of these factors, of course, are deeply alienating alone, and some are partially necessary. It is their sum and their dominating presence in organizing human behavior—extending a minimal necessity into a maximal principle—that produces the pervasive air of human disenchantment and undermines the specific human qualities of interpersonal relations.

For some people—mainly owners and managers—the ill effects of alienation are minimal and the rewards are sufficiently distractive to ignore the question. The magnetic external rewards of ownership and hierarchy have become perhaps the most expansive and abiding game in history. For most people, however, the effects of alienation are chilling and inwardly inhuman, although the majority are convinced that they have been generously compensated for the personal deprivations. Hence, we suffer quietly and typically respond by coating over our emotions, spontaneity, and inner vitality with layers of calcium deposits. The process is called adjustment.

But for others a break occurs. Constructive adjustment does not take place, and society receives a backlash in the form of crime, alcohol, insanity, suicide, or guerrilla actions. And the credibility of illegal, immoral, or debilitating behavior now rises roughly in proportion to the loss of government and corporation credibility as servants and guardians of the body social. In the final analysis, these organizations *are* responsible for the penetrating alienation, because they organized the cities and the social system that give rise to it.

Alienation is perhaps simply another manifestation of the fact that our cities and our way of producing and consuming are personally inorganic and socially dysfunctional. The alienation seems to reflect a society determined to prove Machiavelli right and to convert strategies of power into a general theory of personality. That such a possibility can become a reality has already been solidly proved by totalitarian regimes that have radically reshaped human personality in our time.

And we go on building cities that accelerate fragmented exchange and minimize social cohesiveness, individual wholeness, or human enrichment. The nurturing qualities of interpersonal association hardly enter the debates of city-building, now so deeply oppressed by many powerful physical debilitations.

Devastation of Experience

Let us not mistake the seriousness of what we are doing to ourselves. Alienation is not after-school boredom, a time of youthful adjustment, or a stressful episode in life. It is real, and it underlies vandalism, suicide, schizophrenia, ordinary depression, cold aloofness, and inane cruelty.

Many voices ask why the human spirit takes such a beating when the human promise has risen so high. Why are Americans so anguished at the time of greatest material progress? If in Thoreau's time "the mass of men" led "lives of quiet desperation," how much more desperate are they today, and how much more severely are they obliged to suffer?

Alienation has been variously referred to as the disease of nonattachment, the deprivation of power over one's social existence, an incoherent sense of the self, the divorce of a person from life, the separation of behavior from experience, and absurdity of existence. Those who describe it mention loss of self, anomie, depersonalization, rootlessness, meaninglessness, personal isolation, and lack of community. Sometimes the reference is social, sometimes personal. In any case, alienation involves a separation of the individual from the culturally created and socially sustaining meanings of life. It appears with a decline or breakdown of the interpersonal support an individual requires for a rewarding participation in society.

British psychiatrist R. D. Laing (1967, pp. 78–79) speaks of alienation as the "devastation of experience," a serious distortion in the social order reflected in the foundations of personality. We can say that, *"without exception,"* Laing emphasizes, "the experience and behavior that gets labeled schizophrenic is *a special strategy that the person invents in order to live in an unlivable situation.*" To Laing, alienation appears in the fundamental structure of urban life. "The physical environment unremittingly offers us possibilities of experience, or curtails them. . . . The glory of Athens, as Pericles so lucidly stated, and the horror of so many features of the modern megalopolis is that the former enhanced and the latter constricts man's consciousness."

Although alienation arises from the bedrock of urban forms and institutions, it nevertheless operates even in the smallest interpersonal subtleties: remarks, gestures, unrecognized defenses. These prompt human interaction to become more guarded, conditional, fragmented, abrupt, particularized, and unsure, thereby promoting greater alienation. Persons are but players mutually imprisoned in environments, events, and behavior that they cannot alter. They are not free. They are trapped in a self-reinforcing maze of the physical, organizational, and interpersonal confinements of alienation.

Laing trenchantly describes how socially depraved relations are fostered: "What we call 'normal' is a product of repression,

The Human Toll

denial, splitting, projection, introjection and other forms of destructive action upon experience." The person is deeply estranged "from the structure of being. . . . The conditions of alienation, of being asleep, of being unconscious, of being out of one's mind is the condition of normal man. It educates children to lose themselves and become absurd, and thus to be normal. *If our experience is destroyed, our behavior will be destructive* . . . we are bereft of our humanity."

Laing's insight, although following the tradition of Eric Fromm and Karen Horney, seems to bridge Freudian psychopathology and Abraham Maslow's psychology of being. "The relevance of Freud to our time," says Laing, is "his demonstration that the ordinary person is a shriveled, desiccated fragment of what a person can be." Our humanity is at stake. The sheer loneliness of individual persons amidst millions—cooperating minutely in job and career but unable to reach each other with human affect—illustrates the real specter of modern life. The operational meaning of alienation is the struggle for survival of personality in a society that constantly threatens individual integrity. Wherever we look at today's political economy we find the individual, in ideology as well as in practice, to be dependent, expendable, interchangeable, and transferable. He is, therefore, psychologically formed by the same terms of alienation that shaped the city's forms and organizations.

A Dutch professor of social medicine has suggested that mental health in cities is now comparable to general health conditions two centuries ago. This comparison may be true but it oversimplifies the challenge, implying a number of special remedies and specific environmental changes. General health could be dramatically improved with sanitation, innoculation, and extermination of specific disease carriers, but today's endemic social helplessness strikes at the heart of how society is organized, produces, and governs itself. Our affliction pierces into all that we call modern. It would appear that the challenge is philosophic and moral more than it is scientific and professional.

Put differently, men have spent the last four centuries learning how to use each other to high perfection in expanding production, service, and exchange. Sophisticated management arose and created a new kind of social responsibility (and interdependence).

Our triumph is that we can, in minutes, arrange to travel around the world in twenty flights, mobilizing as it were thousands of persons on our behalf, and be quite certain that schedules will be closely met. This immense feat is human and organizational no less than technological.

While striving to perfect our uses of each other, however, we nearly forgot our human roots, which slowly withered our emotional sources for morality. Our abstractions of good will are superb, but, as Eric Hoffer suggested, "it is easier to love humanity as a whole than to love one's neighbor" (1951, p. 92). To a large degree, that is the way we have organized society. And now the utilitarian cooperation perfected in vast bureaucracies has led directly and indirectly to the atrophy of more intimate, personally rewarding, and socially sustaining interpersonal bonds. We have, in a word, organized love out of our lives.

Antinomies

Although philosophers have struggled to overcome the shortage of love ever since they reflected on organized human behavior, and although the youth of most ages have felt estranged in some way from their family, clan, or village, the abiding concern for oppressive, general alienation belongs singularly to our age. Only the modern age has truly revolutionized the habitational, life-sustaining, motivational, and organizational foundations of human life.

A consciousness of alienation, first appearing clearly with Jean Jacques Rousseau, has grown in each succeeding generation. Much Western writing, which Robert Nisbet (1953, pp. 7-22) calls the "literature of alienation," involves alienation as a conscious or hidden theme. Proust, Eliot, Mann, Kafka, and Joyce were each concerned with the pathology, sickness, and decay in the warp and woof of human behavior. The historians and prophets—Toynbee, Spengler, Sorokin, Niebuhr—similarly wrote of the fateful decline and pervasive hopelessness of our time. Contemporary music and abstract art appear to have incorporated alienation into their thematic structures. Psychiatry has grown on individual breakdown. Psychology and sociology have been seriously preoccupied by personality disintegration, community and family disorganization, and public strife.

These manifestations of alienation are so familiar to us that they are sometimes assumed to be congenital in society. To many persons, personality deprivation ("spare the rod and spoil the child") is a necessary discipline to work, a goad to excel, and possibly a spur to be creative. The arguments recall old debates about slave versus free labor.

It was, to be sure, in terms of freedom that Rousseau raised the issue of alienation. For Rousseau, alienation meant the outcome of growing economic interests that corrupted the character of society, creating the inauthentic condition of man. That condition was represented by a series of dichotomies: being-appearance, nature-society, autonomy-subordination, public and private selves. As a result, Rousseau thought, people sought happiness in appearances, transparencies, and artificialities. They live, he said, "not for the sake of living, but only to give the impression of having lived."

Rousseau's concern that men were living according to a dangerous illusion was felt by many other thinkers. For Friedrich Nietzsche the question was nihilism, which meant that "the highest values devaluate themselves. The goal is lacking: the answer is lacking to our 'why.' " But illusions and lost goals cannot be dissociated from the other facets of alienation. Emile Durkheim, whose study of suicide was monumental, noted that anxiety—the profound uneasiness at the heart of alienation—was generally not found in premodern societies. Kierkegaard wondered whether or not the transformation of a people into a mass society produced a condition in which "the sense of association in society is no longer strong enough to give life to concrete realities." For William James the threatening illusion involved a total anonymity: "No more fiendish punishment could be devised . . . than that one should be turned loose in society and remain absolutely unnoticed by all the members thereof." And to Albert Camus, alienation meant a dichotomy that reduced life to absurdity, an unbridgeable gulf between reason and experience, between the self and what is not the self: "The divorce between man and his life . . . is properly the feeling of absurdity."

Marx, like Rousseau, saw human alienation as an outcome

of economic growth, and to him class interest was the primary tool of corruption. It was the bourgeoisie that had "left no other nexus between man and man than naked self-interest." One of Marx's specific aims was to reduce the effect of self-interest in human relations. And it was his intellectual forebear, Hegel, who sought a "living logic" or "logic of love" that could cope with the antinomies of human experience.

The broad, growing concern for the varied depersonalization we call alienation is now undoubtedly becoming central to society, asking most basically how society perceives itself and governs its own development. The range of concern suggests not only the paramount importance of the separation of the person from civilized personality but also that this endemic condition threatens to upset social responsibility, from local democracy to world peace.

No concern is more critical to human value than freedom. Richard Goodwin (1974, p. 16), in his important book, *The American Condition*, draws vital connections between our materialism, our alienation, and threats to our freedom. He suggests that the promise of Marx was not elimination of private property, but the "abolition of material necessity. . . . liberating individuals to fulfill the more expansive possibilities of their humanity." Marx's promise, Goodwin states, is similar to that in the American Dream. Both the American Dream and the promise of Marx, two guiding assumptions of progressive thought, however, "have now been overturned. Amidst unparalleled productive power, freedom is being eroded and confined."

How does alienation erode and confine freedom? Goodwin's description carries a powerful, if somber, message: "Modern confusion and distress now reveal themselves as a consequence, not of human evil, but of the process which provides material abundance. That process has assumed a vitality and form of its own. Partially independent of human will, its necessities of ideology, value and organization impose themselves on the social order, and thereby define and construct our social existence. The moment of liberation recedes as the 'realm of necessity' continually expands, while the ideology and institutions devised to create the apparatus of abundance have so fused with our environment, life styles, values and

The Human Toll

thought that it is no longer possible to know who is the instrument of the other's purpose."

A number of specific mechanisms contribute to the alienation process, Goodwin suggests. First, "The reduction of freedom to preference and opinion is a sign of advanced social fragmentation and decay. Through the exercise of private liberty we are made to forfeit the possibility of association and intimacy which is the premise of individual power, that is, of unalienated existence." Second, Goodwin notes that the growth of bureaucracy has penetrated our beliefs and behavior, extending "the assault on the forms of shared existence and upon the awareness of our social nature." Third, "The destruction of our relationship with nature is a kind of 'sensory deprivation less complete but far more pervasive and enduring' than recent experiments which deprived persons of their ability to see, hear, smell or touch, and which produced severe emotional turbulence."

To Goodwin, freedom diminishes when the individual transfers, through his alienation, "a portion of his own existence . . . to an autonomous authority. . . . The source of today's alienation is not a ruling class, but a process dominated by bureaucratic institutions." That process secretes itself into the deeper recesses of personality and culture. Goodwin (1974, p. 146) continues:

> Since consciousness, unlike hunger, is the creation of social process, a deficiency in awareness is not an individual aberration but a universal affliction. . . . It is, therefore, expectable that all the significant features of American society should display and fortify the modern consciousness. . . . The disintegration of community, the decline of shared social purpose, the weakening identification between citizen and nation, and the rejection of moral authority superior to individual judgment or opinion are consequences and manifestations of the modern consciousness. . . . The fragmentation of social existence, by weakening the social power of the citizen, enables the ruling institutions of a bureaucratic economy to direct society's resources toward their own aggrandizement. The means of this control are so extensive they

often seem to be part of a natural economic order, as the foundation of production itself, rather than the supporting instruments of inefficient and oppressive economic relationships.

Lewis Mumford, who has spent the better part of his life working against the forces of alienation, also finds the sources of our personal helplessness in our most basic organizations and processes. We have, he said, "a culture that is overorganized, overmechanized, overdirected, overpredictable . . . human beings become 'things' or 'counters' to be treated as . . . brute matter" in the course of this automatic culture. The result, Mumford concludes, is "empty affluence, empty idleness, empty excitement, empty sexuality," that "are not the occasional vices of our machine-oriented society but its boasted final products" (Mumford, 1970, p. 360).

The Illness Among Us

The varied descriptions of alienation we have reviewed have either implied or incorporated some social results. Now we will consider some of these results and complications. They represent a kind of psychic revenge or backlash against society and are unusually varied, including crime and delinquency, alcoholism and drugs, suicide, many mental disorders, and extreme political action (for example, such groups as Minutemen, American Nazis, urban guerrillas). They also include a number of less dramatic attributes, qualities that apply more or less to all people but that are generally identified as inauthentic or undesirable behavior: withdrawal, aloofness, and coldness of personality; orientation to status, money, manipulation, and power; harshness; sudden outbursts of anger.

The unusual diversity of sources, forms, and effects of alienation pose a question of methodology that must be briefly considered. The importance is this: A broad concept of alienation is appropriate and may be necessary for creatures who do not carry specific instincts; whose native proclivities are infinitely variable; whose psychosocial conditioning varies profusely from family to family, neighborhood to neighborhood, time to time; and whose specific models, accidents, opportunities, and expectations are virtually limitless.

In a society in which investigative thought is highly specialized and centers on efforts to isolate specific cause and specific effect, the bewildering diversities of both cause and effect in alienation are, of course, factually illusive and conceptually slippery. Although all social sciences have a bearing on alienation, none relate to it as a whole. Alienation, like its corollary problem, the disintegration of cities, seems to pose a problem of wholeness that our age is ill-prepared to comprehend.

Because alienation itself is not easily quantifiable or testable in terms of specific cause and effect, and hardly amenable to direct experimentation, its province is most properly that of the generalist or philosopher. Although the former is not an organized discipline and the latter has been losing its engagement in social thought for nearly a century, these fields may still be best equipped to compare the disparate sources of information, to judge and direct inquiry, to weigh the hundreds of specialized studies, and to formulate the broad questions, observations, hypotheses, and conclusions.

Although organized society in towns has always suffered varying levels of social backlash and always will—just as some ill health can always be expected—we can say with some confidence that such social maladies as crime, alcoholism, neurosis, and suicide are, to a substantial degree, symptoms of a deeper social malaise. More than most diseases demonstrating multiple symptoms, alienation, reflecting the lack of fit between society and the whole individual, breaks out in a virtually unlimited variety of self-defeating, antisocial behavior.

Rene Dubos and Hans Selye today reaffirm Hippocrates in saying that sickness results from environmental disharmony and that the whole person is sick, not just the heart, lungs, stomach or head. The wholeness of social disease, the wholeness of social causes and individual effects, or of individual causes and social effects, does certainly reflect disharmony in the environment in which the individual thrives or suffers. Today no whole is more important for the individual than the urban environment. And this environment has never been more socially fractured or personally chaotic.

We know all too well the chaotic state of a mutual vandalism now rising in city life, producing an armed-camp mentality. Joseph Lyford (1970, p. 53) has described how the "process" in New York City transmits the ugliness from one generation to the next:

> One of the tidal facts that has impressed me most is the continued waste of human life that is taking place in our city. I am not talking about the murders or assaults that have terrified most of the people I know. . . . I am talking about the destruction of children. . . . Only a small proportion of these crimes have to do with outright physical abuse. From the time tens of thousands of newborn infants are removed from the hospital, they become subjected . . . to a style of existence that usually cripples or destroys huge numbers of them.
>
> I have not been able to discover any good reason why this should be taking place, even an economic one. It is said over and over that the United States and the City of New York together do not have the public or private money to prevent the destruction of children. . . . Later on, when children born clean, ready and expectant, begin to malfunction and cause trouble, hundreds of millions of dollars are appropriated to have special teachers and policemen and youth workers build special classrooms and prisons and mental institutions, and finance hospital beds to get these children under control. The children who do survive this tempering process become adults, but in my neighborhood an adult is a dead child.

Lyford has touched many raw nerve endings of alienation in this description. But in his second tidal fact he gets down to the crux of the matter: "We are, practically speaking, unconscious of what is going on." Such mindlessness is astonishing, for we know of societies, communities, and conditions that do not destroy people. But fundamental corrective action would appear to run counter to the ethic of externalized rewards or to interfere with economic success. Lyford notes that "In the end the justification" for all child-destroying "procedures is that this is the way things have to be done in a system of free enterprise, but in view of the fact that all of the money is wasted, as well as the children, this is hard to believe" (1970, p. 53).

It is hardly surprising that American public faith in public life has plunged dangerously. The ugliest sign is the epidemic of assassinations haunting all public figures, from school superintendents (Marcus Foster, Oakland, California, 1973) to reformers (Martin Luther King), radicals (George Rockwell), and presidents. When the assassins or would-be assassins are considered together, it is evident that conspiracy is rare and that rationally calculated objectives play only a secondary role. Consider Lee Harvey Oswald (John Kennedy), Sirhan Sirhan (Robert Kennedy), James Earl Ray (Martin Luther King), Arthur Bremer (George Wallace), Lynette Fromme and Sarah Jane Moore (Gerald Ford). Unquestionably, a legitimacy for violence is in the air. However, the prominent characteristic underlying these cases is the personal depravity that drove these people to take such extreme and seemingly irrational actions.

Soulless depravity is perhaps better seen in two pointless and merciless mass killings of 1966. The country was shocked when Richard Speck, a drifter and ex-convict, strangled and stabbed eight nursing students to death in their Chicago dormitory. Just two weeks later, Charles Joseph Whitman, an architecture honor student at the University of Texas, climbed a twenty-seven-story tower in Austin and gunned down forty-four persons in a sharpshooting orgy that left fourteen dead, in addition to Whitman's mother and wife, whom he had killed earlier the same day. Why did he do it? A psychiatrist Whitman had visited earlier noted in his journal that Whitman "seemed to be oozing with hostility" and felt like climbing a tower with a deer rifle and shooting people.

These cases are but the tips of the icebergs in the national press. Every local press has its own examples. Most people's hostility, however, is turned inward, suppressed, or diverted to less extreme and more socially acceptable forms of aggression or release.

Society has not evaluated the meaning of the alienation it generates. On Lynette Fromme's attempted assassination of President Ford, *Time* magazine (September 15, 1975, p. 8) noted the paradox that "such a liberal society should somehow generate a sprinkling of warped souls who for dark reasons of their own seek to work out their frustrations by destroying political leaders. The free society has discovered no effective way of identifying and controlling its demons." *Time* here first acknowledges that a free society does "generate" warped souls, but then, quite in accordance with our tradition, looks to "identification and control" that could only lead to more suppressiveness and alienation.

The social mindlessness is also powerfully self-perpetuating. Mary Caroline Richards has made an acute observation that might cause us to reflect. In her book on pottery, poetry, and philosophy, she says that "Wisdom is not the product of mental effort. Wisdom is a state of the total being" (1964, p. 15). A few pages later she notes that in the handwork of pottery she found a wisdom "which had died out of the concepts I had learned in the university: abstractions, mineralized and dead; while the minerals themselves were alive with energy and meaning."

Some years ago Lewis Mumford observed that we send our executives back to the university to leaven their minds when life in the city should have been doing as much all along. Recently, Lionel Trilling raised the same issue for university faculties themselves, worrying about their "growing intellectual recessiveness." Obviously, both the executives and the faculties reside in the same city and are shaped by the same recessive forces. They fail to attain a broader or deeper wisdom than that arising from confined facts and special methodologies.

If fragmentation of life is matched by the consciously specialized ideology and organization of the mind, where is the wholeness out of which a deeper wisdom can grow? "If knowledge does not turn into life, it makes cripples and madmen and dunces" of us all, says Richards. "It poisons just as food would if it stayed in the stomach and was never digested" (1964, p. 18).

Might not a higher deprivation of the mind roughly parallel the stunted mental development found in acutely deprived children? Selma Frailberg at the University of Michigan relates that when a child spends all or most of its first two years without "human partners" or "sustained human attachments," mental functions are sharply impaired. Conceptual thinking "remains depressed even when favorable environments are provided for such children in the second or third years of life." Accompanying this impairment is the children's incapacity to "attach themselves to substitute parents or, in fact, to any persons" and "disorders of impulse control, particularly in the area of aggression" (Frailberg, 1968, p. 49).

Is not the alienated infant a clear model of the alienated adult, although the child is more sensitive, more crucially shaped, but essentially the same in ultimate causes and effects? And if this is true of a child's first "acculturation," how much are we all stunted in our whole human development? How thick are the calcified strata confining or distorting our emotional, intellectual, and social development?

Alienated Will

The inhumanity subtly hidden within our democratic institutions, perhaps within our most progressive forces, helps explain why the human spirit has taken such a battering in these times of high promise.

Today's anguish of nonengagement and nonattachment raises again the old paradox of individual will and general will. This is the paradox of social man, for we are born without specific instinct and are totally dependent on inherited culture to give us motivation and meaning in life, a context for growth, and, not the least, a basis for individuality. If, however, in the name of individuality we begin to isolate the individual and fragment his experience by incorporating him into a nonendearing and fundamentally nonpersonal process, the paradox operates to diminish rather than to build free individuality. Prevalent attitudes of individualism ensure that we perceive ourselves in isolation—as a society of one. When and to the extent that we do so, the social foundation of human growth is inevitably undermined.

The city is, as we have made it, a major part of these processes. We have constructed an urban world where the loss of humanity appears as a silent, unseen petrification of mind and emotion: the artless streets, the natureless pavements, the motorized division of barracked dwellings, the lack of social centering. Somehow, as urban affluence emerged, the growing functional necessities suppressed and distorted rather than amplified our social involvement. In this process we have reversed the traditional bias in societies, where social involvement and incessant festivities often interfere with functional necessities.

Here, briefly, I will consider alienation resulting from what might be called a breach in the social basis of individuality. The question is human freedom.

Richard Goodwin (1974, p. 152) notes that "alienation is the diminution of human life through man's subjugation to his own creations." If we interpret the collective meaning of GNP, full employment, human resources, utilitarian education, and the development of mandatory and sustained consumption in cities, it becomes apparent that society has trained people to be subjugated to a materialism wildly beyond both necessity and freedom. Consider the physical waste of the city, the direct and powerful subordination of experience to the material, and the schismatic *social* randomness by which society is organized. We can make a strong case, in Goodwin's terms, for "our loss of power, the growth of alienation, [being] the consequence of decisive modifications in the conditions of human life; changes which are enforced and accelerated by an increasingly coercive and lawless bureaucracy."

Theorists have told us that freedom rests on delicate balances. We attempted to strike some of these balances in the Constitution. They have fared amazingly well, considering our political trials. But they were only political. The Constitutional fathers could never have anticipated the reorganizing of society by industry in cities for singularly restrictive economic aims. Who could have imagined that the built environment itself—ostensibly created by a free market acting in response to free choice—could undermine freedom?

The most pervasive danger to freedom, I suspect, is that which undermines the social fabric and the strength, stability, and vigor of each individual. Alexis de Tocqueville, who would understand this danger, gave a warning in the 1830s that is more relevant today than ever: "The first thing that strikes the observer is an innumerable multitude of men, all equal and alike, incessantly endeavoring to procure the petty and paltry pleasures with which they glut their lives. Each of them, living apart, is a stranger to the fate of the rest; his children and his private friends constitute to him the whole of mankind. As for the rest of his fellow citizens, he

The Human Toll

is close to them, but he does not see them, he touches them but does not feel them; he exists only in himself and for himself alone." Above such men, de Tocqueville perceived an absolute power, "minute, regular, provident, and mild . . . to keep them in a perpetual state of childhood. . . . For their happiness such a government willingly labors, but it chooses to be the sole agent and the only arbiter of that happiness; foresees and supplies their necessities, facilitates their pleasures, manages their principal concerns, directs their industry" (de Tocqueville, [1835] 1945).

It is a powerful comment on life today that the sharpest threat to our freedom is not in the will of a government, but rather lies buried in a process of fantastic material outpouring. "The true sovereign does not wear a human face," says Richard Goodwin. The suppressions described by de Tocqueville have not changed: "The will of man is not shattered, but softened, bent, and guided; men are seldom forced by it to act, but they are constantly restrained from acting. Such a power does not destroy, but it prevents existence; it does not tyrannize, but it compresses, enervates, extinguishes, and stupifies people, till each nation is reduced to nothing better than a flock of timid and industrious animals." No one has linked oppression so effectively as de Tocqueville to the biting denial of life that is our alienation.

The threat to freedom is not merely that our society has come dangerously close to equating the pursuit of materialism with freedom or that unending economic growth has been projected as a national ethical obligation. The deeper threat lies in two reciprocating causes and effects: (1) building a chaotic and profoundly restrictive set of environments, which then (2) multiply the social and organizational forces of alienation.

The challenges to human freedom are, therefore, social, economic, and physical, as well as political. When we understand that these arise imperceptibly from what we may otherwise believe to be positive and progressive change, we will begin to perceive the wider range of balances on which freedom depends. We may then also learn, as we must, that freedom can be secured only when it is vigorously sought as well as rigorously protected. Then freedom, seen as a positive force, will be equated with the higher possibilities of humankind.

This brings us to a powerful facet of alienation resulting from the breach in the social basis for individuality: the psychological readiness of individuals to join extremist mass movements. A number of important books were produced between 1940 and 1955 that were concerned with the compelling drive of alienated individuals to make a total commitment to authoritarian organizations. The substance of these books, such as Eric Fromm's *Escape from Freedom,* T. W. Adorno's *The Authoritarian Personality,* Robert Nisbet's *Quest for Community,* and Eric Hoffer's *The True Believer,* is that the individual who has lost a significant part of his personal freedom through alienation becomes a threat to the political freedom of the whole society.

The condition converting the individual to authoritarian mass movements results from what Nisbet (1953) has called the "narcotic relief from the sense of isolation and anxiety." These are manifest by "profound dislocations in the primary associative areas of society." The individual struggles, reports Nisbet, "to find in large-scale organizations the values of status and security which were formerly gained in the primary associations of family, neighborhood and church" (p. 49). The driving urge to commit the self to mass appeals rests in an inner turmoil. "Feelings of moral estrangement, of the hostility of the world, the fear of freedom, of irrational aggressiveness, and of helplessness before the simplest of problems have to do commonly . . . with the individual's sense of the inaccessibility of the area of relationship. In the child, or in the adult, the roots of a coherent, logical sense of the outer world are sunk deeply in the soil of close, meaningful interpersonal relations (1953, p. 51).

When Eric Hoffer (1951) said that "faith in a holy cause is to a considerable extent a substitute for the lost faith in ourselves," he was speaking of the collective conditions of individual faith, not individual failings. "The ideal potential convert" to a mass movement, says Hoffer, "is the individual who stands alone, who has no collective body he can blend with and lose himself in and so mask the pettiness, meaninglessness and shabbiness of his individual existence" (1951, p. 39).

What has become dramatically evident is a withering of the roots of freedom in the microsocial setting. Freedom directly and indirectly rests within the local settings and associations that shape the nature of our interpersonal lives. Freedom is literally defined by the engineer and the architect, by social and economic decisions, and in the local environments and institutions that are thereby created.

Perpetuations

It was Marx who described money as a "disruptive power for the individual and for the social bonds. It changes fidelity into infidelity, love into hate, hate into love, virtue into vice, vice into virtue, servant into master, stupidity into intelligence and intelligence into stupidity" (in Fromm, 1963, p. 168). Many of the attributes of money—universal exchange, power and subordination, separability, fragmentation—are identical to those of alienation. Exchange means the alienability of one's goods, one's labors, one's property. Indeed, money might be considered as a symbol par excellence of alienation.

Consider an observation by Northwestern University anthropologist, Francis L. K. Hsu (1973, p. 11): "There is no society in which everyone does everything for love, but a society in which no one will do anything except for money is in serious trouble." To what extent is this a society in which everyone is motivated by money? And is inflation itself a "child of greed," as Arnold Toynbee suggested? If so, how do we begin to diffuse this greed so long building among us?

Once conditions of alienation become imbedded in the physical form of the city, they readily acquire the trappings of normalcy. As Rene Dubos stresses, human beings can and do adjust to very objectionable conditions of life; moreover, the ill effects of these conditions often become masked and disguised as natural and inherent. We too often then become peculiarly accustomed, even dependent on, conditions that are unnatural, which bestows virtue on them and in time gives them a place in human tradition. Richard Farson (1974, p. 48), in *Birthrights,* highlights this paradox, noting in children that the "severely unstable homes are the ones to which the child clings most tenaciously."

The manner in which depraved normalcy perpetuates itself particularly concerns R. D. Laing, who claims the normal condition of this world is one of alienation, in which most personal action destroys both one's own experience and that of others.

Perhaps the greatest self-perpetuating destruction occurs in our inner being, which, as Laing observes, we have become "so estranged from . . . that many are arguing that it does not exist" (1967, p. 33).

In the past, we were subject to the caprices of nature, but we were relatively secure in group life. Now, we are individually much more secure from threats of nature, but our personal security in group life has markedly diminished. Organizational demands have become more selective, specialized, externalized. Yet they put increasing pressure specifically on personality. Unlike members of traditional communities, people today have become directly expendable in the organizations that they depend on most and that demand most of them—the work organizations. People join these groups with personally arbitrary career skills and are pastured out on equally arbitrary conditions at their careers' end.

The groups that once provided unconditional and full membership, those that were concerned with both material and psychological security, have now divided their responsibility to people. Economic security is alien to, and often at serious odds with, endearing group security. Conversely, association and friendship have become heavy personal burdens, which is implied by such terms as *host* and *guest, formal invitations, drinks, dinner,* and *entertainment.* Such necessities of interpersonal protocol are but a preliminary step to close and trusting friendship, not friendship itself, although they have become permanently necessary.

The great social transformation of the last century similarly affected the family, traditionally not only the most protective but also the most utilitarian of institutions. Now stripped down to its nuclear core, made a mobile appendage to economic opportunity, and bereft of its basic functions as a producer, welfare agent, health provider, and protector for the aged, the family has also lost much of its ability to give comfort, love, and emotional security to its members.

Marriage, no matter how romanticized, is precarious. A spouse can die, leave, or fail to provide sufficient emotional response. Perhaps no one person can adequately respond to all emotional needs of another person, yet that is the exorbitant expectation of marriage in a socially fractured society. Little wonder that

The Human Toll

marriage and divorce are becoming horns of a dilemma to so many people.

Nevertheless, in our interpersonally fragmented society, the beleaguered nuclear family is expected to be a virtually self-sufficient society. That cannot be. In a recent speech, Margaret Mead pointed out that "the extraordinary isolation of the young family has never occurred before. . . . The family is too small, too isolated, too unprotected. It needs neighbors, friends, grandparents." Only within a larger context can the family establish a reasonably varied response and depth of security for the individual.

Despite the many external opportunities provided for children in affluent families, the child's foundation to grow and adjust is unusually narrow. Travel, schools, television, and the "kiddie colleges" assure that the child will be knowledgeable and worldly. Such activities cannot, however, provide the lasting human foundation underlying personal growth. They lack the sense of times and places past, the deep feeling of concern and caring, and the substance of a social whole—all of which are conveyed by close and continuous relationships with uncles and aunts, grandparents and close family friends. These fragmented experiences do not provide the full dimension of adult troubles and triumphs, the web of mutual solidarity and commitment, the interweaving of social experience. The technocracized and professionalized experiences of today's children are hollow; by their very nature these experiences are alienating.

No society has been more protective of children than the American society. But, as Margaret Mead says, children cannot be protected without protecting the family and community. Supportive experience relies on the security, meaning, wholeness, and devotion within close human relationships.

Other perpetuations of alienation are revealed in the actions that stretch social distances between people. Utilitarian and pecuniary motives at the heart of many of our most intimate social relations cast interpersonal roles in terms of competitive power, influence, profit, and status. Fragmented and specialized relationships tend to emphasize looks, build, dress, language, and other nonsubstantial elements of personality.

It is no accident, therefore, that many persons who possess

these ephemeral qualities—actors, athletes and exceptionally pretty girls—tend to be very alienated persons. If feminine beauty is often associated with lower intelligence, we may legitimately suspect that at least part of the cause lies in the personal isolation and peculiar conditioning that forces many young women in particular to trade on and build their personalities around looks.

We also alienate fun and culture. Sports, recreation, crafts, music, dance, theater, and art appear to have been socially preempted by the professional, corporate and technical forms of these activities. In cases where the amateur, who strives mainly for inner experiences rather than for external or material rewards, has effectively defended his role, such as in local theater, he usually does so by abandoning the organic context of family, friends, neighborhood, or church and by extensively professionalizing the terms of acting as far as possible: playwrights, directors, ticket prices, facilities, newspaper reviews. The inorganic (and therefore overburdened) efforts of joining together, commuting, and producing a play are unavoidable because they result from an inorganic form of the city. In any case, such efforts increasingly penetrate the behavior of people. The city has made it virtually impossible for children to play football, baseball, or soccer outside organized school athletics or bureaucratic associations, such as Little League.

A final example of reinforcement is found in that "total communication weapon, television," as Richard Schickel describes it. Americans now spend more time watching the tube at home than they spend on any other personal activity except sleeping. Denying oneself TV is socially tantamount to denying oneself participation in life. Yet extensive viewing denies real experience to the individual.

Demanding complete passivity, monopolizing both sight and hearing, and leaving nothing to the imagination, television permits no active role for the individual. Although it portrays endless human drama, the viewer has no involvement and makes no personal investment. In small doses, TV drama adds new dimensions to experience. In habitual viewing, as formats echo one another, alienation begins to deny experience; that is, TV substitutes a vicarious imagery for living, being, and doing, rather than amplifying and extending them as ideally it might.

In alienated society, television offers an easy substitute for group involvement. If group life diminishes in its ability to enrich the individual, becomes more clearly dominated by external motives of power and status, and grows more psychologically abrasive and threatening, then television acquires a special legitimacy for the individual. It closes a cycle of alienation by permitting the viewer to escape personal involvement and to avoid personal threats. But, as its price, television reinforces passivity, promotes personal isolation, and converts drama into a drug.

An observer has noted that, before TV, Detroit appeared to be making the suburban house into a carpeted appendage of the two-car garage, so barren that it would be good only for sleeping. Television changed that and kept the family home. What the observer failed to consider is that the same processes were making the rest of the city as dull and alienated as the suburban vastness. Television filled that void, of course, and rounded out the cycle of human separation and depravement of the city.

Hegel, who coined the term *alienation*, defined it as a *separation of existence from essence* (or, as we might say, a separation of life from experience). This separation or fragmentation of behavior is especially apparent today. Indeed, we have forcefully set forth the elements underlying social alienation as social ideals: objective attitudes, administrative necessity (especially the expendability of persons), technical solutions, specialized effectiveness and validity, money motives, and universal marketability. Ironically, television elevates these sources of alienation to social ideals. We then respond to the overt symptoms of alienation by expanding the professions of alienation: psychiatry, group therapy, counseling, probation, social work, police, attorneys, and judges. And by focusing on the alienated person rather than on the sources of alienation throughout urban society, such professions help perpetuate what they were created to cure.

The Nexus Between Us

Are we not breeding a true social rebellion? We have already seen many early manifestations. To date, the rebellion has been composed largely of disorganized, highly diverse, and basically nihilistic reactions to the destructive irrelevance of our industries, institutions, cities, traditions, and special-interest leadership. The disorganized variety of reactions (from the destructive protests, riots, bombings, drugs, and dropouts, to the constructive liberation movements and counter cultures) speaks directly to the varied sources and forms of alienation. There is no simple enemy, class, or political group in the classic Marxist sense, although these are often a part of specific events. The critical issue today is modernism itself, how the unprecedented changes in society have isolated, fractured, and demeaned human existence.

We may expect the rebellions to grow in each season of trouble as specific issues burst through the well-ordered surface of society. We cannot, however, allow the specific issues to mask the powerful underlying personal anxieties or allow us to misread the more universal desperation. The smooth order characterizing corporate society covers over a quiet seething of tens of millions of acutely frustrated persons who are fully capable of precipitating a "psychotic" break in society no less profound than the shattering events of the Bastille. If and when this event comes, if indeed a single event is precipitative, then we will have the drastic burdens of restoring order in society *before* constructive action can begin.

The challenge today, therefore, is the development of a social context capable of giving new synthesis to the psychological foundations of human personality. That synthesis must simultaneously enlarge the security and congeniality of interpersonal involvement and expand personal freedom and cultural opportunity, creating, in Reinhold Niehbuhr's words, a "social grace."

Before we can begin to constructively rebuild the psychosocial fabric, it is imperative to recognize the myths that propel alienation so deeply into our lives. When will we learn that the dynamic economy has dangerously eroded the underpinnings of individuality by fracturing the interpersonal sources of behavior, especially in the schismatic operations of the market exchange and corporate power systems? And when will we learn that these forces are imbedded in every tissue and in the whole physiology of the city?

Whereas, therapeutically treating one individual so that he or she can function in a less than ideal society may always be necessary, we cannot long ignore the fact that mass therapy by regiments of therapists merely contributes to personal individuation and oppression if the underlying *social* forces of alienation are not also being corrected. Such therapy still leaves people helpless within the social matrix that should sustain and support them. We must learn that urban environments cannot be exploited and still serve us. Our cities are socially bad largely because our mythology says they are bad. How can we reduce the destructive myths surrounding our urban lives?

The biting lesson of human alienation in urban society is that *the worthiness of individual existence is ultimately identical with the worthiness of interpersonal life.* Hsu observes correctly that "the most essential ingredient of human existence is the *interpersonal nexus,* not the individual" (1973, p. 5). All foundations for personal growth, all meanings of healthy individuality—strength, hope, confidence, pride, freedom, challenge, achievement—depend on that nexus. Unless we recognize that a vital and joyously civilized person means human wholeness achieved by a synthesis of the whole social setting, social action is in danger of being reduced to its bestialities, either modern or primitive.

We should be wary of creating special antidotes and particular professions to overcome specific causes and conditions of alienation. This process is too temptingly a part of our tradition. The human promise is great. Dwelling exclusively on social debilitations has long blinded us and stunted our real opportunities for human fulfillment. The only ultimate solution to alienation rests in facilitating human aspiration within a congenial social context. Role relationships characterizing bureaucracy (those stressing money, authority, status, power) need to be diminished and subordinated to relationships based on affective bonds.

But our current tradition, were it to visualize a deeper humanism, might build new programs as alienated as the original causes of alienation—might, that is, continue to deal with the already estranged individual as an unrelated particle of society. Such an approach, however, is based on a contradiction, since healthy individuality can arise only in supportive group life. Programs for the individual in isolation would be money-based, oriented too strictly to service and product, and given over to special-purpose agencies. According to our historic bias, the programs would virtually ignore the formative and cohesive power of the environments and institutions to create the congenial context of individuality. In a few years we would quite correctly label the programs a failure (as we have done even with the fairly broad Model Cities effort) and return singularly to the power game of making and consuming.

One-shot, specialized programs will not do. A new, inspired vision of humankind needs to penetrate all that we do. We can expect success only to the extent that we get down to the basics of organizing life cohesively and congenially for persons. Humanity, if it is ever to soar, must learn the fundamental rules of human flight. With limited exceptions, we have not really tried to soar *as human beings*. Psychologically, we have been burrowing into the darkness of the earth, perfecting machines of ever greater power to burrow. These have diverted our attention from our own explorations of light, sun, and air in a bright verdant setting that affords a magnificent, endlessly variable experience.

It is true, as Emmanuel Mesthene observes, that our technical prowess promises a new freedom, greater human dignity, and unfettered aspiration. To date, nevertheless, we have not been able to free ourselves from the inhibiting and alienating encumbrances we have created.

Consider spontaneity, which the humanistic psychologist, J. L. Moreno (in Otto, 1966, p. 49), compares to the uses of fire. "If the spontaneity is such an important factor for man's world, why is it so poorly developed? The answer may be that man *fears* spontaneity and the uncertainty of it just like his ancestors . . . feared fire; he feared fire until he learned to make it. Man will fear spontaneity until we learn how to unleash it, train and control it."

The human promise rests close to Andre Malraux's belief that human life is expandable by engaging as wide a range of experience as possible. He himself was described as the man of action, living his ideas.

In experience is found spontaneity, cultivation, spirituality, wisdom. These can occur in individuals only when actively promoted throughout the whole society. The two dominant elements are those that structure our behavior and interpersonal relationships: our environments (largely man-made) and our institutions. Herbert Otto (1966, p. 410), another humanistic psychologist with broad visions of the promise, puts the case for institutions very simply: They *"have only one purpose—to serve as a framework for the actualization of the human potential."*

Mary Caroline Richards (1964, p. 35) has put our dilemma in a somewhat different context, suggesting that all the human hungers are "versions of a twofold one: hunger for freedom, and hunger for union, a dance of each individuality with the world."

8

Unkind Traditions

Until the 1960s I believed that America was a favored land—favored in resources and beauty and favored in democratic traditions of equal citizens working out, albiet awkwardly and haltingly, a progressive and continually enriched destiny. Based on our strength and popular affluence, and compared with the long history of wars and poverty abroad, the belief had a certain substance in historic fact.

But history is always new history, even when it seems to be repetitive. And, I fear, it is this boundless faith that America had somehow learned the profound lessons of the old world that now leaves us particularly defenseless against the treachery of new history. No history is as suddenly new as colonized, urbanized, and technologized America.

Unkind Traditions

I was vaguely aware of both the faith and the sense of historic suddenness when I chose to join, in 1952, a relatively new profession, city planning. I felt city planning could be a renaissance profession destined to shape urban history and help maintain the faith. A few years taught me that the profession was far from performing acts of renaissance. Alas, it became clear to me that city planning was born impotent, destined to push paper for the established way of exploitation. The last fifteen years have not provided any major reason for me to change this view. What little useful creativity the field possesses seems to have been injected from the bordering design professions. Meanwhile, city planning has grown rapidly on the rising tide of urban crises it has failed to ameliorate.

The failure of five decades of modern urban planning, of course, has roots far wider and deeper than those attributable to any one occupation. I now wonder whether modern man, at least the American version, has not inherited a profoundly unkind and dangerous set of traditions, especially in the interweaving of causes and effects in human behavior and the creation of human environments. I have alluded to these traditions frequently. Now I will examine some of the underlying traditions more completely.

Axiom of Exploitation

It is common to lament the environmental spoilage wrought by modern man by indicting Christianity and quoting Genesis: "Be fruitful and multiply and fill the earth and subdue it." Lynn White (1967) suggests that the ethos of Christianity has indeed led to our science and technology through its spirit of domination over nature. Unlike other faiths, White observes, Christianity sees man as a specific creation, apart from nature, made in God's image. "Man shares . . . God's transcendence of nature," believing that "it is God's will that man exploit nature for his proper ends" (p. 1205). Thus Christianity became the most anthropocentric of religions and ignored the struggles of such persons as Saint Francis of Assisi to put man humbly back among all God's creatures.

The Christian dualism of man and nature, which removed man from nature, led to an aggressive utilitarianism that White traces as far back as 830 A.D. The Christian did not need to placate the spirits before he cut a tree or killed a buffalo: everything was available, free of religious sanction, for his use.

Following the idea of creation, a linear sense of time emerged, in contrast to the Greek's cyclical concept of time. Creation was associated with time and occurred in a precise sequence, first lightness and darkness, heavenly bodies, the earth, and then life. Finally man was created. Time eventually meant perpetual progress for man.

Science, White explains, followed a similar development, via "natural theology," and became man's way of understanding divine mentality. Every major scientist before Leibnitz and Newton explained his motivations in religious terms. Despite the ethic of objectivity in the laboratory, the Christian anthropocentrism prevailed in the heart. "Despite Copernicus, all the cosmos rotates around our little globe," writes White. "Despite Darwin, we are *not*, in our hearts, part of the natural process. We are superior to nature, contemptuous of it, willing to use it for our slightest whim" (p. 1206).

White quotes Ronald Reagan, then governor of California, who was alleged to have said that " 'when you have seen one redwood tree you have seen them all.' To a Christian a tree can be no more than a physical fact. . . . For nearly two millenia Christian missionaries have been chopping down sacred groves, which are idolatrous because they assume spirit in nature" (p. 1206).

Whatever the historic sources of our earthly destructiveness, science has today freed itself from religion. And, if, as Lewis Mumford (1970) says, science and megatechnics have become a new religion, they have become as well a calculating instrument for society in the supposed struggle to subdue nature. The motive for subjugating nature, rather than creatively responding to it, derives directly from the attitude that humankind stands above nature.

Power as Tradition

The dualism that afflicts us today is not of man and nature but of man and machine, a sharp split between organic existence and naked power. This power is technology, first of all, then its social extension, bureaucracy. Put technology and bureaucracy together in corporate form, as we have, and the organic condition of human life becomes conditional, warped, and attenuated.

Technology today stands at the epicenter of world motivation. While its allure is unprecedented social wealth, its power sweeps aside human traditions of ten thousand years as if these shared understandings giving deep meaning and substance to life were also the foundations of poverty, disease, and ignorance. Yet the technocrat's unreserved faith and power are suddenly facing a sharp, penetrating counterattack. Science and technology, having been effectively fused for about a century, are facing their first historic crisis. That crisis stems from their core: the refusal or inability to recognize limits, whether physical, organic, or moral.

Examined as tradition, the megatechnic approach reveals a faith in endless human power, endless frontiers and resources, endless exploitations, endless put-through and discard. The ultimate meaning of endlessness is lawlessness and meaninglessness, the effects of which are felt in the disorder of cities no less than in the exhaustion of resources.

Thus, when Paul Goodman asks if technology can be human and when Harvey Wheeler considers bringing science under law, they are posing some of the most penetrating questions of our age. The threat of nuclear annihilation is but part of a broader undermining of life created by many of the most intelligent and, presumably, the best educated and most articulate persons in recent history. Evidently, something very basic has gone wrong in the way society develops and uses its highest intelligence.

In its search for objectivity, science sought to avoid moral—that is, social—involvement. Physicist Max Born concluded that the scientific revolution thus undermined ethics, since all action has an ultimate moral effect. As Wheeler (1969, p. 64) notes, the life sciences, using genetics, abortion, life support systems, and so on, are "tampering" with the basic life process, and this, he says, "demands ethical norms" because the "goals, ends and purposes of life" cannot be avoided in the act of acquiring new power over the life process. The best solution, Wheeler suggests, is "to constitutionalize science," since, he says, "science is not the private property of scientists any more than the economy is the private property of businessmen, or the government is the private property of politicians" (1969, pp. 64, 66).

Lewis Mumford has pointed to a darker side of science: "Once . . . scientists decided to exclude theology, politics, ethics and current events from the sphere of their discussions, they were welcomed by the heads of state. . . . their mental isolation made them predestined cogs in the new megamachine." But under the "objective" view, "all living forms must be brought into harmony with the mechanical world picture by being melted down, so to say, and molded anew to conform to a more perfect mechanical model. . . . Unfortunately, the ultimate effect . . . was to devalue every aspect of human experience that could be so treated" (1970, p. 39).

Increasingly, critiques of the technological society have concluded that brilliance has run amuck. "Twentieth-century man is drunk with achievements in one single field of human endeavor: science," wrote Sibyl Moholy-Nagy. "The blind logic of science takes its course regardless of the effects." In melancholy conclusion, Moholy-Nagy remarks that "there is no progress in the realization of man's urban dream, only in mechanical equipment" (1968, p. 12).

The penetrating criticisms of science are now arising more powerfully from within the scientific establishment itself. Nobel Laureate Dennis Gabor has said: "It is not without regrets that I have come to the realization that invention, in the sense of gadgeteering, must come to an end. But the inventive spirit must not perish. . . . It must now be redirected, from 'hardware' inventions toward social inventions" (1972, p. 44). And social invention is inevitably urban invention.

The city itself presents us with a clear picture of the underlying contradictions created by our megatechnic tradition. Built by technology, the whole urban environment is antitechnological by any measure of technological effectiveness. The city has become a medium of perpetual decline overcome by an endless escalation of technology. Furthermore, the rational performance of particular machines in particular situations is contradicted by the conflict and irrationality of such machines in urban systems. The industrial order simply works against itself in the larger order of things, principally in cities. As Paul Goodman has noted, technology in recent years has desperately tried to remedy situations caused by earlier overapplications of technology. Unfortunately, we have come to see the city, at least since the railroads first sliced through them, as a medium for a virtually ungovernable technological mandate.

The city has succumbed—with and under the power of science and technology—to a successive externalization of value that separates people from what they want to be. The strident value is power, which is achieved at the expense of the internal or organic qualities of balanced growth, experience, wholeness, sharing. Bernard Murchland (1971, p. 173) has emphasized "that scientific truth can only be scientifically meaningful. What is directly felt and immediately valued by men—the qualitative dimension of experience—is relegated to a position of inferior status . . . thus bearing out the positivist dogma that that which cannot be the object of exact observation, of scientific analysis, of measurement and experimental verification is unknowable." William James understood this phenomenon many decades ago, saying "this systematic denial on science's part . . . may conceivably . . . prove to be the very defect that our descendents will be most surprised at in our boasted science. The omission that to their eyes will most tend to make it look perspectiveless and short."

Regressive Tradition

Tradition is an evolving inheritance. Our inheritance reveals a great division. Today the traditions sustaining the individual's sense of self have lost their foundations and their vitality, while the traditions we identify with modern development—those that increasingly enlarge exploitive and disruptive tendencies—are virile, built into the foundations of our environments and institutions.

If science lost its motive of revealing divine mentality, that motive was replaced by sanctifying the pursuit of *knowledge for its own sake*. Lewis Mumford has called this motivation a half-truth at best, a self-flattery or self-deception at worst. "As with the holiness of saints," he writes, "the total effect of the scientific ideology has been to provide both the means and justification for achieving external control over all manifestations of natural existence, including man's own life" (1970, p. 106). Science could not defend the pursuit of knowledge for its own sake without tacitly arguing that *all* practical results of its inquiries inevitably benefitted humanity. Yet by so arguing, the scientific habit of power-making is left uninhibited.

Scientific thought, Bertrand Russell once said, "is essentially power thought . . . whose purpose, conscious or unconscious, is to give power to its possessor." Although much scientific knowledge has been sought for its own sake, the general results are increasingly uncontrollable and dangerous. The knowledge that counts is operational—power-generating—and we cannot escape that central fact of science.

The rush for technical capacities described by Mumford (1970) has "only one all-important mission in life: to conquer nature." The subsidiary postulates of science suppose that there is "only one efficient speed, *faster;* only one attractive destination, *farther away;* only one desirable size, *bigger;* only one rational quantitative goal, *more.* . . . The object of human life, and therefore of the entire productive mechanism, is to remove limits, to hasten the pace of change, to smooth out seasonal rhythms and reduce regional contrasts—in fine, to promote mechanical novelty and destroy organic continuity" (Mumford, 1970, p. 173).

Closely allied to the myth of the pursuit of knowledge for its own sake that cloaks the conquering spirit is the mythology surrounding *objectivity,* the dispassionate removal of the scientist's own personality and concerns from the terms of research. Objectivity seen as an ideology rather than as a methodology (that is, considered apart from procedures to ensure validity and reliability) swarms with paradoxes having potentially dangerous consequences.

Mumford (1970) sees two giant fallacies in the scientist's vision of objective reality, originally advanced by Kepler and Galileo. The universe of science "was composed only of isolated physical bodies, destitute of life: 'dead' matter. But we know now that this utter absence of life—or at least of life potential—is an illusion." The second fallacy derived from the first. Mumford notes that Galileo and his successors "treated the mind as if it could function without all the members of the body, as if the eye saw by itself and the ear heard by itself, and as if the brain, equally isolated, was dedicated in its most perfect state to the specialized function of mathematical thinking. . . . To understand the physical world, and ultimately man himself . . . one must eliminate the living soul. . . . In the interests of "objectivity,' the new scientists eliminated historic man and all his subjective activities" (1970, pp. 54–55).

In their effort to overcome the superstitious and all-too-completely-subjective life around them, the scientists neglected the subjectivity inhering in every investigation and thus created another dualism, objectivity and subjectivity. They then began to deny reality to the holistic (unmeasurable) complexity of real-world events and the complete experience of life. Inevitably this denial led to a separation between humanity and reality.

This separation became critical when the highest human qualities, as well as the deepest dilemmas, were systematically read out of the scientific picture, initially reducing people to "irrelevant observers" and, more importantly, to "insignificant effects" in the end. When so reduced, human value systems and problems of ethical conduct became irrelevant, "nonsubjects" of science, even while objective science deeply affected these vital concerns.

Here a major distinction must be made between *functional* and *substantive* objectivity. Functional objectivity, which is necessary for the development and application of empirical knowledge, constitutes our current form of scientific objectivity; substantive objectivity, however, which is concerned with fidelity to human values and goals—setting the higher purposes of human endeavor—is left unattended. Consequently, any new device that is technically and economically feasible under the quixotic exigencies of the moment tends to become, ipso facto, desirable. That device then conditions the "objective" circumstance of the next moment.

Many products and processes—the results of research—that are obviously pernicious and illogical in substantive objectivity become logical and even necessary in the aggrandizing power of functional objectivity. The automobile, which makes good sense in rural areas or in small numbers, becomes completely destructive under a substantive objectivity when it radically reorganizes urban life to meet its own consumptive demands. The auto's functional necessity becomes more profoundly "objective" as each phase of the urban rebuilding proceeds to a higher level of destructiveness.

Science thus not only helps downgrade the human experience, it injects onerous dilemmas into society. Science, by so vigorously and absolutely separating the context of behavior and ethical norms from the investigative processes, creates a pattern of thought that subordinates human purposes to the development and concentration of raw power. Substantive (or ideal) objectivity is subordinated to the functional (or procedural) objectivity.

Objective science has had another direct impact on nature and society, especially in cities, via spectacularly successful *specialization*. Specialized knowledge is inherently power-producing knowledge. Being narrow, it is exploitive and destabilizing rather than integrative and stabilizing (as broader concerns tend to be). Of course, technology is highly integrative in its own way. But this integration is internal to technology itself and retains the specialized, power-exploiting relation to the city, society, and nature. The universities prospered immensely from, and were molded powerfully by, training specialists. Now universities lack both the ethical and the organizational framework to give the critical integrative foundations to society's chief integrator, the city.

Commenting on the philosophical heroes of seventeenth-century science, Rene Dubos (1968) notes that they "separated substances and events into their ultimate components and reactions. The most pressing problems of humanity, however, involve relationships, communications, changes of trends . . . situations in which systems must be studied as a [complex] whole."

How, then, do the scientific traditions of knowledge for its own sake, objectivity, and specialization affect cities, seemingly a distant affair? Knowledge for its own sake is by definition removed from muddling human circumstances. Such "irrelevant" knowledge is also likely to be particularized and isolated, rather than integrated; that is, it is likely to lack the vital context that achieves higher utility, assures social appropriateness, and magnifies human meaning. Specialization and objectivity, when tied as they are to single-purpose and rigorous methods of the mind only, reinforce the fragmentary effects. Unless both purpose and method are broadly conceived for their ultimate and broadest effects, specialization and

Unkind Traditions 229

objectivity cannot serve the complexities of human ideals. Excluded by a narrowness of either purpose or method is a sense of organic function, social wholeness, or the wider and deeper human qualities of observed phenomena—in short, the diverse but specific human potential.

It is precisely these characteristics that are implicit in an urban environment capable of responding articulately to its human inhabitants with grace. So far we have failed to envision, let alone achieve, a higher image of cities. If ideals of the city had inspired a stable organic form and a balance of many human values—or conversely, if organic and balanced qualities had prompted greater urban ideals—we would have very different habitats today. But such orientations are scarce in modern belief and behavior, most of all in the commanding ethos of science.

If the reduction of human wholes to their separate components in science sounds like the reduction of human behavior to the lowest common denominator of market exchange, there is a clear and strong reason: both are methods of acquiring power. Power is best achieved when the object at hand is divided into manageable units, whether protons, products, or political masses. Since the rewards of multiplying powers over nature through specialized science have been dazzling, there has been little comparable reward for correlating and balancing the powers already in human hands to optimize their benefits. Otherwise ecology would have evolved into a commanding science, superior to physics or chemistry. Similarly, a fragmentation or kind of disorder called the free market benefits the enterprise, particularly if that enterprise itself is well organized to maneuver effectively. This need for power is why business has fought—not without certain merit, of course—against governmental planning. And it is the affinity of power that has brought research and development so intimately into the corporate structure.

Again, the point is acute for cities. In science we are taught that specialization (that is, fragmentation) is the golden path to salvation because it offers limitless discovery in countless fields. We view the city, in much the same way, as a completely free medium in which any "power" might be discovered, developed, and used in any way. And in enterprise there is an identical bearing. The free market (an unstructured medium best at promoting goods and services) is today most effective in the unstructured city that demands an increasing quantity of goods and services. And it hardly matters to enterprise that in the last half century much of the demand for goods and services in the city has become pathological. If the unbalanced, inorganic, and highly consumptive condition built into cities becomes widely profitable, then the whole form of the city too easily becomes the next frontier of business opportunity, if not the scientific challenge for new processes, materials, and therapy.

Until we begin to perceive cities as whole and unified entities, delicately adjusted to the needs and aspirations of the individual rather than to promoting new human needs and to socially reshaping human aspirations—that is, until we remake the power-oriented traditions through which urban development occurs—it is doubtful that cities can become habitats of true advantage to the human cause.

We are now learning the acute lesson that endlessly expanding power is not only dangerous but fragile, because it is inherently wasteful and therefore exhaustive. Integrative or organic strength is less dramatic, but it is ecologically balanced and therefore enduring. Whereas traditional villages demonstrate both an organic internal form and an organic relationship with their hinterland, the last century of "development" has largely obliterated that organic stability. Instead of complementing the physical and social unities of town and country, technology destroyed them by unrestrained massing of population, capital, and industry. Instead of regional and world trade filling out the deficiencies of local economies, it has seriously displaced them.

Although there are obvious deficiencies in any locality in serving human needs, the habit of developing massive centralized power tends to bulldoze obstacles and to bring every individual into unnecessary, random, and socially fragmented engagement with *all* others. Tragic illusions are created: the illusion of power that is waste, of utility that is disruption, of control that is destruction, of affluence that is overburden, of growth that is unwanted size, of cooperation that is alienation. This mythical behavior of modernism is not inherent in people or technology or economics. Most earlier

Unkind Traditions 231

societies did not display it. It arises mainly from specific traditions associated with science.

These fallacies are a direct fallout of science. "Increasingly, the 'gross national product' of industry reflects the gross national product of science," observes Mumford (1970, pp. 123–124). "By participating in this transformation, the scientist has forfeited the qualities that were exalted in the past as his special hallmark: his detachment from worldly gains and his disinterested pursuit of truth." The results today could not be imagined by those scientists of the seventeenth century who set society on its present course. Those scientists failed, Mumford continues, "to foresee that society itself might take on the characteristics of an increasingly automatic machine, run by machine-conditioned personalities, in a machine-fabricated habitat, for purely abstract mechanical-electronic ends. These leaders, in short, could not picture the dismaying nightmare of twentieth-century existence."

If irrationalities penetrate the core of our most respected modern activity of the mind, how can we expect the irrationalities to be identified and removed from public life or from the form and functioning of the city? Those irrationalities are both legion and lethal, as Mumford amply accounts.

A. N. Whitehead has described an appropriate role for science, and for all utilitarian behavior, saying that "the function of reason is to promote the art of life." This statement fuses the substantive and functional objectivity we need today. That is, it subordinates scientific "purpose" to human purpose and puts specialized power into a balanced system of natural ecology and social harmony.

Dynamic Decay

For the first time in history, our industrial order has been called into question. The crisis of confidence in technological society burst into the open in 1967 when the hippies began the first general strike against the whole social order.

In an article published in 1955, John von Neumann (p. 106) backhandedly observed one of the basic symptoms of technological failure, saying that the world "is in a rapidly maturing crisis" because the environment in which technological progress occurs "has become both undersized and underorganized." What is now called into question is whether technology itself is not oversized, underorganized, and out of control. It is precisely the weak social context within which technological power is projected that is most directly the cause of our underorganized—and overused—environment.

Although technology has long been set on a collision course with nature, a major confrontation could not occur until industrialization was introduced into a large and highly urbanized population. An individual flying the Atlantic undoubtedly consumes more nonrenewable resources than a soldier of the American Revolution did in a lifetime. Our experience with the initial conflict between technology and the environment might be termed society's first confrontation with nature. The peasant with only a hoe is incapable of a true confrontation with nature. Only a man with a throttle can truly confront nature. Confrontation requires masses of men working with masses of machines.

It is within the city that the technology of man and the natural environment meet most intensively. And it is in the city that technology conflicts most deeply with the environment. There is good reason to say that the undercontrol of technology and the overuse of environment is really an underorganization of the city.

If the city lies at the strategic intersection of man, machine, and nature, it is because it is fundamental in organizing, preserving, and enhancing all three, each in its own way. But such a tradition of harmony hardly exists in either practice or theory, for it runs counter to the powerful combination of scientific-technological exploitation and corporate control of market exchange.

Because cities lack a clear and forceful idealization, they have failed to bring substantial harmony to the precarious dynamism of change. According to Lord Raglan, the English anthropologist, the chief cause of cultural decay in earlier times rested in "the dead hand of conservatism"; today, decay "can be brought about even more rapidly by breaking away from the past" (in Mumford, 1970, p. 282). The unrelenting acceleration of change has become self-defeating because it imposes itself on society with such speed, power, and complexity that anything like normal adjustment processes are impossible. Yet undirected change is central to the ideology of scientific knowledge, technological power, and massive corporate economic growth.

Such a course has been clearly under way in cities for a century. The chaos apparent in urban environments and the dynamic momentum of technology have reached a stage where the two have become mutually generating. This visionless, idealless momentum of stimulus and response is what John Wilkinson calls a passage "from sense to nonsense and from use to abuse." Today it includes the crisis of energy and the massive program of energy development, the problems of economic instability and the promotion of economic growth, the congested deterioration of cities and the emphasis on transportation, escape, and sprawl.

By what vision, then, can we perceive an urban system that avoids the dynamism of decay from which we now suffer? Is it not through search for an organic order capable at once of achieving *ecological* stability and permanence and simultaneously of underwriting a specifically *human* dynamism? Again, as Mumford has observed, it "is in and through the city . . . that man has created a symbolic counterpart to nature's creativity, variety and exuberance" (in Darling and Milton, 1966, p. 729).

What Mumford had in mind, I believe, is elaborated by James Redfield, who implies that "technique" and "second nature" are applicable in the creation of cities: "In a sense technique moves away from nature; technique transforms the natural environment. But in another sense technique moves toward nature. . . . The aim of technique is to produce a kind of second nature by fitting out man with the skills and habits he needs to live comfortably in his environment. The invention of the technique, the remaking of human life, is full of effort, but if the technique is successful, human life, to the degree of its success, is effortless. As Democritus says: 'Nature and teaching are similar, for teaching transforms men, and as it transforms them, it creates nature.' And Euenus: 'The practice, my friend, takes a long time, but then as it comes to completion, it is nature.' . . . So, as man moves from the primitive to the cultivated, he does not simply struggle with the difficulties of his world; he actually creates a new world for himself" (in Platt, 1965 p. 119).

The crucial matter of perceiving cities as human counterparts of nature, as systems having an ecologically valid second nature, has been stated by Rene Dubos (1968, p. 180): "If it is true, as it appears to be, that our environment and way of life profoundly affect our attitudes and those of following generations, nothing could be more distressing for our immediate and distant future than the decadence and ugliness of our great urban areas."

Specialization of Mind

When Max Weber originally described the fundamental qualities of modern bureaucracy—noting firm rules, hierarchy, separation of office from household, specialized training and responsibility—he clearly implied that bureaucracy was also a *habit of mind*. He also noted that the strict procedures of administration were similar to, and compatible with, the objectivity of science. Railroads, he observed, were technological innovations that were useless without a highly articulated bureaucracy to manage them.

Bureaucracy is, to be sure, an exact and essential counterpart of technology. Nowhere could the complexities of a computer factory or an airline be managed by an organization with any less sophistication than the technical process that brought computers and aircraft to their present level of development. In many respects, bureaucracy is as profound as science and technology, and certainly no less awesome.

Our concern here is how specialization, which has proven to be so fruitful in scientific output and so essential in bureaucracy, influences thought and behavior beyond the normal realms of either of these fields, especially in the making of cities.

First, the immense prestige of specialization extends itself into private life as *habit, skill,* and *authority*—a behavioral learning process no less potent than the lengthy process of education, of which it is a major part. The bewildering diversity of knowledge forces all of us to constantly seek out—and be influenced by—the specialist.

Second, specialized work imbues the person with a set of mind peculiar to his field, be it military, medicine, carpentry, or computers, influencing even styles of handwriting, interpersonal relations, and avocation, as well as politics and religion.

Unkind Traditions

Each specialty involves an inner logic, an implicit set of values, and is served by its own system of communications. As specialization intensifies, so do the language and thought patterns. Specialization means separation of a profession from other professions, and the resulting segregation, plus skill and authority, assists in monopolizing a sector of social behavior. Specialization always implies a claim of monopoly in its realm.

In urban affairs, which are (or should be) naturally holistic and integrative, the specialist nevertheless rules over transportation, housing, public works, parks and recreation, education, health. The generalist, the amateur, and the citizen have been reduced in influence, and—contrary to both logic and democratic process—act only within the confines of action left open by the specialist. Specialization dominates the decision-making process because it is identified in the public mind with direct and immediate effectiveness and clear and observable efficiency. We are afraid of failures that directly confront us, afraid of losing a particular battle. That is, we are fearful of the immediate concerns of the specialist. But too easily we fail to guard against the broader failures that do not confront us directly but may cost us the war. Our specialized habit of mind does not recognize the strategic errors, deeper weaknesses, or more penetrating disruptions and alienations that specialization alone inevitably generates.

This specialized habit of mind appears peculiarly susceptible to the belief that if something does not work, more of the same will work. Thus, for example, when a specialization like transportation is in conflict with other specialized functions of the city, the accepted solution is to promote a more exorbitant transportation system, which in turn promotes more exorbitant uses of land. Such a pattern eventually results in a higher level of failure and a greater pragmatic commitment to the failing process itself.

Then, too, specialization of work leads naturally to a specialization of interest. That is, specialization and special interest are virtually identical. Although special-interest groups favor the growth and concentration of established power, they are praised as evidence of a balance of democratic forces. Contrary to Adam Smith's dictum, we do not find the unseen hand of a higher general interest, but rather a standoff among blocks of power.

Yet among the masses of people in cities, only a very small minority has the power to reasonably serve its needs through the special-interest groups. Most citizens are cornered by an ideology of privacy and individual initiative. This ideology prompts them to retreat to their houses and cars, possessory enclaves that, in the present form of the city, separate them and deny them the wider span of mutual support and initiative. Little wonder that hopelessness, frustration, and cynicism have become so universal.

No urban ideal or method effectively bridges the particularization of special interest. The city, built so solidly around privacy and private initiative, on the one hand, and special interest, on the other, is virtually incapable of defining a true public interest. Consequently, cities seem destined to passively accept avalanches of output and development, regardless of their impact and the problems that almost inevitably seem to follow. Only five decades were required for the automobile to pulverize the city after 1920 in just such a public response.

Specializations increasingly arise to meet new problems stemming from special interests. But those new specializations in fact seem to perpetuate the problems they were created to resolve. Consider traffic engineering. Today the automobile has demonstrated a self-defeat of the city on multiple grounds: the congestion and dispersion it promotes; its slaughter of people at a rate of half a million each decade; its poisoning of the air we breathe; its use as a multiple tool to destroy livable urban and rural environments; and, if these are not enough, its industrial, commercial, and direct exhaustion of fossil fuels and other resources.

Traffic engineering first appeared in the 1920s to solve severe congestion and safety problems. But what the profession did was to pave the way for increased quantities of urban automobiles and to vastly escalate the congestion and accident potential. One by one the lower echelon problems were resolved, only to have those problems elevated to horrendous levels with a new magnitude of traffic after midcentury. First, the signals and white lines; then street straightening, widening, and channeling; better pavements and center strips; parking meters, lots, and garages; and, finally, of course, the $10-million-per-mile freeways. All of these public capital investments underwrote and eventually demanded more private cars, since walking was eliminated by the new urban distances and traffic dangers, and transit was destroyed by the congestion, sprawl, and capital starvation.

Each new traffic device or construction typically increased traffic *capacities* by 5 or 15 or sometimes 50 percent. These increased capacities encouraged or forced traffic to grow in volume and distance at a terrible cost of money, air, life, and city livability. Only today are we beginning to discover the deeply hidden defeat imposed by a form of transportation that reduces effective access by each escalation of investment in it. Traffic engineering, which came into being solely to solve the development problems of a deceptive form of mobility, merely delayed the stark realization that the automobile, used as basic transportation, is completely incompatible with the good city. Without traffic engineers, the automobile would have demonstrated its utter futility between 1920 and 1940, rather than in the 1970s.

If smog, accident, money, space, time, and resource statistics are unconvincing, one should reexperience the auto-made environment. First, one should *stand* at least five minutes each at the intersection of two major boulevards, then close to a major freeway interchange, and finally in the middle of a thirty-acre parking lot. Completely see, hear, and feel the kind of human environment that has been created. One should also *walk* at least one mile along one of the great American strips to fully appreciate that "human" environment.

Reexperiencing urban environments is important because we have become accustomed only to operating within their mazes and avoiding their worst debilitations. As it is, we try not to have personal reactions at all. That is, we have submitted ourselves to the specialist's habit of mind and do not react as whole human beings. The automobile and the traffic engineer are, of course, but one demonstration of the profound contradictions that inevitably result when specializations operate independently with the powerful backing of special interests in society and without a sensitivity to the broader course of human events.

The question of specialization affects the entire purpose and spirit in which the human enterprise is pursued. Edith Hamilton has observed in *The Greek Way* that science today, unlike that of

Greece "has kept to the mind alone, and the balance there between the law and the exception, the particular and the general is only intellectual" (1930, p. 245). Ultimately, she stresses, "the balance between the particular and the general is that between spirit and the mind" (p. 243). If we do not pursue a balance of the particular and the general interest—or of the special outlook of the mind and the general outlook of the spirit—what can we expect in the further development of human society now set into such a prodigious momentum? Do we not require a humanistic rebirth?

If the individual is to have real moral power, that power must find expression in the working of things—especially in the environments and institutions that inevitably guide behavior—that fundamentally responds to *individual* initiative, not just in voting or buying, but more deeply in the ways private and public action take shape.

We should not be fooled by the immense successes made possible by specialization. Specialization has a future role to play, no doubt, probably an important one. Yet we cannot forget that any or all special capacities or modes of behavior merely contribute to, and are not the essence of, being completely human, urbane, and civilized; the distinguishing qualities of being human, of being intelligent, are the *general* and nonspecialized capacities of body, mind, and spirit.

A confident, well-developed, fully participating person is the exact counterpart of a unified, responsive city. If specialization continues to grip both the person and the city, both the habit of mind and the structure of action, we can only foresee more conflicting special interests among people and more profoundly destructive divisions of the city. Then, inevitably, both the city and the people will lose the inner wholeness that can enlarge their greatness.

From Scientific to Social Tradition

If we are to shape a valid and completely worthy tradition (valid at least conditionally for our historic circumstance), we can hardly look to science, which has alienated itself from large areas of *human* truth. The social sciences may be useful, but they too have removed themselves from direct human relevance in favor of the objectivity and specialization of the hard sciences. By an ironic twist, the neutrality imposed on the social sciences effectively removes them from the bulk of the human experience, especially human wholeness. The same neutrality in the physical sciences, however, frequently leads to destructive applications of knowledge.

The hapless social sciences have been morally and intellectually trapped by the tradition of the exact sciences. Their subject is the whole human being and the whole society acting in an interweaving of behaviors and environments determined by very inexact philosophies and very mixed ethical values. The content of the exact sciences can normally be judged as means. The social sciences, hardly less than philosophy and religion, however, are continually immersed in unavoidable questions of ends, as well as of the complex relations between means and ends. Hence, to maintain "objectivity," they avoid real issues and major ideas through specialization, methodology, fact gathering, and analysis.

Avoiding many of the most critical human issues has left the social sciences almost irrelevant. The struggle for objectivity operates as a smoke screen that confuses conscious, constructive concern for the human situation. As Kenneth Boulding points out, the so-called laws of science are really possibility functions. Much use has been made of these laws in the physical sciences. But the possibility functions of the human sciences have been minimized. Objectivity too often interposes itself, resulting in neutralized fact-gathering, innocuous hypotheses, and banal conclusions. Social complexity is stressed to the point that significant, clear ideas can hardly arise.

In the end, the emphasis on specialized factual studies and on the fine-grained complexity of every issue creates an aura that appears to justify any condition of society. Fear of fomenting a new Marxism seems to force the social sciences to settle squarely on the status quo. Catherine Bauer Wurster described the process as it applies to cities, saying that "there is a tendency for good studies to make current conditions seem inevitable. And this can lead to a kind of paralysis with respect to issues which require bold innovation. As we have grown more sophisticated about our slums, for instance, it has become ever more difficult to think of anything better to do." Jane Jacobs stated the case bluntly: "There is a quality even meaner than outright ugliness or disorder, and this meaner quality is the dishonest mask of pretended order, achieved by ignoring or suppressing the real order that is struggling to exist and to be served" (1961, p. 15).

Not always, of course. Where the social sciences and social professions have been brought into the direct service of the prevalent technological and bureaucratic initiative, such as in the case of economic growth, advertising, marketing, polling, political campaigning, and industrial management, a directiveness and effectiveness has appeared.

Since basic attitudes transcend particular sectors of society, the idea of objectivity is readily convertible to economic feasibility or, simply, practicability. Being practical means that one responds according to the way society now structures the lines of utility. For example, in the power "traditions" of the construction industry, a series of arbitrary conditions determine how utility is perceived: building and zoning laws, loan practices, the land tenure system, small parcels on small blocks, the tax structure, the particular building design and construction practices.

The habitual lines of utility defined by strictly monetary terms of propelling economic growth do not reflect people. Nor do they reflect an optimum ecology. We are beginning to discover that many of the practical and objective advantages of the moment in the established pattern of decision-making require environmental rape and propel urban decay. Rape and decay cannot be labeled as practical. Yet that is what now happens in the interweaving of private, corporate, and governmental behavior.

We have seen how cities are overwhelmingly dominated by two mutually supporting traditions: science and technology and corporately organized market exchange. The American ideology revolves around them. Yet both are radically new as we know them today. Nevertheless, through the industrial and urban transformations, they have absorbed and redirected the older folk traditions of individuality, initiative, ownership, and, not the least, the idea of progress. Government has been drawn into their service to such an extent that national well-being is understood largely as our relative level of technological superiority and the growth of the corporate economy.

Unkind Traditions

These forces consequently represent a radical turn of social events, especially in their rapid accumulation of immense, untested power. Small, interpersonal groups have lost most of their ability to shape the personal and organizational dimensions of the city. This transformation helps explain the sense of individual helplessness in a still-functioning democracy.

Through this radical convolution, individualism has veered dangerously toward its contrary condition: hopeless individuation. That is the meaning of mass labor markets, mass housing, mass merchandizing, mass media, mass education, and mass politics in the corporate industrial system. True individualism can arise only in groups small enough for the personal qualities of the individual to be recognized and become effective in all of their uniqueness. Wherever there are essentially undifferentiated masses of people, they inevitably come under the control of powerful centralized organizations—economic, political, or religious. Then purposes subtly but powerfully shift toward the establishment. The city, made so overwhelmingly for making and selling, signals this power today.

The deprivations of individuation extend just as sharply to privacy, creativity, meaningful participation, and other conditions that underlie effective personal and cultural growth. The austere procedures of science, the exploitive nature of technology, the demeaning alienation of the market, and the domination of the corporation promote not only an oppressive social massing but also a manipulative standardization of behavior to conform to these dominant models and purposes. When large numbers of people relate to each other in this manner, special interests become their only true bonds.

The primary fact of today's mass society is, of course, the city. Yet cities need not consist of masses at all, regardless of their population. A city will cease to be a mass only when the scale, strength, and distinctiveness of organizations that mediate between the individual and the whole city provide a *locally* secure and responsive framework for individuality. The meaning of mass rests in undifferentation, not in numbers. Masses do not exist in an office or factory. That would mean chaos, disorganization, and a very poor use of skills. But they do exist in the loose, buffeted relationships that people suffer in the city. Urban mass means a lack of social organization or a lack of personal relatedness—a loss of social significance in the individual.

As the radical forces bear down on the individual, privacy too often becomes a mechanism of defense against the psychologically chaotic, meaningless, and threatening city. The defenses that have become a part of privacy arise from participation without personally enduring value, strong organization without deep human bonds, work without freedom to produce, spaces without a clear identity of place, consumption without true leisure. Other parts of the inherited folk tradition have been just as deeply affected: individuality, independence, ownership, initiative. Idealized from the interpersonally more secure past, the tradition has been commandeered, in effect, by "corporate" power, that is, shaped into the radically new mold of science, technology, the market, and the corporation.

Consider in capsule the powerful effects of these prevailing traditions of contemporary life:

1. Science rests on a profound belief that is, by definition, dispassionately irresponsible. Scientific "objectivity" scrupulously avoids the most critical human issues raised by the knowledge it creates.

2. Technology develops specific exploitive capacities for specific organizations. However, these organizations are responsible only for certain immediate impacts, not the accumulative effects, the broad precedents, and the most general disruptions, which fall outside the terms of technological development.

3. The present mode of scientific and technological understanding is deeply antithetic to many basic human qualities of thought and behavior, especially the socially supportive, aesthetic, and spiritual. This understanding does not subordinate itself to human purpose but judges itself to be an ideal form of thoughtful behavior.

4. Market exchange, having extended its authority over both land and labor, as well as commodities, acts to alienate group life, whether the effect is on housing, work, friendship, recreation, or avocation. The family is reduced to a freely mobile unit of economic action.

5. The corporation, which anomalously wields radical power and initiative while defining the conservative political values,

is the prime organizer of science, technology, and the market. Yet the corporation makes no pretense of being democratic in control, organization, and operation, or of equitably distributing wealth.

The potency of these observations increases when we consider that the city—its people, environments, and institutions—is largely governed by the corporate initiative. Not only did urbanization result from the forces of corporate industrialization, and not only did the form of the city reflect new products and industrial output, but the entire urban fabric has been woven as a medium to accelerate both production and consumption. This is the way we speak of the city. We can hardly perceive the city in any other terms, at least when policy is made. The high value we give to the technological mandate and economic growth and the low value we give to the city and the personal integrity of the individual attest to our acceptance of this use of power.

These are some of the results of the reshaped traditions. They reflect the private wealth and public poverty that John Kenneth Galbraith sharply brought to our attention. If the individual and individuality are really a deep part of our faith, why have we not given them a central place in our lives. We have not, simply enough, because it is not part of our heritage. The values of privacy and individuality hardly figure in the thinking of technocrats and bureaucrats.

The social tradition derived from science and organized by the corporation rules the making of cities and the shaping of society. We will not be able to get a grip on the cities we live in until we get a grip on the tradition by which we live. The profound danger is that the new social powers lie essentially outside the traditional political structure. They have also deeply confused the way in which the individual perceives reality. Possibly this uniquely modern tradition is what caused Toynbee to fear a decay in our civilization and to wonder whether our society was making the wrong responses to the challenges before it.

The University and the City

The university has become a microcosm of the modern society, particularly in its power of knowledge, dynamics of mind, and direction of thought. If, as Whitehead has said, the "task of the university is the creation of the future," the university is also a microcosm of the future society. In other words, to a considerable extent, the direction of the university becomes the direction of society.

This relationship between the university and society did not always exist. But today, as knowledge advances and as society becomes more complex, corporate, and interdependent, there is an inevitable centralization and dependence on *collective* social intelligence. The universal scope of the university makes it ideally suited to be the primary institutional generator and integrator of knowledge and collective wisdom in society.

Technology entered the universities in a roundabout way, through the creation of the higher technical school in Europe and in America at the end of the eighteenth and the beginning of the nineteenth centuries. Engineering as a distinct profession was born at that time. In America, the direct applications of scientific knowledge took a big leap with the creation of the land-grant agricultural and mechanical colleges in 1862. Practical utility was their first principle. The arts and sciences were added as a support base. The utility of technology naturally led to the utility of bureaucracy.

The university in the United States then grew into a central and powerful position in society, parallel with the growth of both knowledge and industry. In the process the university was restructured and its character and purpose were remolded to make it a direct and articulated instrument for technological and economic development. After this reformation between 1860 and 1920, the university could respond to all educational and research needs of the high-production, high-consumption society, including such specious subjects of knowledge as the subliminal motivations that increase sales and the social and psychological foundations of industrial management. The deeper social questions that were raised by such research were not fundamentally considered. Utilitarian power dominated the thrust, whether in agronomy, engineering, medicine, or nuclear physics. The university prospered because it was fundamental for new products, processes, and professions. The social sciences, especially economics, prospered where they served the primary motive.

Everywhere the hallmark of change was specialization, reflected in the multiplication of departments in the university. New knowledge, new techniques, and the masses of detail accompanying the new disciplines could best be mastered by the technical specialist and managed by the administrative specialist. Specialization became a virtual synonym for mastery, effectiveness, and efficiency, as well as discovery and development. All of these, of course, were demanded by the industrializing world. Everywhere success was identified with specialization, whether it concerned the development of a new seed or a new steel. Specialization was indeed the central detonator of the kind of development we have experienced.

Of course, planting the new seed or making use of a new steel requires the orchestration of many specialists. This process is now perfected to such a degree, for example, that the huge and incredibly complex Boeing 747 can be created de novo and achieve a fantastic performance and safety record under flying conditions that are inherently dangerous. The record, duplicated in hundreds of fields, is truly inspiring. It is directly attributable to the intensity of specialization—including the specialization of systems planning.

However, the grave problems of our age, I stress again, are the unintended, accumulative, and indirect results of the most extraordinary feats of human intelligence and organization. Modern problems rest most acutely outside the scope of specialists working in multidisciplinary teams. The specialist, working up from narrow purposes and pragmatic foundations, does not meet the generalist, who might work down from broader concerns and deeper ideals of the whole society. There is no creative tension between specialist and generalist to produce balanced and permanently beneficial results from the creation of specific capacities. The sources of initiative and power are thus extremely one-sided.

The broader level of perception and integration represented by the generalist remains undeveloped, even largely unrecognized, because it was not foretold in the application of utilitarian knowledge or organized into the collective intelligence of the university. The tidal force of specialization has made philosophy into just another specialty. The utter complexity and power unleashed in society now reveal a serious misuse of the specialists, which generalists might have corrected. Here I am not obliquely inviting the rule of philosopher-kings, for the problem is perception, not authority.

Perhaps one of our greatest challenges is the multiplication of specialization. That challenge is both a promise and a threat. Put simply, the mass, complexity, power, and interdependence created through specialization demand an altogether new and higher level of integration, for these attributes require their harmony, no less than the parts of a machine. They also raise profound questions of purpose that are not as easily answered as those of effective operation or profit.

The challenge to the university is to deal with wholes—whole human beings and whole societies. And this is a problem to be dealt with by the whole university, not by another specialty, even philosophy. The whole involves human ends and means; complex interactions and ultimate results; liberating diversities and securing unities; interacting environments linked with interacting institutions. Nowhere is the historic challenge more pressing than in understanding the whole human environment, particularly cities.

If the university is in any way a microcosm of the future society, the city is certainly a critical embodiment of the future and probably the best place to achieve rich and gratifying human wholeness. We have a choice: the city can either integrate and amplify or it can fragment and depress the prospects of people in all of their particular behavior. In our society, the purposes and organization of the university will ultimately determine the purposes and organization of the city through the kinds of knowledge thus generated.

In the end, moreover, fulfilling the educational obligations of the university itself will depend substantially on the urban framework. So will the higher future achievements to be demanded of specialized fields, such as economic policy.

To a very important degree, astonishingly, the present conception and organization of the university makes it incapable of dealing articulately with natural and social wholes. A few illustrations:

1. The organization of the university, despite an increasing number of interdisciplinary research centers and institutes, is organized and educates exclusively for specialization. We have no useful tradition of educating or using generalists, and we look down on them as unfocused eclectics. We have almost no generalist methodology. The centers and institutes tend to be congregations of specialists, and they are virtually unable to create general principles and perspectives or to advance a usefully broad dialogue.

Unkind Traditions

2. Scientific objectivity has become the measure of both *method* and *value* throughout the university, preventing a happy union of both. Although value systems pose muddling paradoxes and risk confusion of "exact" or objective knowledge, such risks must be taken. And they will be risks only to classical scientific method; society can only profit by any clarification of the paradoxes. The more terrifying risk before us today is that powerful scientific knowledge is being injected via technology into society without proven need, appropriate integration and restraints, or solid human control. Human control is best when its foundations are ethical, ecological, and politically clear. Sound public decisions are inescapably subjective, introspective, and aesthetic, as well as technical and objective. What we dare not risk is moving ever faster toward unknown ends, which is the threat of naked objectivity.

3. Despite the university's unequaled range of developed intelligence, higher education has but a hazy idea, let alone a worthy strategy, of developing its own potential, its best development, its larger service to society. The Carnegie Commission's unprecedented series of studies certainly filled a vast chasm. Academic and campus planning has taken hold in the past two decades. Yet, despite these important strides, a particularized, almost parochial attitude remains. *Excellence* is a hardly disguised term for elitism of specialized innovation. Planning for higher education focuses mainly on occupational needs. The mission of professional training becomes increasingly a proprietary claim to a sector of social power. Where, then, do we find the directive efforts to give conscious shape to the form and use of all disciplines and to lead them toward a larger humanism? Liberal education requires a massive resurgence to overcome a technicalization of thought and behavior. Given the power of an institution's structure on the way concepts and attitudes are generated, we cannot change the results of higher education without also changing the organization of the university itself.

The ethos of the university, I suspect, is the taproot of both the problems and the possibilities of modern times. It has shown itself to be highly responsive to the creation of the technological order. So far the university has been only incidentally resourceful in bringing a beneficial maturity to the urban and industrial order. It has yet to recognize that its challenge is radically new, and that it must accept larger navigational responsibilities in charting the future, as Whitehead indicated. Answering this challenge may mean making the whole university, in effect, into an institute of the human possibility.

If the university in America early took a clear responsibility to create a society founded, so to say, on the "agricultural and mechanical arts," its responsibility as clearly now resides in adapting the vast human capacities for higher human benefits. First and foremost this responsibility entails making the city into an unequivocally human affair. We are now on a treacherous trail. The highest reaches of human intelligence are squarely confronted. But the university has thus far virtually pushed them aside in favor of an ecclectic proliferation of specializations.

When we look at the awesome dimensions of city life, it quickly becomes evident that old approaches, assumptions, disciplines and organizations will not do. We are no longer after just a better car or the relief of auto congestion. The time is now upon us when virtually everything, including art and music, education and travel, becomes beneficial only in context and balance. Otherwise we face surfeit, chaos, conflict, and a direct diminution of life's potential.

We are now desperately short of the penetrating concepts to give the city meaningful human context and balance. We do not understand the integration necessary to achieve *urban* efficiency and *urban* amenity, to bring nature into the city, or to create satisfying human interaction. What really constitutes urbanity? What is the intellectual or aesthetic or emotional content of a good city? Instead of addressing itself to these questions, the overwhelming force of the university remains focused on the technical questions of machines and, increasingly, on special solutions to the problems created by too many ill-placed machines.

A central issue now is the humanization of higher education. The question that then becomes fundamental is whether a substantial humanization of higher learning can occur without a humanization of the urban framework within which the university operates. If, as Lewis Mumford has stressed, the entire city should impart a liberating and stimulating experience, the university's contribution in research and directive knowledge to the city would ultimately return to the university in building a more spirited milieu

Unkind Traditions

for its service to society. If the university's formal and rigorous role in education acted in concert with the city's informal and provocative educational possibilities, perhaps the universities could truly answer Toynbee's call to "make the benefits of civilization available to the whole human race."

Once more, Mumford (1970, p. 374) moves to the heart of the matter, suggesting that we remove "the university from its commitments to the power system . . . the bureaucratization of learning . . . points and credits and purely formalistic degrees." Positively, Mumford suggests that "the university would no longer be restricted to the detached pursuit of learning, divorced from art, politics, and religion, but would apply all its special resources for intellectual cooperation to revitalizing the whole life of the community."

The university's *urban* challenge may be conceived in four related efforts. The first is to discover and develop a new *vital pertinency* of university teaching, research, and service in urban affairs, paralleling its critical engagement in the specialized fields of development in the nineteenth century. The second hurdle is to bring all fields of knowledge to bear on the city as an *articulate whole*. The third is to make *human values* and goals consciously and directly a part of the concepts, analyses, research, and experimentation in all urban questions. The last effort toward a tradition of organic wholeness—and therefore human freedom—is to recognize that the university itself (its campus, varied institutions, faculty and students) is increasingly moving to the *center stage of life,* as essential to the city as transportation.

The deep challenge to higher education is awesome, almost ominous. Henry Steele Commager has said that world development "will make ceaseless and importunate demands, upon our resources of organized intelligence. That is another way of saying that the responsibility will fall upon the university" (1966, p. 83). Abraham Flexner, who has perhaps influenced American higher education as much as any other man, put the idea another way: "Societies have to act—intelligently, if possible—if not, then unintelligently, blindly, selfishly, impulsively. The weight and prestige of the university must be thrown on the side of intelligence. If the university does not accept the challenge, what other institution can or will?" (1930, p. 13). This is the challenge of the university, especially in its role as a microcosm of the future society, most particularly of the city.

The Intellect and the City

Despite the sheer necessity of advancing collective intelligence in the university and in all institutions, our intellectual tradition is peculiarly and perhaps dangerously confined by the *institutional* stamp on all modern thought. Rarely has creative thought been so monopolized by organizations. At no time has such a confinement been more debilitating to an understanding of the modern phenomena of cities. Yet the debilitation, I suspect, runs more deeply.

Whereas the public conscience of American private wealth has been represented by a surprising number of superb public servants, including Harriman, F. D. Roosevelt, the Kennedys and Rockefellers, there is no comparable roster of minds devoted to a public ideal through an independent intellect, free of an orthodoxy occurring when careers are tied to disciplinary professions and institutions. This pattern is not inevitable. A large part of the eighteenth- and nineteenth-century English liberal intellectual tradition arose from wealth outside the cloistering effects of the university and may owe its vitality to that freedom.

When the city is viewed against the institutionalized, professionalized, and specialized mold cast by the recent American intellectual tradition, we find that both the city and the intellect inherited essentially the same pattern of estrangement. A kind of intellectual alienation appears to parallel social alienation. The effects bite deeply into both the university and the city, as well as into our tradition of liberal thought.

The increasingly alienated city and the increasingly specialized and compartmentalized university seem to affect each other in a dual and reciprocal way. When, as I suspect, the person cannot experience a social vitality of the whole city, the intellect is likely to lose the vitality of the whole university. Neither the person nor the intellect can find the potent stimulus that Vienna apparently gave to the "Vienna Circle" of an unusual number of creative minds around the turn of the century. Because cities have lost much of their value of enlarging perception and motivation, the mind, also blockaded by a singularly narrow academic discipline, can neither grasp nor appreciate the human wholes of the city or the larger realms of the mind.

Partly because the intellectual environment of the city itself has become sterile, the special fields of the university tend to become monolithic. When development of either the mind or the emotions depends on a specialized and narrow base, the social breadth of human development appears to suffer. When the university, which so completely conditions the American intellect, combines its intellectual monopoly with a caste system of degrees, then a club membership and a pecking order are subtly substituted for the excitements of the mind, for the virility of whole human ideas, for the vigorous intercourse of all knowledge and interests, and possibly for intellectual freedom. This condition, I suspect, may be the primary source of the "intellectual recessiveness" in university faculties that Lionel Trilling noted.

The estrangement lies deep and leaves the intellect as seriously antithetic to the city as the American Dream. Peculiarly, even among urbanists there seems to be a bias against cities. That antiurban bias lies far back in the American past; Jefferson, for example, said about cities: "True, they nourish some of the elegant arts, but the useful ones can thrive elsewhere . . . with more health, virtue and freedom." Edmund Faltermayer, author of *Redoing America* (1968), has observed a defeatism concerning urban democracy. Perhaps those to whom Faltermayer refers—Irving Kristol, Nathan Glazer, and Raymond Vernon—are above this defeatism. Yet these and many others do reveal a peculiarly narrow commitment to the assumptions which have been used for generations as rationalizations for the increasingly misdirected technical and economic development underlying the condition of cities today.

Kristol, essayist, editor, and professor, is frankly pessimistic, especially about urban democracy, wondering "how anyone can be blithely sanguine" about the urban condition (Kristol, 1970, p. 30). He says, "no clear solution seems visible even to the most thoughtful among us." What is surprising is to set this view beside an earlier statement of Kristol's: "It is all very well for city planners to laud the Swedish way, and to point out how Stockholm benefits from the fact the Swedes live in high-rise apartments outside the city and commute to work via rapid transit. Bully for them, say I. But Americans are not Swedes. The overwhelming majority of our population, which lives in one-family homes and drives its own automobiles, is not going to veer off suddenly into the Swedish way or any other. The American home has three centuries of homesteading behind it; and the American automobile has three centuries of individualism behind it" (1967, pp. 72-73).

Kristol's use of the rural myths of isolated homesteading and rugged individualism as a critique of contemporary urban development flies in the face of the urban debilitations with which he himself is concerned. Unfortunately, this kind of contradiction characterizes a large part of the urban and environmental thinking today. Although very urbane himself, Kristol does not distinguish between rural and urban essences of things, which is the only way *urban* freedom or *urban* democracy can ever achieve its own validity. He does not recognize how one-family houses and one-family cars convert vital rural individuality into brutish urban individuation, regardless of national ethos.

In taking a stance supporting simple, raw, individual choice, Kristol rejects the reasoning he uses to criticize the pursuit of self-interest as the basis for democratic self-rule. He comes very close to saying that self-interest operating without clear constraint has corrupted urban Americans, who behave, he says, more and more "like a collection of mobs." Kristol knows that *individual* choices are increasingly illusory unless they are built on a carefully prepared framework that optimizes trade-offs in favor of the individual. The Constitution demonstrates this idea politically. The framework of cities today just as clearly reveals the constrictiveness of individual choice, especially when so powerfully directed by the tastemaker merchants who would reduce all choice to product selection on a plane of rising consumption—a treacherous course when *built* into the city.

Another manifestation of both intellectual estrangement and bias against cities is revealed in the surprising chasm between environmentalists and urbanists. In the last decade, hundreds of

Unkind Traditions

books—varying from *Ecocide* and *A Time to Choose* to *The Limits to Growth* and *Resources and Man*—have been written about the environment. These books all raise fundamental issues. Yet, other than an occasional and rather incidental reference, these and the many other environmental works do not seriously raise what is certainly the most basic issue of the environment, the *nature of the urban environments* that we make.

Similarly, a large number of books on the city have appeared. Whether we consider the widely discussed *Megalopolis* and *Death and Life of Great American Cities* or review the professional books in city planning, housing, or transportation, we find a serious inability to consider the critical questions of the deeper *environmental impacts of cities*.

When we ask who has crossed the chasm between "cities" and "environment," we find that the number is very small. Paulo Soleri (1969), known for his brilliant "archologies" (architecture plus ecology) has set forth many penetrating insights of ecological significance. Ian McCarg, in *Design with Nature* (1969), has sensitized us to the dynamics of land and nature in locating and designing urban projects. Barbara Ward and Rene Dubos also come to mind as persons who have veered close to a comprehensive ecological view. Yet their book, *Only One Earth* (1972), was a disappointment in its treatment of the city. The best urban-ecological bridge is Lewis Mumford. His range and spirit of understanding span the successive waves of technology, the meaning of science, and the social significance of cities. And his grasp is solidly human. With historic and philosophic breadth, he underwrites a positive vision of ecologically and socially valid cities.

I suspect that Western philosophy, which laid superb foundations for science, did not provide society with ways to avoid the environmental debacle we now face. No minds set forth a vision of a liberal environmental or urban order comparable to the contributions of Locke and Hume to the Declaration of Independence and the Constitution. Consequently, we are a society that wildly exploits the natural environment and blithely builds destructive urban environments. These two facts are really one, and they reveal a treacherous gap in our intellectual heritage.

All societies have patterns of fortunate and unfortunate

traditions. Today, the traditions that hurt us most tend to be the most dynamic. We have only begun to recognize the gross environmental threats. We have hardly begun to recognize the urban sources of that threat or the accompanying social debilities. We confuse the awesome challenge by blaming population growth (a relevant but minor factor in the industrially advanced nations) and then invoke the old Christian appeal to the conscience of the individual, when the essential challenge rests in raw industrial growth and powerful organizations. Although the city penetrates all other organizations in advanced society, it does not play a creative role in shaping social power.

Toward the end of his career, Frederick Jackson Turner is said to have confessed to the need for an urban reinterpretation of history. More vitally, are not the philosophic foundations overdue that will prepare us for an urban civilization? Had such a philosophy arisen with the scientific and technological forces accompanying the growth of the city, would we lack a valid urban interpretation of history?

In the meantime, we remain without an adequate theory of urban form, a concept that might honor and nurture the highest conceptions of human association, aspiration, honor, and spirit. Our concept of the city is today completely subservient to the hard technologies that permeate it and to the powerful institutions that rule it.

Traditions that were creative and positive in an older context have become destructive in our radically more powerful era. Our pragmatism has become a huge impoverishment. Indeed, pragmatism has become our problem because it specifically assumes a self-feeding and self-accelerating system of need and consumption. A new framework of basic social assumptions is imperative if we are to create cities worthy of the potential of our time.

The Planner and the City

How have each of the many lines of tradition affected urban planning practice? Let us briefly review the premises on which planning, the focal point of traditions affecting the conception and control of city environments, rests today.

Planners operate without a conception of an ideal city. There is no established norm for size with either upper or lower limits. There is no economic ideal, no formula for urban productive or consumptive efficiency. We look as vainly for a social ideal. Despite a fifty-year debate about the neighborhood unit, the concept remains incomplete and exists only partially in a few locations. Urbanity, the quality of environments that stimulate a rich cosmopolitan life, is almost absent in the literature, except as a reflection of particular architectural settings. Although urban aesthetics has been given greater attention, few can argue that it is more than a hopeless idea lost in garish, dingy, declining, and barren settings of the city.

While medicine operates with a vision of health, and law with a distant image of justice, city planning exists without such a simple goal. Its operational objective becomes, in effect, to maintain order, principally to accommodate the technical and economic forces, not to conceive, select, and shape spaces, structures, and functions for health, justice, beauty, personal growth, and social grace. Planning does not select or shape technology to build the good environment, whether we speak of railroads, airports, freeways, or industrial establishments. Each essentially defines its own penetration into the city and alters the city in the process. Regulations are but minor qualifiers.

Order, as opposed to *ideal,* is an objective of last resort. It avoids worst damage but fails to strive for higher possibilities. Even at that, order is achieved only superficially. Planners succeed only where a given municipal interest coincides with that of developers, industrialists, and merchants. Of course, chaos always benefits well-organized business interests. One is often left with the impression that there is no public interest as such and no public will, only private interest and private will.

In the name of jobs and economic growth, cities seek all kinds of new physical development. If, for example, development is distant from the city and requires a freeway or boulevard where only a two-lane road now exists, that freeway will be built as a huge, after-the-fact subsidy. The developer argues economic necessity for each housing project, but the full facts of urban economics are never brought together.

Like social scientists, the planners bury themselves in lengthy, "objective" studies. Both the complexity and the objectivity ultimately justify a low level of order in cities. The possibility of an urban ideal supported by measurable benefits is swept over by the avalanche of urban development that subsequently builds great problems, requires a fantastic public investment, and then demands redevelopment within fifty years. The game is an interplay of private money, power, and status demanding an exhaustive public development of freeways. But congestion, sprawl, and degeneration are the result. The objective studies underlying pragmatic public solutions are but weak public responses to strong private initiative in a process that in the end destroys even the limited order the planners originally sought.

Much of the defeat, however, is incorporated directly into the official plans and policies. The facade of bringing order into urban development in the end sanctifies a larger, deeper level of chaos founded in the huge spaces, huge distances, and their lack of integration. The process, pragmatically evaluated at each step, argued in public hearing, and voted by elected or appointed officials, carries an appearance of public responsibility. But, seen as tradition in historic perspective, the process does little more than paper over the disintegration of the American city.

Any process that does not serve a deep cultural ideal inevitably serves those who wield raw power. Lacking penetrating ideals, planning is dominated by process. Most planners try to make planning serve a higher public purpose by focusing on making *the process* more responsive to the public and therefore more democratic. The general plan concept promoted by Jack Kent was a supreme effort to bring comprehensiveness into the development process. Planning advocacy set forth by Paul Davidoff attempts to put the planning process into the reach of groups disenfranchised by the dominant powers. John Friedmann's transactive planning seeks a better understanding of people's desires through an ongoing dialogue. The urban growth management process currently in vogue attempts to replace the methodological weaknesses found in the last two decades of general planning.

All of these methodologies allow urban ideals but do not envisage or promote them. Urban processes, no matter how democratically based, become dangerous without a commonly accepted ideal of the city that gives them particular content and direction. All have the appearance of working for a better city—and do, of course, make particular contributions—but the possibility of their becoming vitally engaged in the real issues of building genuinely good cities will be slight until new aspirations and idealizations of the city can frame and direct them to that end.

The term *bloodletting* might fairly describe the planning process. However, even bloodletting is inadequate, because it implies a wrong action in protecting the health of an organically unified being. The planning process is theoretically more fundamental and more critical because it *creates* the city, determines its form and function, and defines its organic being. Planning does not merely work to maintain good health. It creates the very *idea* of urban health.

Many of the distortions of planning are revealed in the language of planning, which speaks of division and mobilization rather than organic integration, balanced form, and dynamic stability. Consider the following terms:

Land use. The *use* of land emphasizes what is occupied rather than the functions that occur in the city; implies qualities of exclusiveness, specialization of activities (the uses), and naked revenue; and tends to deny common urban design.

Central business district. Only *business* activities and interests are emphasized in what should be the most diverse and cosmopolitan part of the city, while residential, social, cultural, and religious activities are excluded or downgraded, thus denying integration for cosmopolitan benefits.

Suburb. Quite appropriately, *sub-urb* denotes something less than what is fully urban (or complete), symbolizes private escape, and emphasizes private wealth as against public poverty. It is of interest that the Oxford English Dictionary defines *suburban* as having the "inferior manners, the narrowness of view, and so on, attributed to residents in suburbs."

Zoning. Zones, as noted, *segregate* and *isolate* rather than relate and integrate. They also promote unnecessary mobility and have demonstrated a powerful new leverage for the wealthy to assure exclusiveness and special advantages: better schools, tax enclaves, commercial leverage, and avoidance of general urban concerns.

Planned unit development. The planned unit development is an integrative, "antizoning" provision incorporated directly into zoning ordinances. PUD begins to demonstrate some of the advantages of common design, unified facilities, and social cooperation in the vicinity of one's residence.

Subdivision. This primary process of urban development divides land into its lowest common denominator of use and into a maximum exclusiveness, typically the single-family house, providing it with wide streets, which become necessary to connect the isolated urban fragments.

Conflicting land use. Conflict, almost inherent in great separation of activities, necessarily arises when the free market randomly determines the urban land use through market maneuvers that maximize monetary gain.

Planning standards. Applied mainly as a public means of promoting private consumptiveness (such as large lots with wide streets), standards are often identified with spaciousness (private minispaces), which, however, promote congestion and deny the larger, more varied, socially interactive, public spaciousness. Despite our high planning (and building) standards, the accompanying social sterility, the fluid real estate market, and the impermanent building materials make deterioration inevitable.

Congestion and density. Congestion in American cities does not arise with high density but with the movements attendant on low density. Virtually all modern congestion is transport congestion, which originates from and is promoted by large and poorly used spaces, long distances, and individual transport (automobiles). The geometry of large urban areas requires that true spaciousness can be secured only through articulated high-density clustering.

Center. The use of this term increases as true centrality is fragmented and lost.

Community. Like center, community is used inversely to the reality of its existence and refers to any identifiable group of people or interests. Sometimes the clearest community is negatively defined: the ghetto or slum.

Urban. Virtually any development in any location now

brings it into the urban orbit. The term tends to supplant the word *city*, which infers a clear unity of the economic, political, and social life of a human settlement. Paul Goodman observes that city planning has devolved "into something called 'urbanism.' "

Housing. This term places emphasis on the number, cost, technical standards, and raw quantitative output of shelter units, as opposed to the quality, design, and long-term improvement of all living conditions—the vital context of improving the whole living environment, including health, education, social interaction, and personal growth.

Trafficways. Because they are the most sacred element in urban development, trafficways warrant the bulk of public urban capital expenditures. Such expenditure, of course, promotes more distance, more travel, more segregation, and less centering or integration of urban activities. Wilfred Owen has asked "whether it is possibile to be urbanized and motorized and at the same time civilized." The importance given to trafficways reveals a conception of the city based on a motorized functionalism that has brought the city to its knees.

The American planning tradition supports the idea that the city can grow to any population or expand to any area, which raises the question of whether the city can do anything in real human terms. The planning profession, which became a recognizable profession between 1900 and 1920, hardly represents a serious amendment to the forces that brought the city to its knees. If it did, we would have to look for a sharper break with the past, a clearer theoretic foundation, and, most of all, a powerful set of ideals. One would expect social controversy, but there is little except for the local fights about specific zoning, freeway routes, and the like. Planning is accepted today because it is docile and unable to raise the burning issues of cities that strike at the heart of our problems of modernity.

Planning has not even approached a renaissance. It has inherited without essential questioning the dominant technological and economic traditions. One looks in vain for an innovative core, an independent voice, a vital engagement with the ideas of change.

Planning has become an arm of bureaucracy that is, as Max Weber described it, neutral and therefore obedient to whatever forces are in control. We must therefore look elsewhere for the vision and leadership that can strike a vital dialogue of ecology, democracy, and undiluted humanism in cities and that can responsibly govern change. Innovation is too awesome to be managed by those who profit from it.

Quite abruptly we have invented the future. But we have not considered the requirements that will make it really work, either ecologically or humanistically. Time is urgent. We cannot wait for the slow processes of evolution to adjust us to our revolution. What we require is an inspiration capable of renewing our dominant traditions, which are fast coming to a dangerous climax. The city, as integrator of most human doings, has an immensely creative role to play. That role must be definitive and active, not passive and absorbent.

9

The Urban Implosion of the Population Bomb

Since Wendel Wilkie's 1940 rally, One World, we have witnessed many truly awesome global realities: A world war and many local wars, crises of atomic annihilation, the world population explosion, world food shortages, a struggle for international development, and threats of general energy and material shortages. These make parochial all previous problems of humankind.

The creation of one highly interdependent world ends for all time our animal innocence, robs us of all privileged remnants of savage nobility. From now on we must become completely civilized or face the terror of losing everything. All complexities ultimately become as simple as that.

If the perspectives of this book have even partial validity, no subject is more central to the resolution of world problems than cities, whether we speak of the conditions underlying food production, world resource depletion and pollution, or the psychological propensities for war. No subject is more central than cities to human aspirations and development. Yet rarely has such a serious universal subject been ignored so ominously by the economic or political leadership. The time for tolerable solutions has been running out for decades. We do not know how much time we have remaining. We do know that the mass, power, and complexities of technological development are becoming less and less distinguishable from the monumental crises of society.

We now shift our analysis of the city from the urban problems of the high technology society, already through most of its urbanization, to the poor industrializing society, now just entering the tidal stage of urban growth. To a surprising degree, what the cities of the poor countries are being forced to do is what the cities of the wealthy countries ought to do.

The cities of Asia, Africa, and Latin America, for example, are being forced to reconsider the *process* of growth and change. They would like to follow the Western model but cannot afford to do so in critical areas, even on modest terms. Implicit in what they must do are possibly some of the most profound lessons of life and cities at this stage of human development, East and West, North and South. In effect, governments have had to abandon the model of development prescribed by bureaucracy and technology. They have abdicated to the people themselves. While this act is taken as a temporary tactical retreat, it is in fact a shift of *process* with immense implications for the *goals* of development.

While one third of humanity struggles with industrial surfeit in functionally chaotic and socially destructive cities, the remaining two thirds struggle to learn the treacherous sun dance of Western industrial power. The already greatly overpopulated rural areas in Asia, Africa, and Latin America are spawning billions of would-be migrants to already overpopulated cities. The challenge is to channel the tremendous energies of these people into positive and permanent accomplishments.

The present "development decades" are based on a Western

industrial model that world resources cannot sustain and on a specifically American model of city that seriously erodes the human benefits of development. Moreover, Third World urbanization and industrialization are founded on a number of burdens and imbalances that did not afflict the West at comparable periods of transformation.

The repeated shocks and setbacks of more than two decades of international development, combined with the tough new lessons of Western industrial and urban development, strongly argue not only that the strategies of development are profoundly wrong but that the objectives are seriously misconceived and may be courting disaster. Theobald and Mills (1973) are right when they argue that we must rework our model from the beginning because present theories of development have proved invalid.

Rethinking from the beginning is particularly necessary for cities. Today's urban strategies are hardly strategies at all. National development plans reduce urban development to a minor corollary of economic development, a view consistent with the West's historic vision of the city as a simple container of social development. (Although cities in the Third World warrant independent attention, here I must limit myself to those perspectives that are most relevant to the city in the industrially advanced nations.)

Human Crescendo

Cities are approaching the time when their growth will be more explosive than that of world population. Although their importance is unrecognized, they overshadow and encompass the spread of technology, the expansion of education, the changes in health.

Urban growth in our times acts as a delayed implosion of the population bomb. A century was required for the world to grow from one billion to two billion souls, roughly from 1830 to 1930. The final billion of the 6.5 billion people predicted for the year 2000 will join us in only ten years, or less than one tenth of the time required for the second billion to appear.

Similarly, urban growth, relatively slow in the past, must now also be measured in gargantuan proportions. In 1920 only

270 million persons lived in urban centers larger than 20,000 and three fourths of these were in the industrially advanced countries. By 1970 the urban population was approaching its first billion.

The portentious fact is that cities will expand at least threefold between 1970 and 2000. No less can be expected if the total population reaches or surpasses 6.5 billion persons, for even the urbanization of only half of that figure (3.25 billion) assumes a continued population growth in the already overcrowded rural areas of China, India, Indonesia, Bangladesh, Pakistan, Egypt, Nigeria, Brazil, and dozens of other countries. In gross terms, three billion city dwellers could mean one hundred cities with an average of ten million inhabitants each (such as Tokyo), one thousand cities with one million inhabitants (Brussels), and ten thousand cities averaging one hundred thousand inhabitants.

Unfortunately, the distribution of urban population is not likely to be that well balanced. Some calculations have projected that Calcutta could grow to fifty million or more. Other cities could grow beyond twenty million, as the New York metropolitan area is now about to do. Will those conglomerations be minimally viable? This is a very real and hard question. A diabolical urban magnet seems to be operating, and the reasons for it have largely eluded scholarship.

The implosion of population to the poor cities from the impoverished countryside illustrates what must be faced. In the year 2000, hardly more than one year's urban growth may well equal the world's entire urban population of 1900. Given the population that must be expected, there is no realistic way to stem the rural-to-urban tide. Most rural areas of Java, the Ganges Plain, the Nile Valley, and northeast Brazil are at or near human saturation.

For more than three decades now, the cities of Asia, Africa, and especially Latin America have experienced what seemed to be a fantastic growth. Delhi, São Paulo, and Mexico City each quadrupled between 1940 and 1970. A United Nations report revealed that in Dar es Salaam, Tanzania, more than one third of the population of 273,000 was living in miserable slum and squatter conditions. In Seoul, a city with three times its 1950 population of 1,500,000, some 970,000 families (or about 3.6 million persons)

The Urban Implosion of the Population Bomb

live in only 440,000 dwellings. Yet Seoul continues its growth at about 400,000 people annually. In Guayaquil, Ecuador, half of the 730,000 people live in squatter suburbs, a large part in shacks built on stilts over tidal flats. In Brazil, although all cities over 100,000 are expected to double in less than twelve years, the *favelas,* or squatter settlements, are expected to multiply six times.

This most portentous migration in history does not assure an improved level of living. A study in India found that whereas 34 percent of the rural families lived in one room, the figure rose to 44 percent in the urban areas, 67 percent in the four largest cities, and 79 percent in Calcutta (United Nations, 1968, p. 52). The United Nations has referred to cities as the symbol of failure in development. Robert McNamara, president of the World Bank, has reported that cities are "spawning a culture of poverty" that threatens the economic health of whole nations. Why, when cities grow so rapidly, should they be seen as the sinkholes of development?

Barbara Ward has suggested in a brief United Nations report (United Nations, 1970, pp. 10–12) that the conditions of urbanization in the Third World today carry four disadvantages not present in the period of comparable urban growth in the West during the nineteenth century: (1) Many cities grew to a large size as a reflection of colonial development, rather than as a result of local diversification and steady technical development, and thus preceeded a full system of modernization; (2) The sheer scale of population growth on top of already large populations exceeded that in the West, creating exceptional pressures on the land, capital savings, and public services; (3) Agricultural transformation has lagged, whereas in Europe and America many important changes in farm productivity created surplus food prior to the industrialization of cities; (4) Rapid urbanization today accompanies relatively slower industrialization by comparison with similar periods of development in the West.

These propelling forces do not add up to a logical and progressive condition of world development under assured control of society. Rather, they point up a perilous transition set up by the unleashed forces of industrialization without full or balanced development. For example, the first crisis of international development, the population explosion, resulted directly from the first powerful success of development, simple improvements in public health.

Between 1965 and 1970 it appeared that the miracle rice, wheat, and corn seeds, along with the corollary developments of the Green Revolution, might result in a second major success story of development, an adequate food supply. Some people feared that this success would result in rapid farm mechanization, which would expel extra millions of unprepared peasants from the rural areas to the cities. Such an event now appears likely to occur regardless of whether mechanization occurs or crop yields are substantially increased. Whatever happens in agriculture, the second major development crisis—a bursting of acute urban problems—will inevitably fall on world society. Rural people will be expelled from their villages either by their inability to produce or by a major transformation of agriculture—or by patterns of both.

The really critical problems lie over the horizon, when cities will double or quadruple their present sizes, when the makeshift character of the early decades of urbanization will reveal profound shortcomings of urban development, and when the rapidly expanding demands on scarce metals and energy will begin to throw major new blocks in the path of assumed and planned industrialization. When this stage of development begins to falter—when rising levels of material consumption accelerate the shortage of materials—a series of uncontrollable and perhaps catastrophic events seem destined to follow.

By that time (and the particular time, place, and circumstances will vary), we can expect that the population will have benefited from a degree of education and income improvement— enough to acquire high aspirations of consumption. When improvement is stunted for any extended period, especially when accompanied by privileged groups unaffected by the cessation of development, a critical mass of the ingredients for violent revolution will have gathered. Poor, uneducated rural peasants do not revolt. Quasi-developed urban masses can and do.

The urban masses will be conditioned to revolt when they become psychologically and socially alienated. Massive, chaotic cities reveal a profound potential for personal dislocation. A rapid estrangement of rural-urban migrants who are accustomed to close interpersonal bonds may well result in the transfer of those bonds to groups with revolutionary and tyrannous intent.

It is ironic that the hopes of the poor for a good life rest in the very cities that they themselves are creating through a process of desperation. It is equally ironic that, to the extent official direction and money create the city as a crude medium for economic exploitation, future cities based on the western model will acquire structures with a low level of efficiency, amenity, and sociability— a poverty of vision. Unless we can find a means to steadily broaden our vision to develop a valid urban strategy and provide effective guidance and support to the poor, the future of the city and economic development is dim indeed.

The Poor Shall Inherit . . .

Our concern here centers on squatter and impoverished settlements, for these are the most common and dynamic conditions in world urbanization today. As late as 1940, before cities developed their magnetic power and jumped to a new level of exponential growth, there were relatively few squatters. John Turner (in United Nations, 1968), who has had much creative experience working with squatters, reports that they constituted less than 5 percent of the population of Lima, Peru in 1940. What has occurred since has but scant precedent in history.

As population growth and urbanization gathered momentum, especially in Latin America (which was demographically ahead of Asia and Africa), intolerable crowding first took place in the central slum areas of cities. Since land costs were prohibitive to the poor and since there was no reasonable way for them to achieve minimal shelter, they began to organize themselves and clandestinely seize private or government lands at night. By morning they were prepared to defend it by force. An item in the Mexican newspaper, *Ultimas Noticias,* for May 5, 1965, illustrates one such incident: "Seven thousand 'paratroopers'—a colloquial term for squatters—occupied half a dozen tracts south of the harbor. The owners requested that the 'invaders' be evicted by Federal troops but the authorities seem unable to act. Violence is feared since the 'paratroopers' are armed. When the men leave for work, women take up their posts with rifles in their arms. . . . Word reached neighboring communities and factories that sites can be acquired at 125 pesos. An 'office' was set up, funds collected from interested families and plots of 100 to 150 square meters were staked out. An avalanche of buyers appeared; and overnight, innumerable shacks and shanties sprang up where the land was barren for many years."

Official response is predictable. When the squatter groups are small, they can be physically removed, sometimes after considerable investments in houses are made. When the squatters number in the thousands and a constant patrol of armed guards reveals determination, the concept of squatters' rights slowly develops. The legal dilemma of the rights of the owner posed against the social, humanitarian, and even economic position of the squatters does not resolve itself easily.

Gradually many governments have taken a more tolerant and constructive position. In the late 1960s some governments began to undertake specific programs to provide land to would-be squatters. However, as late as 1971, the city of Nairobi, Kenya reportedly mounted a campaign to burn 60,000 hovels in shanty towns as "unhygienic," as if this act would improve the housing and hygiene of the quarter of a million persons evicted.

Slowly the dynamic and positive aspects of propertyless urban settlers began to be understood. Turner has shown (in United Nations, 1968), for example, how squatter and clandestine settlements are "logical, both socially and economically."

Such settlements must be sharply distinguished from classical slums, which normally become traps and "breeding grounds for discontent and violence" (United Nations, 1968, p. 120). The essence of the squatter's dynamism is the freedom they have to improve their condition of life, unlike slum dwellers, whose environment is physically and organizationally stunted. The squatter builders make improvements themselves or, failing that, they make the "best of a situation for which they accept full responsibility," suggests Turner. Many squatters prefer to take on great new hardships where there is the prospect of making steady improvements on their own.

To Turner, housing is an activity, not a commodity. The

benefits of housing are all the values surrounding the self-improving activity, of which the material and spatial standards of the moment are but a small matter. To fail to distinguish, says Turner and Fichter (1972, p. 152), "between what things *are* . . . and what they *do* in people's lives" leads to absurdities, such as tearing down substandard houses when there is no other place for people to go.

Turner's analysis of squatter settlements begins with *bridgehead settlements,* the act of squatting, followed by *consolidation* or *self-improving settlements,* where land is held securely and permanent investment is then encouraged. Many bridgehead settlements cannot move very far along the path of improvement because they cannot obtain secure freehold title, because distances to employment and services are too great, because the land is too steep or dangerous (subject, for example, to floods or slides), or because critical public assistance is withheld (such as potable water, landfill, and schools).

All hope and progress revolve around the limits of improvability. To expand the range of improvability, a number of governments have developed a variety of aided self-help schemes that are within both their means and those of the masses of urban poor. Some of the more notable actions are: the provision of sites and services (usually a small plot with access to a water tap and sanitary facility), housing shells, and various forms of self-help improvements. The idea is simple but powerful. Most families simply cannot afford a complete, moderate-standard house. Neither government nor private initiative alone is capable of creating a reasonable dwelling. But, working together, they can in time do just that. In particular, the government can provide critical public facilities, small loans for materials, and technical assistance in constructing a respectable dwelling over a period of years.

Yet the major component is the ambition and energy of the family. When people are able to find a condition of basic improvability and hope, they are capable of vast "output" and "savings." When the major input is "sweat" capital, a level of investment is often possible that could never be achieved through ordinary capital investment. Most financial overhead costs are then avoided. Employment, both visible and invisible, is generated. Cooperation and general education are advanced in the arts of building, and new employable skills are learned. In short, very substantial hidden resources are revealed and unleashed.

The bonus of such approaches is the social self-confidence and the inner human growth that can then take place. Although we must be extremely wary of the potential for severe alienation that any large, socially undifferentiated, squatter or sites-and-services settlement can generate, the *process* at least is one in which the individual, the family, and a whole settlement can initially achieve a deep security, pride, and identity.

The danger always exists when an immovable ceiling of improvability is reached. When the inhabitants abandon hope and stop improving their homes and neighborhoods, "Then the fear that a huge belt of recent city growth is peopled by disaffected slum dwellers might well turn out to be true. Should the air of hope vanish and expectations continue to be frustrated, the predicted uprising might occur" (Turner in United Nations, 1968, p. 120).

Although the early achievement of a "reasonable standard" of dwelling remains the acute problem, we cannot be sanguine about the future when even the self-improving neighborhoods of today reach the limits of improvability set by an inauspicious formative period. If we know anything about housing at all, it is that most of today's dwellings have definite limits of improvability. Limits of improvability are set most permanently and absolutely in the physical layout of any settlement. At some point, the old actions and precedents of planning without great vision and acute strategy set arbitrary limits to what can be done. Beyond that, the slate must be wiped clean at great public expense before a new, higher level of urban development becomes possible.

We can be sure, too, that people's aspirations will grow. When they soar above the ceiling of improvability of a neighborhood (whether limited by land and layout, dwelling construction, utilities, community facilities, or whatever), a profound sense of frustration will inevitably set in. Moreover, when this frustration is set against a growing alienation of highly anonymous cities, the new generation of dwellers in ex-squatter areas—the persons who will not be able to identify with the accomplishments of their parents—are going to see themselves stunted in the midst of their ongoing revolution.

Already many large squatter areas are thirty years old. Large inner-city slum areas also remain as fixed environments fit only to escape from at the earliest time. The year 2000 may see between one and two billion people living in urban areas of severe physical, social, and economic debilitations that cannot be corrected short of complete clearance. Many government and private housing projects have the same basic built-in limitations. However, a massive scale of clearance will be even less feasible in the poor countries than it has proven to be in the United States. And in such hovels, social improvement will surely hit dead-end.

At this point a grave theoretic inadequacy protrudes its ugly head. A process of self-help was originally initiated to assist the desperate urban dweller who was utterly without resources. A new promise was opened. But how far along the trail of human freedom, opportunity, enlightenment, and joy will it carry the people whose neighborhood is fundamentally a disorganized patchwork?

Roughly the same theoretic limit to improvability and higher aspiration exists in the industrially advanced nations. Here, houses are ready-made (without personal self-help investment) to the highest standards of plumbing, heating, and electrical convenience. Other than the installation of new appliances, air conditioning, or the addition of new rooms, there is little essential improvability in the American suburban home. Few creative changes are possible that might enlarge the social horizons of the individual or family, let alone remove the ominous overhead created by the consumptive conditions of industrial and urban growth. The most acute limitations are to be found in the dull, dispersed, and highly alienated suburbs created since the 1920s. The dwellings are isolated so perfectly that social evolution based on residential location is all but impossible.

In America there is only one direction a neighborhood can go: down. The ceiling of improvability is reached roughly ten years after construction, when the patio is in and the sycamores reach a useful spread. In the developing countries, the ceiling is likely to be reached twenty or thirty years after first settlement, with house, water, electricity, and perhaps sanitary sewers. For the upper classes, the picture is more like the American condition, except that the typical higher densities in these countries present some opportunities for a social as well as a physical evolution of neighborhood life.

The penetrating question for all urban development is how investments that are realistic for today can contribute most completely to higher human capacities in tomorrow's city. The question asks how we can achieve both permanence and flexibility in the structure of the city and in its dwellings through a process of gradual investment and steadily changing priorities and aspirations. It assumes that present resources are always limited but that the present limitations should not constrict the eventual creation of an urban environment that is environmentally spacious, convenient, and efficient, beautiful and stable, and still very responsive to the social needs of each generation.

At present this paradox is unresolved in both theory and practice. It will work more sharply against humankind as urbanization reaches a massive scale and as more and more improvability ceilings are reached. The limits to improvability will be especially binding when resource problems become more acute and therefore narrow options. Clearly, the favorable developments we hope for in twenty, thirty, or forty years depend on the precedents we set into action today.

Making Improvability Permanent

How do we resolve these dilemmas when the leading role in the uncertain drama of urban development in countries like Brazil, Nigeria, or India is being played by masses of impoverished urban settlers? The people are bursting into the cities partly in desperation, partly in hope, but always without sufficient skills or education.

Hardly a less auspicious foundation could be found to build urban environments for a promising future. Yet these people *are* the urban inhabitants, present and future, and they *are* vigorously building the city, good or bad. Their struggle reveals a great reservoir of development energy and ambition—the only ultimate source of development—that economists find hard to discover.

Residing in the people's own struggles are the creative, restorative, and stabilizing possibilities that are central to both urban and national development. In other words, human development, urban development, and national development perhaps should be seen as essentially one united process rather than as separate sectors of thought and action. Indeed, there is no other means than the people, and there can be no other *purpose* than the people. All else is a subordinate consideration.

It is the city that determines the relevance, effectiveness, and benefits of all particular facilities and activities within its bounds. Heretofore we have used economics (money) as the dominant measure of social relevance, effectiveness, and benefit. Money is, however, monolithic, arbitrary, and personally unreal, although it is obviously flexible, purportedly comprehensive, and absolutely necessary to facilitate exchange. Cities, although they do not provide a ready and simple quantitative measure of "progress," are organic and very real in human life. This means that what does not directly assist Juan Mario in his *barriada* in Lima, either by himself or in free cooperation with his neighbors, is very likely to be spurious. According to Turner, the problems the squatter settlers feel most strongly involve their frustration to work and build.

The huge poverty-based settlements being built around most cities of developing countries are important because they are becoming the dominant form of urbanization, already involving hundreds of millions of persons. Moreover, these settlements provide us with a compressed natural history of urban development. Cities were originally impermanent encampments, then evolved into permanent habitats with numerous lines of improvement, and finally, in some cases, achieved one or more attributes of excellence in performance and beauty: classic Venice, Kyoto, and Isfahan, as well as Athens and Rome. Today part of our lesson lies in the opportunity, choice, and freedom to build in humble settlements. Part lies in the conception of ultimate possibilities.

At best the improvability of settlements with impoverished beginnings now extends ten or twenty years after first settlement. After that, we can foresee, even in the best of humbly founded settlements, a plateau of a decade or two, followed by a general and steady decline into the dead-end trap we call slums. In less fortunate areas, the rise will be of shorter duration, more modest in extent, and the decline more precipitous for the occupants. A corrosive trap will have been set on the human spirit.

How, then, do we find a basis for continuous improvability and a degree of protection from subsequent loss of vitality and deterioration? Experience in the United States convinces us that a rising income alone is not sufficient. On the other hand, rigid standards and codes of construction are impossible to implement in the early and critically formative years.

An initial lesson is found in the illustration of a dwelling passing through its "natural history" of development, a process normally requiring at least fifteen years. Theoretically, such a dwelling could be developed to spaciously accommodate an upper-middle-class family, provided that each step is carried through with that ultimate goal in mind. The important elements for a progressive and smooth construction of a dwelling that will one day achieve adequate standards are: (1) A calculated and controlled improvement of building materials, possibly beginning with temporary use of cardboard, packing crates, tarpaper and tin, but shifting to the use of permanent building materials, such as lumber, stone, concrete, metal, and glass. (2) A coordinated progression to permanent, high-standard methods of construction worthy in design and durability to an ultimate (although flexible) house plan. (3) Provision for eventual incorporation of all utilities and appliances. Underlying any successful program depending on self-help methods is articulated and flexible assistance by government, especially financial and technical.

Although strict building codes cannot be imposed in the early stages, government could create a "development code" in which building regulations would apply differently at each stage of development within a particular settlement or neighborhood. Perhaps each step of a graduated development code might be adopted on motion of the people themselves through their official association or council. This procedure would maintain maximum local freedom while encouraging the neighborhood to perceive its goals clearly and to cooperate in achieving them. Government assistance might be designed to act as an incentive for a neighborhood to shift to higher standards of construction at reasonably early dates.

The Urban Implosion of the Population Bomb

So far, so good. The dwellings of a neighborhood may be expected to noticeably improve each three or five years, and in a way that will encourage progress toward very substantial excellent homes over a period of, say, fifteen or twenty years, possibly as long as thirty. Still, the longer term barriers to improvement have not yet been removed. They are more complex and rest in the physical setting of the whole neighborhood and the extent to which the whole urban pattern encourages improvement and maintenance of each dwelling: the schools, parks, community facilities, shopping and other services, as well as utilities.

This dimension of improvability is only primitively perceived, although it has vast implications. Inevitably it rests on higher organization abilities, always on government to an important degree. Yet, for the same reasons that squatter settlements are dynamic when they have the freedom and encouragement to build, a maximum degree of locally organized initiative should always be encouraged.

Thus, perceiving a steady neighborhood evolution is as basic as the steady improvement of the dwelling itself. Aside from being essential to the protection and enhancement of property values, an astute long-term neighborhood strategy is critical if economically ruinous and socially disruptive slum clearance is to be largely avoided in the future. Equally critical is the necessity of creating vigorous communities capable of sustaining identity, cooperation, multiactivity association, pride, and tradition—avoiding the vacuous alienation of tract-built suburbs or block-built apartments. Local initiative, local autonomy, and local power are foundations for stability and improvement. The primary role of government is to encourage and support them, as the essence of both development and democracy, creating the conditions in which social growth is possible.

The neighborhood imprint that lasts longest is the first to be created: the property and access lines, easements and public spaces, and the clear definition of the neighborhood. Therefore, a vision of ultimate neighborhood development must be astutely set in the initial layout, regardless of how many years its realization may require. Basic changes may be possible at later stages and may even be incorporated into the original scheme of the neighborhood. But, as we shall see, the possibility of making nondisruptive alterations to an ultimate plan is dependent on a long-term plan that encourages future vigor and cohesiveness of the neighborhood or continuous improvability.

Quite precisely, our objective is, in the words of a 1963 United Nations report, to promote "the physical framework in which man's human, social, economic and cultural resources are released, enriched and integrated" (United Nations, 1963, p. 1). Can it be any less without courting common disaster?

The Higher Potential

The ultimate question, therefore, is how urban development can concretely release, enrich, and integrate the highest human potential.

As incongruous as the idea may seem, I believe that both the problem and the potential of cities are seeded in the dynamism revealed in the uncontrolled settlements around Ibadan, Allahabad, or Davao. Admittedly, the accomplishment will not be easy. But I believe it can be done through building a human ethic of development, an inspiration of what cities *can do* and *can be* in everyone's life.

Two ingredients are essential at the outset: (1) a conception of the urban potential, and (2) a wide span of experimentation to demonstrate the specific opportunities and realities, accompanied by an understanding of the stages and conditions needed to fulfill the potential. Although one is a conception of ends, the other of means, each is best established if fused with the other.

Let us start with assisting urban settlers to obtain the simple sites and services. Planners in the *barriadas* of South America have found that a few public services, mainly potable water and simple sanitation, are initially more essential than formal shelter. Once a plot, minimal services, and temporary shelter are available, the beachhead stage shifts, in Turner's classification, to the self-improving stage, in which the settler builds his own permanent shelter, room by room. Although emphasis in this period is necessarily on private improvements, several community questions become increasingly pressing—notably a school, transportation to employment centers, and commercial services.

Typically, after some years, when the household reaches its first level of adequacy (basic permanent shelter), another stage of development begins: the qualitative improvements, including appliances and the house-connected water, electricity, and sewers. Unlike bare shelter, every internal improvement then depends on a neighborhood improvement: the pipes and wires that connect them to the house, as well as the source facilities. The importance of collective action becomes prominent once again, as it was at the outset.

To date, these three stages—beachhead, basic shelter, and qualitative additions—represent the maximum improvability that a typical poverty-initiated settlement can normally expect. Significant progress into a fourth stage is largely denied, not by income but by a poor original layout and the lack or poor quality of the common spaces necessary for the new improvements. These are essentially the factors that can improve the whole range of neighborhood quality: *good* school grounds and park facilities; *aesthetic* appearance of the dwellings; general *landscaping; convenient* and complete commercial services; transportation *frequency, flexibility,* and *convenience;* and *quality* and *range* of the school program.

It is at this time—between the third and fourth stages—that those families which have most steadily improved their own circumstances are most likely to relocate into a contractor-built neighborhood. When they do, they exchange organic growth for class status. They assure the end of the growth process in the original neighborhood by denying it the improvement energies and monies it otherwise might have had. A new family that moves into their dwelling is likely to be at an earlier stage of self-improvement and unlikely to continue improvements because its resources must be devoted to paying for improvements already made. When improvement throughout the neighborhood begins to falter, the neighborhood changes its role to that of a social stepping stone, until finally it becomes an environment of social degeneration and deprivation.

For the new middle-class family, the move represents a shift into stage four. Most contractor-built mass housing—whether in the central city or suburbs—represents stage-four achievements, although public transportation and certain local conveniences can be ignored if the family then owns an automobile.

Today more neighborhoods than dwellings falter in the improvement process. Neighborhoods require more sophisticated concepts and more sophisticated organization. They require the assistance of government. They require an effective local organization, a local mechanism to give impetus to freedom through collective means. Hence, continuing neighborhood-wide improvements are rare. Organic growth is stunted and fails to evolve the fuller, open-ended human possibilities because these possibilities were not perceived or incorporated into the neighborhood's original genetic endowment and aspiration. The aspirations, the physical pattern, and the institutional form were not equipped for long-term growth.

That higher development—or what might be called an open-ended stage five—is today beyond both the vision and capacity of middle-class neighborhoods. Such neighborhoods are designed to be guarded, isolated, and sterile—nondevelopable. Some of the important elements of higher neighborhood development include: a strong and vigorous neighborhood council with numerous active corollary organizations; vigorous local traditions (including the tradition of improvement), celebrations, and festivities; diverse community facilities (pools, gyms, dance and art studios); a variety and quality of personal, social, and cultural opportunities; and a close interweaving of neighborhood activities. Together these elements create a unified whole in the perceptions and behavior of the individual.

This last stage should be understood as unique to each neighborhood, reflecting the particular social interests of its members. I therefore refer to it in a suggestive rather than definitive way. What is important is that stage five cannot occur without a positive human ideal of the city and its local living units. The material benefits and environmental qualities are at this stage mainly preparatory and supportive of an open-ended range of social opportunity.

It is useful to plot the five stages to clarify the major components of improvability or growth and to show the relative importance of family, neighborhood, and governmental involvement at each stage. Figure 1 gives a hypothetical outline for improvability.

Several critical factors emerge in Figure 1. First, each stage has validity to the extent that it represents a major barrier to or a threshold into a new potential of improvement and growth. That

Figure 1. Hypothetical Continuous Habitat Improvability

Stages and Relative Requirements

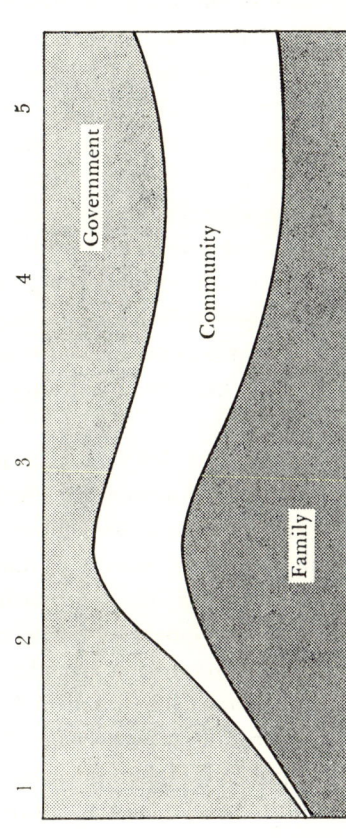

Stages and Improvement Roles

	1	2	3	4	5
Government	Sites and services	Schools, transport, technical assistance	Utilities and connections	Complete all facilities	Respond to aspirations Facilitate social and cultural growth
Community	Organization of council	Manage water and sanitation; organize self-help cooperation	Start community center; promote social organizations	Expand social services and improvements	Broaden family and individual horizons
Family	Temporary shelter	Basic shelter	Shelter improvements; plumbing and appliances	Dwelling refinements and broaden basic opportunities	
Time range	1–2 Years	2–8 Years	5–15 Years	5–15 Years	Indefinite

is, ceilings of improvability are more likely to occur between than within the stages. Each stage involves not only a new set of circumstances but also a new kind of perception before it can be seriously undertaken.

While I have stressed the role of government, especially in planning, assisting, and guiding each community unit of urban development, one of the most important objectives is the creation of a general community organization that steadily increases the locality's ability to act willfully on its own behalf. Community strength and self-reliance will be improved by delegating as many functions as possible at an early time to its direction and management.

At this time, a general conception of stages one, two, and three are influencing policy on urbanization problems in many of the poor countries. Stage four is understood mainly as a standard of development in contractor-built housing projects. There is little recognition that living areas that have passed through the earlier stages are capable of becoming high-standard stage four neighborhoods.

Stage five, although quite hypothetic at this time, is a necessary concept if the city is ever to humanize development. As it is, the dominant bureaucratic ideals are antithetic to actions that would remove people from the socially alienating system of bureaucratic power. This higher stage of development is nevertheless essential to understand and initiate at the outset if its potential is to be reasonably achieved within, say, three to five decades.

The perception of ultimate importance illustrated in Figure 1 is the essential role of multilevel cooperation at every stage. Without highly articulate and timely support of higher governmental bodies, all human settlements face unbridgeable chasms. Moreover, the development of the higher social potential requires a form of community that can respond directly, intimately, and holistically to the individual in a cohesive local setting. Perhaps one day the most strategic role of national or municipal governments will be the development of self-reliant community.

It is not desirable to impose a rigid timetable for the stages. Every neighborhood is different and must meet each challenge on its own terms. Then, too, some elements of one stage may occur in another, as fortuitous or debilitating circumstances appear. However, it would seem that a neighborhood could not normally move solidly from humble origins into stage five in less than about thirty years; although, with broad vision, perhaps many elements of social development could be initiated in the earlier stages.

What I have done here is project the concept of human growth and social health on one of the most important physical and institutional organs of the city: the community. Community is an idea of social unity, as is the idea of the stages of development. The city badly needs measures of human well-being. The stages leading to an ideal form, such as social community, offer a start, especially in unifying our presently separated and sterile conceptions of physical, economic, and social development. The stages also bridge the radically different conditions of cities in both the industrially advanced nations and urbanizing Third World.

It is the conceptual unification of urban development at both poles of today's economic development ladder that may set us on the trail of a common ideal for urban living. That ideal can encourage immense diversity in specific tradition and form while also establishing universal criteria in humanizing the instruments of change.

Ends and Tools of Development

What are the city's logical and necessary roles in world human development? Here I say "human" rather than "economic" development because the latter has become seriously estranged from the former. If Western cities have imposed a specter on human worth and progress, as well as set the stage for ecological tragedy, then shaping the wildly growing cities of the Third World into the destructive Western mold certainly courts unrelenting social tragedy and irreversible natural disaster. Under narrowly conceived economic development, the city is no more than a medium endlessly accelerating production and consumption. Such a concept neither recognizes nor consciously uses the whole city—its location, size and form, or its generative and integrative power.

Nowhere do we find in development planning a clear conception that the city itself is one of the central *objectives* of the development process—as well as one of its most basic tools. Created environments are possibly the most articulate achievements and penetrating conditions of social progress. How life is enhanced, how beauty is created and perceived, how human growth is underwritten, how freedom is expanded—all these reach to the essence of development. All are creations or conditions shaped and given vitality by the city. By reducing development to a multiplication of output, society degrades its human members at every stage, regardless of the lure of gross material wealth.

If we are to bring the individual to the forefront of development, we must make the *nature* of the city faithful to his purposes. And it is in the *nature* of the city that we can best achieve savings, investments, and technical advancements—and make them beneficial in life. The city's organization is the foundation, not only for aspiration but for human commitment. Savings are not only the dollars that finance industrial growth. They are also the endearing and affective assets of the city that call forth pride and encourage personal growth and hard work by every person.

Economists have taken for granted the cultural heritage of a society. They forget that they are creating a new world society. Should economics become, as seems likely, virtually the sole objective of development, economics will also become the content and the limits of the culture that is coming into being. Economists are not prepared for this burden. And if technology and management are effectively the sole operative means to create the new world economic order, then we may truly fear the end results.

When we perceive the city as a fulcrum for development, however, we can begin to perceive each of the special areas of development in a new light. For example, a high priority would be given to that form of industry which builds the city: construction. Already economists know that national investment in the perennially short housing market can be highly rewarding in classical economic terms. United Nations reports have stressed how, among the paradoxes of the city, construction, one of the oldest technologies, is today one of the most retarded. It is no accident that backwardness of construction and backwardness of the city exist together.

The backwardness of cities and our perception of them as passive containers has seriously distorted the role of industry. The excessive or misplaced production in the economically advanced nations is founded largely on excessive distances and wasteful forms of transportation. This bias is taking hold in the newer nations. Workers in Bombay and Lagos now commonly spend a large part of their low income and three or four hours per day in commuting.

Similar distortions are appearing in public services where socially destructive conditions are imbedded in the urban development process. As a consequence of disorganization in the early stages of urban growth, epidemics appear and then demand scarce highly trained health personnel. Costly flood protection is provided to areas that should not have been developed in the first place. Rising crime rates force the expansion of already burdensome and questionable police forces. The cars of the wealthiest 5 or 10 percent of the population command huge public investments for streets, parking, and even freeways.

If Jane Jacobs' argument in *The Economy of Cities* (1969)—that towns grew *prior to* and promoted agriculture in our neolithic past—is correct, perhaps a strategy of urbanization is the most acute step that could be taken in modernizing agriculture in the poor countries. The case is very substantial. If a regional plan of deliberate urbanization were to promote an eventual pattern of cities varying in population from twenty thousand to five hundred thousand in areas now basically rural, a series of positive and powerful forces could be set in motion.

First, the planned expansion of selected small towns into full urban centers providing a wide span of services at closer distances to rural people would improve the range and quality of services, especially education in villages within twenty to forty miles. Many rural elementary schools now operating without a framework of literate behavior lose the impact of literacy. To obtain and retain literacy, people require reinforcement and use, which distant and backward villages cannot provide. Four, six, or eight years of isolated schooling are just not enough. In the first generation of education for a family or village, a secondary education is generally required for a permanent and general impact. But a secondary education is largely an urban affair. Small and medium cities are ideal places to establish these crucial secondary schools or agriculturally oriented universities. Such a pattern of small cities also offers opportunities of informal education through frequent casual contacts with the village people.

Second, varied rural extension services at well-located town centers will increase their effectiveness by being physically near the farms and by reinforcing each other. Urban tools, skills, advice, and money encourage the use of better seeds, fertilizers, and pest controls. Improved buildings and equipment can be provided only by cities of reasonable size. Cities close to the farms also encourage better processing, storage, and transport of farm produce. Tragic quantities now rot or are lost to rodents and insects.

Third, when rural people who now live in a hard-to-improve cultural isolation are brought into close contact with the attitudes, institutions, and services of a growing town, they unconsciously prepare themselves for the urbanization that most of them are likely to make in this or the next generation. If the nearby town is growing vigorously, they can move there, rather than to the larger, more distant, and more alienated city, while still maintaining regular contacts with their families in the nearby villages. A continuity is maintained that is impossible if the move is hundreds of miles.

Rubbing shoulders between urban and rural lifestyles has always been stimulating. Now it can be used as a constructive vehicle of development, particularly if the city is not too distant, large, and inscrutable to the rural peasant.

An examination of the ingredients necessary for human development reveals that, initially at least, they are amazingly few and often very simple, compared with that demanded by megatechnics. At the outset the requirements are simple improvements of health, food, and shelter. The primary foundation for all of these is education. Moderate incremental investments, small as today's investments go, can underwrite them. No fantasy of thousands of nuclear power plants. No IBM giants. No rush to drill for oil under the sea. Industry is essential, of course, but subordinate. It is best developed in smaller doses and in better balance.

When these concrete and primary objectives of development are underway, the role of education becomes even more central, concerned more with the ends of development, the individual himself, and the cultivation of new values that replace or, better, modify and enlarge on the older comforting but confining traditions of the

The Urban Implosion of the Population Bomb

people's rural past. At this point the values and processes of education and urbanization become united. They can be encompassed in one great goal: the building of the city and its diversely enriching and challenging opportunities. When environments that genuinely serve human aspirations interplay with an equally exciting growth of knowledge and understanding, the entire development process directly underwrites human growth.

A new, somewhat larger level of industry then becomes both necessary and desirable, but again the purpose is entirely supportive rather than basic. Consumer goods will expand, but their sheer quantification will have no meaning. The encumbrance of too much will become immediately evident, unless of course the city is organized to promote waste and the society is driven by conspicuous consumption.

Humankind has learned enormously during the process of industrialization, but in the last few decades that kind of learning has become destructively one-sided. The future of creative learning and of human development lies in imaginative environments: made and modified environments interweaving with the natural; environments that relate human beings affectively; environments that educate; environments that are works of art and that promote the arts and humanities; environments that enlarge human value, including a sharper sense of the past and a clearer inspiration for the future. The framework, content, integration, and balance of the human environment will be as limited or as far-reaching as our vision of the city.

The meaning of the urban environment is doubly important in the newly developing countries. The human pressures are greater. Resources will be more limiting. Time is short. The dead-end of irrelevant, uncontrolled industrialization is becoming known and can be avoided in these nations.

Some persons have said that the fate of development lies with the billions of poor peasant farmers. This is a distractive and dangerous pastoral sentiment. Our fate rests with the direction people are going, not where they have been, only partly where they are now. Those who shape urban environments shape the content of the future. The unlearned peasant has little to offer development except his ability to respond to the opportunities before him, most notably those opportunities stemming from the cities. If our fate in any way does rest with the peasant, it will be on that momentous day when he puts down his wooden plow and walks barefoot into the city. The question is how we are to prepare for him.

It is a sad commentary on human intelligence that world society should stumble into industrialization and development crisis by crisis. It is a pity that we promote industrialization as if we were compelled to consume the entire storehouse of the earth within a century. We manufacture almost anything to consume but build very little of human essence and create even less of lasting value. "There is not only a world-wide crisis of urbanization," the seventh Delos symposium concluded (reported in the *ATO-ACE Newsletter* of September 1969), "but there is also a basic distortion of values in society's failure to allocate resources for the improvement of human settlements, the upgrading of the total environment, the strengthening, protection and education of the young, and the equalization and enlargement of individual opportunity . . . we must establish the condition that will release the human will to act."

10

Can We Build Good Cities?

Society is awakening to two sets of apparently contradictory facts. The first, gradually rising in everyone's consciousness over the last four hundred years, is a vast working order based on highly sophisticated science, complex technology, huge corporate bureaucracies, and an incredibly successful exchange system of economics.

The second set, hitting us bluntly only within the last two decades and felt deeply as yet by only a very small part of the population, is the recognition that the vast working order is rapidly undermining the premises on which it was built, indeed, is undermining life itself: the store of energy, metals, and other resources; the natural ecology of plants, animals, and habitats; and, not the least, the emotional and cultural sensibilities of the human beings who are chained to its compelling demands.

The summary message of several hundred books appearing since 1965 is that time is exceptionally short to make fundamental corrections. But the corporate powers seem to be constitutionally unable to read the urgent messages. They prevent democratic government from either awakening to or acting on the closing circle of realistic options.

Yet the literature is not just a doomsday report. Either hidden or explicit is a new promise for human life. Many writers could be cited. Here I quote Bernard Gross (1971, p. 295) of Hunter College, "We find no other animal species that has been as savagely destructive as humankind. In moral terms, civilization is something that has not yet existed . . . might humankind perhaps build the first civilized human society?" That challenge is both a historic crisis and a great promise.

The hopes that lie ahead inevitably rest on a vision of the human habitat. Today cities are a mixture of known and unknown, fantasy and fiction, truth and ignorance. They contain dangerously stagnant backwaters of unbelievably dynamic science, technology, management, and economics. More than any other sector, the virtues of cities have become villanous and their power to create degenerative.

Cities are the eye of the rising storm of an unprecedented conflict between man and nature. They are misunderstood, built with incredible recklessness. They connect the magnificence of our time and the destructiveness of modernism.

It is deeply disturbing to observe that the problems of society that are coming to count most are those that seem to be understood least. World achievement arises only where there has been general aspiration and keen awareness. Unfortunately, cities have not shared in society's central consciousness. Yet cities frame all other questions, directly or indirectly, whether crime, the arts, emotional stability, or simply the maintenance of society on the planet. Progress in the next half century will rest deeply on how the centrality of the city in human life is recognized.

The city is now the ghostly framework of both our problems

Can We Build Good Cities?

and our possibilities. It is for us to create cities as the constitutional foundation for the human potential.

Logic of Unreality

The modern city has become a structure that diabolically creates new necessities for products and services that are not inherently necessary and not original to the individual. Too often one finds oneself driving alone in a four-thousand-dollar vehicle at perhaps five miles per hour in stop-go traffic on a $10 million-dollar-per-mile freeway between oversized places with overspecialized services. The mammoth services and transport facilities are too small for the size, volume, and demand of the machines we build. Driving one's car for repairs to an auto dealer on a ten-acre site on the other edge of the city reveals the compelling futility. Then our vaunted pragmatism of science, technology, management, and economics appears as a cruel charade, unreal and degenerative in the maintenance and conduct of life.

Today each separate activity on a separate property, determined by the so-called free market, demands a fragmentation of the city to the limit supportable by transportation. A wide street in front of every property symbolizes both the waste generation and the social division. The overlayed pattern of boulevards and freeways assures larger spaces, longer distances, and more mandatory travel.

The city then becomes insatiably mobile: the increase in individual movement and the industry to maintain it; the increase in consuming more resources and destroying more environments; the increase in the isolation of the individual and the compulsion to travel in more directions to meet one's increasingly synthetic needs.

Americans, more than most peoples, have attempted to remove themselves from the limits of nature, not only from the elements but also from time and place. The American tradition of living directly on large and isolated farmsteads remains deeply within us. As the pioneer broke through and cleared the wilderness, he succeeded precisely to the extent that he could subdue and reshape it.

The development of cities also departed from nature, ironically in a nostalgic idealization of the rural past. The urban lot was the new homestead, the job the new cash crop. But whereas the farm had been a relatively self-sufficient unit of production and consumption, the urban homestead became solely a unit of consumption. As it grew in size with affluence and suburbia, the more consumptive it became.

The automobile—the greatest prize of commercialism—was especially powerful in promoting and then demanding private mobility, private spaciousness, and private recreation (including recreation rooms, pools and barbeques, as well as radio and television). It was hardly noticed that as work became more demanding on personality through enforced socialization of production and office routine, free time became more ardently private and isolated in the single-family house and car. Concomitantly, association became more defensive and less free in the name of privacy and individuality. Private life became synonymous with nonwork life, and privacy became a narcotic relief from enforced socialization on the job.

It is therefore hardly astonishing, despite the known privations of rural life, that according to George Gallup in 1972 only one fifth of the people living in cities with populations over five hundred thousand would reside there if they could live where they wished. Is this part of a pathetic inversion of social behavior? Is this not one of many human unrealities we build into cities?

Psychiatrists have long observed that psychotic individuals not only make wrong judgments about reality but that their observations of reality are cognitively wrong. If that is the case with individuals, can it not be true for society? Is there not evidence of a streak of psychosis rising from the deeply radical changes and forced adjustments occurring during the last one hundred years: migrations, urbanization, industrialization, mass media, depressions, and wars?

Should we not seriously ask whether society has not acquired a kind of psychosis relating to collective life in cities? Are not many of our most common observations about cities cognitively wrong? A mere listing of some subjects we have considered reveals wide and serious gaps between observation and reality, value and value achievement, and causes and effects. Recall, for example:

Can We Build Good Cities? 291

- Spaciousness and compactness (high land consumption and urban congestion)
- Privacy and one-family cars and houses (or human isolation and individuation)
- Individual transportation and flexible and convenient travel (actually forced auto travel at huge public and private costs)
- High urban development standards and urban stability (the fifty-year cycle of decay and escape)
- Wealth and urban quality (where does the wealth result in great achievements of urbanity?)
- High mobility and effective access to services, friends, and opportunities (the growing inaccessability and alienation)
- Open land markets and desirable urban form (inefficiency, lack of amenities, low cultural opportunities)
- Productive efficiency and consumptive efficiency (forcing everyone to consume arbitrarily)

Faulty perceptions imbedded in these examples underlay the degenerative paradoxes of the city. They represent a kind of truth not fully understood by empirical science, cause-and-effect mechanics, direct-authority administration, exchange economics, specialization, and objectivity. The city, like the body, is boundlessly complex, not only in the way it functions but what it functions *for* and how behavior changes through experience and growth. Scientific truth allows for no opposite truth, no higher truth than an experimental proof. More important, the subject of the city is not critically considered with the same idealism and purpose—or objective pragmatism—that we apply to, say, product development or business management.

If the city is anything at all, it is a pathway for many kinds of truth, many processes of becoming, each uniquely valid to individuals. As such, the city is value-seeking rather than right or true. But since our history and philosophy is nonurban, if not antiurban, in origin and sentiment, the truly urban potential easily becomes clouded and suppressed.

Our pragmatism is based on acting according to narrow self-interest (or group special interest). Have we not yet learned that the greatest self-interest arises from the broadest human interest? An individual's range of potential fulfillment grows directly as the context of interests grows with others, such as the diversity of opportunities presented by a whole city. The widest human opportunities are, after all, the gift of civilization. Sooner or later, the practical realities of narrow self-interest pursued as a social manifest become impractical illusions. The automobile was grand, indeed, when it was new and few, but it dominates and debilitates the whole human environment when it has been multiplied a hundredfold.

Today's city embodies the brilliance of thousands of valuable particular innovations. More tellingly each decade, however, the city embodies an accumulative illogic of the same innovations profusely strewn among us, changing the whole city into a burden and destroying the city's simple livability.

According to the current growth ideology, the city can grow to any size and take on any form. But in today's reality, the result is always a dinosauric massiveness. Weighty imbalances are set right by equally burdensome counterweights or armor plating—the social defenses, the social disciplines, the therapy. Note the sense of desperation with which we built the fantastically expensive freeways and parking facilities for fantastically expensive individual transportation. Our per-capita income has doubled about every fifteen years since 1920. But are we more than three times better off? Hardly. Although no one can doubt the many specific benefits occurring in those decades, the sheer overhead grows and reinforces itself.

Promotions continue to be the solution to the problems caused by promotion. Lee Thayer suggests that it is insane to continue believing that we can solve our ecological crisis from the same ideologies that originated the crisis. Our contradictions now bite so deeply that we stand in danger of having to build a synthetic environment to replace the natural setting we are so assiduously destroying. That environment, if workable at all, will inevitably distort all that remains in our earthly treasure and all that is human. Drinking water will require increasingly complex processing. Air will have to be filtered for many. As wood resources diminish, we will use more synthetics fashioned as wood grain.

Of all of our harsh realities, it is the transiency of the good and the permanence of the bad—such as saying that "we will have to adjust" to the degenerative direction of things—that is most ironic. We have excellent designers, but they cannot create more beautiful and permanent environments. They create advertisements. They design bottles, packages, and labels for lotion. They make fashions for one season. They mold cars for the next model year. These impermanent arts, however, contribute to permanent waste: the mountains of garbage, the costly recycling and the permanent loss of fossil fuels. Much of the most imaginative architecture is similarly done for six-month expositions. Many fine buildings, such as the Imperial Hotel in Tokyo or Penn Station in New York, succumb to the feasibility of more "economic" uses of land.

A final irony is beginning to appear in the return-to-earth movement by those adhering to a simple ecological ethic and subsistence ideal based on nineteenth-century farming practices. In this disguise of bucolic nature, we may find the worst ecology of all. This movement may have something to say to society while it is small, involves but a small population, and demonstrates the benefits of "organic" farming overlooked by the massive agricultural functionalism. We do need to learn more about subsistence economics, about work that is individually productive and creative within a framework of modern knowledge, and about communes and human values under varying kinds of sharing and intimacy.

As a model for any large population, however, the back-to-earth movement can do little more than create vast belts of Appalachia with hard-rock poverty and acute human deprivation. The American population has grown by nearly one hundred million persons since our rural population hit its peak on 6.5 million farms in 1935. It is difficult to imagine any worthy enlightenment or "prosperity" occurring with a high rural population density. A very small population might perhaps live comfortably on the fringes of a wealthy society. A large population decidedly cannot.

The new ruralists may believe that the affluent society will collapse. But if that were to happen, we would have an entirely new order of problem, a disaster of unthinkable magnitude. The promise of ecologically sound and socially inspiring cities is that we can avoid such a collapse.

Money Against Cities

Viewed in classical terms, the modern economy is extraordinarily productive and beneficial. However, there can be no justification for the destruction of cities or nature. Yet, in the practice of economics—that is, in the realities of money—a ruthless process promotes destruction of whole cities and whole environments.

Contemporary economics is a growth machine that knows no limits, prized precisely to the extent that limits are exceeded. When Garrett Hardin (1968, p. 1244) wrote "The Tragedy of the Common," he rightfully asked us to "exorcise the spirit of Adam Smith" who popularized the "idea that the individual who 'intends only to his own gain,' is, as it were, 'led by an unseen hand to promote . . . the public interest.'" Such an ideology resting in the power of a corporate economy combines wild fecundity with eventual mass suicide. Such a situation closely parallels the behavior of lemmings. However, in the case of industrial man, the first cycle of industrial expansion and death may be the final one. The unseen hand may have made a full turn.

The economic problem, wrote John Maynard Keynes in 1930, has been the most pressing problem of humanity: "If the economic problem is solved, mankind will be deprived of the traditional purpose." With uncommon prescience, Keynes asked, "Will this be a benefit? . . . I think with dread of the readjustment of the habits and instincts of the ordinary man, bred into him for countless generations, which he may be asked to discard within a few decades" (1963, pp. 366–367). And in but a few short decades, many elements of the traditional economic problem have been solved.

Since we have valued money and have not valued cities, it may be useful to compare them. The city, more than money, reflects the real commonwealth of society. The city is physically real and therefore basic; it constitutes the physical and institutional framework for the things that are most human. Money is a

Can We Build Good Cities?

lubricant for social exchange. The city is fundamental in determining how we share and works best in making all things possible and accessible. Money, however, favors power and elitism. When the city loses its democratic and social vitality to moneyed power, then great internal walls guarding privilege are built into the structure of the city, easily dominate it, and in so doing, reduce the benefits to everyone.

A pervasive influence of money in society presents a double treachery to the human qualities of the city. First, the rapid growth of money and goods acts as an incessant bribery of the body, mind, and spirit. The mind is excited by visible gadget improvement and comforted by the security of paid vacation, health, and retirement programs. The spirit is intoxicated by the games of goods. The intoxication is promoted by advertising, the most powerful and pervasive propaganda ever conceived. The individual is, quite directly, bribed away from conditions of well-being and vital living to gross consumption.

This treachery is reinforced by a second invidious effect. Deteriorating cities promote growth of the GNP, as I have demonstrated (see Chapter Five). Conversely, an excessive growth of private goods directly causes deterioration of the urban environment. Then private goods, once nonexistent or unimportant, become *essential*. When *public* facilities or amenities decline or do not keep abreast of the human possibilities, then much larger volumes of *private* purchase must fill the gap. Private goods then heighten the disparities between the rich and the poor. These disparities are particularly vicious because high consumption becomes necessary for effective membership in society. Goods purchases become not only increasingly necessary but a matter also of personal competence and status. Economic growth, when based on inefficient or undesirable cities, thus moves deeply into the recesses of human motivation.

Today our measurements of money and goods are highly sophisticated. They ostensibly measure a social good—wealth—but they provide no indication of effective *use,* either of personal or public wealth.

If social value is to be enhanced and protected, many measures (representing many values) must vie with each other in estimating personal well-being or social health. We are beginning to employ a few measures, such as the numerous special censuses (especially of housing, transportation, manufacturing, retail and wholesale trade), the *Social Indicators* (ranging from health and housing to crime and recreation) published by the Office of Management and Budget, and the Environmental Protection Agency standards for air and water quality. Still wanting are better measures covering such matters as basic urban efficiency (especially the consumptive efficiency of individuals); the kinds, levels, and qualities of urban amenities; the quantity and quality of various natural and built environments; the conditions that promote health and informal education; the variability and flexibility of opportunities provided by organizations; growth of freedom; and the variety, vigor, and excellence of human endeavors.

Transportation provides an example to demonstrate a potential breadth of evaluation that we might apply to each given element of the city. Here I suggest five things to measure.

1. How well does the urban system *minimize the need to travel?* That is, how accessible is each function of the city to the individual? What portion of an individual's time must be spent in necessary movement?
2. To what extent does the urban system *utilize the most effective forms of transport* and plan them to achieve their full potential? We have not measured environmental/transport effectiveness of walking, transit, cycling, and automobiles in relation to various urban forms.
3. How well do the transport arrangements *minimize land consumption, environmental degradation, energy, and other resource use?*
4. What are the overall urban costs, efficiencies, conveniences, flexibilities, and reliabilities of various transport solutions?
5. How does the transport system and each of its elements support the economic, social, and cultural goals of society?

The measures that help evaluate city life inevitably rest on our expectations of the city. When our expectations are narrow, as they have become with money, our actions and evaluations also become restrictive and distorted.

Urban Inflation

The concept of inflation has a powerful and peculiar relevance to cities. By analogy, the American city can be said to suffer from acute and aggravated inflation of its land, resources, machines, and goods. Unlike the devaluation of money, which we all watch closely, the devaluation of urban environments is only partially recognized.

While urban inflation continues seemingly without end, a companion process operates, which Grady Clay aptly describes as "a run on the environment." In cities, the self-propelling engorgement of things causes the urban environment to become too much with us. Conversely, the engorgement demands the "run" that propels a constant and partly unrecoverable depression of the storehouse of nature. We have seen how the debilitating space-distance-mobility sequence operates in a circular fashion to arbitrarily accelerate consumption, how the process is embedded in our ethic of development, and how the process assures decay and escape. This sequence is but the most visible dimension of the urban inflation.

The response of individuals in cities follows the classic formula of behavior under runaway monetary inflation. People anticipate the relative shift of values, they speculate on it, and they accelerate it. Only government can bring it under control. Governments, although they attempt to slow economic inflation, are themselves serious offenders in the inflation of cities. They sanctify and partly require sprawl in planning and zoning. They then subsidize the inflated urbanism with immensely costly boulevards and freeways, water and sewer lines, police and fire protection, schools and busing.

Inflation may be one of the best single indicators of the sickness of today's cities. Comparable to an "overheated" economy or high temperature in the body, it signals serious maladjustments, a challenge to basic performance and, in extreme, a threat to existence. The analogy could well lead to important insights about the nature of cities.

No question is more pressing than the raw consumption of land. Fortunately we have many clues suggesting that the benefits of the environment increase precisely to the degree that human intervention is minimal, selective, and concentrated. A modest intervention in nature is not only better ecologically, as the conservationists argue. It is also better functionally, as mass production and micro-miniaturization suggest.

The inflation of land, resources, machines, and goods of the city ultimately points to a shortage of land, resources, machines, and goods. Since they are never put into balance, each forces the endless expansion of the others. Tragically, this expansion means a depression for people as well as nature.

From Problem to Promise

No matter how many hard reasons we find for society's dismal failure to produce humanly satisfying and workable cities, the question of *why* we fail continues to plague our conscience. Although I have focussed on the traditions and more direct causes of failure, I could have made a case that we should have built better environments under our present traditions. It is obvious that our traditions were not shaped to create the vision, organize the resources, and build a distinctive basis for urban truth, beauty, and justice: a vision of human truth of collective living, of human fulfillment in man-made environments, of fuller grace and intimacy in living, learning, and growing together.

But still we are plagued with the question of why we did not do a better job. This question, I suspect, will bother us in the future like a lost battle that by all odds should have been won. Perhaps the best answer at this time is that as a society we do not yet realize how crucial the battle is or how badly we could lose. Perhaps we think it is for play when it is very much for keeps, a side skirmish when it is the crucial engagement. Perhaps I am wrong, but the many ominous issues of society point to a central dynamism that we seem to have missed.

Perhaps also the history of modernism is passing through

its greatest watershed, where the individual's motivations and inner being, and with them the economic and political forces, are fundamentally realigning themselves. Technology has now made possible what Mumford refers to as plenitude. A new range of the human spirit seems to be on the horizon, an observation gleaned from artists, humanists, hippies, mystics, psychologists, and individuals who perceive a society, not in nineteenth-century utopian or perfectionist terms, but in terms of inner and interpersonal potential, a more meaningful experience for every individual.

Never before has this level of human potential really existed, perhaps not even for the upper class, for they had to constantly defend their elitist position. Defense saps energy, confines aspiration, alters values and goals. True equality makes trust and openness—the prerequisites for individual growth—possible.

Our past and current revolutions can reveal the wider dimensions of simultaneous creativity and destruction, trained brilliance and congenital ignorance, release and confinement, humanity and brutality. These things were crystallized in the eighteenth and nineteenth centuries as a manifest destiny and resulted in the creation of what we know as the *Establishment*—power creating, privilege promoting, centralized, and singularly exploitive. As such, progress was technical, instrumental, specialized, inorganic, un*whole*some, and unable therefore, to serve the wholeness demanded of things human.

It is presumptuous to say in these complex times that any one thing will bring salvation or real fulfillment. I do not think it is presumptuous, however, to say that the city is deeply involved and may be central in giving our complex circumstances a coherence for the individual to behave creatively and to grow on his own terms.

Whatever our perceptions of the good and the possible, we can no longer allow our immense and really superhuman powers to operate outside the vision and direction of a human parliament. Unlike the rest of nature, from which we have now so effectively set ourselves apart, the only effective restraint on powerful human action is the collective human intelligence. At minimum, an antitrust act is necessary to prevent an unstable technoeconomic monopoly over intelligence itself.

With justification we can say that we do not have a workable science and profession of city-making. It is instructive that Abraham Flexner (1930) found city planning to be unworthy of inclusion in the university curriculum. If planning were based on a simple grid layout, Flexner would be right. But if the city is central in the ultimate science of ecology and in the ultimate profession of design, then following his advice would directly undermine perhaps the most urgent question of the university's development of higher intelligence today.

Unfortunately, the professions and sciences of urban development operate without a demanding ideal. Our values and goals stand in arrested development. We strive hard in a frantic race for change. But we are not clear about what we are striving for. Every sector of urban life cries out for a sophistication of *purpose* to match the onerous sophistications of methods and operations.

But society has a great capacity to learn. When the questions are posed effectively and recognized widely, important solutions can be expected. The grave challenge today, as I have frequently stressed, is time and perception. The momentum of the past requires between twenty and fifty years to redirect. Every year lost makes the present momentum more ominous.

Urban Gift of Freedom

Reduced to its essence, the human significance of all theory and design of the city is freedom. We are sorely overdue in recognizing this dimension of freedom.

Freedom is, of course, complex, often paradoxical, and always in question. I take as a point of departure the idea that freedom is intimately connected with human value, a position well stated by Julian Huxley (in Gutkind, 1962, p. 91): "The well-developed human being is, in a strictly scientific sense, the highest phenomena of which we have any knowledge; and the variety of individual personalities is the world's greatest richness." The connection of value to freedom has been stressed by Jean Paul Sartre: "Once man has seen that values depend upon himself . . . he can will only one thing, and that is freedom as the foundation of all value. . . . And in thus willing freedom we discover that it depends entirely upon the freedom of others and that the freedom of others depends upon our own" (in Goodwin, 1974, p. 121). No interdependence underlying freedom is greater than that created in cities.

If our interdependent freedom rests on the interdependence built into cities, that freedom is today in double jeopardy: from the abiding chaos that binds us to the maintenance of the overbuilt, underorganized urban environment and from the well-organized powers that profit from the chaos (ironically in the name of freedom).

We note, in Richard Goodwin's (1974, p. 189) words, that "the most traditional form of bondage is that imposed by material necessity." Ours, however, has become a bondage of surfeit, waste, and inner destructiveness. As William James put it: "Lives based on having are less free than lives based either on doing or being."

Goodwin has, I believe, defined freedom in a manner that is genuinely valid and significant to our time. He says freedom is "The use and fulfillment of our humanity—its powers and wants—to the outer limits fixed by the material conditions and capacity of our time" (1974, p. 24). He further stresses that freedom is not the creation of a particular kind of social order, but rather a "statement of historical possibility." Implied is a delicate balance of the material, organizational, and environmental conditions that broaden freedom *for the individual*. Freedom is not protective and static, but a positive setting of vigor and growth, limited only by human imagination and abilities and symbolized by the aspirations and hopes of people throughout their lives.

The demanding question for cities is how they can be shaped to achieve what Friedrich Engels has called "the leap from necessity to freedom." Commenting on Engels' phrase, Kenneth Boulding (1968, pp. 100–101) suggests that "We begin to make this leap when our knowledge of social systems rises to the point at which some sort of control becomes possible so that the future is no longer in the hands of necessity and chance. . . . The more inaccurate our knowledge of the social system, of course, the less the element of freedom in it."

Put in these terms, the city, as the most critical embodiment and organizer of our modern social system, is an instrument for freedom to the degree that we understand and develop its potential. It will achieve higher potential only to the extent that we incorporate that knowledge into all facets of urban life. Unless we understand how dynamic and deeply social freedom is, how dependent on the positive actions of society, we well never recognize the range of freedoms that the form and function of the city can radiate or suffocate.

In today's city, many freedoms are either blatantly or subtly tyrannized. We are not free to expend our "high" incomes as we would wish: we must purchase goods that we do not really need or want. People stay home for fear of life and property, threatened by persons who are deeply alienated and deprived by the city. Participating in (or trying to expand) the cultural life of the city is an exponential burden posed by the urban logistics of facilities, management, cooperation, and transportation. We must drive even for a loaf of bread and are prevented from taking recreation walks because of forbidding and dangerous environments. All restrictions are legal, but all deny our being or doing in some vital way.

Building the good city is a way of building freedom—positively, dynamically, and creatively—building for human choice, human diversity, human experience. The good city creates opportunities for a wider span of human intimacy, trust, and faith. If "society does not *provide* ways to choose," says Goodwin (1974), the choice is excluded from its notion of freedom (italics mine).

Our concept of freedom has been narrowing with the complex and more demanding urban condition. Truth and well-being are increasingly identified with institutional interest. Public affairs are seriously reduced to economic feasibility, essentially profit. Ironically, the billions we have spent to relieve traffic congestion merely induce traffic and compel the spending of billions more to serve the newly induced traffic.

Somehow, our passiveness about cities, our aggressiveness about economic growth, and the simple-minded pragmatism connecting the two have virtually made increasing urban necessity into an ethic. A psychology of suppressing freedom in cities for survival and profit arises among us, parallel with the growing legitimacy of violence. As we have observed, many ideas of freedom—privacy, private ownership, private initiative, and honest individuality—are fostered in a setting of social chaos that rebounds to infringe on or deny those same freedoms. Private action in a mass, complex society is illusive. In Goodwin's words again, "To say that people wanted cars, that production simply responded to demand, is to claim that individuals, alone and as members of society, also decided to devastate and reconstruct . . . human existence" (1974, p. 299).

The city is a structure of human behavior and, if good, a structure of freedom. Such conditions are discernable, designable, buildable. Such conditions can be constitutionalized in the form of the city. When society begins to seriously debate social and environmental rights, the lines for a constitution of cities will become clearer.

The constitution of urban freedom will need to recognize the urban paradox. For each right, each freedom, there is an opposable right and freedom: private *and* public life; great "compactness" for intense human behavior *and* great openness; places of permanence and security *and* places for experiment; ownership *and* the possibility of nonownership; easy mobility *and* immediacy of access; high productivity *and* an efficiency of consumption, with a permanent and easy system of recycling.

Freedom means diversity but not chaos. Although often appearing as freedom, chaos is really a process of deterioration and disintegration and therefore a denial and a threat to the individual. Freedom means many avenues created for individual and group choice, for *ad hoc* initiative, for spontaneity and interplay among the serious and the trivial things of life, for the organized and the casual, and for both the permanent and the passing. In the end, I suspect that the social dimensions of freedom will approximate our ideal of the city and our idea of its organic forms and functions.

One writer suggests that our one-sided notion of *E Pluribus Unum* be modified to *In Pluribus Unum,* which would strive for plurality no less than unity, a unity that now threatens our national heritage of diversity. The deathly singularity of suburbia, in tandem with homogenized, finely graded education and a vision of the good life as an inundation from the horn of plenty, reveals a reverse swing of the pendulum from the time when regional and old-world divisions of population challenged American unity. Our traditional diversity now permits us to glory in and to develop a richer national tapestry. A new richness is no longer to be expected from another immigrant wave, although immigration might continue to freshen the national character, but rather from nurturing the incredibly wide possibilities of human experience.

The urban ideal of freedom, we must also note, is antithetic to privilege, status, and power because the best city is primarily a perfection of dynamic sharing. To be sure, cities historically emerged with a concentration of social power that underwrote people-dividing privilege and personality-rigidifying status. But mature concepts of freedom and equality are also urban in birth and development. The challenge before us in enlarging urban freedom is to make it fundamentally equalitarian. I submit, therefore, that if the city is the frontier of freedom, building urban freedom demands that we do battle with inequality and privilege in all of its forms.

Democracy can truly exist in a large society and people can have power over their personal destinies only when the individual's primary dealings are framed small enough, close enough, and responsive enough to be relevant to their individual human aspirations. We have lost much of that freedom and that potential in the functionalism of cities. The impersonal market and its driving forces of alienation are incapable of buying and selling either the humble or the great human satisfactions. The corporation is socially out of control because it effectively shapes social action and urban form in such a way that one can respond only to power and money. How can a society be free when the components of freedom more basic than law are restrictive and yet compelling, frighteningly isolated, and narrow the base of personal stability?

In human terms, where do we find an ethic of urban development? In our time, is not the deficiency of an ethic a part of the deficiency of urban form?

A difficulty of any age is to perceive the pressing questions of the next. There are powerful reasons to believe that the vital issues of the next decades at least will revolve deeply around the nexus of interpersonal behavior and that the crucial determinants will be found in the organization of urban life.

If we begin to perceive the city in profoundly human terms, we will, I believe, also perceive it as the fertile medium for a high-energy democracy with social, cultural, and spiritual dimensions that each rise to equal our political heritage. Democracy can, if we will it, blossom in a new springtime, boundlessly flourish with new genetic vigor. But the city can be a medium generating the unfathomed richness of the human spirit only if successive visions and cultivations operate at the "microscopic" human scale of our gargantuan metropolitan areas.

One day we may understand that freedom is a gift of cities, perhaps in the future more than direct political action itself. The urban importance of freedom has been growing for more than two centuries in our country. By some accounts, an American nation was impossible until the mere half dozen towns of Colonial America had grown large enough to gestate an "urbane" or mature perspective of national life during the decades prior to the Revolution. Today the city's equally important gift of freedom remains undeveloped, muted, confused and in danger of deep erosion.

Toward Awakening

"We need a general theory which encompasses physical, biological and cultural evolution; which contains an intrinsic value system; which includes criteria of creativity and destruction and, not the least, principles by which we can measure adaptations and their form." Interestingly, this statement, with its immense implications, was written not by a philosopher or social theorist but by an ecologist with a background in landscape architecture: Ian McCarg (in Smithsonian Institution, 1968, pp. 216–217).

McCarg's statement, although by no means unique, strikes at the root of social theory. It is *unifying* in character and *purposive* in intent. It looks toward a *human* future directed by a civilized process rather than by undirected particularistic exploitations. Human *diversity,* human *value,* and human *growth* are founding assumptions. Social and ecological *harmony* are implicit. The roles of science, measurement, and monitoring are envisaged to maintain harmony and stability. Yet a vibrant, vigorous, free, and challenging life for individuals is clearly the prospect. What McCarg and many others are beginning to say is that we are finally awakening to the revolution we have created.

Out of the travail, chaos, injustice, and insecurity of our time seems to be arising a new outlook no less spectacular than the rise of that vision of life we call modern. It is premature to fully understand the shift, of course. But we cannot escape the responsibility of giving it direction.

Western man has prided himself on being the measure of all things. Eastern man has prided himself on being a part of all things. Perhaps our awakening is that humankind is completely a part of and yet the measure of all things, able to achieve that Godlike quality of self-creation that might endow our enormous powers with the inner restraint of form and function exhibited in the natural evolution of the higher species. In this, we may find a merger, suggested by Goodwin, of Marx's idea of "returning man to himself" and the American ideal of the "pursuit of happiness."

We are experiencing an emergent rebirth of humankind, founded, if you like, on our morass and confusion. Voices are rising with new perceptions and fresh determinations telling us, in Ivan Illich's (1971, p. 93) words, that "the human adventure is just beginning." Illich calls on us all "to say one great 'Yes' to the experience of life." When we do begin to discover a new and courageous spirit, the super evolution called civilization will brighten with an inner and perhaps greater human inventiveness.

These words may seem to be delusions of grandeur. My answer is that human evolution lies solidly in human hands and that only in our time are we beginning to become conscious that we *can* write our history in the future tense. We can at least broaden freedom to the limits of our historic possibility. Rene Dubos (1968, p. 215) relates his perception of that possibility, saying that "The most spectacular achievements of the first seven decades of the twentieth century would pale in significance if we did manage to create environments in which human beings, and especially children, could safely express the rich diversity of their genetic endowment." But this possibility, Dubos adds, will require a change in the course of science and technology.

The new and not yet widely accepted field of humanistic psychology may have discovered the outcroppings for a profound human advance. The chief mentor, the late Abraham Maslow, suggested that the new psychology is part of "a new philosophy of life, a new conception of man, the beginning of a new century of work" (1968, introduction). Maslow daringly proposed a humanistic science to develop the capability for creating "one good world."

Maslow felt that human nature is either neutral or good in foundation, without the depravity and evil requiring constrictive control by society. Human destructiveness and cruelty, he said, do not seem to be intrinsic but rather reactions against frustrations and deprivations of basic needs, emotions, and capacities. This approach is beginning to be recognized in areas of endeavor with which Maslow himself remained unconcerned. I refer, of course, to the environment and particularly to the environments we make—and the way that they in turn remake us—one of the most ignored subjects of modern learning.

Slowly, some of the gaps are being recognized, among them environmental psychology. We find some early dialogues taking place between environmental and humanistic psychology. For example, Mayer Spivak, working with concepts of Roger Barker, has postulated a theory of *archetypal places,* specific settings that serve particular human needs from eating to interpersonal relationships (Spivak, 1973). When some of the settings are absent or inadequate and the need is unfulfilled, a setting deprivation occurs. Spivak notes an acute case in the treatment of mental patients. The more sick the patients became, the more restrictive their environments were made—a cause and effect relationship of deterioration—until they were transferred to a ward for intractable patients.

Setting deprivation exists in the city when functional places are in conflict with or isolated from each other. "Opportunities may be too far away for walking, and walking may be the most desirable way to get there. . . . Access to some settings may be restricted to the wealthy. . . . For people without a car, the trip length, the time and the expense may render such trips either infrequent or impossible" (Spivak, 1973, pp. 45–46). What people do in reasonably adequate settings is make a *place* out of a *space.* When we fail "to provide a complete range of archetypal places within our communities, and if we do not compensate in the larger community for those we no longer can contain within our homes," says Spivak, we "may produce feelings of rootlessness, disorientation and a dissolution of the cohesive bonds present in more healthy states of social organization." The direct implication of the theory of archetypal place—and of other theories awaiting creation—is, as Spivak asserts, "a higher architecture" aspiring to enrich human behavior.

The obviousness of depraving or enriching environments, however, seems to have been lost in the raw quantification of goods and the rude accumulation of power over nature. When Rene Dubos (1968) says that human potentials are expressed only as far as circumstances favor them, we too easily interpret this to mean special advantages or a particular kind of opportunity for favored individuals: books, travel, elite schools, or entree into business, the professions, or politics. How barren and fragmented have our efforts been to create a superior setting for all persons? How long will it be before we discover a great new commonwealth of human growth, a setting for a qualitative change in life no less significant than the commonwealth of material affluence obtained through perfection of a particular kind of sharing for industrially produced goods? Again Dubos (1968) has alluded to this horizon, suggesting that the latent potentials of human beings may surface "when environment provides a variety of stimulating experiences." As more people express more of their biological endowment in different situations, society and civilizations grow and benefit, as Dubos notes.

The city cannot be viewed as anything less than fundamental in organizing life, not only for the minimally essential archetypal places but for all higher human development. Within such a perspective the city embodies two sets of cause and effect relationships governing human behavior. First, the city profoundly defines both the physical environment (such as the quantity and quality of spaciousness) and all social institutions (such as their human scale or their democratic responsiveness). These mold our attitudes, stimulate (or dull) our thinking and aspirations, give us security (or threaten us), and shape our behavior. Subsequently, our changed behavior is reflected in specific pragmatic changes in the environment.

Second, in the much larger frame of history, the powerful environments and institutions redefine or re-create the entire ethos and ideology of the society. The scientific tradition evolved in recent centuries represents one such shift, for it massively transformed

Can We Build Good Cities?

our way of perceiving purposes, values, and challenges—how society characteristically defines and responds to its problems and possibilities.

Because all valid theory of human development rests inevitably on ideals of life, we cannot honestly escape building ideals for the city. The major hurdle to perceiving worthy urban ideals is the tendency to reduce all values to one measure, whether we speak of cost-benefit calculations of specialized projects or a purely material and monetary measure of success. A theme is required that translates our revolutionary changes into a setting of life that will amplify human experience.

Organic City

To perceive the city as an organic entity is to perceive urban life in a whole and unified way, with a definable condition of good health and human fulfillment. Also implied is an aspiration guiding a process of evolution toward a higher definition of good health and fulfillment.

The phrase *organic city* suggests that, like organisms in nature, the city has an inner form, a symbiotic pattern of organs, tissues, and cells that maximizes potential with a minimum of internal bulk or burden. That quality of form, resulting in strength, economy of action, special capacities of each species, and unique beauty and graceful performance—superbly revealed by a running cheetah or gazelle—must be consciously built into the city through a new kind of design that creates the necessary wholeness and unity (as well as diversity).

Although all living things clearly do not display equal endowments of form, all demonstrate wholeness and unity as a necessary principle of existence. *Wholeness* means identity, a clear distinction between what an organism is and what it is not, the primal separation between organism and its external environment. Identity permits the integrity of biological functioning, whereby each internal organ is dynamically balanced with all others. Balanced form and function are only possible with a well-defined wholeness, a body that does not grow endlessly or indiscriminately merge with other organisms. Medically, a break in wholeness is a wound or infection that threatens the integrity or life of that organism, for which the body is endowed with defenses.

Unity is equally vital, and involves the ability of the body to perform coherently, to constantly adjust for internal balance, and to perform purposefully in an environment. Unity means a centeredness, biologically a nervous system integrated by the brain, an endocrine system guided by the pituitary, and a sensory system that screens stimuli to create coherent and meaningful perceptions.

Wholeness and unity are always present but never complete or perfect in any species or in any single organism. Both are present in life and disappear only on death. Both wholeness and unity involve not only an inner form and harmony, but also a harmony within the environment. That harmony is also never perfect, but it is suggestive of an ideal and a condition of health.

In nature, many hardy plant or animal species become threatened by changes in the environment within which they evolved. Others with specific genetic weaknesses can prosper if man puts them in special environments and cultivates them. Perhaps this protection is necessary, but it promotes weakness. The cultivation creates a dependency, which occurs in most domesticated plants and animals through long periods of "unnatural" selection. We have learned to breed new genetic lines, often thereby creating an even greater dependency on particular environments and particular forms of cultivation.

The urban "genetic" endowment has proved to be exceptionally fluid. Fundamental genetic reformation is possible in a relatively short period of time. So also is genetic deterioration and dependency. As yet we hardly recognize this possibility, despite the radical changes occurring in the last hundred years. We have put the city into a completely new context of industrialization without giving it a genetic constitution by which it can withstand change and prosper. Consequently, the city deteriorates under the impact. Most of what is lost in the city's ability to respond is made up by an inordinate cultivation (material support and effort) by the historically new industrial system.

Cities depart from the biological analogy in at least one critical way. Whereas the value of living things resides in their

Can We Build Good Cities?

organic whole rather than in the individual cells, the value of the city rests in individual human beings, not in the whole, organic city. Human purposes reside entirely in the person, not in the urban collectivity.

Still, the legitimacy of individual human life derives from organic urban environments. Apart from healthy, fulfilled human beings, a concept of a healthy city is irrelevant and meaningless— and apt to become tyrannous. Although the city, like the cell, may therefore be considered organic, both the city and the cell are completely subordinate to the one organic entity where all purpose in life resides: each living human being. The cell is the organic basis for human life. The city is the organic environment for human fulfillment.

The tragedy of cities becoming less organic, almost anti-organic, is that human growth is stunted in favor of megamechanical growth, which is founded on the disunity of urban sprawl. The massive scale promotes a faulty urban performance that destroys the vitality and spontaneity of people. There is no guiding endocrine system to establish size, function, relationships, balances, or make the "biological" adjustments necessary for best functioning or highest individual freedom.

Analogies, of course, are easily carried too far. Their value exists only in being provocative. The value of extending the organic analogy to cities is that nature has evolved many species with long lists of superb qualities that carry direct inferences for both human excellence and the ecological stability of cities.

Being organic involves a working relationship among all parts and processes of a plant or animal that enlarges inner capacities and bestows inner freedom to the individual. Freedom— to grow and develop and to experience with others in each individual's own way—is the essence of our stay on earth. Our mind is generally free of instinct, except for a pattern of behavior that is culturally acquired. The challenge of society is to assure that our culture helps us to grow while it also enlarges our freedom and cultivates our inner worth. Nature has freed us of binding instincts. Our culture can now free us of binding social inhibitions.

Of course, we are bound to our bodies and their needs. But nature has opened to human beings a wider scope of life, permitted us, so to say, a metaphysical and metaorganic life through the self-directiveness of our intelligence. Now it is time for our new nature, our culture, which has created fantastic new capacities, to free us for a new metacultural horizon. That will happen only when a collective intelligence and common vision come to understand how individuals can be infinitely enriched by their interactions with fellow humans and with the environment. The physical and social environments can raise the vision. The vision can raise the environment to a higher level of human possibility.

Yes, in Goodwin's terms, freedom is a statement of historic possibility, positive and dynamic rather than guarded and static. The options of cities are infinitely profuse before us, perhaps as great as those existing in the period of the transition from the cold-blooded mesozoic reptiles to the warm-blooded mammals, or the development of noninstinctual intelligence of *Homo sapiens*.

Here the concern for cities is acute because they now endanger our future. They have set arbitrary upper limits to freedom and taken many freedoms out of the reach of law. It is time to consider cities as human possibility sets in creative interplay.

Society's Master Mechanism

How, then, should we begin to think about cities in organic terms? When we ask this question we are saying, in effect, that we can build genuinely good cities that are as improved over those we know today as the giant Boeing 747 compares with the Trimotor Ford air transport of the 1920s or as organ transplants compare with bloodletting in medicine.

Good cities will not be built until Americans decide to write the city into the American Dream. Cities are not just commerce and industry, jobs and economic growth, or suburbs and shopping centers garnished with some parks, universities, and Red Feather societies. Cities are the stuff of civilization. Civilization will be no more profound than the ideals, love, and imagination we build into our cities.

The validity of the city rests on two overriding questions. The first is *how the city relates human beings to nature:* to nature's resources and the living environment, to its reserves of life-giving elements, to its variety and beauty, to its natural history and the awe of life itself, and to the exhilarations of both natural wildness and human order. The second is *how the city relates people to each other:* to achieve security and comfort, to establish opportunity and develop creative challenges, to foster the most fundamental kinds of companionship and human warmth, to kindle the human spirit in its thousands of manifestations, to relish the diversities of the human mind and emotion that find expression and growth only in the flow and force of collective life.

These two questions are the essences of cities. They are the city in continual change. Our recent history, however, reveals a confusion of unprecedented emergence combined with unprecedented denial. The urban essence we foresee does not disregard the prosaic functions of production and exchange, but rather gives them purpose, focus, and an esprit beyond thoughtless profit.

Our social future is being determined by the city we have so foolishly neglected, so wildly overbuilt, so badly structured. If the city may be described in economic terms as being the most useful "machine" and also the most valuable "product" of industrial society, should we not then perceive it as a master mechanism of society, more profound ultimately than economic policy? But we have not yet discovered (or created) either an urban equivalent to the simple balance of supply and demand in economics or to the feedback controls in automated production.

To build substantially better urban environments based on growing ideals and aspirations, we must first clearly perceive how we went wrong in the environments we have built. Let us therefore summarize some of the more basic lessons of urban development derived from the present analysis.

1. *Cluster for Spaciousness.* Cities are inherently concentrations of human activities, and it is the management of compactness that makes for effective and good cities. Cities of old often managed compactness quite well. Today we have the capacity to do it much more dynamically. Cluster development has received much attention for over a decade, but most of the proposals have been too limited, too partial, and too undeveloped to establish an effective human environment.

In clustering, there are two critical considerations. First, when carried out with good design, clustering promotes human effectiveness by complementing and combining activities to bring things together to work in larger wholes. Making multiple use of spaces and facilities, reducing transportation, shortening communication, and providing for less rigid interpersonal relations. Second, spaciousness, within either man-made or natural environments, results from a conservation and effective use of all space, that is, clustering spaces to their most effective scale rather than multiplying burdensome dead spaces, such as useless yard spaces, or promoting wasteful movement and excessive vehicular spaces.

2. *Integrate for Efficiency and Amenity.* The good city depends on *how* things are joined to work together and avoid conflict. Our history of functional segregation through zoning, however, has destroyed urban integration, built new conflicts, and added new space and distance requirements while increasing the demand for otherwise unnecessary industry, commerce, energy, and pollution. Massive individual transportation reduces rather than increases access to all things we need and want. We commute long distances by car because we want to escape the chaotic degradation that has resulted from these actions. The process is pragmatic in specific decisions but totally illogical as a collective consequence.

The future art and science of city-making will be founded on how living, working, shopping, transporting, and recreation activities can be *united* in full harmony for all individuals. This unification can be accomplished in part through a kind of microminiaturization, in part through systems that optimize bulk, weight, and energy (such as that used in the design of a jetliner), and in part through systems that make effective use of urban geometry, improved construction, and advanced lighting, air conditioning, and communications. Integration is the ripe challenge of urban design.

3. *Cluster in the Third Dimension.* Integration works best in contiguity. The possibilities of contact without conflict multiply with the articulate use of three-dimensional space. Only then can urban life really become dynamic, that is, achieve the full advantages of compactness *with* great spaciousness. However, the real dynamism is not activated by simple stacking and concentration of activities in one-use, high-rise structures. Rather, it will operate

fully only when many activities are integrated at many levels of space. Today this burden of integration is put almost completely on the second dimension or ground level.

For this reason, the third dimension remains possibly the largest "undiscovered" resource of cities and awaits theories of urban geometry that will demonstrate compatibilities and complementarities that we do not yet believe are possible. To date, multi-storied buildings are woefully unimaginative and take little account of integration made possible by basic advances in construction, heating, lighting, air conditioning, energy conservation, or solar energy.

4. *Multiply Nature in the City.* Clustering the built environment allows clustering open spaces into very large acreages, enormous by any measure of today's urban parks and playgrounds. And the very large and more varied urban open spaces would also be much more accessible than today's scarce nature in the city. Consider how gathering thousands of useless sideyards and unwanted front yards alone would multiply the natural areas within most cities. These valuable areas of unlimited potential could multiply again if we drew on the half of the urban land that is now preempted by roadways, parking areas, and auto services. It would then be possible to explore the many possibilities of urban farms, urban forests, more diverse parks and playgrounds, more golf courses, pastoral meadows and lakes with farm or wild animals, long hiking trails, special sanctuaries and habitats.

The benefits would be enormous, varying from less storm water runoff and cleaner air to nature education, natural beauty, recreation, and significant output of food and wood. The vastly increased open spaces would also help create distinctive urban form and improve the validity of the whole urban system.

5. *Build Clusters as Complete Urban Growth Units.* Community provides a simple building block for rational, integrated, and efficient urban development. The location, scale, and form of community growth units can be organized to optimize the highest possibilities of the city: to the individual, to the community itself, and to the city as a whole.

Community units should function close enough to the individual to respond directly to him *as a person,* to give him a sense of power in determining his course of life, and to encourage him to be a vital participant in society. Community should provde a sense of place, a social context, and a personal continuity necessary for a personal integrity in society. The current massive, undifferentiated form of the city demands large, specialized programs that do not suit people and that leave them powerless and frustrated.

The community itself could become an effective unit of production and consumption (including the provision of goods or services, from electronics to tourism); a valuable unit of ecology (from minimizing the need for resources to efficiently recycling used material); a vigorous social center (including highly varied recreation, religious, and cultural endeavors); a unit of government (making local self-determination a reality of urban democracy); a focal point unifying transportation (walking, transit, and automobiles—without conflict); and a highly articulated unit of social intercourse and analysis (understanding the wider range of human problems and possibilities).

To a city or metropolis, the community establishes a local, self-reliant element of civic and social development. Metropolitan government could be freed of all matters without metropolitan significance. Communities become natural forums for vital civic dialogue through varied and informal, yet powerful and pointed, interpersonal and group communication. Diverse communities also provide varied, continuing experimentation on hundreds of important questions of human settlements.

6. *Reduce Mobility.* When we realize that we can *radically reduce the need to travel while improving the freedom to travel,* we will add a major new element to the mutually reinforcing lessons we are setting forth. All of the lessons considered here help to reduce mandatory movement. Reducing the need to move supports all other lessons. And unless the lessons do clearly reinforce each other, there can be no real integration.

Reducing mandatory travel will occur when clustering, integration, the third dimension, open spaces, and community growth units are unified in a way to optimize each of their specific possibilities. Travel requirements will decline as a general result.

Although we equate mobility with freedom, enforced mobility directly denies freedom and becomes personally deadening and environmentally destructive. Our aim, therefore, is "free" mobility, freedom to live well and diversely at home, freedom to travel when the legitimate benefits of travel beckon us.

7. *Rationalize Mobility.* A critical corollary to reducing mobility is rationalizing the modes, routes, and the man-made environments that serve mobility. In environments built at a human scale, no system of movement is more efficient, pleasurable, and economic than walking. Within such environments one would not need to walk more than is now required to walk to and from the inhospitable parking lots and garages. Still, the possibilities for pleasurable walking on promenades or paths are endless and can be inexpensive, as transport investments go.

When cities consist of concentrated community units, we can make the most efficient use of the most efficient form of mechanical movement: transit. When we do so, transit will acquire the convenience, flexibility, and utility we once thought we had with the automobile. Transit's demand for land is but a tiny fraction of that commanded by automobiles; its use of energy is about one third. With rational and minimal routing, many lines can be located underground, especially in the vicinity of the three-dimensional communities, where stations would be located in the basement and cause not a flicker of conflict with other urban functions.

The role of the automobile then becomes like that of a boat or personal aircraft, oriented more to recreation than to necessary movement. Then, once again, it will become the joyous plaything that excited automobilists the first two decades of this century.

8. *Strengthen City Centers.* An essential counterpoint to distinctive communities is a strong cosmopolitan center. A diverse and complete urban center is vital to integrate the life of the metropolis, be it production and exchange or transportation and cultural life. The urban center, like the cell's nucleus, is the basis for urban existence, providing the unity that organized life requires. A strong urban nucleus was mandatory to achieve minimal urban performance and public participation in the past; our gross development of industrial power, however, transferred much of this huge burden to transportation, which necessitates a rate of resource consumption that cannot long continue and which promotes a literal disintegration of economic, social, and cultural life.

9. *Build at the Human Scale.* The lesson penetrating all others is that city environments work best at a human scale, instead of a scale designed to suit the power, speed, and consumptiveness of machines. The term *human scale* refers not only to the visual bulk of things in relation to the individual, as architects debate, but how the things of life work in human terms: space, distance, time, numbers of people, size of institutions and services.

Human scale means human relevance, the integrity given to people by the structure of the city. Scale is the level at which the individual operates most efficiently on his daily rounds. Human scale directly affects how we form human relationships, how we develop trust, bond, and good will. In urban terms, whether in a building, a plaza, or a park, an appropriate scale of the human setting is also a necessary part of a serenity of behavior, a casualness of association, a freedom to choose when and how the chores and pleasures of life are composed.

10. *Grant Local Self-Determination.* Everything modern, it seems, has shifted power to larger and larger bodies, in social and cultural affairs hardly less than in economics and politics. Self-determination by groups close to the individual is a basic and profound part of freedom. Yet we have little theory and less inheritance in granting, promoting, and supporting the local roots of freedom that give power to the individual over the conditions of his existence in metropolitan areas. Today the instruments of *social* democracy are at best distant, fragmented, and unresponsive to the individual.

Politics burst out of the reach of individuals with the emergence of metropolitan masses. The impact of mass urbanization reduced democracy to the bare elements of voting, having confounded the lines of common interest (through undifferentiated masses and confused jurisdictions), popular dialogue, and indigenous leadership, while building the power of naked economics and special interests. Perhaps we need to consider a bill of rights around the *local* and *individual* significance of the urban environments, economic processes, social relations, and cultural opportunities. These intimate dimensions spanning all of urban life are essential if we are to rebuild grass roots democracy according to the realities of the metropolis. Otherwise cities will continue to be altered principally for profit and power.

We hardly need to detail the vast practical benefits that might arise from these lessons. In broad scope they include great savings of individual time and institutional expense, reduced resources use and pollution, greatly reduced need for fire and police protection, diminished public works, improved productivity, and a dramatically better economy of consumption.

The independent validity of each lesson can be demonstrated on many grounds. More importantly, the effectiveness of each lesson greatly increases when united with the others. Happily, too, the benefits to natural ecology are simultaneously benefits to social humanism—a magnificent complementarity our society seems to have lost.

11
The Urban Future

When traveling and living abroad in a number of less industrialized countries I was impressed, like many observers, by the way people were completely immersed in the chores of just maintaining life. Many of these chores seemed unnecessary, repetitious, unduly burdensome, sometimes futile. On returning to the United States, however, I was deeply struck by the same observation. This time, however, people seemed to be as completely immersed in the chores of maintaining the Establishment—corporate, governmental, union, health, and education. In perspective, many of these chores also seemed to be unnecessary, repetitious, unduly burdensome, and frequently futile. Since then the process of development has taken on a completely new meaning for me. What we did in our development of great industry was transfer social maintenance from a local, communal, personally supportive system to one in which behavior and values are externalized and depersonalized in a centralized, bureaucratic, and technical system.

I do not mean to suggest that we should retrace our steps to poverty. The process of development has, of course, resulted in a vastly wider range of choices in life. Yet we must ask ourselves whether we have really made the best of our sophisticated systems of organizing and making things. When I set out some years ago to obtain a dwelling, what I acquired had little to do with what I had originally sought. Despite my deep concern for the debilitations of suburban life, my family ended a long real estate search by buying a house in an area that was indeed suburban: large lots, mixed urban and rural development, four miles from downtown (a metropolis of but one-third of a million persons), services scattered to the reaches of stamina. Within months we were *forced* to purchase a second automobile, as well as a mower and numerous garden tools. Soon we found that we were not only chauffeuring the children to their friends and activities but also denying them privileges and opportunities they otherwise would have had.

These events were especially dismaying because we knew that each of our "choices" reinforced the current market pattern, that is, the demand for suburban houses, a second car, the mower, and hundreds of lesser items. We wondered, too, how many tens of thousands of equally basic choices in this one urban area are forceably bent every year by the same distortion in the market mechanism.

Is this lack of choice not a basic question of freedom? Is it not also a basic question of the technology, bureaucracy, and economics that create such constrictiveness of behavior? In short, is not lack of choice also the basic problem of the city? When we have become overwhelmed by the maintenance of the establishment, are we not really talking about the arbitrary burdens built into the city?

Our age demands a new humanism. The question we cannot fail to raise is whether we can build a humanism of technology, organization, and economics without simultaneously pioneering a new humanism into the cities we are still in the process of creating. The city is the necessary context for all three of these commanding instruments of modernism in our lives. The city defines their relevance, fitness, and usefulness; that is, their fidelity to human ends.

Urban Humanism

The present course of society rests on a momentous wave of change. Man has given a narcotic meaning to this change, which we call success. Success has signified the removal of natural obstacles and the breaking out of a terrible confinement into, it sometimes seems, an ecstatic infinity of discovery, money, and power. Yet how much do we learn from success? A success that has outlived its usefulness may prove more harmful than failure, as Peter Drucker has noted. Is not the trilogy of technology, organization, and economics our greatest success? And does not the enormity of this success, which in many ways is no longer of use, also mask an equally enormous failure in our cities?

As the momentous power of business—the locus where technology, organization, and economics join together—continues to find new crests at ever higher levels of success, we begin to feel deeply the vacuity of humanism, which has penetrated the roots of all human organization—the anonymous, manipulative workings of bureaucracy, no matter how lofty the purpose—as well as the increase of corruption. "There is a widespread questioning of the legitimacy of institutions, especially on the part of the youth who would normally move into elite positions," writes Daniel Bell. "The major consequences of this crisis—I leave aside its deeper cultural dilemmas—is the loss of *civitas,* that spontaneous willingness to obey the law, to respect the rights of others, to forego the temptations of private enrichment at the expense of the public weal. . . . The loss of *civitas* means either that terrorism and group fighting ensue, and political *anomia* prevails, or that every public exchange becomes a cynical deal. . . . One may forego interests yet still retain beliefs; or lose beliefs yet have an interest stake in the society. But where trust in a society and its institution is battered, and where interests fail to gain the recognition they feel entitled to, there is an explosive mixture ready to be set off" (1974, p. 46). Unfortunately, such a criticism rests on much fact.

Some critics are less polite. Seymour Betsky argues that America "is a culture without a central intelligence, without a comprehending mind, without a sense of order and control." Betsky concludes that because we encounter so few "convincing celebrations of love . . . we can affirm that culture has virtually wiped it out," and that America "builds in forms of schizophrenia."

Whether one rejects the indictment or qualifies it as being a transitional condition of a society on the leading edge of change, an undeniable problem of serious proportions nevertheless confronts us, especially when considered against the broad base of issues raised by persons of the stature of Arnold Toynbee or by huge numbers of social dropouts. Nor can one ignore the incessant turmoil of economics, national affairs, local affairs, or the family.

But, neither can one deny that an entirely different kind of age is on us. What it is, we do not yet know. That it involves a fundamental metamorphosis of social existence is certain. What now challenges us profoundly is the need to give the new age an indelible stamp of humanism.

Humanism has not played a significant role in our aspirations, except as defined in the foundation documents of the American nation or perhaps as a logical extension of the development trilogy of technology, bureaucracy, and economics (for example, high wages and great purchasing power of the worker). The laboratory and factory, the office and counting house, and even the formal classroom and sophisticated hospital hardly signify the places where humanism is forged. Given the Establishment's sheer prevalence, its talent for achieving disciplined performance and redirecting human motivation, and its restructuring of the physical and social environment in its image, little wonder that the subtler questions of humanism have been clouded or suppressed.

Now, in this new age, something powerfully fresh is happening. So far the primary symbols of the new turn of events are the social dropout, the deepening social chaos, the growing social schizophrenia—hardly the inspiring foundation for a new humanism. Yet these are accompanied by a profusion of grass roots social experiments ranging from meditations and love projects to ecology movements and neighborhood corporations. Specifically rejected by the new movements are the high technologies, powerful hierarchies, and big money of the American success. Still lacking is a common ethic, a restatement of our traditional terms of success, and an acceptable social strategy to make a new system both workable and diversely human. These are also the minimal requirements for acceptance by middle America.

So far, society is unprepared to declare its independence from the establishment it created, to rewrite human interdependence in a new union of self-motivating individuals, to use the higher paradoxes of life as a dynamic interplay of human growth. That is, we are not yet prepared to commit ourselves to Aristotle's definition of happiness as the full use of one's essential nature or to Goodwin's definition of freedom as "the use and fulfillment of our humanity . . . to the outer limits fixed by the material conditions of our time" (1974, p. 24).

What we are speaking about is a richer cultural setting created for a higher image of human personality. Pericles described something akin to this personality in the citizen of Athens, who "in all the manifold aspects of life, is able to show himself the rightful lord and owner of his own being, and to this, moreover, with exceptional grace and exceptional versatility." Human personality is indeed a fulfillment without limits. Can there be any higher motive for a declaration?

A richer cultural setting for a higher fulfillment of human personality forcefully returns us to the burning issue of the city. The city remains the pervasive framework of life that barely figures into political theory; the critical environment that is almost completely absent in philosophy; the central structure of human behavior without basic human ideals; the medium of industrial development lacking principles of unity, efficiency, or economy. Until society focuses astutely on this indispensable medium of culture, this genesis of personality, this fundamental physical context for the diverse functions of society, there can be little hope for a new humanism. How else can we found a renaissance guiding the new explosive capacities of society?

If the city is, as this work asserts, a central controlling fact of life and the critical frontier for a highly variable humanism, then it is the central controlling instrument of our future. Yet the city has been an almost inoperative instrument, although it is complementary to all that has happened in recent history. But, unfortunately, the city is unable to integrate, moderate, and give undiluted value to the thousands of specialized technical developments. Each innovation follows an independent course and interacts wildly in the highly sensitive conditions of urban development or decay. Under these circumstances, the apparently positive lines of specialized development, whether automobiles, boats, or aircraft, easily become the bitter poisoned fruits of industry.

The city is the logical focus for a new social creativity and a new social will. If I am at all correct, the city will become a new central arena for ideology. The focus of urban ideologies, I would hope, will be the whole person. The only way to deal with the whole person is with the whole living environment. If the future does indeed focus more directly on the growth and fulfillment of individual personality, the form and nature of the city will provide the means to relocalize social life and revitalize the crucial intimate contexts of human behavior.

With the late Charles Abrams, we can justifiably say that the city is the frontier. It is the frontier of emerging social issues, human development, human destiny. The city is the frontier of theory of all things human and the fountainhead of new realms of human creativity. The city is the frontier of freedom.

Urban Imperatives

These frontiers give rise to clear urban imperatives. Our question is how to build on past achievements while redirecting our specific powers to more closely serve human purposes.

The first and absolute imperative is to create an urban ecology that assures indefinite human survival on this earth with a sufficient margin of resources to eliminate fundamental stringencies, suppressions, conflicts, and wars over a diminishing foundation for life. I hope these pages have demonstrated, in at least a preliminary way, the possibility of greatly improving the prospects of life while drastically reducing human burdens on the environment.

While working toward a valid urban ecology we can consider the means of bringing the fullest range of humanism to every individual. When we put our minds to the task in any socially serious way, especially if objectives are wholly and clearly defined and the social will is established, we will discover that we can make headway in many areas with about the same assurance and momentum that occurred with technological knowledge during the last hundred years. The limits to our genetic endowment, Rene Dubos (1968) assures us, are not yet in sight. Nor do the environmental and institutional arrangements yet reveal their limits for greater human fulfillment.

One of our greatest challenges is clarifying and defining human ends. Such clarification is best accomplished through an interplay between theory (broad and far-reaching ideas) and practice (pragmatic development of specific ideas, including ideas that emerge from human interaction). However, we need interim definitions of human ends as a basis to proceed on a new course. I suggest the following as a point of departure: Personal fulfillment arises when an individual experiences as broad or profound a range of civilization as possible and displays great spontaneity and creativity in integrating that experience into his or her own being.

This definition emphasizes that every individual is a new expression of the culture and represents a new integration of its immense diversity. Obviously, no individual can experience (let alone absorb or understand) a very large part of world civilization. Civilization nevertheless represents the range of experiences open for a person to experience. That possibility presents us with an immense horizon of the human potential.

Although we speak of world civilization, we place emphasis on the individual and on the diversity and richness of the local environment that, of necessity, constitutes the major realm of individual behavior, especially in the first and last stages of life. Our definition involves an interplay between the personal and the cultural dimensions of life—between the unique expressions and the universal possibilities. And the uniqueness of the individual and the universality of civilization meet and find concrete expression and experience in the local community.

A focus on the individual demands an emphasis on the local setting of life—the realm that nurtures personality, that builds the individual's capacity for experience, and that is real to the body, the emotions, and the mind. Distant peoples, times, places, things, and events become real and can be experienced only when the local life is vibrant, challenging, and responsive, as well as supportive

The Urban Future

and secure. In other words, a rich and unique local environment is necessary to appreciate as well as sustain a rich and diverse world environment.

What emerges from this perspective of the individual's experience is a very different kind of city than we have today. Its form will not be organized to produce and consume in a massive and quite meaningless functionalism, depriving us of the ability to learn and experience. Production and consumption will be moderated and organized to be consistent with a person's experiential growth.

New Horizons

At this point in our history, we can say that the potential of cities is vast, enormously constructive, and virtually unrecognized. The real urban potential is simply an unprecedented humanism in society. Yet the thinking that might realize the potential is hopelessly confined by the radical imperialism ruling our times.

Somehow, therefore, we must find a new sense of the possible, a sense of what the human setting might nurture in every individual. To give just a glimpse of a different horizon, consider some of the important urban dimensions of the human potential:

- Creating the city as the basic foundation for a valid, stable, and propitious *human ecology*
- Creating the city as a basis for *least means* in production, consumption, conservation, and resource recycling
- Creating a system of urban space and mobility with immense *convenience, efficiency, and resource saving*
- Creating the city as a social ameliorator (minimizing social disorganization and alienation)
- Creating the city as a comprehensive vehicle for an unprecedented range of *social development* and human opportunity
- Creating the city as a constitution of freedom and as an articulate means to evaluate *social democracy*
- Creating a system of urban governance and management that flexibly responds to the needs and aspirations of people through *local self-determination*

- Creating human environments for *informal education, creative provocation, and ethical inspiration*
- Creating the city as a work of, and as a stimulating medium for, the *arts and humanities*
- Creating the city to enhance the *integrity, spirit, zest, and meaning* of every person
- Creating urban unity and diversity to serve as an integrator of means and an optimizer of ends
- Creating a city that can change itself creatively in response to new aspirations and yet preserve worthy environments and customs

This list of brief, interlocking statements suggests a vision of a challenging life that knows no boredom; that will be open, trusting, and spontaneous; that will steadily rid itself of the social dimentia arising from alienation; that is engaged in limitless creative endeavors (practical, artful, and monumental) that flow in a stimulating interplay and give great meaning to communal celebrations.

With a common vision and but a moderate political will, we can now create a high level of security for every person: physical, environmental, economic, and social. On a firm foundation of security, individuals become willing to experiment; become free, open, and spontaneous; enlarge their capacity to be curious and learn; nourish their love of involvement with others. In short, they increase their capacity for experience.

Humanism in cities, I submit, is the proper study of our time. Such a direction of events is imperative if the root issues of human worth and aspiration are to become the objectives that society pursues most diligently. For example, consider the significance of creating environments and conditions in which love can become the primary source of human motivation and action, perhaps as a major displacement of the money motive.

We can build environments that will ensure opportunities to know a reasonable number of persons in trust. Trust is necessarily founded on understanding another person's whole personality through varied kinds of interactions with oneself and within one's groups. However, an open lattice network of friendship promoted

The Urban Future

by the present forms of the city deprives persons of complete experience with others by all senses and under many conditions. Only a shallow level of trust is then possible, and this is based on special arenas of action, credentials, and sanctions. Shallow trust inevitably promotes defensive actions, which too often then give suspicions a foundation in reality.

We require environments that minimize confrontation and conflict, that also provide ready avenues to resolve the conflicts that do arise. Yet, to an astonishing degree, we have evolved an adversary system of interpersonal relations in the physical and institutional setting of cities. Today we build physical environments that not only fracture and divide us, but also instigate ugly episodes: the automobile and its traffic tensions, pedestrian intimidation, and citations; the isolated house and its emphasis on property rights and defensive privacy; and the total and unbreakable anonymity of street, freeway, and parking spaces. The institutional sources of tension are as widely based: bureaucratic hierarchy; sharp distinctions of opportunity and power; accumulative and inherited wealth; private wealth and public poverty; the proprietary underpinning of most human interactions; the emphasis on competition; the personal isolation in the urban mass; school classifications and grade levels. All these are supported by machines and organizations that mediate or intervene in human affairs. Together, they cause and even demand an abrasiveness between persons. We have structured our existence to keep huge organizations running smoothly at our own expense.

When people are free to participate fully in many activities, their shared interests can lead to the creation of deeper human bonds. Affective involvements normally occur when organizations can promote a common aim while encouraging individual creativity through interaction in small, highly personal groups.

Similarly, I suspect, if behavior can be even partly freed of the compulsions of defense or escape from forced behavioral relationships, especially that characterized by large factories, offices, and mass merchandising, then an individual's involvement is likely to reflect more basic satisfactions of association and creativity.

The urban settings favorable for human growth—those that encourage self-expression and facilitate cooperation—are also the settings in which varied and common underlying values, trust, and love can grow. The socially destructive nature of today's human environments allows little foundation for such ideals to arise. When the need for facades, defenses, and sharp maneuvers diminishes, we will find the basis for a new honesty within each individual, between individuals, and in the functioning of organizations. We can then become open to ourselves, to others, and to our larger possibilities.

New Reality

To what extent can environments and institutions be consciously designed to achieve significantly higher levels of trust among people? We do not know because society as a whole has never seriously attempted to design completely human settings.

We can, however, be confident of the possibilities of environments and institutions, as their demonstrated repertoire in many areas is enormous. Of course, traditional villages achieved high levels of interpersonal trust. Bureaucracy itself has achieved extraordinary levels of effective trust in the limited areas required by factory and office performance. This feat of bureaucracy is extraordinary, especially because it is devoid of the deeper interpersonal foundations we normally associate with human trust. We can observe the amazing degree of human trust underlying the invasion of Normandy in 1944 and the Apollo moon landings in 1969. If high levels of trust can be mustered for great external social objectives, we should be able to establish the foundations for a deeper personal trust among ourselves in the way we organize environments and institutions in our massive metropolitan areas.

Because of the peculiar emphasis of our society on organizing to produce goods and our general indifference to the creation of congenial settings for life, we are far more astute about institutions than we are about environments. We are also more astute in organizing for smooth performance of a corporation than in promoting smooth interpersonal relationships and personal growth. Even our schools are organized completely for external performance, including the marching order of classes, grade levels, examinations, semesters, and report cards. Hence, the achievements of society are to be found only where its objectives and efforts have been focused.

One day, when we do positively seek new interpersonal quality in our lives, I am confident that we will find notable achievements in a relatively short order. Initially, we can borrow achievements from the past. Plazas designed with a feeling for the human drama will create a foundation for casual and familiar responses among people, as well as a sense of a community center. Many other initial elements of more human environments are deceptively simple: protected and yet stimulating promenades, common places for doing and sharing, quiet places for repose and conversation, varied places for casual learning and recreation, and more immediate and simple access.

Contrary to most current thinking about cities, the first step to achieve these objectives—and the first step toward greater interpersonal trust—will bring people closer together. If this can be done without the heavy overburdens and divisiveness of transportation, congestion ceases to be a problem. The essential ingredients bringing people together—spaciously—are contiguity and multiuse of spaces at a human or community scale. With good community access, contiguity allows people who use pools, gyms, recreation rooms, studios, and special classrooms to meet frequently by chance in the lobbies, lounges, promenades, and plazas, as well as by plan within specialized activity spaces.

Insofar as the individual has easy access to groups or organizations with a wide variety of attractions and can move easily among them, the groups and activities coalesce in ways that sustain the individual and support interpersonal trust. Organizations that cut across age, sex, career, and status lines in favor of individual aspirations and inclinations are also likely to develop more open, free, and trusting relationships.

Do not mistake the powerful significance of the changes that will be necessary to reshape the organizations closest to the individual in the city. Recall, however, that bureaucratic organization is radically new in its pervasive envelopment of the individual. Bureaucracy is, of course, exceptionally well-suited to large-scale bodies, to technological enterprise, to particular purposes (such as profit), to particular functions (such as the provision of products or services), and to strict lines of authority and responsibility (especially in government). Bureaucracy, however, is inept in serving people as *people*. Only people—performing through affective bonds—can do that.

We can expect, therefore, that organizations that nurture, support, and stimulate the person will change as much in the coming decades as physical environments. And organizations require a fundamental strategy no less than physical environments. Our concern here centers on the kind of organization that might directly serve people in rebuilt urban environments. The characteristics of such an organization, I believe, will combine some features of municipal governments, some of corporations, and some of voluntary organizations. Historically we have rigidly separated the three types of organizations. Yet it is precisely a breakdown of the hard barriers between these types of organizations where they most affect persons that we can build a model to serve people in their urban habitat.

The bureaucratic ethic labels direct responses of government to individual needs as corruption, and the corporation has found it injudicious to so involve itself with people beyond pay and certain fringe benefits. Consequently, the voluntary organizations have been left quite alone to carry out an increasingly important role. But they are quite outside the mainstream of society's resources and power. As a result, individual needs tend to be assuaged by private purchases—boats, skis, campers, sport vehicles, and home recreation equipment. These continue to rob the individual of the vital continuing participation that highly evolved voluntary organizations might have provided. Although boat, ski, and sport vehicle clubs abound, these activities remain largely individual or family affairs, and the clubs do well to hold a few meets each year. Social fragmentation thus becomes self-reinforcing, encouraged by the lack of organizational support for combining strong personal interests with interpersonal associations, and the tendency to be seduced by material purchases.

If, then, our organizations are seriously inept in providing adequate social anchors in support of the individual, it is vital that we create a new form of human organization capable of multifaceted and highly articulated support for the individual. We look for more unity and more diversity, more organic oneness of many organizations, in serving every reasonable ambition of the person in his or her living setting. We have built incredibly complex life-support systems, such as the space capsules. Now it is time to develop the same level of sophistication in our life-expanding institutions.

New Creativity

The marvel of being human is that, although we are created, we yet create what we become. The process of self-creation is the meaning of civilization in its long span of evolution. But it is also increasingly the possibility of individual persons in their shorter span of development.

When civilization expands the ability of each person to consciously create himself, the individual can then also experience more of what civilization has evolved and possibly add to humankind's storehouse of experience.

Might the city, remade into a completely human habitat, become a dynamic cradle of personal self-determination? Might we create thousands of new Athens to liberate the deepest wellspring of mind and spirit? Might our new Athens unleash a thousand lines of creativity, possibly enlarging the scope of truth and beauty, just as that single, underdeveloped, *polis* on the rocky terrain of Greece did so daringly nearly twenty-five hundred years ago? Might the city itself, through the wholeness in which it integrates life, shape a higher living truth and manifest a more exalting beauty for the entire human enterprise? Might we return to the quest where the Athenians left off?

The promise of an *urban* truth and an *urban* beauty is matched by the promise of *urban* freedom. Never as a society have we recognized the wider reaches of social and environmental freedom. Both diversity and unity are necessary to make social and environmental freedom possible. *Diversity* is the individual's foundation of choice. *Unity* is the consistency and reliability that the individual requires in doing his daily tasks and in following his ambitions. Without either a fund of opportunities or a security in pursuing them, there can be little freedom beyond protection from simple tyranny. And both opportunity and security are fundamentally dependent on the physical and organizational setting of the city.

References

ADORNO, T. W., and OTHERS. *The Authoritarian Personality.* New York: Harper & Row, 1950.

ALEXANDER, C. "The City Is Not a Tree." *Design,* February 1966, pp. 46–55.

ANDERSON, M. *The Federal Bulldozer: A Critical Analysis of Urban Renewal.* Cambridge, Mass.: M.I.T. Press, 1964.

APPLEYARD, D., and LINTELL, M. "The Environmental Quality of City Streets: The Residents' Viewpoint." *Journal of the American Institute of Planners,* March 1972, pp. 84–101.

BARBOUR, I. G. (Ed.). *Earth Might Be Fair: Reflections on Ethics, Religion, and Ecology.* Englewood Cliffs, N.J.: Prentice-Hall, 1972.

BARNETT, J. *Urban Design as Public Policy.* New York: Architectural Record Books, 1974.

BEL GEDDES, N. *Magic Motorways.* New York: Random House, 1940.

References

BELL, D. "The Public Household." *The Public Interest,* Fall 1974, pp. 29–68.

BOULDING, K. *Beyond Economics: Essays on Society, Religion, and Ethics.* Ann Arbor: University of Michigan Press, 1968.

BRADY, R. A. *Organization, Automation, and Society: The Scientific Revolution in Industry.* Berkeley: University of California Press, 1961.

CALLOW, A. B., JR. (Ed.). *American Urban History: An Interpretive Reader with Commentaries.* New York: Oxford University Press, 1969.

CANTY, D. *The Campus and the City.* Berkeley, Calif.: Carnegie Commission on Higher Education, 1972.

COMMAGER, H. S. "The University and the Community of Learning." In T. B. Stroup (Ed.), *The University in the American Future.* Lexington: University of Kentucky Press, 1966.

Committee on Resources and Man. *Resources and Man.* San Francisco: W. H. Freeman, 1969.

Council on Environmental Quality. *Environmental Quality.* Washington, D.C.: Council on Environmental Quality, 1970.

DARLING, F. F., and MILTON, J. P. (Eds.). *Future Environments of North America: Transformation of a Continent.* Garden City, N.Y.: Natural History Press, 1966.

DUBOS, R. *So Human an Animal.* New York: Scribner's, 1968.

ECKBO, G. *The Landscape We See.* New York: McGraw-Hill, 1969.

FABUN, D. *The Dynamics of Change.* Englewood Cliffs, N.J.: Prentice-Hall, 1970.

FADIMAN, C., and WHITE, J. (Eds.). *Ecocide . . . And Thoughts Toward Survival.* Santa Barbara, Calif.: Center for the Study of Democratic Institutions, 1971.

FALTERMAYER, E. K. *Redoing America.* New York: Harper & Row, 1968.

FARNESS, S. "Resources, the Metropolis, and the Land-Grant University." Amherst: University of Massachusetts Cooperative Extension, 1964.

FARSON, R. *Birthrights.* New York: Macmillan, 1974.

FLEXNER, A. *Universities: American, English, German.* New York: Oxford University Press, 1930.

FOGELSON, R. M. *The Fragmented Metropolis: Los Angeles, 1850–1930.* Cambridge, Mass.: Harvard University Press, 1967.

Ford Foundation. *A Time To Choose: America's Energy Future.* New York: Ford Foundation, 1974.

FRAILBERG, S. "The Diseases of Non-Attachment." *Current,* March 1968, pp. 46–53.

FROMM, E. *Escape from Freedom.* New York: Irvington, 1941.

FROMM, E. *Marx's Concept of Man.* New York: Frederick Ungar, 1963.

FRUIN, J. *Pedestrian Planning and Design.* New York: Metropolitan Association of Urban Designers and Environmental Planners, 1971.

GABOR, D. *The Mature Society.* New York: Praeger, 1972.

GALBRAITH, J. K. *The Affluent Society.* New York: Mentor, 1958.

GOODWIN, R. N. *The American Condition.* New York: Doubleday, 1974.

GROSS, B. M. "Planning in an Era of Social Revolution." *Public Administration Review,* May–June 1971, pp. 259–271.

GUTKIND, E. A. *The Twilight of Cities.* New York: Free Press, 1962.

HAMILTON, E. *The Greek Way to Western Civilization.* New York: Norton, 1930.

HAMMER, T. R., COUGHLIN, R. E., and HORN, E. "The Effect of a Large Urban Park on Real Estate Value." *Journal of the American Institute of Planners,* July 1974, pp. 274–277.

HARDIN, G. "The Tragedy of the Common." *Science,* December 13, 1968, pp. 1243–1248.

HEILBRONER, R. *An Inquiry into the Human Prospect.* New York: Norton, 1974.

HOFFER, E. *The True Believer.* New York: Harper & Row, 1951.

HOWARD, E. *Garden Cities of Tomorrow.* Cambridge, Mass.: M.I.T. Press, n.d.

HSU, F. "Kinship Is the Key." *Center Magazine,* November–December 1973, pp. 4–14.

ILLICH, I. *Celebration of Awareness.* New York: Doubleday, 1971.

ILLICH, I. "Energy and Social Disruption." *Ecologist,* February 1974.

Intertechnology Corporation. *The U.S. Energy Problem.* Washington, D.C.: National Science Foundation, 1972.

References

JACOBS, J. *The Death and Life of Great American Cities.* New York: Random House, 1961.

JACOBS, J. *The Economy of Cities.* New York: Random House, 1969.

JAY, A. *Management and Machiavelli: An Inquiry into the Politics of Corporate Life.* New York: Holt, Rinehart and Winston, 1967.

KEYNES, J. M. "Economic Possibilities for our Grandchildren." In *Essays in Persuasion.* New York: Norton, 1963. (Originally published 1930.)

KRISTOL, I. "It's Not a Bad Crisis to Live in." *New York Times Magazine,* January 22, 1967, pp. 23–73.

KRISTOL, I. "Urban Civilization and Its Discontents." *Commentary,* July 1970, pp. 29–35.

LAING, R. D. *The Politics of Experience.* New York: Pantheon, 1967.

LAMBERT, J. Quoted in "Prometheans and Epimetheans" by F. S. Hopkins. *The Futurist,* June 1974, pp. 131–134.

LYFORD, J. "In My Neighborhood, an Adult Is a Dead Child." *Center Magazine,* November–December 1970, pp. 49–55.

MC GARG, I. *Design with Nature.* New York: Doubleday, 1969.

MC KELVEY, B. *The Urbanization of America, 1860–1915.* New Brunswick, N.J.: Rutgers University Press, 1963.

MC KELVEY, B. *The Emergence of Metropolitan America, 1915–1966.* New Brunswick, N.J.: Rutgers University Press, 1968.

MASLOW, A. H. *Toward a Psychology of Being.* New York: Van Nostrand Reinhold, 1968.

MASOTTI, L. H., and HADDEN, J. K. (Eds.). *The Urbanization of the Suburbs.* Beverly Hills, Calif.: Sage, 1973.

MEADOWS, D., and OTHERS. *The Limits to Growth.* New York: Universe Books, 1972.

MILL, J. S. *Principles of Political Economy.* (Abridged version.) New York: Appleton-Century-Crofts, 1885.

MOHOLY-NAGY, S. *Matrix of Man: An Illustrated History of Urban Development.* New York: Praeger, 1968.

MUMFORD, L. *The Pentagon of Power: The Myth of the Machine.* New York: Harcourt Brace Jovanovich, 1970.

MURCHLAND, B. *The Age of Alienation.* New York: Random House, 1971.

NEUMANN, J. VON "Can We Survive Technology?" *Fortune*, June 1955, pp. 106–152.

NISBET, R. A. *The Quest for Community*. New York: Oxford University Press, 1953.

OFSHE, R. *The Sociology of the Possible*. Englewood Cliffs, N.J.: Prentice-Hall, 1970.

OTTO, H. A. (Ed.). *Explorations in Human Potentialities*. Springfield, Ill.: Thomas, 1966.

PLATT, J. R. (Ed.). *New Views of the Nature of Man*. Chicago: University of Chicago Press, 1965.

PLATT, J. R. *Perception and Change: Projections for Survival*. Ann Arbor: University of Michigan Press, 1970.

POLANYI, K. "Our Obsolete Market Economy." *Commentary*, February 1947. (Reprinted in *Ecologist*, July 1974, pp. 212–220.)

RAGATZ, R. L., and ASSOCIATES. *Recreational Properties*. Eugene, Ore.: Ragatz and Associates, 1974.

Real Estate Research Corporation. *The Costs of Sprawl: Detailed Cost Analysis*. Washington, D.C.: Council on Environmental Quality, 1974.

Regional Plan Association and Resources for the Future. *Regional Energy Consumption*. New York: Regional Plan Association, 1974.

REPS, J. W. *The Making of Urban America: A History of City Planning in the United States*. Princeton, N.J.: Princeton University Press, 1965.

REVELLE, R., and LANDSBERG, H. H. (Eds.). *America's Changing Environment*. Boston: Houghton Mifflin, 1970.

RICHARDS, M. C. *Centering in Pottery, Poetry, and the Person*. Middletown, Conn.: Wesleyan University Press, 1964.

SCHNEIDER, K. R. *Destiny of Change: How Relevant Is Man in the Age of Development?* New York: Holt, Rinehart and Winston, 1968.

SCHNEIDER, K. R. *Autokind Vs. Mankind*. New York: Norton, 1971.

SCHUMACHER, E. F. *Small Is Beautiful: Economics as if People Mattered*. New York: Harper & Row, 1973.

SCHUMACHER, E. F. "On Inflation." *Resurgence*, May–June 1975, pp. 14–15.

References

Smithsonian Institution. *Smithsonian Annual II.* Washington, D.C.: Smithsonian Institution Press, 1968.

SOLERI, P. *Arcology: The City in the Image of Man.* Cambridge, Mass.: M.I.T. Press, 1969.

SPIVAK, M. "Archetypal Place." *Architectural Forum,* October 1973, pp. 44–49.

STEWART, D., and OTHERS. "Carboxyhemoglobin Levels in American Blood Donors." *Journal of the American Medical Association,* August 26, 1974, pp. 1187–1195.

THAYER, L. "Man's Ecology, Ecology's Man." *Main Currents in Modern Thought,* January–February 1971.

THEOBALD, R., and MILLS, S. *The Failure of Success: Ecological Values Vs. Economic Myths.* Indianapolis, Ind.: Bobbs-Merrill, 1973.

TOCQUEVILLE, A. DE *Democracy in America.* (H. Reeve, Trans.) New York: Knopf, 1945.

TOFFLER, A. *Future Shock.* New York: Bantam, 1970.

TUNNARD, C. *City of Man.* New York: Scribner's 1953.

TURNER, J. F. C., and FICHTER, R. (Eds.). *Freedom to Build.* New York: Macmillan, 1972.

United Nations. *Report of the Ad Hoc Group of Experts on Housing and Urban Development.* No. 63.IV.1. New York: United Nations, 1963.

United Nations. *Urbanization: Development Policies and Planning.* No. E.68.IV.1. New York: United Nations, 1968.

United Nations. *Urbanization in the Second United Nations Development Decade.* No. E.70.IV.15. New York: United Nations, 1970.

U.S. Bureau of Mines. *Mineral Facts and Problems.* Bulletin No. 650. Washington, D.C.: U.S. Bureau of Mines, 1970.

U.S. Forest Service. *The Outlook for Timber in the United States.* Forest Resource Report No. 20. Washington, D.C.: U.S. Forest Service, 1973.

WARD, B., and DUBOS, R. *Only One Earth: The Care and Maintenance of a Small Planet.* New York: Norton, 1972.

WARREN, C. "California's Response to the Worldwide Food Crisis." *California Today,* October 1974.

WEBBER, M. M., and OTHERS. *Explorations into Urban Structure.* Philadelphia: University of Pennsylvania Press, 1964.

WEBER, M. *The City.* (Translated and edited by Don Martindale and Gertrud Neuwirth.) New York: Free Press, 1958.

WHEELER, H. "Bringing Science Under Law." *Center Magazine,* 1969.

WHITE, L., JR. "The Historical Roots of Our Environmental Crisis." *Science,* March 10, 1967, pp. 1203–1207.

WIENER, N. *God and Golem, Inc.* Cambridge, Mass.: M.I.T. Press, 1964.

WOLF, P. *The Future of the City: New Directions in Urban Planning.* New York: Whitney Library of Design, 1974.

ZUCKER, P. *Town and Square: From the Agora to the Village Green.* New York: Columbia University Press, 1959.

Index

ABRAMS, C., 325
Access overburdens, 57
Accidents, tolerance of, 81
ADAMS, H., 53
ADORNO, T. W., 210
Advocacy planning, 119
Affluence and alienation, 186
The Affluent Society, 169
Agriculture: lagging development of, 265; and urbanization, 283–284
Air pollution, 132–133
ALEXANDER, C., 193
Alienation: and analogy to physical health, 197; in arts and sports, 213–214; in children, 206–207; of commodities and real estate, 186–188; defined, 184; descriptions of, 196; as devastation of experience, 196; and diminution of life, 208; diverse forms of, 202–203; elements of, as social ideals, 215; of goods, 188; harsh effects of, 195; of individuals, 197; and inorganic city, 195; institutional, 190–195; literature of, 198–200; and loss of placeness, 189; and money, 211; physical, 186–190; as problem of wholeness, 203; as province of philosopher and generalist, 203; results of, 194–195; and specialization, 212; subtleties of, 196; summary of factors producing, 193–194; as theory of personality, 195; and TV, 214–215; and tyranny, 208–209.
ALINSKY, S., 119
America, believed to be favored land, 220
American cities: epic irony of, 118; self-destructiveness of, 116
The American Condition, 200

American Dream, 22, 37, 53, 200, 251, 312
American house, as model of separation, 74–75
American Land Development Association, 127
American Museum of Natural History, 52–53
American Nazis, 202
American Revolution, 232
ANDERSON, M., 120
Anomie, state of, 193
Apartments, 96–99
Appleyard and Lintell, 188
Archetypal places, 307–308
ARISTOTLE, 22, 324
Assassinations, 205
Athens (Greece), 8, 24, 273, 333
Atlantic City, 51
ATO-ACE Newsletter, 286
The Authoritarian Personality, 210
Autobank, 83–84
Autokind Vs. Mankind, 77
Automobile, 10, 15, 65, 81, 132; and accidents, 81; direct cost burden of, 80; effect of, on cities, 88–89; and energy consumption, 150; and environment, 237; importance of, 61; and land and material extravagance, 77; mammoth dimensions of, 77; one-family, 72; and one-family house, 66; phenomenal growth of, 61–62; services, 79; space given to, 78–79; and traffic engineering, 236–237; and urban paradox, 81; and urban transformation, 79; watershed years for, 62

BAILY, F., 47
Bank Act, 173
BARKER, R. 307
BARNETT, J., 106–107
Barriada, 273, 276
BARZUN, J., 175
Bastille, 216
Behavior, utilitarian, 194
BEL GEDDES, N., 63
BELL, D., 322
BETSKY, S., 322–323
Bill of rights of urban environments, 318

Birthrights, 211
BLETHE, H., 153
BLUCHER, W., 120
Bombay, 283
BORN, M., 223
BOULDING, K., 141, 239, 301
BRADY, R., 9
Brazil, 264
BREMER, A., 205
Bridgehead settlements, 269
Broadacre City, 55
Broadway, 106
BROOKS, P., 139
BROWN, H., 175
Buddhist economics. *See* Economics, Buddhist
Building codes, 274
Bureau of Mines, 151
Bureaucracy: broad repertoire of, 330–332; fundamental qualities of, 234; growth of, 201; as habit of mind, 234; ideals of, 189

Calcutta, 246, 265
California farmland, 93
California State University, Fresno, 112–113
California Today, 94
The Campus and the City, 29
CAMUS, A., 199
Canada, 32
CANTY, D., 29
Capital improvements maps, 110
Carbon monoxide of nonsmokers, 133
CARNEGIE, A., 7, 52
Carnegie Commission on Higher Education, 29, 247
Cedar Riverside, 122
Census, urban growth, measured by, 47–48
Central business district, 88, 257
Central city population decline, 59
Central Park, 51
Central Valley farmland, 93–94
Centralization, illusions of, 230
Cheap building, 168
Chicago, 34, 48, 52–53
Children, 213; attachments of, 206–207; destruction of, 204

Index

Christianity: doctrine of, 15; and dualism of man and nature, 221
CIBOROWSKI, A., 130
Cincinnati, 51
Cities: of Africa, Asia, and Latin America, 262; alienation of, 186; and automobiles, 72–73, 77–82, 88–89, 237; built for industry and input-output, 131; built for privacy and private interest, 236; as catalysts for broader freedom, 178; centrality of, in society, 288; and civilization, 312; commerce and industry in, 82–85; conflict of man and nature within, 288; continuing fragmentation of, 38, 195; creation and destruction of, 22–26, 131; and decline from promise of 1900, 68–69; degeneration and decay of, 31, 116–120, 231–234; as determiners of relevance and effectiveness of development, 273; distrust of, 7; and ecology, 182, 312–319; ecology and humanism as social forces in, 16–20; economic underpinnings of, 155; environmental struggle in, 10; evaluation of elements of, 296; and the failure of society, 35; fundamental in organizing life, 308; and the good life, 22; growth and modernization of, 259, 262, 265, 292; as heart of civilization, 21; hopes of the poor in, 267; house and automobile as structural elements of, 72–73; and human will, 207–208; humanizing economic life, 177; ideal, 8, 255; importance of, 262; and inflation, 297–298; and intellect, 250–251; in jeopardy, 5; man, machine, and nature in, 232; as means of development, 282; and money, 294–297; natural history of, 274; organic, 309–312; portrayal of, 29; potential of, 327–328; and prevailing traditions, 242–243; and private and public wealth, 169; and profit, 70; and psychosis of collective life, 290–291; and public policy, 39; and quality of life, 167; and recreational properties, 129; and reduced movement, 150; revenues and expenses of (by size), 167; and social power, 254; as society's master mechanism, 313–319; and specialization, 229–230; and studies reinforcing status quo, 239; success and failure of, 67–71, 298–299; universities and, 206, 243–250; as urban market, 73; and urban planning, 254–260; vacuum of purpose in, 43–44. *See also* Economics; Role of cities

City beautiful movement, 64
City centers, 10; components of, 87–88; European, 86–87; strengthening, 317–318; and technology, 87; transportation and decline in, 88–89
City planning, as renaissance profession, 221
Citymaking and profits, 48
Civilization: challenge to, 32; cities as the heart of, 21, 312; fear of decline in, 243; and the individual, 326–327; morally nonexistent, 288; new tact for, 186; and self-creation of the individual, 333
Civitas, 322
Class, decline of, 216
Class struggle, lost urgency, 176
CLAY, G., 297
CLOUD, P., 141
Club of Rome, 99, 141
Clustering, 313–314
Colonial America, 305
Columbian Exposition, 53
COMMAGER, H. S., 249
Commerce, changed use of space in, 82–85; and land, 91–92
Committee on Resources and Man, 141
Commodity Exchange, 194
Community, 258; children and family as, 213; development of, 278–279, 281; disintegration of, 201; improvement of, 275; inability to create, 58
Congestion and density in cities, 258
Conservative forces, 14

Construction of housing, backwardness of, 74
Consumer economics. *See* Economics, consumer
Consumerism, appearance of mass, 61
Consumption, 3; growing unendingly, 116–117; and waste, 33–34
COPERNICUS, 222
Corn Laws, 173
Corporate enterprise, 42
Corporations: ruling the making of the city, 243; tradition of, 242
Costs of Sprawl, 150, 158–159, 160, 161, 166; summary of comparative costs of, 162–165
Council on Environmental Quality, 133, 159
Country Life, 15
Crowding. *See* Lower East Side (New York)
Cultural challenge, depressed by modern age, 185–186
Culture: decay of, by breaking from past, 232; overorganized, 202; of poverty, 265

Dar es Salaam, 264
DARLING, F. F., 38, 152, 233
DARWIN, C., 222
David and Goliath, 26–29
DAVIDOFF, P., 256
Death and Life of Great American Cities, 253
Deaths, automotive and battle, 132
Declaration of Independence, 253
Delhi, 264
Delos symposium, 286
Democracy: high energy, 304–305; and individual's primary relationships, 304; and social stability, 176
DEMOCRITUS, 233
Density. *See* High density; Low density
Design with Nature, 253
Detroit, 7, 53
Development code, 274
DRUCKER, P., 171, 322
DUBOS, R., 30, 36, 203, 211, 228, 234, 253, 306, 308, 326
DURKHEIM, E., 193, 199
Dwellings, rural and urban, 66–67

E Pluribus Unum to *In Pluribus Unum,* 303
ECKBO, G., 186, 188
Ecocatastrophy, 144
Ecocide, 253
Ecological crisis, 292–293
Ecologist, 148
Ecology: and economics, 176, 182; and humanism, 16–20, 312–319, 326
Economic development, initiation and culmination of, 40–41
Economics: benefits of stationary, 179–180; Buddhist, 181–182; and the city, 154–183; consumer, 171; and determinism, 173–174; disservice, 165–172; and ecology, 176, 182; feasibility and scientific objectivity of, 240; and feasibility of urban projects, 175; freedom from, 180; ideals of, 189; market, 172–174; modern, 294; and physical sciences, 157; as politics, 181; stable, 179–180; and urban thought, 155. *See also Costs of Sprawl*
Economists: determining content of culture, 282; metaphysical blindness of, 158
Economy: of goods, 37; social and ecological control of, 176
Economy of Cities, 283
El Segundo, 84
Electricity, 51
ELIA, S., 87
Elizabethan England, 24
Energy: car and house as gluttonous users of, 146; damage, 148–150; increased use of, 145, 152; investments for Project Independence, 152; nuclear power as, 153; projections, 147; projections to 2040, 151; and technology, 152; and transportation, 159–160; U.S. consumption compared, 145–146; waste, 145–148
ENGELS, F., 301
Environmental Protection Agency, 134, 159, 296
Environmentalists and urbanists, chasm between, 252–253
Environments: beautiful, 1–2; crea-

tive possibilities for, 285; distressing effects of, on future generations, 234; destructive, 22–23; inefficient, 2; random and fragmentary, 188; restructuring, 24; run on, 297; spectacular possibilities for, 306; ugly, 1–2
Escape from Freedom, 210
Essence, separated from existence, 215
Establishment, chores of maintaining, 320–321
EUENUS, 233
Excellence, as disguise for elitism and specialization, 247
Exchange value: of ourselves, 157; replaces use value, 188
Experience, devastation of. *See* Alienation

FABUN, D., 138
FADIMAN, C., 167
FALTERMAYER, E., 251
Family, 212
Farmland, cities threat to, 93–94
FARNESS, S., 157
FARSON, R., 211
Favelas, 265
The Federal Bulldozer, 120
Federal Energy Administration, 152
Federal Road Act of 1916, 62
FEISS, J., 152
FICHTER, R., 269
Field Museum of Natural History, 52–53
FISCHER, J. L., 152
FLEXNER, A., 249, 300
Florence (Italy), 24
FORD, G., 205
FORD, H., 7, 170
Ford Foundation, 147
Forest Service, 151
FOSTER, M., 205
FRAILBERG, S., 206–207
Freedom: and alienation, 199–200, 208–209; cities as catalysts for, 178; denied in corporations, 191–192; to despoil the city, 70; in double jeopardy, 301; from economics, 180; as foundation of all value, 300–301; good city, a way of building, 302; hunger for, 219; illusion of, 38–39; from instinct and social inhibitions, 311–312; for machines and organizations, 28; of movement, 140; opposable forms of, 303; reduced to preference and opinion, 201; social, economic, and physical, 209; as statement of historic possibility, 312; and technology, 218; as urban ideal antithetic to special privilege, 304; as use and fulfillment of our humanity, 301; withering roots of, 210
Freeways, 63–64; costs of and alternatives to, 80; results of, 70
Fresno, 75, 80, 83–84, 94, 105–106, 112, 113–115
Freudian psychopathology, 197
FRIEDMANN, J., 256
Friendship: burdens of, 212; semilattice, 193
FROMM, E., 197–200
FROMME, L., 205
Functional renewal, 123–124
Future, oppressive anticipation of, 176

GABOR, D., 224
GALBRAITH, J. K., 69, 169, 170, 243
GALILEO, G., 20, 226
Gallup poll, 290
Ganges Plain, 264
Garden City movement, 68
General theory, need for, 305
Generalist and universities, 245
Genesis, 221
Georgetown (Washington), 118
Ghirardelli Square, 1–2
GNP, 148, 295
God and Golem, Inc., 13
Good city, as way of building freedom, 302–303
Good life, 8
GOODMAN, P., 223, 225
GOODWIN, R., 200–202, 208–209, 301, 302–303, 306, 312, 324
Government, role of, 42; role of, in neighborhood improvement, 278–280; and urban inflation, 297
Grand Central Station, 87
The Greek Way, 237

Greeks, 23, 47
GREELEY, H., 27–29
Green Revolution, 266
GREER, S., 122
Gridiron plan, 46–57; changed meaning of, 66; new scale of, 56
GROSS, B., 288
Guayaquil (Ecuador), 265

HADDEN, J. K., 56, 60
HALPRIN, L., 189
Hammer, Coughlin, and Horn, 168
Handicapped, 28
Happiness, pursuit of, 306
Hard organizations, 190–192
HARDIN, G., 153, 294
Harper's Weekly, 15
Health: and alienation, 197; environmental, 132
HEGEL, F., 200, 215, 237
HEILBRONER, R., 176–178
HENARD, E., 87
High density, on urban periphery, 59
Highway expansion, 63–65
Hippies, strike against society by, 231
History, 220
HOCH, I., 167
HOFFER, E., 198, 210
HORNEY, K., 197
Hospital design and management, 191
House: duplication of equipment in, 75; ecology of, 76–77; one-family, 66, 72; as structural element of cities, 72–73; suburban, 70; utility and street connections for, 75
Housing, 259; as activity/commodity, 268–269; and neighborhoods, 119–120; standards, 270
Housing Acts of 1937, 1949, and 1954, 119–121
HOWARD, E., 68
HSU, F. L. K., 211, 217
Human: adventure, 306; attachments, 206–207; defeat, urban locus of, 12; development, ingredients of, 284; ends, challenge of defining, 326; evolution, 306; future, 305; opportunities, as gift of civilization, 292; parliament, 299; revolution, 44; scale, 318; settlements, improvements of, 286; spirit, 185, 305; truth, 239; will to act, 286
Human beings: become things, 202; as highest phenomena, 300
Human potential: of cities, 23; new levels possible for, 299; urban dimensions of, 327–328
Humanism: and ecology, 16–20, 312–319, 326; of technology, bureaucracy, and economics, 321–322; urban, 23–24, 322–325
Humanity: learning to soar, 218; love of, 198; at stake, 197
Humankind: destructive, 288; as measure of all things, 306; robbed of animal innocence, 261
HUME, D., 253
HUXLEY, J., 300

ILLICH, I., 131, 138–139, 148, 306
Immigrants, 49
Imperial Hotel, 293
Improvability, 269, 271, 274, 275, 277–278; ceilings of, 271–272; chart of continuous, 279
In-place urban renewal, 123
Income projections to 2020, 157
Individuals: and civilization, 326–327, 333; and democracy, 304; expendable, 194, 197; focus of value of, 310–311; to forefront of development, 282; production and consumption by, 171; wants of, 169
Individualism, shifting to individuation, 241
Industrial city, turn of century, 49–50
Industrial output excessive, 65
Industrialization and urbanization, 135
Inflation, 3; as child of greed, 211; and justice, 156; and poverty, 171; in world economy, 178
Inhumanity of democratic institutions, 206
Inner city, escape from, 55
Institutions: for actualization of human potential, 219; hard and soft, 190; massive, rigid, and alienating, 81–82; questioning legitimacy of, 322
Integration: of city center, 86; by

Index

design, 42; for efficiency and amenity, 314; of the human habitat, 41–42; by movement, 89
Intellect: and alienation and recessiveness, 206, 250–251; and the city, 250–251; institutionalized, 250
Intelligence, bad development of, 223
Internal Revenue Service, 112–113
Interpersonal life and individual existence, 217
Interpersonal nexus, as essential ingredient of human existence, 217
Intertechnology Corporation, 151
Invention, 224
Isfahan, 273
Isolation and fragmentation, 187

JACOBS, J., 189, 239–240, 283
JAMES, W., 199, 225
Java, 264
JAY, A., 191
JEFFERSON, T., 7, 47, 251
Journal of the American Medical Association, 133
JOUVENEL, B., DE, 168

Kansas City, 53, 89
KENNEDY, J., 205
KENNEDY, R., 205
Kennedy Center for the Performing Arts, 189
KENT, T. J., 256
KEPLER, J., 226
KEYNES, J. M., 18, 294
KIERKEGAARD, 199
KING, M. L., 205
Knowledge: for its own sake, 225, 228; as human problem, 20; and relation to life, 206
KRISTOL, I., 251–252
Kyoto, 273

Labor market, 172
Lagos, 283
LAING, R. D., 196–197, 211–212
Land, 32; as commodity, 172; consumption of, 91, 298; as foundation of cities, 90–91; market, 92, 172; and metropolitan growth, 93–94; misuse of, 35–36; paradox of, 91; reform laws, 173; and road development, 48, 57; rural farm, 93–94; and space, 94; tenure, 42, 55; and urbanity, 98–99; use, 257–258; values and crowding, 48
Language of planning, 257–258
Las Vegas, 126
LEIBNITZ, G., 222
Liberation of mind and spirit, 333
Liberty, restricting, 178
Libraries, 52
Lima, 267, 273
The Limits to Growth, 99, 141–142, 253
Lincoln Center for the Performing Arts, 189
LINDSAY, J., 106
Livability of streets. *See* Streets
Locality, 230
LOCKE, J., 18, 253
Los Angeles, 27–28, 34, 36, 56, 58, 93, 126
Lot, typical use of, 75–76
Love: logic of, 200; and money, 211; of neighbor and humanity, 198
Low density: and the motorcar, 55; and nature of city, 97–99
Lower East Side (New York), crowding in, 96
LYFORD, J., 204–205

MC CARG, I., 253, 305
MACHIAVELLI, N., 119, 195
Machiavellian structure of interpersonal relations, 190
MC KELVEY, B., 69
MC NAMARA, R., 265
Macro order, 43
Maginot lines, 39
MALRAUX, A., 218
MALTHUS, 41
Malthusian nightmare, 136
Man: eastern, 306; not flourishing, 175; in God's image, 221; modern, 38; over nature, 222; returning to himself, 306; western, 39, 306
Management, sophisticated, 197–198
Management and Machiavelli, 191–192
Manhattan, per-capita energy consumption of, 149
Manufacturing, 84–85

Index

Market: distortion of choice in, 321; economics, 172–174, 181; free, 181; power and values, 73; tradition of, 242; transformation, 49–50
Marriage and community, 212–213
MARTINDALE, D., 193
MARX, K., 18, 193, 199–200, 211, 306
Marxism, fear of, 239
MASLOW, A., 197, 306–307
MASOTTI, L., 56, 59, 60
Mass: movements, 210; urban, 241–242
Master mechanism, 313
Material necessity, abolition of, 200
MEAD, M., 213
MEADOWS, D., 99, 141
Means and ends, 239
Medical College of Wisconsin, 133
Megalopolis, 253
Megalopolis, eastern, 31–32
Membership, unconditional, 212
MESTHENE, E., 218
Metropolis, changing nature of, 60–67
Metropolitanism, 49–53
Mexico City, 264
Michigan, University of, 206
Micro order, 43
Microcosm of society, the university as, 243
Middle Ages, 2
MILL, J. S., 41, 179
MILLS, S., 263
MILTON, J. P., 38, 152, 233
Mind and spirit, 238
Minutemen, 202
Mobility: and alienation, 187–188; ascendence of, 56; rationalizing, 317; reducing, 316–317
Model Cities, 123
Model T and the city, 169
MOHOLY-NAGY, S., 224
Mojave Desert, 110
Money, 155–156; and alienation, 211; and cities, 294–295; disruptive power of, 211; and love, 211
MOORE, S. J., 205
MORENO, J. L., 218
MOSES, R., 64
Motor homes, 125
Mott Foundation, 111

Movement: incoherence of, 188; misplaced emphasis on, 100–101
Multiple dwelling, 99
MUMFORD, L., 24, 37, 85, 169, 202, 206, 222, 224, 225–227, 231, 232, 233, 248, 249, 253, 299
MURCHLAND, B., 188, 225
Museums, 52–53
Mutations, social and technical, 15–16

NADER, R., 151
Nairobi, 268
National Science Foundation, 151
Nature: in cities, 315; freed us from instincts, 311; man over, 222; and technique, 233
Necessity, leap from, 301
Neighbor, love of, 198
Neighborhood: and houses, 119–120; structure, 275
NEUMANN, J., VON, 231–232
NEUWIRTH, G., 193
New Jersey, 34
New-towns-in-town, 122
New York City, 1, 10, 34, 47, 50–52, 95, 96, 106, 122, 149, 189, 204
New York World's Fair, 63
Newarks of America, 35
NEWTON, I., 222
NIEHBUHR, R., 216
NIETZSCHE, F., 199
Nile Valley, 264
NISBET, R., 198, 210
NIXON, R., 146–147
No-man's land, 97
Noise, 133–134

Objectivity, 226–227, 239–240
Office of Economic Opportunity, 123
Office of Management and Budget, 296
Offices, 84–85
One World, 261
Only One Earth, 253
Orderliness, human and bureaucratic, 3
Organizations: best characteristics of, 332; special purpose of, 190; roles fixed and standardized in, 191
OSWALD, H. L., 205

Index

OTTO, H. A., 218–219
OWEN, W., 70

Palo Alto, 84
Paradox, 9; of cities, 35; of economic and industrial growth, 30; of social man, 207; of urban age, 22; of urbanism, 131
Parks, effective size for, 139–140
Passage versus place, 101–102
Peasant farmers, 285–286
PENN, W., 47
Penn Station, 293
Pennypack Park, 167
People, and their struggle for improvement, 272–273
Person, as counterpart of unified city, 238; shriveled, desiccated, 197
Personal development, 185
Personal helplessness, 36
Personality disintegration, 199; psychological foundations of, 216; schizoid urban, 193
Ph.D. degrees, 52
Philadelphia, 47, 68, 118, 167, 253
Philosophy, made into a specialization, 245–246
Phoenix, 126
Pittsburgh, 7
Placeness, 100; loss of, 189
Places, archetypal, 307–308
Planned unit development, 258
Planning: and ecology, 300; standards, 258
POLANYI, K., 172–174
Polis, 333
Pollution: mechanical suppression of, 135; and population growth, 135–136; and technology, 135
Poor Law Reform, 173
Population, 32; central city decline in, 59; and density and crowding, 95; growth, 40–41, 263; growth and pollution, 135–136; growth and sheer scale, 265; metropolitan, growth, 54; reactions to high density, 96–97
Power, 222–223; and science, 226; in the urban tradition, 243; wasteful and exhaustive, 230
Princeton, 84

Privacy and one-family house, 76
Private initiative and public responsibility, 57
Private wealth, 69–70, 169, 243
Process in urban planning, 256–257
Production, emphasis from Depression and World War II on, 69
Productive excesses, 181
Project Independence, 146–147, 151
Protestant ethic, 3
Psychosis: of collective life in cities, 290–291; public, 3–4
Public: faith, 204; interest, lack of, 255; poverty, 69–70, 243; services, 110; spaces, 187

Quality of life in cities, defeated by wealth, 30–31
Quest for Community, 210

Radical forces, 14
RAGLAN, LORD, 232
RAY, J. E., 205
REAGAN, R., 222
Real Estate Research Corporation, 150, 159, 160, 165
Reason, to promote the art of life, 231
Recreation, as urbanites' last escape, 125–129
Recreational properties: and cities, 129; and conversion to primary residence, 127; decline of, 128; distances from, to primary residence, 127–128; improvements in, 126–127; and sense of community, 128
REDFIELD, J., 233
Redoing America, 251
Regional Energy Consumption, 149
Regional Plan Association, 149
Relations, dominant-submissive, 194
Renewal: characteristics of, 121; creative possibilities for, 123–124; with preservation, 123; questions about, 122–123; from strength, 124; of transit and walking, 124
Repression, 196–197
REPS, J., 47
Resources, 41; and exponential growth, 143; imported to U.S. 143;

nonrenewable, 143; and science, 152; shortages of, 152; urgency of, 141
Resources for the Future, Inc., 152
Resources and Man, 253
Reston, 44
Return-to-earth movement, 293–294
REVERE, P., 18
Revolution: good, 13; urban, 20
Revolutionary times, 12–13
RICARDO, D., 18
RICHARDS, M. C., 206, 219
Riverside, 134
Roadways, three levels of, 56–57
Rockefeller Center, 44, 87
ROCKWELL, G., 205
Roles, single-purpose, 193
Role of cities: in human development, 281–286; in social change, 260; in society, 177
Roman Empire, 3
Rome, 273
Roosevelt Island, 122
ROUSSEAU, J. J., 198–199
Rural: communes, 293–294; overpopulation, 264–266; urban migration, 264–265
RUSSELL, B., 226
Russian city planners, 167–168

Saint Agnes Hospital, 115
SAINT FRANCIS OF ASSISI, 221
Salt Lake City, 47
San Fernando Valley, 58
San Francisco, 1, 10, 34, 47, 68, 93, 188
Sao Paulo, 264
SARTRE, J. P., 300
SCHICKEL, R., 214
Schizophrenic behavior, 196
SCHNEIDER, K. R., 77, 130
Schoolgrounds, 110–111
Schools, rigid order in, 191
SCHUMACHER, E. F., 3, 156, 158, 181
Science: analysis of, 225; and Christianity, 222; and devaluation of human experience, 224; and ethics, 223; ideology of, 19–20; laws of, 239; and power, 226; and resources, 152; tradition of, 242; trust in, 142

Science and technology, as first historic crisis, 223
Seagram building, 189
Self-determination, 318
Self-interest, 193
SELYE, H., 203
Sensory deprivation, 201
Seoul, 264
Settlements: improvement stages in, 277–278; self-improving, 269
Sewer systems, 50
Shopping centers, 57, 89, 92, 105–106, 139
Shut-ins, the young, old, poor, and handicapped as, 137
SIRHAN, S., 205
SLOAN, A., 62
Slums, 267, 271
Small Tract Act of 1938, 126–127
SMITH, A., 18, 235, 294
Smithsonian Institution, 168
Social: Darwinism, 48, 191; decay, 11; fragmentation of existence, 201; grace, 216; indicators, 296; irrelevancies, 39–40; magna carta, 174; sciences, 239–240; wholeness, 185, 246
Society: awakening to contradictory facts, 287–288; freeing man from inhibitions, 311; and the university leadership, 249
Society Hill, 118
SOCRATES, 13
Soft organizations, 190, 192–193
SOLERI, P., 253
Space: and human scale, 100; and land, 94; loss of, 139–140
Spaciousness, cluster for, 313–314
Special interest: destructiveness of, 33; groups, 235–236
Special purpose agencies, 217–218
Specialization, 228–230; in bureaucracy and technology, 234–238; future role of, 238; and modern problems, 245; of organizations, 191; and special interest, 235; and universities, 244–245; and urban affairs, 235
Species, best size and form for, 8
SPECK, R., 205
Spirit and mind, 238

SPIVAK, M., 307
Spontaneity, learning to develop, 218
Sports and urban growth, 51–52
Sprawl, and increased automobile and energy consumption, 150
Squatter settlements, 257
Stanford University, 84
STEWART, D., 133
Streets, livability of, 188
Structure and capacity, 119
Sub-urb, 54, 60
Subdivision of land, 258; lowest common denominator for, 91
Suburb, 257; escape to, 36; overturning the metropolis, 60
Suburban house, 70; and TV, 215
Suburbia, 55–56
Subways, 1–2, 50
Success: enormity of, 33; mythology of, 190–191
Super-evolution, 15
Swedes, 252
Swiss Family Robinson, 74

Taxation, debilitating effects of, 108–109; two roles of, 108
Technique and nature, 233
Technological dynamism, self-defeating, 37
Technology: appropriate, 6; and bureaucracy and economics, 9, 19; in the city, 232; in collision with nature, 232; and energy, 152; as epicenter of world motivation, 223; fighting against limits, 142; and pollution, 135; and power, 223; traditions of, 242; and universities, 244
Telephones, 51
Tenements, 48, 95–96
Texas, University of, 205
THAYER, L., 292
THEOBALD, R., 263
Theory, 5
Third dimension, cluster in, 314–315
THOREAU, H., 195
Timber, 144
Time: deprivation of space and, 140; loss of, 138–139
A Time to Choose, 253
Time magazine, 205–206

TOCQUEVILLE, A., DE, 156, 208–209
Towns in Colonial America, 305
TOYNBEE, A., 3, 211, 243, 249, 323
Traditions: great division of, 225; that hurt us most, 253–254; megatechnic, 223; of science and technology, 225–231; summary effects of, 242
Traffic engineering, 236–237
Trafficways, 259
Tragedy of the Common, 153, 294
Transit: public, 31; renewal of, 124
Transport and urban decay, 31
Transportation: and consumption of BTUs, 150; and energy, 149–150; as evaluation of city, 296–297
TRILLING, L., 206, 251
The True Believer, 210
Trust, environments promoting, 329
Truth, human, 239
Tucson, 126
TURNER, J. F. C., 254, 268–269, 270, 273
TV, 214–215; and suburban house, 215

UDALL, S., 30
Ultimas Noticias, 267
United Nations, 74, 130, 264–265, 268, 270, 276, 282
U.S. Constitution, 253
U.S. Department of Health, Education and Welfare, 133
U.S. Department of Housing and Urban Development, 59, 159
The U.S. Energy Problem, 151
U.S. Geological Survey, 134, 152
U.S. Office of Interstate Land Sales, 126
Unity of organic life, 310
Universities: as challenge to cities, 248–249; and the creation of the future, 243–244; ethos of, 247; incapacities of, to deal with social wholes, 246–247; and relationship to society, 243–244; urban, 52
Urban: anatomy, revolutionary changes in, 63; center, 86; challenge to the university, 249; chaos, 188; conflict, three levels of, 35–36; defeatism about democracy,

251–252; development objective, 276; disaster, 29; disorder and degeneration, 119; environments, destructive, 22–23; freedom and paradox, 303; genetic endowment, 310; growth units, 315; history, 45–71, 254; inflation, 297; land, critical role of, 94–95; lot, 74–76; paradox, 4, 81, 303; plans, 42; population growth, 263–264; problem, futility of special responses to, 66; promise, 333–334; revolution, 20; settlers, 46; space, creation of, 94–95; transport improvements, 50–51; values, 4; wholeness, 4–5. *See also* Environments

Urban Design as Public Policy, 106

Urban development: basic lessons of, 313–318; and escape, 58; game of, 57–58; irony of high standards of, 118; rural image of, 55

Urban planning: and emphasis on order, 255–256; failure of, 221; process, 256–257; summary of distortions of, 257–259

Urbanism, ultimate paradox of, 131

Urbanist. *See* Environmentalists and urbanists

Urbanization: and agriculture, 283–284; disadvantages of current growth in, 265; and industrialization, 135, 265; of third world, 263

Utility charges, 109

Utopian movements, 68

Values, confusion of, 14–15
Venice, 273
Vienna, 24
Vienna Circle, 250–251
Villages, European compactness of, 74

Violence, legitimacy of, 205
Virginia City, 53

Walking, 56–57; renewal of, 124
WALLACE, G., 205
WARD, B., 253, 265
WARREN, C., 94
Washington, D. C., 118
Waste and wealthy districts, 35
Water: filtered, 50; pollution, 134–135; runoff, 134
WATT, K., 144, 166
WEBER, M., 48, 193, 234, 259–260
Westwood Village, 84
WHEELER, H., 144, 223
WHITE, J., 167
WHITE, L., 221
White City, 53
WHITEHEAD, A. N., 231, 243
WHITMAN, C. J., 205
Wholeness: as challenge to the university, 246–247; of organic life, 309–310
WIENER, N., 13
WILKIE, W., 261
WILKINSON, J., 233
Will, individual and general, 207
Willamette River, 134
WIRTH, L., 193
Wisdom, as state of total being, 206
World society, micro and macro order of, 43
WRIGHT, F. L., 55
WURSTER, C. B., 239

Zoning, 73; case for, 107; contradictions inherent in, 104; facts of, 64–65; and privileges of power, 105–106; and segregation of activities, 103–104; as segregation and isolation, 257–258; theoretic difficulties of, 103